*Local Public Library
Administration*

LOCAL PUBLIC LIBRARY ADMINISTRATION

Completely revised by

ELLEN ALTMAN, *Editor*

in cooperation with the

INTERNATIONAL CITY MANAGEMENT
ASSOCIATION

SECOND EDITION

AMERICAN LIBRARY ASSOCIATION

Chicago 1980

**Cover photograph by Bill Engdahl,
Hedrich-Blessing, Chicago**

Library of Congress Cataloging in Publication Data

Main entry under title:

Local public library administration.
   First ed. published in 1964 edited by Roberta
Bowler.
   Includes bibliographical references and index.
   1. Library administration. I. Altman, Ellen.
II. Bowler, Roberta, ed. Local public library
administration. III. International City Management
Association. IV. American Library Association.
Z678.B8 1980   027.4   80-20168
ISBN 0-8389-0307-X

Contents

Illustrations

Tables

Foreword

Learning is a growth activity in the United States. Although college enrollments are down as of the early eighties, the growth in almost all forms of continuing education—or lifelong learning—is remarkable. It is evident in the enrollments in community colleges, with many of the students past thirty or even forty years of age; in the unprecedented number of short courses, workshops, and institutes in hundreds of different fields; in rising book sales reported every year; in the diverse activities of local park and recreation departments, extension agencies, churches, YMCAs, YWCAs, and other community agencies; and in the expanding work of the local public library.

It is within this value setting that *Local Public Library Administration* shows how the library administrator and staff can plan, develop, and administer services to meet community needs. The library administrator has to be involved with the social and political environment of the community, has to have empathic understanding of the amalgam of forces that make up the polity, has to be both an external and internal manager of a governmental agency, has to know the techniques of management, and has to know professional library methods to work with professional staff. It also helps for the library administrator to know enough about library buildings to deal efficiently with programmers, architects, engineers, and library board members.

The range of subjects that falls within the purview of librarianship is suggested by the chapter titles for this book. Both city and county managers and library administrators will find *Local Public Library Administration* of great value in blending policies, methods, and self-appraisal to help in building better library services for all elements of the community.

One of the authors, Ira Sharkansky, states: "If the local library ever was isolated from the pressures of other affairs, that is no longer the case." How true! Like the city manager and the county manager, the library administrator finds that his or her world is intergovernmental, permeated with citizen participation, and premised on technology, information flow, information access, and information exchange.

At a time of public distrust of government and other institutions, of budget cuts and reduced services, of inflation and energy limits, it is well to remind ourselves of the worth of the local public library. Just as the laboratory serves the scientist for observation and experiment, so does the library serve the citizen for learning, leisure, reference, and validation of his or her values and choices. The effective library blends administration with learning, community values, and media resources to provide an educational dimension for all.

The International City Management Association is pleased to have had the opportunity to work with the American Library Association in planning and developing *Local Public Library Administration*. A worthy successor to the first edition that was published by ICMA in 1964, this book will be valuable not only for local government administrators and library professionals, but also for teachers, students, and others concerned with the quality of life.

MARK E. KEANE
Executive Director
International City Management
Association

Preface

Over the past seven or eight years I have spent a lot of time on airplanes. Quite often the stranger in the next seat and I engage in that pass-the-time conversation common to travelers. These people frequently ask what kind of work I do. When I say that I teach people to become librarians their uniform response is usually one of polite bewilderment—what is there to teach except how to check out the books? I no longer point out that materials must be selected, ordered, and organized for efficient retrieval and use because most of my traveling companions do not see these activities as meaningful technical skills. I have found the reply they can best understand is that libraries are complex organizations, sometimes employing a hundred or more staff members and spending budgets well in excess of a million dollars. I stress that libraries have the same function to perform as most other organizations in our society: planning the efficient utilization of human and financial resources, organizing and directing the work efforts of staff, preparing and justifying budgets, and satisfying the desires of clientele. These activities have become increasingly complex since the original edition of *Local Public Library Administration* was published in 1964.

Rising expectations on the part of staff for meaningful and satisfying work situations and the desire to participate in management decisions require new and adaptive management styles and more effective organizational communication. At the same time the number of laws and government regulations relating to employment and employees has increased enormously.

An awareness that public library administrators must be more adroit in the political process at the local, state, and national level has also become more important as governments' and citizens' commitment to education and social welfare programs has decreased and, hence, budgets allocated for such programs have not kept pace with the skyrocketing costs of providing these services. As a result, library administrators have had to become more knowlegeable about government financing and budgeting. Terms like revenue sharing and zero-based budgeting were unheard of in the early 1960s.

When the 1964 edition appeared, library networks were just beginning to organize. Today, nearly every library in the country has the opportunity to participate in at least one kind of network. The tremendous growth in computer technology and its applications in libraries requires that library administrators possess a level of technical understanding undreamed of fifteen or twenty years ago.

Considering both the changes that have occurred in the intervening sixteen years since publication of the first edition, the need for this revised edition is readily apparent. This edition has the same purpose as its predecessor—to provide a reference guide for library supervisors, librarians, trustees and local government officials and, in addition, to serve as a text for library school students. The eighteen chapters written by experts in librarianship, law, management, and social sciences present the principles of good practice and their application for effective library management.

I want to express my appreciation and thanks to the chapter authors, all of whom were gracious, patient, and willing to cooperate to bring this project to completion despite long delays. Special thanks are due Bunny Lockett who spent countless hours checking footnotes, catching errors, and generally getting the individual chapters into a unified format.

ELLEN ALTMAN
Editor

1   The Contemporary Society

RALPH W. CONANT and ALAN SHANK

The intent of this introductory chapter is to help librarians understand changes in our society that have an impact on library services, so that library administrators might effectively adjust their policies and planning to conditions that lie ahead. The perspective of this chapter includes a broad sampling of the main forces at work in the society and sets the stage for the practical issues discussed in chapters that follow.

The American society is experiencing sharp breaks from long-standing values and traditional ways of life. Such changes stem from a wealth of breakthroughs—for example, (1) in media transmission technology that puts within the reach of librarians and information specialists the means to keep up with the awesome expansion of published knowledge; (2) in medical science that is producing a healthier, longer-lived population and decreasing birthrates; (3) in communications and transportation that are moving the nation's divergent cultures toward common experiences; (4) in land and environmental planning techniques that have a scientific rather than an arbitrary base. America's openness to innovation and its propensity for invention and exploration, coupled with its great wealth of resources, are the driving forces behind such changes. Only in our inability to maintain access to cheap energy does the break with our past give reason for despair.

We examine first some major population developments and their related effects upon individual and group life-styles; family formation and structure; economic development; race, ethnicity and social stratification. Subsequently we look at the related matters of political structure in cities and urban regions.

During the 1970s it became evident that population growth and economic expansion in the United States were slowing down. The previous thirty years of explosive growth, especially in urban areas, impelled the federal government to encourage local and state development planning, a course of action that has improved the decision-making capacity of government at all levels. On the other hand, the United States has developed national economy, anchored in industrial, financial, transportation, and marketing firms of national and international scope and paralleled by the vast domestic activities of government. A provincial nation has thus been transformed into a mobile, cosmopolitan society whose customs, tastes, and daily routines now approach homogeneity.

Overt racial and ethnic hostility has seemed to decline, but a class structure coalescing along social and economic lines is being reinforced by segregation in elementary and secondary education. The gradual aging of the population, from an average of twenty-seven in 1970 to thirty-seven in 1980, is lessening the emphasis on youth values and shifting the focus to middle-class materialism and the status quo—thus providing an impetus to social and political conservatism. Yet national election results in 1974, 1976, and 1978 indicate voter skepticism with "business and politics as usual" coupled with considerable public concern over governmental responsiveness to public problems. In recent years voter confidence in public officials has declined not only in the United States but in other Western democracies as well.

Trends for the 1980s point toward a period of economic uncertainty characterized by inflation, unemployment, and an era of relatively declining gross national product and personal income. The efforts of government leaders to achieve peace among nations, especially among the major powers, will if successful contribute significantly to worldwide economic prosperity and therefore to political stability. At the same time the nation and the world are likely to experience localized conflict so long as the economic gap between the haves and the have-nots continues to widen. Terrorism throughout much of the world is only the most dramatic form of such conflict.

Advances in communications technology since the close of World War II have revolutionized techniques for information dissemination, and this development in turn is enhancing man's capacity for producing new knowledge. These advances are having a profound effect upon the mission and the organization of libraries and are promoting the movement toward regional, statewide, national, and international library and information systems. For example, laser beams carried on bundles of fine glass fibers will soon be capable of transmitting massive amounts of information instantaneously, perhaps rendering obsolete most contemporary modes of communications.

Population Trends and Movements

A few years ago much of the world, including the United States, faced a rate of population growth that threatened the earth's capacity to support a tolerable standard of living. Most experts were projecting a doubling of U.S. population every seventy years. In 1965–70, however, it became apparent that the decline in birth and fertility rates (which had begun in 1957) was likely to continue. In 1967 demographer Donald J. Bougue predicted a general leveling of the world's population by the turn of the twenty-first century. His calculations were based upon worldwide studies of trends in the use of birth control techniques by women in childbearing years. Many governments have included birth control incentives in their national planning programs. Also, there has been a steady increase in private and public resources for birth control research. The ready availability of oral and intrauterine contraceptives has also contributed to a dramatic shift in attitudes toward premarital sex, thus removing a primary incentive to early marriage.

The Facts

High birthrates, characteristic of primitive and developing societies, persisted in the United States as long as infant mortality rates were high. By the 1930s, life expectancy had reached sixty years, and the birth rate dropped to an unprecedented low of 18.9 per 1,000. 1936. The rise in the birthrate following World War II persisted through 1957, when it peaked at 25.3 per 1,000. From that point it declined steadily until by 1976 it reached a historic low of 14.7 per 1,000. Thus the population "explosion" after World War II turned out to be a "bumper crop" of babies. In absolute numbers, however, births continued to rise until 1961, when 4.3 million were born. In 1976, in spite of the larger number of women in the childbearing years, only 3.2 million babies were born, reflecting a decline in the *fertility rate* from 123 births per 1,000 women between the ages of fifteen and forty-four in 1957 to 67 in 1975. By 1975 this sharp decline brought the average number of children per family to 1.8, as compared to 3.8 in 1957. The statistical replacement rate is 2.11. Demographers calculate that an average of

1.8 children per family would cause the U.S. population to level off by the year 2020, provided that death rates hold at 9 per 1,000 or decline, and immigration does not increase. Further, groups that traditionally have had the highest birthrates have shown the sharpest declines. Between 1960 and 1970 the fertility of blacks fell 37 percent, of Native Americans 45 percent, and of Hispanic Americans 30 percent. The decline among urban whites during the period was 27 percent.

The effects of the gradual leveling of the U.S. population may be summarized as follows: A shift is likely to occur in both public and private productivity from an emphasis on a quantitative response to a qualitative one. For example, as fewer classrooms and physical facilities are needed for schools, the quality of teaching and programs could be improved. The principal impetus to an expanding economy under conditons of slowing population growth is the scientific and technological advancement that provides new opportunities for technical and professional manpower and new levels and types of services for an affluent society: vastly improved health maintenance and medical services, communications and transportation technology, homemaking facilities, and the like. Among the most important technological advances must be the organization and dissemination of knowledge and information of all kinds—a natural function of libraries.

The Causes

The decline in birthrates is traceable to educational and professional opportunities extended to women and the development and general acceptance of effective birth control methods. Women have gone to work also to increase personal and/or family income and to escape from the menial duties of housekeeping. In recent years working wives have provided the extra income that has guaranteed middle-class living standards for millions of American families. By 1977 women made up 48.9 percent of the work force. The intermingling of these factors has encouraged the women's liberation movement and has had a major impact on family formation.

Although universal public education has been a goal of Americans for more than a century, vocational and university education until the postwar period was generally limited to young men (except in such "female" professions as teaching). Most young women did not regard education beyond high school as necessary to their futures as mothers and homemakers, or they could not afford it, or their families did not encourage it. This pattern was broken in the 1950s when state universities expanded and more families reached levels of affluence that permitted them to send daughters into higher education. By 1979 women outnumbered men in undergraduate schools; in law and medical schools they occupied one in four places. Meanwhile birth control technology produced "the pill" and several effective intrauterine devices. By the mid-sixties a revolution in premarital and extramarital sex was in the making. Young people no longer took for granted the necessity of marriage as the only safe and acceptable route to satisfying their emotional and sexual needs. By the mid-seventies the old taboos were disappearing; coed dormitories on college campuses had become commonplace; young couples who wished to live together encountered fewer social difficulties in postponing marriage and child rearing. Between 1960 and 1976, the proportion of women in the United States still single at age twenty to twenty-four rose from 28 percent to 43 percent.[1]

Beginning in the early seventies, liberalized state abortion laws have had a major impact on the birthrate and may have been the principal factor in the subsequent sharp decline in fertility rate. The abortion taboo held firm until the late sixties: according to a 1968 Gallup poll only 15 percent of the population favored abortion on request. By 1971, during the period when proabortion groups attracted national publicity in their attacks on state abortion laws, a majority registered approval of abortion on request. In 1973 the United States Supreme Court ruled that the decision for an abortion in the first three months of pregnancy was between the woman and her physician; beyond three months the states could regulate the abortion procedure; and in the last three months a state could declare abortion illegal except to preserve the life or health of the woman.

Court and legislative action on abortion since 1971 has generally resulted in making abortions safe and inexpensive.[2] The U.S. Commission on Population in 1971 estimated that more than 1 million abortions were performed annually in the United States. Bogue asserts that "whenever abortion has been legalized and allowed as a legitimate medical activity under hospital conditions, there has been a swift and substantial decline in the birth rate."[3]

As discriminatory barriers have receded and family responsibilities have been postponed and minimized, younger women have moved rapidly into the labor market and into professional careers. Trial marriages and temporary liaisons have breached the traditional pattern of women's role as housewife and child rearer although many still want marriage. A recognition of women valued for their professional contributions has reinforced the inclination of many to remain free of the menial aspects of family life; if married to have an explicit, sometimes contractual, understanding of equality in partnership. Consequently, there have been strong trends toward later childbearing as compared to previous generations; toward having fewer children; or toward having no children at all. The size of the average family dropped from 3.8 in 1957 to 1.88 in 1975.

It was not uncommon to find older women who had married early seeking independence in a late career or a divorce. According to the U.S. Bureau of the Census, there were 63 divorced persons for every 1,000 married persons in the United States in 1974 compared with 47 in 1970 and 35 in 1960. At 1976 rates, 40 percent of all marriages will end in divorce—a rate double that of a decade earlier.

In sum, the principal changes in the status of women included the postponement of marriage for an average of several years; an increase in the incidence of divorce among couples who married early; postponement of child rearing; a decrease in the number of children per family; and a slight increase in the proportion of childless marriages. These trends point to a long-range slowing and, if they hold, a gradual leveling of population growth. In the 1980s and 1990s, researchers who follow the reading habits of library users will probably observe a trend among female clientele away from light-fiction reading and toward professional and recreational interests.

In areas other than monetary, the nation has done very little to meet the needs of the elderly. In 1978 there were 23 million persons over the age of sixty-five in the United States—roughly 10 percent of the population. By the turn of the new century there are likely to be at least 28 million in the age-group called "elderly," and the numbers will continue to rise as the post–World War II bumper crop of babies reaches the seventh decade of life. The impact on society of increasing numbers of the "aged" will rival the impact the same people had on schools, colleges, and the housing market from the 1950s onwards. By the years 2010–15, when the first of the postwar babies will become "senior citizens," most of the institutions of the society will have anticipated their demands. Probably the age sixty-five will no longer be the customary dividing line between active employment and retirement. Already the compul-

1. Paul Glick and Arthur Norton, "Marrying, Divorcing and Living Together in the U.S. Today," *Population Bulletin*, October 1977.

2. The usual cost of an abortion in 1975 was $150 to $250.

3. Donald J. Bogue, *Principles of Demography* (New York: John Wiley, 1969), p. 8.

sory retirement age has been advanced in most occupations; compulsory retirement may someday be a relic of history. A result will be continued economic self-sufficiency and a brisk market for goods and services in demand by an older population. The principal ones are leisure activities (especially travel), health services, educational and cultural opportunities, efficiency housing (most in well-serviced metropolitan centers). As the elderly increase in number and in economic power, their political influence will be disproportionately felt.

Older political leaders are likely to be more readily elected. Probably the first president to enter office at age seventy or more will be elected in the first or second decade of the twenty-first century. Surely the majority of the nation's wealth will pass into the hands of the over-sixty-five agegroup within three decades.

Public institutions and services desired by the "elderly" will begin to take precedence within the next two decades. Those having the foresight to anticipate demands and needs of the "elderly" in the years immediately ahead are likely to prosper in the first half of the twenty-first century. For example, carefully planned "retirement centers" that include efficiency housing, an interesting variety of quality eating facilities, ready access to health and medical services, appropriate recreational opportunities, and a broad range of educational and cultural facilities are likely to attract an increasing clientele among the elderly population after 2010.

Well-stocked, diversified libraries utilizing a variety of media are likely to be popular among the "elderly" where such facilities are readily accessible. The favored "retirement centers" of the twenty-first century will feature imaginatively planned libraries and media centers. Central city libraries, especially in the larger metropolitan areas, are likely to experience a gradually increasing demand for recreational, informational, and educational library services by older residents who occupy middle- to upper-income housing. Bookmobiles will become more widely used to serve older people who choose to live in rural and suburban communities. In some places meals-on-wheels and library services are likely to be continued for the benefit of older persons who are confined to their houses. Among the library services that will be in demand among older clientele will be tape cassettes of novels, short stories and plays; videotapes of old and current films; books in braille for the blind; informational services on health problems; recreational programs and employment opportunities. Librarians who seek to serve the elderly and the aged need to bear in mind the vulnerability of older people to the dread disease of ennui.

The Economics of Qualitative Consumption

Expanding economic activity is likely to raise average family income from $10,000 in 1970 to at least $20,000 (in 1970 dollars) by the year 2000.[4] By the mid-1980s half the population may be living as well as the top 15 percent did in 1970. Although fewer people may be poor, the differential between those who stay poor and those who are better off will probably widen. As the youth of the 1960s and 1970s advance in their jobs and professions, their sheer numbers may increase competition. This situation will be exacerbated by the large increase in the numbers of working women more than by any slowing of corporate or public sector growth. However, a greater percentage of the population will be in the work force because the proportion of children will be lower, and so per capita disposable income will rise. Thus working adults will have more to spend on themselves as compared to preceding generations who supported larger families.

The increased affluence will result in increased spending on leisure activities. Yet there is evidence that people whose affluence is growing, when given the choice, tend to choose more income over greater leisure. A worker who earns ten dollars an hour, given the opportunity to work overtime, is likely to feel that he cannot afford to pass up the extra income. Professionals expect to put in whatever time the job requires; they gain higher incomes by earning a reputation for dedication and productivity. Thus the demand for library services in the future is likely to continue the trend toward users seeking education and information, and away from recreational ones. It is no accident that library public relations emphasizes the information function. The more we have the more we want, and achievement is the driving force of an affluent society; leisure is for the unemployable poor and the unemployed rich.[5]

Doubling of family income over the next twenty years would mean less poverty. Although income differentials between the poor and the affluent might not change very much and might continue to widen, absolute dollar income would increase substantially at all levels of society. If the economic gap between the educated and the poorly educated continues to widen, the cause will be the relative inability of the uneducated to take advantage of job opportunities in other locations. Never-

---

4. $16,000 by 1985.

5. Lee Rainwater, "Post-1984 America," *Society*, February 1972, p. 25. See also Steffan Linder, *The Harried Leisure Class* (New York: Columbia University Press, 1970).

theless, the poverty groups of 1975 with $3,500 a year for a three-member family will probably have incomes of $10,000 (in 1970 dollars) by the year 2000. Moreover, public services—including information and recreational services provided by public libraries—may be more widely demanded by the less affluent during the next two decades. The broader demand, however, will depend upon what new services for the less affluent are offered by libraries. Some suggestions are made in later sections of the chapter.

Welfare Reform to Eliminate Poverty

For many years antipoverty policy has focused on various combinations of cash aid and services to the poor. The primary emphasis was on services until we realized that social service workers either did not know how to deal with the problems of the poor or they lacked the resources for undertaking the task. In recent years policy goals have shifted to various plans for income maintenance. Such plans assume that the main problem of the poor is lack of money. In the mid-1960s several income maintenance plans were put forward, but a skeptical Congress and a reluctant public would not accept any of them. Many Americans believe that the poor receive welfare payments because they do not want to work. The work ethic runs so deeply in American culture that it has obscured the need of millions who are cognitively or situationally incapacitated and who therefore cannot work regularly.

After years of experience and experimentation with a variety of assistance programs for the poor, we have come to recognize: (1) that some categories of the poor require permanent assistance both in cash payments and in service (e.g. the disabled and the elderly); (2) that other categories require only temporary assistance—for example, dispossessed immigrants who are otherwise able; and (3) that there are millions who require a cushion of insurance and services to keep them from poverty in times of crisis (e.g. the marginally employed and the low-income elderly).

The future should bring more effective and humane antipoverty programs, including assistance for the permanently and situationally disabled through regular income that supports an acceptable standard of living. For others, unemployment and health insurance is likely to be designed to bridge crisis periods of unemployment or extraordinary health or medical problems. Such programs would not only eliminate poverty but would also contribute to national prosperity. A minimum income would place millions of disabled people squarely in the consumer market and pro-

vide an additional basis of stable economic expansion. A universal health insurance program developed in conjunction with a reorganized health and medical care system could be a major factor in shifting the emphasis in health care from treatment of acute problems to preventive medicine and adequate maintenance care.

The public library could make a substantial contribution to the plight of the poor by continuing to expand library service at the neighborhood level where access is easy and the library environment can be made comfortable for local residents. As we pointed out a few pages back, a great deal has been done in the past few years to extend library services to the poor. The lessons learned from recent experience indicate that library service in poor neighborhoods should emphasize educational services that are designed to help adults gain the knowledge and information they need in the job market.

A problem is that librarians have had trouble adjusting their attitudes and their training to modes of services that would benefit the educationally or culturally disadvantaged. If librarians do not choose to provide the needed educational and informational services, then they should consider employing educators to do the job. Progress has been made in branch library services, in developing special ethnic collections, and in attracting to the profession increased numbers of minority librarians. Local public libraries need to persist in maintaining this facet of service as a priority—against a growing trend nationally away from special services for the poor.

Population Movements and Urban Concentrations

The migration patterns within the United States in the early to mid-1970s were largely away from low-income, economically depressed and rural areas which characterized the older settlements of the interior. Many of the metropolitan areas of the Northeast and Midwest have experienced slowed growth compared to the rapidly developing urban areas of the Southwest and South. The main factors contributing to this trend are abundant resources, favorable climatic conditions, and lower living and production costs. The principal growth areas are Dallas, San Diego, Memphis, Phoenix, San Jose, Jacksonville, and Houston.

A new trend barely discernible in 1980 is the move to rural areas. According to Calvin L. Beale, the nation's nonmetropolitan counties, which experienced a net out-migration of 300,000 per year in the 1960s, were gaining about 380,000 persons a year in the 1970s.[6] The preference for rural or semirural areas years ago created the outlying suburb with building lots of an acre or more; the automobile served by a modern highway system made possible vast suburban expansion. In the decades ahead increased affluence and improved air transportation and telecommunications will enable people to live where they prefer and in many cases to work where they live. Gordon F. DeJong, a sociologist at the Pennsylvania State Population Issues Research Office, has established that persons moving away from cities are on the average seventeen years younger, have two more years of education, and are in occupations with higher socioeconomic status than persons who remain in metropolitan areas. They also have fewer children and more stable family lives than those who stay in cities. DeJong concluded from a 1974 survey that many more wanted to move to smaller communities than did so; the most prevalent reason given for not moving was high commuting costs.[7]

A significant factor in current migration is that people have improved information about areas of opportunity and therefore are able to judge the advantages and disadvantages of one location over another. Most people in the labor market know where unemployment is high or low; where opportunities are open to them; what are the relative costs of living, climatic conditions, and so forth. Americans are also traditionally mobile and have little concern about putting a continent between themselves and kin. The increased mobility of the American work force—from professionals to skilled and unskilled laborers—has contributed to the flexibility of the economy and thereby its capacity for expansion. Many of the rigidities of location of resources, markets, and labor force have disappeared.

By 1978 population in metropolitan areas had increased to 74 percent of the nation. Within these areas, however, population densities will have decreased from 6,580 per square mile in 1920 to 3,800 in 1985. The proportion of population in suburbs will have increased from 39 percent to about 45 percent.

Within metropolitan areas, populations have dispersed from once-crowded central cities into less-densely settled suburbs. The inner-city slums have been thinning out since the mid-1950s, when densities reached a postwar peak. By 1970

one-third of central cities over 50,000 had lost population. As suburbs grew, business and industry also dispersed, encouraged by construction of limited-access highways and ready availability of skilled office workers. In 1972 the U.S. Bureau of the Census reported that for the first time a larger proportion of business and industry was located in suburbs than in central cities. This trend did not mean the central cities were dying out. Some of the most vital ones have an economic momentum that is not likely to fade in the foreseeable future. Chicago, Houston, Boston, and Atlanta were continuing to develop at a pace that matched that of their suburbs.

Not only are these cities attracting a substantial share of new commercial and industrial development, but they are drawing affluent singles of all ages, younger couples without children, and middle-aged and older couples for whom suburban living is no longer convenient or economical. The upswing in new apartment and condominum construction and a corresponding decline in new single-family housing throughout metropolitan regions are a strong indicator of movement into the cities of the affluent middle and upper classes. One account of the return of middle-class professionals was given by Ellen Karasik and Elizabeth Duff in a Knight Wire Service feature:

> Urban pioneering, brownstoning, or rehabbing—that is, buying a structurally sound but shabby home cheap, fixing it up, making the immediate neighborhood more attractive, thereby attracting other professionals to buy other homes and thus touching off an upward spiral in a once declining area—is becoming a new urban dream.

Karsik and Duff were not describing an isolated phenomenon. Such projects, privately initiated, have been going on in Boston and New York at least since the early sixties and have in recent years spread to Chicago and other cities. Further, the growing popularity of condominiums may be an attempt of many people to have the benefits of apartment living and ownership of a home without the disadvantages of either.

The federal urban renewal programs of the 1950s and 1960s prepared the groundwork (quite literally) in clearing slums to make way for new commercial as well as residential development. Though the improvements were supposed to benefit the poor by replacing old housing with new low-cost housing, the programs seldom worked out that way. Instead the cleared land usually was sold at subsidized prices to private developers who put the acquired land to its most profitable use. In this way many cities made run-down sections

---

6. Calvin L. Beale, "Renewed Growth in Rural Communities," *Futurist* 9:196–202, Aug. 1975.

7. Gordon F. De Jong and Ralph R. Sell, "Population Redistribution, Migration and Residential Preferences," *Annals of the American Academy of Political and Social Science* 429:130–44, Jan. 1977.

attractive for affluent commercial and residential use. Thus the housing that was built in urban renewal sites was mostly in the medium to high-rent class—for example, Boston's West End. In many cities the land was used for new office buildings or civic or governmental centers.

From the mid-1960s onward the working classes and increasing numbers of the poorer classes left the urban renewal areas and other older sections of central cities to resettle in the nearby suburbs or in more remote older communities beyond the middle-class suburbs. In spite of these trends, the numbers of impoverished in central cities have not decreased, because many of the larger coastal and industrial cities are still attracting poor immigrants from rural areas, the migrant labor streams, and settlers from abroad. It is likely that the inner-city ghettos will continue to serve as staging areas for these newcomers—a trend that is rooted in our nation's past urban development.

Immigration—especially illegal—will continue to be a signficant demographic factor in certain of our largest cities: New York, Chicago, Los Angeles, Houston, San Francisco, Miami, and San Antonio. In additon to the 5.5 to 6 million illegal aliens who are already in the United States, another million or more enter the country annually, according to the Immigration and Naturalization Service. One and a half million aliens were apprehended by the INS in 1975–76, but INS estimates that for every alien apprehended another goes undetected. Legal aliens entering the United States number 494,000 each year. As population pressures grow in Latin American countries, especially Mexico, the numbers of illegal aliens are likely to increase.

The central cities are not yet attracting, indeed are still losing, middle-class families with school-aged children. These families continue to populate the more affluent suburbs, although by the mid-1980s their declining numbers are likely to cause a slowing of population growth in these areas. The decrease in children is already noticeable in suburban public schools.

The greatest volume of population movement in the nation is *within* metropolitan areas as families move from suburb to suburb seeking to adjust housing needs to job location and to social aspirations. The most common reasons for such moves are the search for the better school districts; the more homogeneous or prestigious neighborhoods; convenience to desired social, cultural, and recreational amenities. As a consequence metropolitan areas are developing clear patterns of social and economic segregation. Vance Packard illustrates the point in quoting a relocation consultant:

I can take a transferring family from Darien, and in any metropolitan area of the United States I can put these people in approximately the same environment as far as schools, types of neighbors, same income bracket, same family background, same education, anywhere across the country. They will not be changing their environment, they will be just changing their address.[8]

The Metropolis as "Community"

Yet the longing for community persists, perhaps more acutely for the movers than for the stayers. Our large-scale society has tended to breed anomie, separation between home and work, a weakened family structure, and community government managed by professionals. Participation in public decision making in communities often seems artificial except for permanent residents. Americans maintain strong attachments to grass-roots localities, at the same time as we are attracted to the more challenging and intellectually satisfying activities and institutions that are metropolitan and national in scope. Although we try to preserve our small communities, we grudgingly recognize that regional government and planning must be utilized to deal with the most complex problems of our urban society.

The development of new forms of local government in which people can play a major role has taken some inventive courses. In the past two decades there have been many efforts to make larger cities out of smaller ones, such as Miami–Dade County, Nashville–Davidson County, Jacksonville–Duval County, Indianapolis–Marion County, and many others. In some of our largest cities, efforts to create neighborhood governments have occurred to make public services more effectively serve the everyday needs of people. Both centralization and decentralization of local government structure and services are essential in that people need the social intimacy of neighborhoods and certain community-level activities as well as the benefits of efficiency and economy provided by regional services.

In response, local libraries must continue to adapt their services to purely local needs, and at the same time they must help to promote linkages with other libraries and library systems that put the

---

8. Vance Packard, *A Nation of Strangers* (New York: McKay, 1973). Quoted in the *Wall Street Journal*, May 8, 1973.

local community in easy touch with all types of collections everywhere. While impressive efforts have been made in this direction by some of the states and a few groups of states as well as by several national and international groups, library and information networks that connect local communities with each other and with national and international collections were in the late 1970s still at a rudimentary stage of development.

The Future of Local Self-Government

The struggle to maintain a democratic system in America has largely been one of balancing local power against national power. This balance is maintained because political power in America is preponderantly in the hands of state and local leaders and their constituencies. The Congress, which controls the purse strings of the federal government, must be responsive to local interests or risk the loss of vital support. Nevertheless, because of its vast resources and relative ease of taxing power, the federal government is in a position to initiate policies and programs from civil rights to environmental protection; to be the instigator of local and regional planning and cooperation; and to serve as the provider of services that state and local governments or private enterprise cannot manage effectively or equitably. Local and state governments, on the other hand, are face to face with the taxpayer, who finds it far easier to resist new tax proposals at these levels than at the federal level. The differential between the federal taxing power and the state and local ones is the crucial difference in the power to provide services. Libraries traditionally have been regarded as primarliy a state and local responsibility. The national government for its part has been hampered in recent years, since the great social programs of the 1960s, by a deepening skepticism of the ability of the public sector to solve social problems. Local and state governments may be further hamstrung by a growing resistance to the property tax as was dramatically demonstrated in 1978 when Californians voted overwhelmingly to roll back the level of property taxes (Proposition 13). It was hard to say at this writing how widely tax revolt might spread in other areas of the country in the next few years, but it seemed reasonable to assume that local political leaders would be wary of proposed expansions in budgets.

As the national government has increased its role in domestic affairs, it has also been pressed by local interests to strengthen the capacity of state and local governments. To the degree this policy has succeeded, the states and localities have been less the instruments of the federal government and more the testing grounds for adaptations of federal policies and programs. Even though the national government has increased its capacity enormously during the past five decades, local government has not lost influence in the political system. Political leaders and citizens insist upon the superior capacity of localities to understand and conduct their own affairs. People uphold the value of local self-government as a hedge against "undue" centralization because they fear encroachment upon their liberties. They think of local government as an instrument of political education and an opportunity for schooling in citizenship. They believe that the most important responsibility of local government is to provide the forum for citizen participation in planning and development decisions. In the future, major central cities will need to reconcile the demands for neighborhood participation with overall community policies and programs, because, as John Bebout cautions, "in no case should decentralization within a city destroy the integrity or ultimate authority of the whole city."[9]

Neighborhood as Community

The regional viewpoint came into focus in the 1960s and 1970s at a time when some local leaders—especially those representing people in minority and ghetto sections of large cities who believed they were being cheated out of a fair share of public services—began to argue for "community control." One objective of community control was to tailor services and facilities to the special needs and values of minority and poverty areas. It was argued, for example, that schools should have curricula and instructional staff attuned to the predominant educational aspirations of the communities they served. In ghetto neighborhoods, police service would be transformed from a "force of occupation" and "agents of oppression" to a protective body dedicated to crime control. Health services would be made available in local clinics staffed by professionals familiar with community attitudes about health and medical services. Library services would be designed to cater to the information, education, and recreation needs of the community. Planning and administration would be done with participation of community residents.

Except in poverty communities, the principle of "community control" is already well established in

---

9. John E. Bebout, "Centralization and Decentralization" (Houston, Tex.: Institute for Urban Studies, Univ. of Houston, 1973), pp. 20–21.

the American system. Local political party organizations have traditionally used districts, wards, and precincts as election units and as "listening posts" for citizen complaints. Demands for "community control" during the past decade came largely from groups who felt deprived of adequate representation in local, state, and national government when the local political organizations passed them by. The community control movement, however, had a short lifetime, roughly 1968–72, and focused largely on public schools in a few large cities including New York, Detroit, Washington, and Boston. Nevertheless, the movement precipitated a radical shift in several big-city school organizations that had been highly centralized. They instituted various forms of decentralization, some of which provided for community participation in local school policy. Decentralization of services, however, is different from community control in that decentralization leaves control of policy in the hands of the dominant community, thus minimizing the influence of minority interests.

Anticipating the community control movement by several years and providing the organizational base from which it was launched, the federal government in the early 1960s sought to creat opportunities for participation of the poor in the Community Action Program of the War on Poverty (1964) and in the Model Cities Program (1966). The Community Action Program required "maximum feasible participation" of residents of affected neighborhoods, while the Model Cities Program required resident participation in establishing community priorities. The participation aspects of both programs were deemphasized by the federal government after 1968, partly in an effort to stem the rise of new political leaders in the expanding black areas of cities. By 1970, a majority of the nation's electorate believed that too many concessions had been made to minorities and that antipoverty programs should be dismantled. Moderate leaders cultivated new opportunities as barriers to political advancement disintegrated. Although the dominant society could not tolerate radicalism, it welcomed minority leaders who were willing to work within established channels.

By 1975 the politics of racism had nearly disappeared. White candidates who aspired to office in areas where large numbers of black or Hispanic voters resided had to cater to these groups to win their votes. Minority candidates were numerous, and localities with large black or Hispanic populations were electing their own to public office. By 1975 more than 3,000 black politicians held elective office as contrasted with less than 200 in 1965. Thus the traditional pattern of American politics

proved as viable for recent urban immigrants as it had for earlier ones—once exclusionary barriers were down. The decline of racist politics is an important development, but social and class distinctions based upon race and national origin continue to affect our political life.

Some progress has been made since the 1960s in improving library services in poor communities in both urban and rural areas. Most of the improvements have been initiated in federally funded experiments in providing information and reader services at branch libraries in cities, in mobile rural units, and within suburban library systems. Their strength and cogency has been in the participation of community residents at the planning and implementation stages. Reduction of federal funds for such programs has caused many of them to fade for lack of local financial support. Vigorous new efforts are needed to revive library services of this type.

Institutional and Societal Changes

Mass Transportation

Mass transportation innovations may provide American cities with opportunities to create systems of individualized transportation that could eliminate the extensive use of private automobiles in congested areas. Such opportunities exist in cities not yet committed to old-style rapid-rail systems. Individualized forms of mass transportation systems have been invented over the past three decades, but the federal government has not provided funds on sufficient scale to test those systems that might work best in American cities. Two policy enactments in 1974 may encourage innovations in mass transit. First, Congress and the president agreed to use part of the Highway Trust Fund for mass transportation. Second, the National Mass Transportation Assistance Act of 1974 provided $11.8 billion in operating and capital subsidies to urban mass transportation systems, the first such federal support for this purpose.

By 1973 a few cities had begun to develop plans for automated rapid transit systems. Denver, for example, was developing a system that featured twelve-passenger vehicles to carry commuters from suburban to downtown points with few stops. The system was planned for flexible scheduling and routing and for nonstop service in rush hours. Projections were for limited operation by 1978 and completion by 1983 (federal funding, however, was cut off in 1976). Other cities whose suburban population densities do not warrant heavy investment for rapid transit train systems may follow suit. Predecessors of the Denver plan are short-run systems at the Dallas–Fort Worth Regional Airport and Tampa International Airport and a 3.5-mile test system in Morgantown, West Virginia. Some cities may limit the use of private automobiles in downtown congested areas or impose incentives that encourage car pooling and extensive use of public transportation. Other possibilities are that private automobiles may be equipped with low-emission or nonpolluting engines or that alternatives to the internal combustion engine will be developed.

Although such efforts are promising, their impact upon the organization and services of public libraries is not likely to be felt much before 1985, except in a few cities. Even with federal subsidies, the development of new mass transportation facilities will take several more decades in a large number of metropolitan areas. Changes in the habits of automobile users could take even longer. The few cities that do make significant improvements in public transportation are likely to be followed by other growing ones over the next half century. The lack of public transportation services in suburbs and small cities greatly reduces access to libraries, especially for the children and the elderly. Energy shortages, if they materialize on a large scale, may further reduce access. Library administrators need to make their influence felt in the planning stages so that public library facilities can be adapted to demands generated by the increased accessibility made possible by new transportation systems.

Health Services

The United States has some of the finest health and medical facilities in the world. Our medical and health scientists have been leaders in medical science and technological developments that have contributed to the nation's capacity to maintain health and to control disease. The trouble with the health system as it exists in 1980 is that it is not organized to provide ready and economical access to its vast services and facilities. Access to adequate health care is frequently beyond the financial means of substantial segments of the population, especially the elderly and the poor. If progress is to be made toward improving access, the federal government will have to take the lead in encouraging and assisting in the provision of neighborhood diagnostic, emergency, and health maintenance clinics organizationally related to diagnostic and treatment centers. Such centers would have a more sophisticated level of services than clinics, and they would serve as the principal links between the clinics and the great hospital and health maintenance centers. The latter already

exist as "medical centers" in several of our largest cities, for example, Houston, New York, and Boston. Neighborhood clinics would be located throughout metropolitan areas for easy access by the entire population.

It is apparent that the health and medical profession is moving toward system organization. A major influence has been the federal planning requirements of the 1966 Health Services Act, which incorporated incentives for the development of state and areawide comprehensive health planning. The National Health Planning and Resources Development Act of 1974 has thus strengthened the prospects for effective health planning. Also, existing and pending federal health insurance programs require improved cooperation in health systems planning.

A crucial aspect of access to the health facilities of the future will be information that provides incentives to use them. Public libraries could play a major role in providing the public—especially the least-educated segment—with materials that inform people of health problems, of preventive measures, and of the facilities and services available for health needs.

Crime Prevention and Control

Crime is one of the worst problems of cities. Although scientific and technological applications are available to help bring it under effective control, local police departments in many cities are still utilizing primitive and haphazard methods of crime control: emphasis has traditionally focused on crimes committed rather than on measures to prevent criminal activities. Consequently citizens in many urban communities are not safe inside or outside their homes either day or night. Drugs and drug pushers are in nearly every school and neighborhood—rich and poor. American cities need federal and state assistance and cooperation to develop scientific crime-control systems. Local police agencies have made gains under the Safe Streets Act of 1968 and subsequent amending legislation, but more federal assistance is needed for crime-prevention programs, particularly in central-city ghettos and suburbs, where the crime rates are highest.

The greatest danger in a high crime rate is in the conditioning of society to its presence. The more crime people experience, the more they tolerate, until it becomes a part of the culture, a condition that can lead to the demoralization and corruption of law enforcement itself. Once the framework of law enforcement has crumbled, the very basis of the social order is threatened. A symptom of the breakdown in law and order in the United States today is the widespread vandalism in public institutions, which have become targets for discontented and undisciplined youth. As with riots, once the scenarios are set by a few well-publicized incidents in which the vandals go unpunished, like-minded imitators multiply.

A consequence of rampant crime and vandalism is a breakdown of sense of community and a pervasive fear of routine use of public facilities. According to James Q. Wilson, this may create a condition of "urban unease," which is the result of crime, violence, rebellious youth, racial tension, public immorality, and delinquency.[10] Wilson argues that "improper behavior in public places" causes a great deal of community concern and contributes to tensions among different groups and particularly in the relationships between white and black residential areas. Recent evidence suggests that in extremely unsafe areas and in vandalized neighborhoods there is considerable housing abandonment even where low-income residents have limited choices in relocating elsewhere. Police patrols and surveillance cannot prevent the deterioration of such neighborhoods. Intensified community disruption reflects more than the level of criminal or antisocial behavior. More likely, the seeds of despair and discontent in such areas have persisted over long periods of time.

The public library can do little or nothing to reduce crime, but library administrators in cities have an obvious stake in its effective control. Public libraries, along with schools and other educational and recreational institutions, are especially vulnerable to crime and vandalism. Library administrators should involve themselves directly in public and private efforts at crime control and should offer whatever anticrime informational services are needed by crime authorities and the public to support such efforts.

Education

Public education at the elementary and secondary levels has fallen on hard times in the nation. Money has been short because of taxpayer resistance, and the quality of education has suffered as a consequence. Some claim that taxpayer resistance increased as quality slipped. Probably both observations are true. Public education has always been considered the function and responsibility of the states and localities, and these taxing jurisdictions have never supported public schools at a level that would attract our most talented young people into teaching. If the public has been disillusioned with its educational system, it has got

what it paid for: mediocre instruction, discipline problems, a hampering of instruction because of the discipline problems—in short, a vicious circle. The consequences are evident in declining central city and even suburban public school populations, abandonments of school buildings, and increases everywhere in private school enrollments.

To break the vicious circle, cities should consider alternatives addressed to the multiple problems of public education. One such alternative that has not been fully explored by any large city school system is a system of educational parks, each planned to incorporate recreational, health, information, and other needed facilities. Each could be located for easy access by foot, bicycle, auto, and bus or rapid-rail transit. A city of 1 million, for example, could design twelve to fifteen such campuses to accommodate a social and economic cross-section of the city's population. The campuses could occupy unused city spaces, each sufficiently extensive to avoid concentration of students in time or space. The facilities of a high school and two-year college might be placed at one end, thus enhancing the functional relationships between the two. Kindergarten and preschool areas could be remote from the upper-grade and adult segments of the campus and could be designed on a scale suitable for young children. In addition to general purpose education, each campus could have specialities that would attract students from all parts of the city. The campuses could be linked by a transportation system that would be an integral part of the city's transportation system.

The campuses would have a range of community facilities, programs, and services within easy access of all residents. These might include a health clinic complete with diagnostic services and health maintenance services; a library and information center, or on each campus a series of such centers to serve different kinds of information and research needs; recreational facilities that would be designed physically and programmatically to serve the entire community.

A restructured educational system should be thought of as a physically and socially integrating concept. Future public education systems should serve all of the formal educational needs of the society and therefore should serve the entire society, not just persons of "school age." The present-day world requires that education be a continuing process. American school systems should provide such opportunities on a basis that fully meets the educational needs of society. A student attending school on a campus of the scale and diversity suggested here would be exposed to opportunities that would mirror the real world of work and creativity. Such a facility would head off the de-

---

10. James Q. Wilson, "The Urban Unease," *The Public Interest* 12:26 (Summer 1968).

velopment of a stratified class structure. Public schools designed to assure social mix and educational quality would reaffirm the nation's dedication to a democratic society, to equality of educational oportunity, and thus to the appropriateness of merit as the basis of achievement in society. Moreover, our nation cannot afford to educate its children in tight little islands of authoritarianism operated on minimal resources by professionals of modest talent.

The American public is not likely to give serious consideration in the near future to any radical restructuring of its public school systems. Moreover, there are presently no incentives for substantial integration of education and other public facilities, and none are likely to emerge in public policy at any level in the foreseeable future. Therefore, the library profession must continue to make its contributions to public education as opportunities present themselves. The targets of maximum opportunity in the years ahead may lie with "preschool" children who have been placed in nursery schools or day-care centers by working mothers, and with community college students, whose library facilities are expanding at a rapid pace.

It is commonly known that the public schools have not been able to educate or train large numbers of young people who find themselves virtually illiterate after years of compulsory public schooling. Possibly the most challenging task the public libraries of cities could undertake would be the one of meeting the needs of young people who are educationally disabled. Hardly any institution is better equipped for the job.

The State Role

State constitutions and court decisions establish local governments as extensions of state government, although the more independent local governments are in conducting their affairs, the less likely are state governments to assert their prerogatives. Until recently, most state governments have been somewhat passive even when many local problems could not be managed by local governments.

Library services are among the public functions for which the state has a primary responsibility. State inaction in these areas can effectively frustrate both national and local efforts to deal with problems that arise from new demands and changing societal conditions. Moreover, when localities are forced to look beyond state governments to the national government for assistance, local control over these functions is usually reduced. Specifically, it is the state's responsibility to promote library and information services. While

this service traditionally has been regarded as a local or private responsibility, a highly educated society needs well-organized sources of knowledge and information to maintain technologically based commerce and industry. Of equal importance is the availability of information upon which governmental decisions are made. Libraries and information services are not exclusively a state function, but every state has a responsibility to maintain adequate support to and accessibility of library and information services.

To the extent that public libraries fail to provide the extensive information services vital to the functioning of our society, they are being superseded by specialized organizations. However, such organizations cannot serve the broad needs to which libraries could readily be adapted. There is an integrative function in the organization of *all* knowledge and information that must continue to be the responsibility of public libraries and of library systems.

Libraries and Communication

Knowledge and information have come to be recognized as one of the nation's most valuable resources. As sociologist Lee Rainwater has observed, modern communications in the context of urban society have "the effect of exposing the average citizen to a much wider range of information, and a much wider range of perspectives for interpreting that information than has ever been true in the past."[11] In recent years librarians and information specialists have been concerned with organization and storage to meet the retrieval demands of diverse and often unpredictable consumers. This problem has been partially solved by librarians through improved and expanded systems of classification; through the development of specialized collections that utilize mechanized networks to serve their users; and by state governments that encouraged the reorganization of ordinary public libraries into regional systems. A major complication of the regional network organization today is the diversity of media and the locations for storing them. Despite the hesitancy of some who fear federal controls, a national network is clearly indicated.

A permanent National Commission on Libraries and Information Science has proposed the establishment of a national network of library and information services based upon regional and statewide systems. A national network would tie together not only all local and state public libraries,

---

11. Rainwater, "Post-1984 America," p. 20.

but the federal and academic libraries as well. If a national system of library and information services is established, as seems likely, it should include the major research libraries of both public and private institutions. It should also bring together the unique information resources of private vendors of information services. A national network of library and information services, as outlined by the national commission, is a necessary step toward facilitating access to all of the communications resources of the nation and the world, including print and nonprint materials.

While there are substantial technical, organizational, and political problems affecting the development of a national system of library and information services, such a system is long overdue. The main problem is that the states and the federal government have not given high priority to a national library system as one of the basic domestic improvements, as was demonstrated by the modest funding of the commission's early work. The tentative federal commitment also recognized that major technical difficulties could be overcome only through cooperative efforts of library institutions at all levels of government as well as between the public and private sectors.

Federal, state, and local governments have not vigorously promoted the comprehensive development of libraries. Priorities in library service have focused narrowly on specialized collections by groups to whom the services are critical—but even these groups tend to resist participation in regional and national library systems. Independent libraries cannot easily accommodate the growing knowledge and informational demands of the society, particularly those demands that cut across traditional areas of specialization. Library services should accommodate specialty interests, but they also should serve problem solvers who draw upon a diversity of information and expertise. In our complex society, problem solving frequently requires information and resources that are hard to mobilize. The extent to which libraries can develop effective capabilities for mobilizing critical problem-solving information depends upon their provisions for maximizing available resources.

Up to 1978 the permanent National Commission on Libraries and Information Science was funded at a fraction of the level needed for design and promotion of a national network. A few years earlier the Nixon administration had declared that public libraries were not a national responsibility and underscored the point by attempting to terminate all federal aid to libraries.

In a nation with common economic and social problems, the availability of education, of knowledge and information is the key to past and future success of resource development. Various types of libraries are the nation's major educational and cultural institutions, a national resource of incalculable value. The great national libraries, such as the Library of Congress, are the responsibility of the federal government. The great research libraries of our public and private universities should also be treated as national resources and should receive substantial federal support on the conditions that their collections be available to responsible users and that they become a part of a national system of libraries. All public libraries should be organized into regional and state systems for accessibility of resources and for economy. Regional organization of public libraries should be a condition of federal support.

As part of planning for a national system of libraries and information services, an appropriate division of support should be established among the federal, state, and local governments. In promoting a national system of information resources, a reasonable level of support might be one-fourth federal, one-fourth state, and one-half local (the last supported by an areawide tax). State and federal support of libraries and library systems must be stabilized in the future to remove the financial barrier to their development. National legislation to this effect should be formulated jointly by the American Library Association and the national commission. The two groups acting together could be a potent force in Congress. An alternative would be a vigorous ALA Action Commission charged with developing an ALA plan for a national network of library and information service and organizing the profession to press for its adoption in Congress.

Meanwhile, an increasing number of local and regional public libraries have been transformed by imaginative leadership from introverted, book-oriented institutions to gregarious, multimedia institutions bent on serving diversified community interests. Among the newer services in the nation's public libraries are these examples:

Any resident of Bexar County, Texas, can call the San Antonio Public Library at any time, twenty-four hours a day, and order a book to be mailed to his home. The library guarantees mailing within twenty-four hours, if the book is available, and there's no charge to the borrower.

Public libraries in Miami, Atlanta, and a number of other cities are now offering college-credit studies under the sponsorship of local colleges.

Brooklyn's public library system plans to set up a computer-operated urban-information system for citizens needing answers to problems they have with city agencies and other official bureaucracies.

It has become common for libraries to have media resource centers that provide overhead projectors, slides, microfiches, filmstrips, cassette players, and portable television-recording equipment. Many libraries have become community centers—the equivalent of the small-town general store, the settlement house, Grange hall, church, or town meeting—where people get together and find out what others are thinking and doing.

Concluding Observations

We believe that American society has the potential for self-improvement despite major setbacks of the past two decades—a draining war, an economy plagued by inflation and unemployment, a failure to solve problems attending poverty, a deterioration of public education, and governmental scandals and corruption. The opportunities for advancement may be elusive. We have wealth beyond the dreams of our ancestors, yet we cannot bring ourselves to improve its distribution for the common benefit. We educate our youth, but we have difficulties in improving educational opportunity and quality. We pour endless resources into medical research, yet we put off organizing health services so as to make the best use of medical knowledge. We set foot on the moon, yet we provide no more than meager support to research and development of mass transportation facilities for our cities. We police the world, yet we seem unable to control crime in our neighborhoods. We are leaders in systems analysis, yet we have not mastered the fluctuations of inflation and recession in our economy. We produce scientific and technological breakthroughs, yet we allow our scientists the luxury of eschewing responsibility for beneficial societal applications. We boast of a free political system, yet we are unable to control abuses of public power. We constantly produce new information and knowledge in every conceivable field, and yet we neglect to arrange for ready access to library resources.

Our creativity and our waste are both a product of our freedom and our democratic system. If this is true, then our freedom is both our salvation and our nemesis. Until we resolve these contradictions, the American dream will be less a reality than an unfulfilled promise.

2 Expanding Environments of Library Administration

IRA SHARKANSKY

If the local library ever was isolated from the pressures of other affairs, that is no longer the case. The image of cloistered study and contemplation is more apparent in architectural features of the older buildings than in their administrative offices. Library authorities must compete with numerous other claimants for their shares of local, state, and national government budgets; they feel the effects of increasingly assertive clients and staff; and they catch the turmoil of changing mores about proper collections and the proper audiences for books, magazines, films, and records.

In this context, library administrators cannot take a narrow perspective of the environment. It is not limited to users, staff, and the professional community of other librarians, but includes the cultural traits and economic resources of the community and the actions of other governmental bodies that make relevant decisions on funds or programs. Even if library administrators did limit their perspective to the narrow confines of users and staff, they would need to show the same openness and flexibility under fire as administrators who were sensitive to the larger environment. Gone are the days of quiescent clients and subordinates. Libraries have become a target of citizen groups wanting a voice in the design of their public services and demanding—among other things—useful information and due regard for their distinctive cultural heritage in the materials to be available. The public's image of the demure, submissive librarian has been rendered obsolete by librarians' concern for making their services more relevent to citizens, a concern that may lead to efforts at organizing users into an articulate force, and to making demands on their administrative superiors and their library boards.

The classic image of public administration is only partially useful in understanding the operation of a public library. The official institutions of library board, chief librarian, department heads, and subordinate personnel, plus the outline of responsibilities assigned to each, portray only the formal structure. The organizational chart, with boxes, lines, and indications of which unit makes what kinds of decisions may actually hide more than it reveals. To say that the board sets policy—perhaps within the limits made possible by the city council's budgetary actions and with the advice of the chief librarian—says nothing about the actions taken by various library personnel or community groups to exert their influence on the chief librarian, the board, or the city council. Also, the awesome position of the chief librarian on the organizational chart does not indicate the difficulties encountered by a weak administrator in that position or the frictions produced by issues of policy or personality among key members of the staff.

The great variety of stimuli that impinge on library administrators makes it necessary to devise a model that can portray relevant information in a systematic manner. The model of an administrative system is appropriate. It comes from more general efforts to portray the influences on public administrators,[1] and it can be adapted to the specific features of the public library. The system outlines the setting of administration by highlighting the components of—

1. an *environment* that both stimulates administrators and receives the products of their work
2. *inputs* that carry stimuli from the environment to administrators
3. *outputs* that carry the results of administrative action to the environment
4. a *conversion process* that transforms (converts) inputs into the outputs
5. *feedback* that reflects the weight of output in the environment and transmits the outputs of one period—as they interact with features in the environment—back to the conversion process as the inputs of a later time.

All of these features interact with one another. Together they form the administrative system, as it is outlined in figure 2.1.

---

1. See Ira Sharkansky, *Public Administration: Policy-Making in Government Agencies*, 3d ed. (Chicago: Rand McNally, 1975).

15

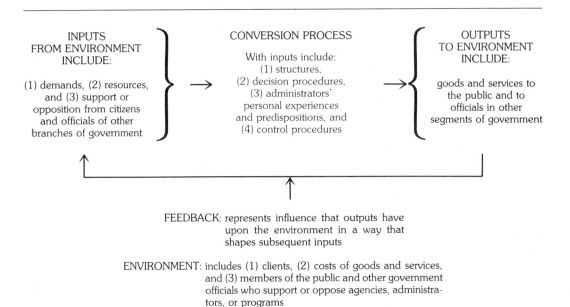

Fig. 2.1. The administrative system

SOURCE: Ira Sharkansky, *Public Administration: Policy Making in Government Agencies*, 4th ed., copyright ©1978 by Rand McNally College Publishing Company.

Environment

Inputs

The environment includes the host of social, economic, and political conditions that present problems to the policy makers and that subsequently assist or confound their efforts to resolve these problems. Within the environment are: the clients who are to benefit from a policy; a market that sets costs for the goods and services to be consumed by a policy; plus interest groups, members of the public, and other units of government who provide support for—or opposition to—a policy. While some features of an environment facilitate policy-making and the solution of social problems, other features "harden" the problems and frustrate the policy maker's efforts to cope with them.

Inputs come from the environment to the conversion process of the administrative system. They include: *demands* for policy; *resources*; and *support, opposition,* or *apathy* toward the actions of administrators. People demand goods and services for their own use: branch libraries, longer hours of operation, larger or more specialized collections. They also demand intangible or symbolic policies, like the celebration of patriotic, ethnic, or religious holidays. A "demand" is an analytic concept; it does not necessarily describe the nature of the citizen-administrator interaction. A demand may take the form of a routine request for service, such as filing an application for a library card or asking for certain acquisitions; it may be a statement that an agency should introduce a new service; or it could be a public confrontation with all the hoopla of placards, civil disobedience, police, and tear gas.

Resources include personnel, skills, material, facilities, technology, and money. These inputs reflect the qualities that employees or citizen groups bring to their library activities: in the budget voted for its programs; and in the buildings, collections, and equipment that are provided. One library may exist in a setting where it is conceived in traditional terms as a depository for books with nothing more complex than a rubber stamp and cards to process their flow. Another library may benefit from an environment that expects a full range of media in the collection and sees advantages in computers to administer the movement of the collection, to identify those items that have the most use, and to provide justifications for subsequent budget allocations.

Support, opposition, or apathy shows itself in the willingness of a population to pay taxes and to accept established procedures. It is also evidenced by clients' patience in the face of adversity and by their sentiments toward administrative personnel. Sentiment can range from the enthusiasm of "Support Your Local Police" to the animosity of a campaign to oust a schoolteacher, principal, or librarian. Between these extremes are the more typically passive attitudes toward public employees. The status of public administrators in the United States is below that of numerous other professional or technical groups. This has an implication for public policy: because many people consider government service to be an undesirable profession, government recruiters may not attract a sufficient number of applications from highly qualified college graduates.

The private sector is not the sole reservoir of inputs to the administrative system. Other governmental units also provide inputs. The executive, legislative, and judicial branches of government send demands to administrators in the form of statutes, instructions, requests, or judgments. They also supply resources and support or opposition in the form of funds and legal authority to perform services. Some governmental inputs are informal. Administrators receive suggestions and recommendations from legislators during hearings and throughout the year as the legislators clarify the intentions behind enacted statutes. Administrators also anticipate demands that they might receive from other branches of government. They do this by extrapolating from existing committee reports, court decisions, or the public speeches of elected officials. Administrators try to discern what the desires of another official will be—or whether an official will be so irked by a contrary administrative action that he will invoke sanctions.

Conversion Process

Conversion of inputs to outputs occurs within the agencies of the administrative system. In libraries the conversion process involves central and branch unit facilities and personnel, including both superiors and subordinates. Inputs are not the only influence on actions of administrators. Features of the conversion process itself affect them. These features are given a separate label in order to distinguish them from the inputs that come from the environment. Since they originate within the conversion process, they are called *withinputs*. Withinputs include: chains of command and other formal structures found within agencies; the procedures used by ranking officers to make their decisions; administrators' personal experiences and predispositions; and the procedures used by administrative superiors to control their subordinates.

Administrators must take account of numerous issues that are relevant to their major decisions and must find some way to assess costs associated with each of the principal claims. Because each major issue may involve a number of claimants from other units of government as well as from the private sector, there are times when the decision makers feel badgered and alter their procedures for making choices. Among the features that may be found in the conversion process are: conflicts between the formal rules of the organization and the personal values of administrators; clashes among administrators that increase the problems in producing outputs; decision makers' use of routine procedures to simplify complex and numerous inputs; and tendencies toward rigid maintenance of the status quo in the face of innovative demands. An agency's leadership and staff may disagree about proper salaries, working conditions, and service to the agency's clients. Like other segments of government, administration is usually involved in some controversy. Indeed, it is partly because of its numerous relations with other social, economic, and political systems that administration is affected by differing assessments of its own proper activity. There is frequent conflict among administrators themselves, as well as between them and the suppliers of inputs or the recipients of outputs.

Outputs

The outputs that administrators provide to their environment include services, tangible goods, and regulations, plus gestures, statements, and activities that give symbolic messages to those who are tuned in. Library administrators provide for many of the cultural, recreational, educational, and symbolic needs of the citizenry. They also provide direct benefits to officials in other government units: information, technical advice, and concrete proposals that are necessary for policy formulation. Legislators and public executives make their living by promising and delivering services to voters. Yet most of these services must come ultimately from administrative agencies, including libraries. While the politician can supply the necessary resources to the administrator and can urge the administrator to make the desired product for the public, it is the administrator who generally implements the statutory power that is enacted by the legislature and makes the actual delivery of public service. The administrator's failure to provide desired services may offend both the citizen and the elected members of the legislative and executive branches. Such failures are "negative outputs." They carry short-term deprivations for persons in the administrator's environment, and they threaten long-term deprivations for the administrators themselves.

It is helpful to think of outputs as including both policies and performance. Policies are the goals and actions of administrators that are undertaken in the effort to shape the quantity or quality of public services. Yet policies do not always produce their intended results. Conflicting policies, being pursued by the same or different administrations, may produce a net result of zero. The efforts of branch librarians to serve the needs of cultural groups in their communities may come up against budget restrictions that are designed by the central library administrators to placate a city council adamant in resisting an increase in property taxes. Often the social problems that are the targets of policies are more substantial than first believed. Certain children remain "hard to reach" no matter how much money is spent on personnel and facilities in their schools. Conflicting demands from the environment lead officials to compromise their objectives, and so their programs may not perform as intended.

While policy represents efforts of administrators and other officials, *performance* represents the work that is actually produced. Policies can aim at services by defining expenditures, salary levels, employee workloads, and the rules that govern the treatment of clients. Performance may reflect the influence of policies, but the measures that have been developed may also reflect the influence of the various factors that complicate the delivery of policy intentions.

It is often difficult to evaluate performance, partly because a policy may have several goals. But even if a major policy has several intentions that are more or less spelled out, it remains necessary to measure the performance of each goal. Public education, for example, tries to impart basic skills of language and calculation; plus substantive knowledge across a range of academic fields; plus a measure of social amenities and patriotism. Libraries tend to pursue several of these same goals for children and adults, plus certain forms of recreation for their clients. For each policy there may be different ways of measuring performance: by the frequency with which services are actually made available or used; or by the quality of services as judged subjectively by clients or professional experts or judged objectively according to established criteria. Insofar as the determination of "successful" or "unsuccessful" performance is likely to influence a policy's future (and that of its administrators and clients), the choice of instruments to measure performance and the interpretation of the results are likely to be matters of some controversy.

Feedback

Feedback represents the influence of earlier outputs upon the environment, and the demands, resources, support, or opposition (i.e., new inputs) that administrators receive. Existing taxes, for example, influence the flow of economic resources into administrative agencies. Public services affect citizens' satisfactions and thus shape the later demands they make.

Feedback mechanisms are evident in the continuity of interactions among administrators, the many sources of their inputs, and the recipients of their outputs. Citizens, legislators, and the chief executive are seldom satisfied once and for all times. Some always ask for more. They may demand improvement of existing services, expansion of the magnitude of services to provide for increased population, and expansion of the scope of a program to provide for certain needs that are left unmet by present activities. The annual budget cycle requires an agency staff to defend its activities of the current year and its proposals for the coming year in hearings before officials in both the executive and legislative branches. On these occasions, evidence of program accomplishments and of unmet demands comes back to administrators in the form of program instructions and budget ceilings for the coming year. Groups that receive an agency's services join with allies in the legislature and try to alter the programs of an agency or its level of appropriations. In less formal ways, client groups and legislators are always making some effort to get administrators to change particular policies.

The Systems Framework

The environment, inputs, conversion process, outputs, and feedback relate to and interact with one another in the manner shown in figure 2.1. An entire set of these elements and their interactions is called an administrative system. A system is not simply the administrative unit that is contained in the conversion process. An administrative system is the combination of the administrative unit and all the elements and processes that interact with the unit. A system such as this is a useful framework for treating individual items; it focuses attention not merely on a simple description of discrete parts, but on the importance and relationship of these parts to one another. As a conceptual framework, an administrative system helps us think about public administration. It is not a fixed set of actors and activities. It can be used to guide our ideas about universal happenings—generalization about administrative activities in all govern-ments—or about particular happenings—admin-istrative activities in certain settings.

By thinking about public administration in a systems framework, we should discipline ourselves to ask about the relevance of the indi-vidual components: What implications for outputs are to be found in the ways that various features of the conversion process respond to inputs from the environment? What kind of constraints over out-puts are exercised by the amount of resources that come into the conversion process from the en-vironment? This kind of questioning establishes the relevance of public administration to politics, to economics, and to other features of its environ-ment.

The linkages among environment, inputs, con-version, outputs, and feedback may appear to be a closed system in which decision makers respond continuously to the impact that their own previous decisions have had upon their environment. Fig-ure 2.1 may suggest such closure to some readers. However, the diagram only shows which items in a system may interact with others; it does not portray the character of these relationships. There is much slippage among components of a system. In the real world, there are numerous features that can influence the decisions of the participants. New inputs continuously come from the demands of citizens and citizen organizations. Officials have many options in reviewing the feedback from their previous decisions. Administrators differ in the weight they assign to precedent, to the demands that come from citizens or from other officials, and to their own assesment of the success of current activities.

An administrative system may attain stability if its decision makers succeed in satisfying demands and in living within the resources that are conve-niently available. For real-world administrators, however, stability is—at most—an elusive goal. For many participants, stability is neither apparent nor desired; they prefer major changes in their agency or in its surroundings. For some, the quest for stability is frustrated by an environment that provides not only shifting and ambiguous goals, but also resources and supports that change in response to numerous and complex determi-nants.

Examples of Systems Interaction

The model of the administrative system is com-prehensive and should allow a place for each of the elements that affect library administrators. Rather than attempting any comprehensive cov-erage of the elements operative in the system, however, we can see its workings by reference to a small number of important elements that have received considerable treatment in the literature.

Economic and Governmental Environments

An environmental issue of considerable impor-tance concerns the availability of funds for local institutions. How much money is available? Where does it come from? What economic and political features serve to constrain the resources that are available or to channel funds to competing claimants? As we shall see, the answers to these questions depend partly on the availability of pri-vate wealth in a jurisdiction and partly on the capacity of local authorities to extract resources from their communities. Such capacity does not depend on the sheer effort of officials, but to large extent on static features of their surroundings: for example, the character of governmental structures in metropolitan areas that keep local authorities poor despite an abundance of private wealth, with these problems lessened to some extent by finan-cial aids of state and national governments. As libraries and other local institutions find an increas-ing share of their budgets coming from outside the local arena, their officials must become wise in the ways of state and national authorities in order to maintain some control over local affairs.

The amount of wealth in a community—as measured by such indicators as property value, population, and median family income—is one factor that governs the money available to local authorities.[2] By and large, the wealthier a com-munity, the more its officials have to spend. Yet there may be a marked discrepancy between the private resources in a community and the afflu-ence of the public sector. The urban areas of the United States offer the greatest concentrations of private wealth in the society, but the governments in those areas complain almost uniformly about their inability to raise adequte funds locally. Much of the problem lies in the heterogéneous nature of local communities and the fractured nature of lo-cal government boundaries. The affluence of urban areas also creates problems by attracting disparate elements to the population. Urban pros-perity attracts migrants who want better opportu-nities. Many such newcomers require city services that cost substantially more than the value of the contribution they in turn can make to the city's

2. See Robert L. Lineberry and Ira Sharkansky, *Urban Politics and Public Policy.*

economy. Urban slums represent the attractions of the city for the poor, plus the inability of many immigrants to be successful in the urban environment. Slums also provide a stimulus that sends affluent families and business firms to the suburbs. The ironies of urban wealth appear in the affluence that begets poverty, even while it reproduces wealth, and a magnitude of resources that is not sufficient for local authorities to satisfy intense demands for public service.

The fractured nature of urban government is an important element in limiting the revenues available to libraries and other public bodies. Boundaries between neighboring cities, counties, suburban towns, school districts, and special districts divide an urban area into a surplus of jurisdictions. Often they compete with each other to keep taxes low. Some local jurisdictions have a greater tax base than required to support their services, so their levies can be low. Other jurisdictions have needs that surpass their resources. While they may raise taxes to the legal or political limits, there remain untapped resources in neighboring jurisdictions. One New Jersey school district had an assessed valuation of $5.5 million per pupil, and a neighboring district had only $33,000 per pupil.

State constitutions and statutes add to the problems of urban governments by limiting the kinds of taxes they can raise. Restrictions keep most localities to the regressive and unpopular tax on the real property that lies within their borders. The regressive nature of this tax restrains its contribution to local treasuries during periods of inflation; tax rates do not move automatically higher with inflation, as they do in the case of the progressive federal income tax. The unpopularity of the property tax dampens the frequent rate increases that are needed to keep revenues up to increases in prices and service demands. And since such a tax may only be levied on locally situated property, cities cannot tap various other economic resources of their area—for example, the income suburbanites earn in the city and the suburban retail purchases they make with this income.

A frustrated reform movement. The first major response to the problem of metropolitan jurisdictions having surpluses and the segregation of resources from needs came during the 1950s and 1960s; it sought to integrate the separate jurisdictions. There were several approaches to this goal:

1. Municipal regulation of real estate developments in the rural fringe outside city borders
2. Development of metropolitanwide districts
3. Annexation and city-city consolidation
4. Consolidation of the city with the urbanized county surrounding it
5. Federation of several municipalities.

Few of these reform efforts were successful. Voters tended to be apathetic, and most established elites were hostile. Officials of local governments, political party chiefs, leaders of unions and the black community were accustomed to the existing structures in which they had come to power—and feared dilution of their political bases in any aggregation of diverse communities.

Out of forty-seven referenda on metropolitan reorganization undertaken in thirty-six of the nation's 212 Standard Metropolitan Statistical Areas during 1946 to 1968, only eighteen produced favorable votes. Even this figure overstates the success of reform campaigns. It reports only those campaigns where reform forces were strong enough to put the issue on the ballot, and few major reforms were undertaken in the largest metropolitan areas.

For a period during the 1960s the more prominent movement in metropolitan areas created *more rather than fewer* jurisdictions. There has been a greater impetus in the 1970s toward consolidation, but whether the trend of the 1980s will be toward consolidation is still a matter for speculation. Between 1857 and 1967 the number of local governmental units other than school districts increased by 7,579. This was largely a result of continued suburban development, but the growth also affected sentiments in the metropolitan core. The central city movements had several names: decentralization, neighborhood control, community control, control sharing. Some arrangements would actually decentralize the power to make program decisions, and others would merely provide representation on a centralized policy-making body to program clients. All such arrangements would further complicate the task of financing services in urban areas, with many problems focused on the issue of who would pay for the services provided in self-styled "communities."

Most efforts at decentralization occurred in black ghettoes, but any explanation of the move toward additional governments within central cities must take account of the earlier blossoming of suburban units. Spokesmen for inner-city decentralization justified their demands by reference to the suburbs. Ghetto leaders wanted for themselves the benefits of local autonomy.

With the failure of metropolitan integration to rationalize local government boundaries, the taxing and spending powers of state and national governments came to the fore. These governments collect taxes from throughout a metropolitan area regardless of municipal borders. Moreover, their levies on personal incomes are progressive and help to keep revenue collections ahead of prices during inflation. Both state and national governments have increased their financing of local services. Moreover, state and national aids are going increasingly to local governments with the largest populations, and—presumably—the most difficult social and economic problems.

Intergovernmental support of the largest cities. Much of what passes for "municipal government" in the largest cities is actually the program and funds of state and national governments. These superior levels of governments use municipal authorities to administer their activities and focus their efforts on the largest cities. Table 2.1 shows the weight of intergovernmental assistance in city budgets. In the largest cities (over 500,000 population), 46.7 percent of expenditures comes initially from Washington and state capitals. For all other cities, the percentage received as aid is only 32.8. Since the most dramatic takeoff of new federal social programs in the 1964–65 period, the largest cities' per capita receipts of intergovernmental aid have grown by $322.33 and 554 percent over their 1964–65 base, while those of other cities have grown by only $73.55 and 389 percent.

Table 2.1 Large Cities' Receipt of State and National Aids

Combined State and National Aid as a Percentage of City Expenditures

	Cities of at least 500,000 population	All other cities
1977–78	47.5%	35.6%
1976–77	46.6	37.3
1975–76	46.7	32.8
1964–65	24.0	18.1
*Per capita receipt of aid**		
1977–78	$404.47	$116.63
1976–77	371.52	113.09
1975–76	380.53	92.45
1964–65	58.20	18.90

*Population figures: 1977–1978, 1977; 1976–1977, 1975; 1975–1976, 1975; 1964–1965, 1960.

SOURCES: *City Government Finances in 1977–1978* (Washington, D.C.: U. S. Bureau of the Census, 1979), and earlier years.

There has been a growing federal role in local and state finance since 1961. Federal aid as a percentage of state and local government expenditures increased from 12.6 in the last budget of the Eisenhower administration to 21.8 in 1975–76. Yet this federal aid brings problems along with its benefits. Washington controls the use for much of its money, and the schedules of federal lawmak-

ers and bureaucrats determine when states and localities know how much they will receive.

State governments also deserve credit for their awareness of urban affairs. Cities over 500,000 population received $3.4 billion from the national government during 1975–76, but $7.9 billion from the states. Admittedly, some unknown portion of the states' $7.9 billion came initially from Washington. Table 2.2 shows that the states, like the national government, are giving the greatest aid to the largest cities and are increasing most the aids to those cities. From 1964–65 to 1975–76, state aids per capita to cities over 500,000 population increased by $216.54 and 439 percent, while state aids to all other cities increased by $39.78 and 265 percent over their 1964–65 base.

Table 2.2 Large Cities' Receipt of State Aids

State Aid as a Percentage of City Expenditures

	Cities of at least 500,000 population	All other cities
1977–78	29.9%	19.4%
1976–77	33.6	19.3
1975–76	32.6	19.4
1964–65	20.9	14.3
*Per capita receipt of aid**		
1977–78	$254.92	$63.44
1976–77	267.97	58.52
1975–76	265.89	54.77
1964–65	49.35	14.99

*Population figures: 1977–1978, 1977; 1976–1977, 1975; 1975–1976, 1975; 1964–1965, 1960.

SOURCES: *City Government Finances in 1977–1978* (Washington, D.C.: U. S. Bureau of the Census, 1979), and earlier years.

State governments not only are providing financial aid but also are changing their constitutions and statutes to permit local authorities more flexibility in raising their own revenues. Historically, localties have been limited to the tax on real property. In 1976, however, twenty-six states allowed their local governments to collect a sales tax, and ten states permitted local income taxes. Agencies of forty states pursue active programs to improve the administration of local property taxes. These typically involve systematic comparisons between market values as determined by actual sales and local property assessments. The sales-assessment ratios serve to equalize the distribution of those state aids that go to local governments on the basis of local property values and to identify local areas that need additional attention from tax assessors. Such procedures can minimize tax competition between local governments and keep assessments reasonably equivalent across that state for properties of similar value.

State governments are also making greater direct expenditures in metropolitan areas. These take the form of state clinics and hospitals, parks, intraurban expressways, and urban branches of state universities. Most states also have a department of local affairs. Twenty-six of these appeared during the 1965–69 period alone. Some departments integrate the distribution of state financial aids to local governments, and some offer sizable state supplements for such urban programs of the national government as public housing, mass transit, urban renewal, and manpower training.

Public libraries have not done as well as other services in competing for the funds of national, state, or local governments. As of 1973 federal aids contributed only 9.7 percent of state and local library expenditures, compared to the 23.5-percent federal contribution for all state and local services. During the period of great expansions in local spending (1964–73), library budgets increased by only 114.0 percent, while all other local government spending climbed by 152.8 percent.

Revenue sharing. The year 1972 saw a major new departure in the nature of federal aid. Revenue sharing began with grants of $2.6 billion to the states, with two-thirds earmarked for local governments. Annual disbursements under revenue sharing reached $7.3 billion in fiscal year 1977. The allotments to individual states and localities reflect various characteristics of the recipients, with revenue increasing along with population; the effort shown by states and localities in taxing their own resources; and poverty as reflected by income per capita. The requirement that two-thirds of a state's share go to local governments, plus the formula that rewards jurisdictions with large population and high tax effort, should continue the recent trend of increased intergovernmental aid to the largest cities.

Revenue sharing differs most dramatically from traditional federal aids in its lack of "strings." The money goes to states and communities as a matter of right, without detailed applications. Recipients can spend money at their discretion, subject only to the following restrictions:

1. State governments have no program restrictions in allocating their shares.
2. Local governments must spend their allotments within certain "priority" areas: public safety, environmental protection including sanitation, public transportation, health, rec-

reation, libraries, social services for the poor and aged, financial administration, and "ordinary and necessary" capital expenditures.
3. Discrimination on the basis of race, color, national origin, or sex is not permitted in any program financed with revenue-sharing funds.
4. Funds may not be used to match federal funds provided under other grant programs.
5. Construction workers paid with revenue-sharing funds must be paid at least the wage prevailing on similar construction activity in the locality.
6. Recipient governments must publish plans and publicly account for the use of revenue-sharing funds.

While the lack of detailed controls on revenue sharing appeals to certain local officials, this feature disturbs other actors in the local arena.[3] Supporters of individual programs have no guarantee that the money will be spent on their favored projects. With the traditional grants-in-aid, program supporters concentrate their efforts at the national level and count on state and local officials to carry out requirements in the federal statutes.

Interested groups can now examine the mandatory reports of revenue-sharing allocations by state and local governments to determine the percentages used for libraries and other services. With this information, it may be possibile to judge the advantages to each service of allowing local officials, rather than Washington, to determine the program allocations of federal money.

Local program continuity. While local governments have come to depend on increasing contributions of revenue from state and national governments, localities have retained major responsibilities as the ultimate administrators of programs. Since 1960 local governments have made between 36 and 38 percent of the ultimate, direct expenditures that provide services to the people; this figure has remained stable despite all the expansions of new programs since 1960 and despite the growth in national and state funding. What this means, of course, is an increasing separation of responsibility for raising revenue and making expenditures. Two implications flow from this.

First, local officials spend much of their time in the pursuit of funds. This means negotiating with those national and state agencies that exercise discretionary control over the intergovernmental funds they have available. The mayor of Provi-

---

3. See Michael D. Reagan, *The New Federalism* (New York: Oxford Pr. Univ. 1972).

dence, Rhode Island, expressed some widely held sentiments in an address to a training conference of the U.S. Civil Service Commission:

> I could not hope to raise locally the kind of money which was going to be necessary to undertake the massive effort which lay ahead. In fact, my career as a municipal administrator has been formulated by the Lees and Cavanaughs across the country who were putting their cities into the mainstream of political life by being effective disciples of the art of grantsmanship. I became a student of their experiences, and of their lively encounters with the federal establishment, and with the programs which they had developed. . . . We worked long and hard to satisfy regulations, federal officials and our own community. But for Providence it has worked very well.[4]

Second, there is also a good deal of negotiating among the agencies of a local government receiving intergovernmental aid. The funds of numerous national and state agencies meet together in common local jurisdictions, where the process of combining the different program requirements leads inevitably to trade-offs and compromises with the goals of individual donors and recipients. It is not possible to maximize the transportation criteria built into the federal highway programs at the same time that recipients also maximize the relocation criteria of federal housing legislation or the environmental protection criteria of other federal programs. Efforts to maximize low- and middle-income housing construction under programs from the U.S. Department of Housing and Urban Development run afoul of efforts to maximize racial integration in criteria of U.S. Department of Health, Education, and Welfare; concerns for racial balance and neighborhood schools, and local opposition to the development of public housing outside the central core, do not fit together into any neat package consistent with the guidelines from several Washington offices.

The Conversion of Inputs to Outputs

The lack of money is a major impediment to local authorities, and it is important to understand the problems that minimize the funds available. Yet money alone does not provide services. Once the major problems of resource availability are faced, it is still necessary for the staffs of local agencies to plan activities, pursue the funds

through the stages of legislative and executive approval, and then translate the money into equipment, supplies, and personnel, plus the policies and procedures that render all of these into services actually delivered to clients. Other chapters will deal with the details of recruitment, the training of staff, and the design of policies and procedures that are appropriate to libraries. Here we can deal with some general problems faced by local administrators in various departments.

One perspective on the working of local agencies is that of a social critic who views administrators as integral to the pathology in American cities. Another perspective emphasizes the constraints on administrators and urges them to be more assertive in making their distinctive contributions to the local scene. While neither of these perspectives may reflect perfectly the situation of local librarians, they do pose some parameters of the urban setting within which library authorities must work.

Norton Long has written numerous articles about cities and their administrators. At an earlier point in his career, he described administrators in positive terms as widely representative of the population in their personal background and as infusing professional and creative forces into government. In his most recent work, however, he paints a depressing picture of urban pathology, with the local bureaucrats (including, perhaps, librarians) among the worst components.

> The tragedy of the growth of the local public sector is that while it provides income to those it employs, it has no necessary connection with increasing the viability of the local economy and, all too often, is too much dead weight dragging it down.[5]

Long's assessment of the local bureaucracy reflects, in part, the fractured nature of jurisdictions in the metropolis, He sees a loss in the sense of community. To paraphrase the title of his book, *The Unwalled City*, the city no longer has walls that its citizens feel compelled to defend. The urban area is a hodgepodge of separate entities, with each one of them useful only insofar as it meets certain of a person's economic needs. The city resembles a market more than a community, and it cannot call upon the emotional commitments of people who take *citizenship* seriously. Especially for the affluent, the central city in a metropolitan area is a place only to earn a living, if that much. One's residence is most likely in the suburbs, and one's attachment, if any, may be to a

4. Douglas M. Fox, ed., *The New Urban Politics: Cities and the Federal Government* (Pacific Palisades, Calif.: Goodyear, 1972), p. 91.

5. Norton E. Long, *The Unwalled City: Reinstituting the Urban Community* (New York: Basic Books, 1972), p. viii.

distant place that was home during childhood. Private employees look to the city as a place to work or shop—or to avoid altogether. City employees have little incentive to show any greater attachment. To them, according to Long, the city is an employer that will pay a salary but not demand high-quality performance. Long writes about "stagnant, costly, unenterprising, consumer-be-damned behavior of centralized, irresponsible, and unresponsive bureaucracies."[6]

Long's writing helps us look ahead to a discussion of the policy-performance hiatus in the local administrative system. He is especially critical of bureaucrats who do not know which constellation of inputs produces good service, and who seem not to care about their ignorance.

In bargaining with the unions, officials make little attempt to relate wage increases to productivity . . . most elected officials show far more interest in contracts, buildings, and jobs, the inputs of the political system, than in the outputs, the delivery of goods and services to the citizen.[7]

To Long, bureaucrats contribute to the lack of concern with performance by seeking to maximize their own benefits at the expense of their clients. He sees them hiding behind their unionism and their job protections, perhaps not intending to exploit the city for their own economic gains, but having little incentive to do otherwise.

While Norton Long ascribes many of the city's problems to self-centered administrators, another perspective sees administrators as the potential saviors of the city. This view would have administrators throw off constraints on their freedom of action and take the lead in representing their clients' interests. Such a view emerged most prominently during the latter years of the Johnson administration and was of a piece with the general theme "maximum feasible participation" in the war on poverty. *Advocacy administration* is one label for this view. Its practitioners do not wait passively for clients to assert their needs but seek to help clients formulate as well as promote their demands. In some views, the administrator as advocate would stand alone on the policy-making stage with his clients, with other officials relegated to subordinate positions. In the view of advocacy administration, there is limited concern for the historic issues of administrative control or coordination by elected officials. The administrator as advocate would use overtly political tactics to gain control over the chief executive and the legislature:

Public Administration . . . must find means by which it can enhance the reelection probabilities of supporting incumbents . . . building and maintaining of roads or other capital facilities in the legislators' district, establishing high-employment facilities, such as federal office buildings, county courthouses, police precincts, and the like, and distributing public relations materials favorable to the incumbent legislator. . . . As a consequence it is entirely possible to imagine legislators becoming strong spokesmen for less hierarchic and less authoritative bureaucracies.[8]

This kind of patronage is standard operating procedure in relations among the elected chief executive and members of the legislature. Yet an aggressive administrator would disperse patronage to reduce the control of the chief executive and legislators over the bureaucracy. Just which administrators would have the opportunity to engage in this kind of politics? This is not clear.

This and other writings on behalf of advocacy administration received their most prominent expression at a conference on "new public administration" at the Minnowbrook Conference Center of Syracuse University in 1968. The "Minnowbrook perspective" has several themes:

1. Society is experiencing revolutionary ferment and change.
2. Government is repressive and not responsive to the demands of racial and low-income minorities.
3. Young people are mature beyond their years.
4. Social scientists, including specialists in public administration, should identify with the interests of powerless minorities and adopt explicit value orientations to promote equity in income and power.
5. Public administrators should assume overtly political roles.
6. The political process should emphasize confrontation rather than negotiation and compromise.

What is surprising in the Minnowbrook papers that advocate more power for undefined personnel in the administration is the virtual lack of concern that the devolution of authority may turn against the values expressed by the writers. What would control the brutality of an unrestrained police officer; the racism of a schoolteacher, li-

---

6. Ibid., p. 93.
7. Ibid., p. 114.

8. H. George Frederickson, "Toward a New Public Administration," in *Toward a New Public Administration: The Minnowbrook Perspective*, ed. Frank Marini (Scranton, Pa.: Chandler, 1971).

brarian, or social worker; the undisciplined infantry lieutenant or general? Each of these was a feature of the era that prompted the Minnowbrook conferees to advocate more political and policy-making activity by administrators. Yet the conferees seemed blind to the possibility that the freedom they urged upon administrators would loosen vital control procedures and unleash more of the forces they abhorred. One writer recognized that the "politics of love" might become the "politics of suppression." In his final sentence he could offer only "hope" that things would go the right way.[9]

It is not possible to reconcile the divergent positions of Norton Long, who laments the powers of local administrators, and the spokesmen of advocacy administration who would free administrators from many of the controls on their activities. Each perspective has some following among observers of the local scene, but each is conceived without any systematic survey of local administrative behavior. In this sense each perspective is more a piece of social criticism than a hard-headed social-scientific assessment of real conditions. As such these perspectives may present the outer limits of conceivable culpability or inherent social responsibility among local agencies, within which practicing administrators might try to place themselves and their organizations.

Policy, Performance, and Feedback

Policy, performance, and feedback are all products of local administration. From the perspective of the client, they are the real meaning of government and public service. If they are not right, or cannot be changed to suit citizens' desires, then the faults may challenge their sense of satisfaction with government, and their sense of control over its activities.

We have noted before that it is not possible to speak lightly of policy and performance as if they inevitably work in tandem. If a librarian would maximize a community's exposure to a variety of cultural media serving the widest spectrum of tastes, then it may be necessary to integrate the policies of several bodies in the public sector (elected legislators and the chief executive, plus libraries, museums, schools) as well as policies of other institutions in the private sector (theaters, bookstores, churches, private schools, and colleges). All too often, a policy is not delivered because of faulty administration, or because the problems are more complex than first believed, or because the policy comes into collision with other policies that operate in counter fashion.

People who formulate policy goals may have only scanty knowledge of just what tangible achievements are desired by the other policy makers and by the various clients or interested citizens, and perhaps even less knowledge of just what course of action will produce the benefits desired by each party. Certain theories of policy making speak glibly of the greatest benefit for the greatest number, or a balance of benefits over costs, presumably meaning satisfying the most "important" desires—however determined—while at the same time threatening the least harm to those not currently satisfied. However, such platitudes lead to no easy calculus that works in the real world.

It is not possible in this context to provide a thorough treatment of the problems that will foil those who would define the goals of policy, or translate policy goals into acceptable performance, or achieve desirable kinds of feedback. It is possible, however, to note five of the questions asked most often by political scientists and economists who write about policy, in order to gain some understanding of the problems that will trouble the naive.[10]

What choices are made and at what cost? Policy making involves choices among alternatives. Except in an ideal world, all choices involve costs. Costs are not only monetary, but social, psychological, and political as well. The costs are measured by the dollars to be spent on the chosen projects and by the disappointments, dislocations, damage to staff morale, and community opposition that result from the failure to choose other alternatives.

A policy alternative is never *free* because all choices involve opportunity costs. A dollar invested in building a branch library is a dollar that is not invested in education, a public park, improved housing, or a film collection at the central library. Opportunity costs, in other words, pertain to the courses of action that are foregone in order to undertake some particular policy. Opportunity costs represent no problem at all if we know that a dollar invested in some policy will bring greater social utility than investing it any other way. Unfortunately, we rarely know that with any certainty.

Who benefits and who loses? The burdens and benefits of public policy fall differentially on the urban landscape. Policies can make the rich richer and the poor poorer, or they can redress social

---

9. Orion F. White, Jr., "Social Change and Administrative Adaptation," in *Toward a New Public Administration*, ed. Marini, p. 83.

10. See Lineberry and Sharkansky, *Urban Politics*, pp. 184–89.

and economic inequalities by giving advantages to the disadvantaged. For each policy alternative, we can ask, who benefits and who loses?

A few urban policies are pure public goods that can be enjoyed by one person without diminishing the consumption of the same good by another person. At the national level, defense is said to be a public good insofar as it protects all of us. At the local level, pollution control and fluoridation are public goods that can, at least potentially, benefit all members of the community equally.

Some policies are delivered unequally to citizens but still have aspects of public goods. Some neighborhoods may have excellent, and others poor, school and library services, even while the general programs provide some benefits to the community as a whole. We all benefit, at least to some extent, by having a high level of education available, even though some of us may benefit more readily or more directly than others. Likewise, public health services may go only to cetain groups, but everyone benefits from having tuberculosis held in check.

Do library policies make the rich richer and the poor poorer? At least indirectly, yes. Insofar as they are supported mostly by the regressive tax on real property, and are used disproportionately by the well educated and the relatively well-to-do, library programs provide upward distributions of resources and benefits. They are redistributive policies, taking from one group and giving to another. Yet there are counter policies that aid the poor at the expense of the affluent: public health, compensatory education, subsidized housing, and antipoverty programs. A study by the Tax Foundation concludes that the total tax structures of state and local governments are regressive, that is, they favor the rich, but that state and local expenditures are sharply progressive in their totality and favor the poor.[11]

What difference does money make? Few public policies involve no expenditures of money. The questions of the total size of the public budget and of desirable tax burdens are among the most critical issues in most urban political systems. Officials pay a great deal of attention to budget making, and expenditures are widely viewed as a common denominator with respect to items that actually produce service. Although spending does not by itself meet popular demands for service, it does buy many of the things that do.

Yet we must be aware of the "veil of money": the image that money is the real cost or measure of a public service. Many citizens as well as officials feel that an increase in spending will purchase a corresponding incease in service. This is the spending-service cliche.[12] The amount expended may be important to citizens, policy makers, and economic analysts. But the generosity of expenditure may have little relation to the quality or quantity of services actually delivered to the public. To understand actual performance in an administrative system, we should be concerned more with the performance and impacts that result from money spent; that is, with what is purchased rather than with the price tag alone.

What are the impacts of policy? The output of a public policy does not necessarily accomplish its goals. Although the elements of a service may be delivered by a local agency, the performance may not have its intended impacts. Impacts may be intended or not. Some are planned and anticipated by policy makers. Others—called *spillover effects*—represent the unanticipated products of policy. The elusive hope of policy makers is to design policies whose major consequences are intended and whose unintended impacts are either minimal or benign. Federal programs for urban renewal and urban freeways have produced great controversies over their social and economic impacts. They are not simply programs of physical clearance, construction, and transportation; depending on one's perspective, they offer great promise or great threat to the opportunities of certain citizens for suitable dwellings, jobs, or investments in the city.

The impacts of library policy include the immediate and long-range changes in information, attitudes, and values of the clients, plus those people whom clients reach with the ideas acquired in the library. The range of impacts and spillovers extends to the far reaches of speculation about what the reading of various people will do to their beliefs and behaviors. The research on these questions is limited, and the valid information available to policy makers is scarce. Policy is made at least partially "in the dark" and based on insufficient information about probable impacts.

How shall policies be evaluated? Policies can be evaluated in terms of two principal issues: Are the goals pursued by the policy desirable social ends? Do the policies actually accomplish the stated goals? If one dissents from the stated goals, the likely choice is to oppose the policy. Yet matters are more complex, because most policies carry noble but abstract goals. Library policies are said to purvey knowledge and skills relative to consumer choice and job qualifications, to provide cultural

11. "Allocating Tax Burdens and Government Benefits by Income Class" (New York: Tax Foundation, 1967).

12. Ira Sharkansky, *The Routines of Politics* (New York: Van Nostrand Reinhold, 1970), ch. 7.

enrichment, and—through all of this—to help eliminate poverty. The tough question is whether the policies actually accomplish these goals—and whether they accomplish them more effectively and at less cost than alternative policies.

The term *policy analysis* has numerous meanings, including the kinds of evaluation noted here. At the extreme of simplicity, policy analysis requires only a specification of an agency's programs, together with an outline of the services provided within each program. More elaborate analyses indicate the amounts of resources used for each program, together with some justifications in terms of the number of people receiving benefits from it. Still other analyses seek to "model" the way in which a social problem may be solved, then develop and test alternative policies for coping with the problem.[13]

Increasingly, policy analysis—or evaluation—depends upon measurement. The rising status of precise measurement and quantitative analysis is evident, not only in academic studies of the causes and implications of certain policies—what might be called basic research—but also in applied studies that attempt to measure various cost-benefit ratios of public policies.

Cost-benefits analysis and planning-programming-budgeting (PPB) are techniques currently being touted by some government management specialists. Cost-benefit analysis attempts to estimate the costs of each policy option, including as many spillover costs as can be identified, and to sum up the benefits of each policy. PPB was originally developed as an aid to budgeting in the U.S. Department of Defense and, at President Johnson's order, was then applied to all agencies of the federal government. Under the prompting of management analysts, and sometimes with the funding of private foundations, PPB has been adopted by a few state and local agencies. Its elements include:

1. Defining the major programs in each area of public service
2. Defining the principal outputs of each program in ways that can be subjected to precise measurement
3. Defining the inputs relevant to each program (e.g., various combinations of personnel, facilities, funds, and ways of rendering services)
4. Computing the costs of alternative combinations of inputs and the economic value of the various combinations of outputs likely to be produced by each combination of inputs
5. Calculating the cost-benefit ratio associated with each combination of inputs and outputs.

But recipes for analysis do not solve all the complex problems of measuring variables. Economists have claimed some success in surmounting problems of measurement, but their fundamental unit of analysis—money—readily lends itself to measurement. Other social scientists have found measurement to be a more difficult problem, with such concepts as culture and learning not lending themselves to measurable units that are acceptable to social scientists having different perspectives.

Summary and Conclusions

This chapter examines some basic concepts in public administration. The organizing model is the administrative system, which arrays an administrator's world into environment, inputs, conversion process, outputs, and feedback. No item is alone in the system. The participant who would understand it must consider the implication of each part for the others. The model of the administrative system should help the reader throughout this book, as it suggests a context for each of the particular concerns treated in other chapters.

The contemporary librarian must be alert to many issues of a complex scene, including implications for the library that come from unequal distributions of demands and resources throughout the municipalities of a metropolis, and the role of intergovernmental aid in library support. Views of proper administrative behavior in such a context range from active advocacy to passive dependence on actions taken by legislative and executive bodies. In choosing an appropriate role, an administrator had best be aware about the ingredients of effective policy making and policy delivery, including costs and benefits, the role of money and other inputs, and problems of evaluating impacts of policy.

---

13. Kenneth L. Kraemer, *Policy Analysis in Local Government* (Washington, D.C.: International City Management Association, 1973).

Bibliography

The items below are chosen for their comprehensive coverage of major areas relevant to public administration and for their extensive references to additional material.

Kraemer, Kenneth L. *Policy Analysis in Local Government*. Washington, D.C.: International City Management Association, 1973. A brief but comprehensive outline of policy analysis principles and techniques, written for the administrator who must be sufficiently informed about this field to direct the work of policy analysts and to interpret their findings.

Lineberry, Robert L., and Sharkansky, Ira. *Urban Politics and Public Policy*. New York: Harper and Row, 1978. An introductory text covering the structures of local governments and the character of local politics plus substantive issues: taxation, education, poverty, race, crime, transportation, environmental protection, housing, and urban growth.

Nigro, Felix A., and Nigro, Lloyd G. *Modern Public Administration*. New York: Harper and Row, 1973. An introductory text showing more concern for the techniques of public management than Sharkansky (see below), with less concern for the political context of administration.

Schick, Allan. *Budget Innovation in the States*. Washington, D.C.: The Brookings Institution, 1972. Reviews various efforts to rationalize the budgetary process. Primary focus on state governments, but with an exceptional review of budget theory in general. Aware of both the benefits and problems associated with various reforms, although more sympathetic to these efforts than is Wildavsky.

Sharkansky, Ira. *Public Administration: Policy-Making in Government Agencies*. Chicago: Rand McNally, 1978. An introductory text in public administration, written from the same perspective as this chapter. It emphasizes the understanding of public administration in its political context, more than techniques of public management.

Wildavsky, Aaron. *The Politics of the Budgetary Process*. Boston: Little, Brown, 1974. A description of government budgeting that stresses the pervasive influence of "incrementalism." Outlines major budget strategies followed by agencies, the chief executive's budget office, and the legislature. Reviews efforts at the systematic analysis of budget requests—for example, planning-programming-budgeting—emphasizing their inability to replace incremental procedures.

3 The Library and the Political Processes

PHYLLIS I. DALTON

The success of a library administrator depends largely upon an understanding of and an ability to operate within the context of the political process. Library administrators have, in many instances, held themselves aloof from politics, ignoring political reality and thus allowing the political aspects of library service to be handled elsewhere. In the second half of this century, and especially within the last decade, it has become evident that this attitude has cost public libraries severely, in both status and financial capability. A failure to understand and utilize political processes has resulted in the lack of needed legislation and adequate tax support for public libraries.

Because political processes are not restricted to any particular size of jurisdiction, type of library, organizational structure, economic situation, or thrust of library service, all library administrators will be successful to the extent that they can cope within the political milieu. Politics involves influence and the influential. A major skill in working in the political process is advocacy. But first there must be an understanding of the political process itself—how libraries are organized in terms of other governmental functions, relationships of library administrators with government leaders, responsibility for policy making, and intergovernment relations.

Governmental Organizations

Nationwide, many types of governmental organizations exist at the local library level. Regardless of the type of organization in which the public library functions, its administrator is involved in policy making, problem solving, and coping with hard decisions involving substantive issues of policy and programs. All of these responsibilities can be successfully carried out through whatever governmental organization exists. Libraries are subject to different systems of governance. One system is the board. There may be an appointed administrative or advisory board at one level. At another level there are elected or appointed boards such as the city council, the public library

district boards or school district public library boards, all of which represent political jurisdictions. At a third level, the librarian's responsibility is to an administrator in a larger department or to the city manager. The most common organizational patterns at the local level are described below.

Administrative Boards

Administrative boards are groups responsible for managing departments and agencies within a local jurisdiction. They have the authority to set policy. The members (trustees) are appointed, usually by either the local legislative body or the chief elected offical. The board is directly responsible to the appointing authority for the administration of the library and advises that body or person on matters of library policy as defined by the appointing authority. The board submits an annual budget to the appointing authority but usually does not have the authority to set tax rates. Most boards have the authority to employ and to dismiss the library administrator, to whom it delegates such authority and responsibility as it considers appropriate. Other library employees may be responsible to the board or to a separate personnel board with responsibility for the library or for several agencies. The administrative board controls library use, regulations, and, generally, book-selection policy. In most cases the administrative board's powers are established in state library law, in the municipal charter, or in some other "constitution" that establishes and regulates the local government agency. A general stability is provided as these laws and charters are not readily changed.

Advisory Boards

The members of an advisory board have lesser powers than those of an administrative board. Usually advisory boards are established by ordinance or resolution, with the consequence that the authority and even the existence of such advisory boards can be challenged with ease. The method of selecting members of advisory boards is usually

29

similar to that for administrative boards. Often the responsibility of advisory boards is limited to acting in an advisory capacity to the legislative body, to the library administrator, to the chief administrative officer, or to any combination of these groups, and on any matter that the legislative body may direct. The library is administered in a manner similar to that of any other local department, with the library administrator directly responsible to the legislative body or an appointed official for administrative matters.

Public Library District Boards

These special districts may or may not have boundaries identical with other political jurisdictions. The members of public library district boards are often elected but sometimes are appointed. If elected, the board members usually have an administrative responsibility. In this case, they generally can levy a tax for the support of the library. If the members are appointed, the board prepares the budget and has general advisory powers regarding library service but does not have a tax-levying power.

School District Public Library Boards

The school board, elected to manage a school district, may also be empowered to administer public libraries. In some cases school board members are also the public library board members for the district. In other instances, the elected school board members appoint a public library board for the district. The elected officials can levy a tax for the support of the public library. The public library board is responsible for the library operation and appoints the public library director.

City Council or County Board

In some instances, the public library may be controlled more or less directly by the city council or county board. In this form of organization, the elected members usually divide the responsibility for the various municipal or county departments among themselves. Thus, one member will serve as a liaison with the library and the library administrator. The council maintains tax-levying authority and budgeting control and is responsible for making policies and regulations pertaining to the public library, often on the recommendation of the public library administrator.

City Manager

The city manager is the chief administrator for all municipal departments under the council-manager form of government. In this form of government, the library administrator is responsible to the city manager, an official employed by the city council. The public library administrator has direct access to the city manager, as do the other department heads. The library operates directly under the city manager or a delegated deputy.

Library as a Subdivision of Another Department

A variation of the pattern of governance in which the library director is responsible to another administrator occcurs when the library is a subdivision of another department. Examples include those in which the library is combined with a city department such as parks and recreation or cultural affairs. A public library administrator can operate an effective library service as a subdivision of a larger department, but such a governmental structure complicates the political process. The public library administrator must compete with other programs within the department for priority and funds. Resistance to such combinations of departments is common because the disadvantages usually seem to outweigh the advantages. It must be noted, however, that various combinations do seem to operate with comparative success as long as the public library administrator is adept both as a manager and as a developer.

Regional Jurisdictions, Library Systems, and Networks

The broadening roles of state and federal governments have given encouragement to the creation of regional jurisdictions for planning, and service. Many types of regional libraries, library systems, and networks have developed as a result of this trend. There are even cases of interstate cooperation. The regional cooperative or regional library may operate under its own board or may be a part of the multipurpose planning agencies that have been formed in the Standard Metropolitan Statistical Areas throughout the several states. Some of the libraries have a strongly structured regional organization with a board of trustees and/or a professional library board. The governing board appoints the administrator and operates the library organization, but it usually does not have tax-levying power. In other library systems, the chairman of the professional board acts in an administrative capacity.

The Legal Basis for Library Administration

Charters, statutes, ordinances, resolutions, and/or other acts of legislative bodies establish the legal basis for most libraries. Executive orders and judicial decisions often serve to interpret and/or modify these legal provisions. Awareness of the "basis in law" under which the library operates is of high priority for administrators. They must determine the source and nature of authority provided. It may be that the administrator will find that the authority is based as much in tradition as in law. In many instances, much authority, or lack thereof, is the result of the use of the delegatory powers of superiors in the hierarchy.

It is important to understand that the legal basis for administration is not static. Rather it is continually evolving as a result of many forces. Social stresses, environmental changes, political forces, economic conditions, and legal interpretations create pressures that result in news laws, regulations, and judicial decisions. In most cases, however, change of laws lags behind rather than precedes needed changes in our social institutions. Knowledge of the law and accompanying regulations that concern public libraries in any given circumstance need not inhibit the development of creative programs of service designed to meet current needs. Legal provisions should be interpreted in terms of what they allow the library administrator to do rather than being used and viewed as limiting. Should the laws appear to be restrictive, the library administrator has the obligation of bringing this to the attention of the proper officials and seeking remedial legislation.

Role of the Administrator in Government

For any public library administrator to be on the edge of the political processes in our special-interest society is never really a safe position. Library administrators, like other public administrators, are forced to play the role of politician effectively. To a large degree, success for the library will be determined by the relationships its administrator maintains with the local political power structure.

Active participation in the political processes has not been a characteristic of public library administrators in many instances. The paucity of services and facilities, the poverty of library resources that stifle progress in many communities now are the results of the isolation of the public library administrator within the government. Participation in gov-

ernmental affairs does have its hazards as well as its rewards. For this reason, many administrators have preferred to remain on the edge of the political process rather than risk public crisicism, pressure from other government officials, adverse publicity including critical "letters to the editor," and the possible loss of position.

While no library administrator should pursue a cause without good reason, it is doubtful that most communities are best served by such timidity. By avoiding action that might bring criticism or pressure from certain factions, the library administrator may be missing a crucial opportunity to increase public support by better acquainting the community with the library's objectives and programs. By taking advantage of such opportunities, the administrator's counterparts in government frequently gain additional leverage for their departmental programs. Sound library management directed to supplying services and resources needed by the community requires participation in the political processes regardless of the risks involved.

It must be recognized that the public library administrator is both a political manager in the governmental structure and a creative developer of library services. To facilitate these responsibilities, a substantial portion of time must be spent in developing effective relations with superiors and coworkers in government. The actions of all department heads, including planners, finance directors, personnel administrators, intergovernmental representatives, city and county administrators, and others, both elected and appointed, have a direct effect upon the library as an agency in the total organizational pattern. For example, land use becomes important in planning services, in shifting the emphasis of kinds of service being provided, and in planning buildings. A good public transportation system facilitates the use of public library services. Public order and safety are related to both the planning and the operation of the building. Both the public health and personnel departments are important to the well-being and development of staff and, as a result, have a definite effect on library service to the community.

Disinterest in interagency and departmental jealousies and a freedom from fear of loss of power and prestige will follow the realization that personal emotions do not have a place in the political processes. A public administrator will know that success is gained through accurate communications that flow from top levels of governmental organization to the lower-level members of the agencey to obtain effective delivery of library services, commitment to organizational goals, and objectives of the library service.

Within the political processes, the public library administrator realizes and communicates the capacity for choice that exists within the overall government for the delivery of library service. There must be an ability to cope effectively with the problems at all levels, as well as interpersonal trust for assisting the library in developing an effective and built-in capacity to change.

As part of a political sense, the chief administrator must develop a sensitivity to which role—that of manager or developer—is foremost at any given time. Although both roles are compatible, at times as manager the administrator will be required to modify plans that are desirable from the perspective of a developer. For example, even though a proposed service is needed, wanted, and practical, such a service may not be economical from a cost-benefit point of view. It will be necessary for the director to make the hard decision concerning which course should be followed. In the process of considering working with other libraries on a cooperative basis, a conflict can easily occur between the manager and the developer roles. As a manager of a successful library operation, the administrator may see risk in cooperation with its attendant problems. On the other hand, cooperating would probably promote development of improved services.

Constant changes will occur, and the public library director must never be caught unaware of any information pertinent to the roles of manager and developer. The chief librarian must keep up to date on such diverse subjects as copyright, revenue sharing, appropriations prospects for any level of government, and should also acquire an ability to identify the trends that will prove most helpful. Probably the most important aspect of current knowledge is an ability to forecast trends. With this ability, the administrator can plan for financial stability for services, take advantage of new funding for experimental programs, and respond positively to the library needs of the people before they are formally expressed. If the administrator is secure in a position that has favorable status in relation to other department heads—for example, the director of finance, the director of public works, and the planning director—effective communications about present needs and future requirements will flow freely among departments.

Intergovernmental Relations

Intergovernmental relationships (regional, state, or federal) are probably more significant than city, county, or local-regional relations, if less well understood. Intergovernmental relationships require the administrator to provide operations and services that function on a broader geographical and organizational base, since state and federal governments may decentralize programs through regional and local outlets. Since few public library directors have had the training or experience to design and manage systems and networks involving all levels of government, there is a need to understand the significance of such involvement. While library administrators may be responsive to the needs of intergovernmental structures, questions remain about whether they are ready to respond.

Depending on the particular library involved, the administrator must anticipate a growing involvement with all levels of government. An appreciation of the roles of each and of the nuances of the political processes involved is necessary. Moreover, the head librarian must be aware of the relationship of the local library with each of these levels of government.

The library administrator should explore and participate in intergovernmental relationships at whatever level is desirable and practical. The decision to participate will be made on the basis of what is best for the library and its services to the community, and on the nature of the larger unit that will result from the new involvement. Community involvement is a means of overcoming obstacles to change and to intergovernmental relations. Without community involvement, shortcomings in budget and staff may keep the administrator so preoccupied with daily operations that keeping pace with needed changes and anticipating change is impossible.

Justification for local control rests on a belief in divided political powers. In the melding of libraries into intergovernmental organization, the local units must first be very strong, well organized, and effective. If such is not the case, an intergovernmental organization will be made up of weak and ineffective library units. It is essential in the urban areas of the nation that coordinated planning of facilities and activities by local governments become a joint program of comprehensive planning.

Councils of regional government are now found in most urban areas of the United States. Although they differ significantly in organization and activities, there are common characteristics: (1) they are voluntary associations of local government organized to deal with problems that are regional in scope and require regional solutions; (2) most have a degree of comprehensive planning responsibility; (3) many were formed when the federal government made such coordinated planning a condition for receipt of grant funds; and (4) some may be strengthened by state participation in council membership.

Regionalization of libraries may be an idea whose time has come. A regionalism of local governments—including libraries—divides responsibilities for local and regional functions, assigns these to appropriate governmental levels, and shares functions that are logically (or practically) cooperative. The public library director should be aware of the politics of regional organization, for any form of regional planning will have an effect on library services. Regional government, in many political and administrative forms, already exists. The critical question is, Who shall control regional library activities: local, regional, state, or federal government?

Regional library services have become realities, with or without formal regional councils. Public libraries have handled federal, state, and local library funds to set up integrated cooperative library systems. Some have moved toward regional systems of multitype libraries, to interstate library cooperation, and on to the national network of the future. But even without regional applications there must be a broader outcome.

Few local library administrators are adequately sensitive to the intergovernmental process to manage within this larger and more diverse system. Lacking educational background in and formal experience with the problems of interjurisidictional political processes, the director will need formal education in these processes. In any event, the director must keep abreast of intergovernmental relationships at the various levels.

In so doing the director may learn that other agency departments have already developed useful ties with related urban departments and to their counterparts in city, county, federal, and state departments. For example, it may be more beneficial to use resources developed by local planning agencies for a library community study than to use the less-helpful upper-level agencies listed in more general handbooks or directories. Elected officials in most local governments maintain regular contacts with representatives at the state and national levels and frequently hold informal meetings with such representatives to express local concerns and interests. The library administrator should seek to be included in such meetings, stressing the role of the public library as a line of communication externally, with the public, and internally, as a legislative and executive reference bureau.

With increasing frequency, the local library director is called upon to assist in state and federal legislative efforts affecting libraries. It is, therefore, imperative that the local administrator make every effort to understand the viewpoints and positions of state and federal officials elected to represent his area and to cultivate communications on a first-name basis when suitable.

To be effective in dealing with state and federal officials, the administrator must ensure that partisan politics does not enter into the relationship—unless, because of funding or special rules regarding partisan political activities, such a restraint applies only to the work-oriented situation. The library administrator will, of course, vote at the polls according to desires and beliefs. Judgment should govern the personal activities of the library administrator in partisan politics and in nonpolitical civil rights activities. The realities of the political processes require the chief librarian on the local level to retain an impartial stance regardless of the whims and vagaries of partisan politics and the elections that climax their activities. For the local library administrator, the right to exercise partisan and civil rights beliefs remains an essential right of civil liberty. It must, however, continue to be tempered by political reality.

Policy Making

A clear understanding of how the library administrator participates in policy making is prerequisite to successful management of library services. Some of the most serious instances of maladministration have occurred because of failure to understand and/or to observe the relationship of the administrator to policy making. The library administrator is an appointed official and, like those in most other appointed positions, is directly responsible for carrying out the policies established by elected officials. Confusion sometimes results because elected officials delegate the power of policy making to those they have appointed to membership on boards and commissions.

The theory of the separation of powers established in the Constitution and reaffirmed in state constitutions and the charters and statutes providing for local government is clear. The legislative prerogative—the power to create policies—is reserved for those who are elected to legislative offices. While they may delegate the responsibility for policy in certain instances to appointive bodies, the latter retain a legislative rather than an executive or administrative function.

The public library administrator is empowered to implement policies established by the legislative body to which the library is responsible, but not to create those policies. Such a separation of powers would appear to be clear-cut and unmistakable. In practice such is not the case. Local public administrators do become involved in policy matters unavoidably. This occurs for at least two reasons: (1) legislative bodies require accurate information from administrators, which often requires those administrators to submit solutions to current problems in the form of proposed policies or amendments to existing policies; and (2) policies approved by the legislative bodies are often so broad or open to interpretation that implementation by the administrator necessitates the formulation of regulations that in effect may actually be policies.

There should be no question that legislative bodies have sole authority to create policies, and executives or administrators to determine regulations for implementation; but in practice clear distinctions can not always be drawn. An interpretation of a policy that an administrator must make may itself be a new policy. As administrators must sometimes make decisions rapidly, it is inevitable that they sometimes must create a policy and justify it later on. However, administrative policy making is caused by a lack of understanding as to what constitutes a policy and what is a regulation. Policy is often involved when a question of direction or purpose arises. A policy may be defined as a settled course that is adopted and followed by government, an organization, or informed individuals. Such a definition, however, does not take into account the new policies that must be formed to accommodate the changing situations. A regulation is a rule developed by the administration to carry out the policy that has been established. Its authority rests in the policy decision and in the library administrator's full administrative control within the library to carry out policy decisions through rules and regulations.

Because most legislators have limited time and little expertise in library matters, library administrators are often asked to formulate policies or amendments to existing policies for legislative consideration. This responsibility must never be construed to be a delegation of authority to approve policy, however. A recommended policy should be carefully written to embody philosophical concepts in clear terminology that later can be translated into workable regulations. Suggested statements may be solicited directly by a member of the local legislative body or by an executive responsible to such a group. Channels of communication should be carefully observed during this process to maintain good relations between the executive and the legislative branches.

In preparing regulations by which policies are to be implemented, the public library administrator must observe the philosophic concepts and intent of the policy to avoid misinterpretation. Also, the administrator should make sure that the regulations do not exceed the scope of the policy and thereby create *ipso facto* new policy. At this point, many grievous errors could occur to plague the library administrator. If an effort to implement policy turns up deficiencies in the legislation, the administrator has the obligation to request revision of the provisions by the legislative body.

There is, of course, another side to policy making and implementation. This is the more informal side and applies to day-to-day administration. The chief librarian is recognized as a capable individual who has been employed to lead the development of library service—one who is knowledgeable about present programs and policies in library service and who has the capacity to institute change. The service that the library delivers to the public will have an impact on society, so the administrator has a social as well as managerial responsibility. As a manager, the public library administrator works with counterparts in the larger organization, with elected and appointed officials, as well as with the library staff. The administrator should not rely solely on external criteria such as satutes and regulations to guide action but rather must resolve issues on a person-to-person level. The library administrator will by experience acquire and provide continuity, as elected officials move in and out, and the ability to manage with enlightened intelligence.

Administrative Procedures and Techniques

The ability of the public library administrator to communicate accurately and effectively with all is essential to the performance of duties and responsibilities. Timely feedback to others who are responsible for any segment of the service program is vital. It is advantageous for an administrator to provide for simultaneous observation and presentation. Such a program of communications, which involves aggressive planning and delegation of responsibilities, is vital to successful management. In communications, especially to those unfamiliar with the terminology of librarians, care should be taken by the library administrator to relate unfamiliar concepts and terminology to the context of the personal and professional lives of the participants. Time in communication is as important as every other aspect of the administrator's work.

Communications form an intrinsic part of meetings. In some instances the public library administrator will be an observing member of a meeting; in others, a participating member or the leader of the group. Although adherence to a program should be maintained during a meeting, occasions will arise when the administrator will realize that associated objectives will allow sufficient flexibility to permit the participants to consider particular needs as they emerge in discussion. The public library administrator serving as a group leader should know the goal of the meeting and be committed to the objectives stated in the call for the meeting.

The public library administrator also serves in a resource capacity to elected policy makers. The administrator should be prepared to provide the answers to questions concerning library services and their relationships to resources and economics involved in funding. The administrator should be well-versed in national library policies and programs and be able to interpret the need for library service policies as determined by the governing board. The library manager can then develop them along with the staff, who function as technical assistants and managerial advisors. In the political processes, the public library director will assume the resource role with service clubs and other community groups participating in informal discussions when new plans are being proposed either by the library administration or by the community. It is incumbent upon the library administrator to institute change and to keep pace with change through continuing education.

Position Papers

One of the most useful techniques the administrator can master is that of preparing position papers. Clear, concise, and well-reasoned statements that set forth the reasons for a particular viewpoint on a course of action are often required so as to encourage movement in a given direction. Such a statement should begin with a carefully worded declaration of the matter at hand, followed by a succinct analysis of various alternatives. The alternative or alternatives chosen for support are then stated, with advantages appropriately detailed.

Position papers, when properly prepared, often carry much weight among those who must make policy decisions because the issues involved are worked out and a solution is presented with the supporting evidence. The preparation of a position paper provides the administrator the opportunity to study a given problem in depth, to explore various alternatives, and to arrive at a solution that can be supported by substantial data. In addition, the administrator can detail facts and utilize language in a more accurate manner than may be possible in a simple discussion or debate when time is a limiting factor.

Reports

As a part of participation in the political processes, the library administrator may be required to submit reports on a variety of subjects. Regardless of content, certain rules apply that result in clear and concise exposition. The purpose of a report should be clearly stated at the beginning, with a well-defined statement of scope and any other limiting or explanatory factors. Data should be developed in a logical and progressive manner; frequently such a presentation is made more orderly through the use of headings and subheadings. Conclusions and recommendations derived from the data must be stated in language that is free of ambiguity. Where a plan of implementation is required, it should be designed around a framework that is logical and precise. A lengthy report may begin with an abstract and conclusions and/or recommendations. While the length of many reports exceeds that justified by the subject matter, others by their unnecessary brevity fail to provide a sufficient data base and/or explanation of conclusions and recommendations. Reports frequently fail to hold the attention of the reader because the writer has not mastered the elements of word usage, sentence structure, and syntax. Accuracy in word usage can be improved dramatically by courses in report writing and through practice.

Reports of group meetings are also a necessary part of the work of the administrator. Minutes of the meeting should be handled by recordings, stenotypists, taping, or shorthand notes. The duty of the administrator should be that of preparing a report that summarizes the action taken by the group. Extreme care should be taken to include the sense of the discussion and decisions. Motions passed by the organization should be conveyed with absolute accuracy. Words chosen must express the meaning of the participants. Failure to accurately reflect the viewpoints of the speaker or the intent of the motions and actions is not only a disservice but also may precipitate complaints of bias.

Agendas

Just as the political processes inevitably involve meetings, so the orderly conduct of meetings requires agendas. Political bodies and many other organizations have a predetermined format for their agendas established by law or tradition. Less formally organized groups—particularly those that represent citizen action groups, special interest committees, and the like—are apt to be more informal in the conduct of meetings.

The library administrator should have the opportunity to construct an agenda or to develop its design. It is important, therefore, to recognize the fact that an agenda plays an important part in the political process. Agenda items should reflect logical progression from one subject to another. If the items bear no such relationship, then care should be taken to place items where they are most apt to receive considered discussion. For example, placing an item with high public interest at the end of a long agenda may be a disservice to those with deep concern for the item.

Great care should be taken in wording agenda items. The wording should be concise and yet carry the full sense of the intended presentation or discussion. For instance, listing as an agenda item "Library plans" has much less merit than a slightly longer but more explanatory "Plans for a library outlet to be located in the southeastern portion of the city."

In many cases, when submitting an item to a body for inclusion on a forthcoming agenda, the library administrator should indicate a preference for the position of the item on the agenda. Likewise, it is often wise to submit in advance copies of any position paper, report, or other supporting data that may be useful in the consideration of the item. An inquiry to the official responsible will indicate the procedure to be used and the number of copies required. Many political bodies close their agendas to new items several days before their meetings, and it behooves the library director to know and abide by such deadlines. Attempts to force items onto agendas after the deadline sometimes are construed as moves to push decisions through without proper consideration, thus creating resentment on the part of public officials.

Parliamentary Procedure

The library director must have a thorough grasp of parliamentary procedure in terms of principles as well as actual rules. Contrary to the belief that such rules impose limitations and impede action, parliamentary procedure, when properly understood and employed, provides the logical structure within which the discussion leading to action can best be directed. Many local library administrators will be working with organizations that conduct meetings in accordance with a particular system of parliamentary law. An administrator who understands this procedure can be much more effective in the deliberations than one who does not.

Public Speaking

The library administrator must be active in the political processes as an effective speaker and discussion participant. The ability to express ideas and data convincingly in an oral presentation or as a part of a discussion is often paramount to success in the political processes..

The director will frequently be in a position to serve as a discussion leader. This role requires some of the skills of the presiding officer. The ability to encourage participation, to lead without dominating, to keep discussion focused on a particular issue, and to summarize and interrelate discussion can be acquired through training and experience.

The Power Structure

A power structure exists in every community regardless of size. The library administrator must become thoroughly acquainted with the power structure of the community if success in the political processes is to be attained. Administrators who are not politically aware often assume that those in authority in the community—most often those elected to office or appointed to the most prestigious positions—compose this elite group. But this is not necessarily true. Many of the most powerful people in any community have never held an elective or appointive office and have seldom had their names appear in the press. Sometimes they are very wealthy citizens; often, but not always, they represent families of long standing in the community. Not all, of course, maintain such anonymity, but the attainment of a highly visible role in community affairs does not necessarily denote one who possesses great political power. The reason that it is important for administrators and policy makers alike to become acquainted with the most influential members of a community is that some of them will prove supportive. The power structure in a community is seldom monolithic. The larger the community, the less likely will influentials have a single outlook. For the influentials will tend to organize around issues and a larger community must resolve issues that are more complicated.

The library director must learn the power structure through attendance at meetings, perceptive observations, and conversations with informed leaders. In large communities, it is not uncommon to find that more than one such group exists. By tacit arrangement, each group maintains its position in a particular field of interest. Usually there is sufficient multiplicity of interests to prevent the groups from being mutually exclusive.

The power structure is a dynamic arrangement of individuals and is, therefore, subject to continuous change. The most influential member may, for a variety of reasons, be replaced by another. The administrator must develop a sensitivity to such change. More often than not, a few individuals hold the key to the support required for approval of a new library program and the increase in funding required. While working with the power structure does not necessarily guarantee success, failure is much more frequent when this simple fact of the political processes is ignored.

The Community

A complaint is frequently voiced about the communications gap between community residents and the local government. A similar problem can exist between the residents and the public library administrator as well. Residents may believe that problems of major concern are not explicitly stated by those who attempt to solve them, or that their concerns are inadequately acted upon.

To bridge this gap the administrator must involve people in the community to gain support for library programs and services. Reacting to expressed community needs is commendable, but planning ahead for future communities and their services really makes the difference between an administrator who is only reactive instead of proactive.

It is important, therefore, that the public library director work with the people of the community. Some types of contacts seem particularly productive—for example, coffee hours, round-table discussions, and casual conversations with people within and outside the library.

A truly involved advisory committee that represents all of the community is the administrator's key to the constructive expression of community opinion in revitalizing the library program. If the community, via groups, individuals, or organizations, becomes involved in studying community needs, it may become aware that the library has inadequacies in such areas as mobile library service, reference and research, and shut-in service. If members of a community group are then involved in discovering the solution to those problems, they become committed to pursuing the plan they devise; also, the planning and the service can be more effective, realistic, and vital than if they had been done primarily by the library administrator and staff. Almost any library that has actively involved the community as advisors, as artists, as teachers, as story tellers, and as planners has a success story.

Only in rare instances do community representatives initiate involvement in the library. There-

fore, it is incumbent upon the library director to draw people from the community by organizing voluntary programs, establishing councils, and seeking out persons to help with educational programs, counseling, and other activities. The administrator has the further duty to educate the people of the community concerning the library system, its goals, and its policies. Once community involvement and education have begun, the library has a powerful and self-perpetuating ally in the struggle to reach its objectives.

To work effectively with both the governmental bodies and the community, the public library administrator must:

1. Diligently and consistently make intelligent and creative use of library standards
2. Employ persons of vision to work on library programs and activities
3. Inform the governing bodies of the new plans and accomplishments of libraries
4. Plan, develop, and implement public relations presentations and programs and include the political leaders, labor, business services, and other groups in the presentations
5. Be available and ready any time or place to speak on libraries
6. Create interest and pride in library programs
7. Work hard on programs at the administrative level because it is only through such diligent work that the other six developments can take place.

If all seven of the above activities are carried out, community involvement will be assured. These activities provide the administrator with a built-in correction system that will automatically change the program according to the needs of the community. The administrator knows the people, resources, and services and is constantly listening to governmental officials, to the staff, to the residents of the community, and to their representatives. Through these processes, political knowledge, the perception of the community, and the delegation of authority, the public library administrator will succeed in developing a delivery system of public library service capable of changing as changes are required.

4   Community Analysis

DOUGLAS ZWEIZIG

Community analysis is described as an indispensable tool of public library management. But, for all the praise that it receives in the library literature, community analysis is still a blunt instrument. In its very conception as a one-time study that seeks to identify all significant variables affecting library use, it provides a static picture of community life and provides imprecise guidance for implementation. The considerations involved in turning community analysis into an effective planning tool are the concern of this chapter.

The literature of community analysis is frustrating because it characteristically glosses over key issues. For example, the literature asserts that the purpose of community analysis is to allow the planning of more relevant and appropriate programs of service for the particular community. But it is in translating community analysis findings to library service programs that the literature offers least guidance. Further, community analysis is recommended as a tool of library accountability. But accountability also requires that the administration be able to give explicit justification for why a study was conducted in a particular way: Why was this phenomenon investigated as opposed to another one? What will be the effect of the study? Will the study be cost-effective? Here again, the literature is mute. This chapter cannot remedy all of the deficiencies it will identify, but it is intended at least to sort out some of the complexities so that public library administrators will be aware of the issues and be able to make better-informed decisions in community analysis design.[1]

Community analysis can be defined as a process of community study by an agency, self-assessment of the agency, and comparison of the results of the two investigations. The results of the comparison are used to provide *planning data* for the agency. In practice in public libraries, community analysis involves casting a wide net for the community study. Census data, municipal and public utility plans and surveys, directories of various kinds, daily newspapers, annual reports, special files, and other sources of secondary data are all examined for evidence of community characteristics. In addition, primary data collection may tap community reading interests, frequency of library use, attitudes toward the library, and so on. Self-assessment includes inventories of library services, resources, and facilities. Occasionally, a study of library users is conducted in which persons using the library are surveyed in terms of the use they are actually making of the library and their demographic characteristics. The comparison of the results involves a high use of professional judgment and intuition. The common advice is to involve as many people as possible in the comparison effort so that action implications can be more clearly discerned.

For a long period, community analysis was an activity that was urged on public librarians but was little used in the field. Such studies as were done were often made by consultant agencies or individual social scientists from outside the library. Community analysis, however, has become more commonplace and has more often been conducted by the library staff themselves, sometimes with the assistance of outside experts. Further, with the recent progress of the Public Library Association's Standards Development Project, community analysis is now seen as essential to public library planning.[2] Fortunately, along with the increasing requirement for community analysis has come an increase in instruction in its procedures and an increasing understanding of the process.

In addition, the link between community analysis and planning has become more clearly understood and applied in the library field. From among the great variety of planning models, the library field has selected the CIPP (Context, Input, Process, Product) model as the most appropriate. This model has an important emphasis on the

1. Also see Vernon E. Palmour, "Planning in Public Libraries: Role of Citizens and Library Staff," *Drexel Library Quarterly* 13:33–43 (July 1977). Note especially "Pitfalls in Obtaining Planning Information," pp. 37–40.

2. Vernon E. Palmour, Marcia C. Bellassi, and Nancy V. DeWath, *A Planning Process for Public Libraries* (Chicago, ALA 1980).

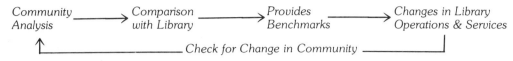

Community ⟶ Comparison ⟶ Provides ⟶ Changes in Library
Analysis   with Library   Benchmarks   Operations & Services
↑ ⎣_____ Check for Change in Community _____⎦

Fig. 4.1. CIPP planning model

investigation of the environment in which service is occurring: the context evalution. The point of context evaluation, like that of community analysis, is to establish the environment in which planning is taking place so that resulting objectives and priorities will be relevant to those to be served. CIPP provides the added emphasis on evaluating the effect of the implemented plan in meeting objectives.

The overall planning model, and the place of community analysis in it, would then look like figure 4.1. Note that the checking for change implies a repetition of the community analysis process to assess changes in the community.

In this planning context, then, we should ask what community analysis can be expected to do for the library and what it cannot be expected to do.

What Community Analysis Can Do

Community analysis will enlighten all involved in it. Portions of the population with special service needs will be identified. Information sources in the community will be discovered and recorded. Incorrect preconceptions about the population will be challenged and revised. The place of the library in the life of the community will be established. Because the process produces learning for all involved, it is important that as many people as possible be drawn into the study process: library staff, library board members, members of the community itself. Each person involved will be affected by the process and will become much more effective in planning and providing resultant library services.

Community analysis will also sensitize the library to trends in the community that will affect planning: movements of population, such changing characteristics of populations as increasing educational levels or decreasing numbers of children, employment patterns, etc. By informing itself about changes and trends, the library can become anticipatory in its planning and not merely reactive to already established change.

Community analysis will allow the library to target unserved portions of the community, whether their lack of service results from geographical isolation, lack of education, lack of rel-

evant programming, or other causes. And subsequent community analysis will allow the assessment of whether targeted populations are better served than in the past.

Community anlaysis can allow the linking of some demographic characteristics with topic or program interests. For example, identification of the number of one-parent families, increasing numbers of older people, significant numbers of adult functional illiterates, and so on, can suggest specific library program topics, areas to emphasize in acquisitions, or other activities. While this capability of community anlaysis needs to be pointed out, however, the suggestiveness of demographic descriptors for library response is more notable for its poverty than its richness.

The study of community organizations and groups through community analysis will allow the direction of library service toward their group information needs. This is possible because many groups are characterized by their topics of interest—for example, scouting, 4-H, sports, church activities, gardening, hobbies, and politics. Since library materials are primarily classified by topic, a matching of materials with topics of group interest can provide tailored and direct service to groups.

Community analysis can clearly identify access issues that relate to library service. Access problems may be physical—for example, distance from library facilities, mobility of population, geographical barriers to access, or hours of service. Or the problem may be psychological: lack of knowledge of the library's location, hours, or capabilities for service; lack of literacy to use conventional library materials; or negative attitudes toward or expectations of the library. Up to some unknown point we may assume that, as we remove barriers to access, the use of library services will increase.

Community analysis can increase the support of the library in terms both of funding and of use. Data can be provided to justify budget requests and to marshall political support. Concrete proposals can be made to address identified service gaps. Involvement of the community in the analysis will itself increase knowledge of and interest in the library. Partner agencies in the community, such as schools, social agency information services, and planning offices, will become more aware of the library and its functions. The library will be able to present a rationale for its service program in terms of community characteristics and its response to them. Finally, as Martin pointed out, the report of the community analysis provides information to those who are generally interested in the community: new residents, community planners, students, and others needing convenient information on the community's character.[3]

What Community Analysis Cannot Do

Community analysis cannot result in a static plan for the library. The key word here, of course, is *static*. Although most planning models appear to be linear, proceeding, in order, from assessment through the development of a plan, to implementation, to evaluation, in practice the environment of the library is changing even as the community analysis is being conducted. Attempting to capture library reality in a plan is as frustrating as was Samuel Johnson's attempt to capture correct usage in his *Dictionary of the English Language*. In his preface, he lamented "that while our language is yet living, and variable by the caprice of every one that speaks it, these words are hourly shifting their relations, and can no more be ascertained in a dictionary, than a grove, in the agitation of a storm, can be accurately delineated from its picture in the water." This is not to say that the exercise of attempting to describe a community should be abandoned, however. After all, Johnson's *Dictionary* stood as the authority for the language for a century. But the planners should not expect that the task is ever finally completed. The community analysis and the resulting plan is, then, a momentary snapshot that must be continually revised and questioned. Community trends, sudden events, changes in library staff, programs, policies—all must be evaluated in terms of how the picture is changed and how the library plan should be modified.

Community analysis will not produce simple systems change. The reasons are linked to the nature of the library organization itself and to the nature of the community it serves. The stance of most public libraries is that they exist to serve the needs of their communities. The rationale for community analysis is, therefore, to determine the needs of the community so that the library may respond to them. But the nature of an organization established to respond to its environment is such that it will not act to change that environment. As a result, libraries have great difficulty determining

new roles for themselves or exerting much power in their communities.

The second reason that libraries cannot produce simple systems change is that they are not alone in being concerned with the information needs of their communities and cannot alone attempt to meet all the needs they may identify. In recognition of this complexity, the recent "Mission Statement for Public Libraries" charged the public library with the task of coordinating the information services of its community.[4] This charge requires that the public library take on two roles in addition to serving the community's public directly: becoming an information specialist for other agencies in the community and becoming an agenda setter for the community to see that community needs are addressed.[5] These service and coordination tasks will not be easy. The number and complexity of other agencies in the community may be great. In a recent survey of social agencies serving the residents of Seattle and surrounding King County, Washington, 1,072 agencies were identified.[6] Of these, 405 described themselves as performing an information and referral service for their clients. The number of social agencies serving information needs outnumbers the public service librarians serving the information needs of the same population.

Community analysis will not result in direct identification of community information needs. False expectation is associated with community analysis. It is raised by the rhetoric that urges community analysis so that we may be "responsive to the information needs of the community." Some suggest that we can approach the study much as a doctor conducts a diagnosis: by studying the community, we can diagnose information needs and prescribe appropriate materials and services. This approach is so commonly expressed that it has become our primary way of thinking about our function.[7] But the metaphor only serves

3. Lowell Martin, "Community Analysis for the Library," in *The Library in the Community*, ed. Leon Carnovsky and Lowell Martin (Chicago: Univ. of Chicago Pr., 1944).

4. ALA Public Library Association, Goals, Guidelines, and Standards Committee, "A Mission Statement for Public Libraries: Guidelines for Public Library Service, Part I," *American Libraries* 8:615–20 (Dec. 1977).

5. See Margaret E. Monroe, "Community Development as a Mode of Community Analysis," *Library Trends* 24:497–514 (Jan. 1976).

6. Brenda Dervin et al., "The Development of Strategies for Dealing with the Information Needs of Urban Residents: Phase II—Information Practitioner Study" (Final Report on Project #47 AH 50014, Grant #G007500617 to the Office of Libraries and Learning Resources, U.S. Office of Education, Department of Health, Education, and Welfare, Feb. 1977). ERIC #ED 136 791.

7. Charles Evans, "A History of Community Analysis in American Librarianship," *Library Trends* 24:441–57 (Jan. 1976).

to conceal our ignorance from even ourselves. "Information need" is a concept that our literature never clearly defines. It is presumed that because people use our services they must do so at the urging of a "need." Thus, if we could study the need directly, we could anticipate service demands. Study of general population information needs has involved all the dedication of microbe hunting (the medical metaphor again). We have asked people to tell us about their information needs only to be greeted by a nonplussed reaction from the respondents. We have asked them if they have information needs regarding such topics as housing, education, public affairs, etc. Attractive as this concept is, however, we have not isolated information needs or been able to design library programs on the basis of what we've found.

A number of flaws in the approach can be identified. First, "information need" is only our idea, not necessarily something that exists in the minds of our patrons. If "information needs" do exist at all in nature, they may be like some atomic particles that can never be directly observed;[8] we can only infer their existence by observing their traces in library use, as we observe the trace of a particle in a bubble chamber. Second, for our own convenience, we would prefer to label information needs by topic. Since we organize our materials by topic, we could then directly match needs with materials. But when a study asked respondents what information they, in fact, sought in actual situations, the respondents did not relate the information they sought to topics but to how they wanted the information to function for them. They said that they sought information in order to learn such things as what resources are available, who are the decision makers, what are better options, what caused their situation, whether others agreed with them, what information they could get, etc.[9] These findings have advanced our understanding of individual information seeking but, as libraries are presently organized, the findings do not provide guidance on what programs to plan or what materials to buy.

An additional difficulty with the notion of information needs is that there is no reason to believe that the distribution of information needs in a community will remain stable over time. Even if we were able to identify information needs

satisfactorily, we would not be able to infer that those information needs that predominate for the community would be the same the next day. Therefore, a finding that 20 percent of a community had information needs relating to public affairs at the time they were surveyed could not be used as a guide to what materials to purchase over the following year. As a planning tool, the determination of information needs may be of only illusory value, although the concept continues to be appealing to researchers and community analysts alike.

Community analysis will not give clear direction to library decision making. It is reasonable to suspect that one reason community analysis is little done is because previous experience with it has been disappointing. Community analyses are begun so that library programming can be more appropriate, but when the data are collected, the realization dawns that they do not provide clear guides for program design.

This is because the data themselves do not have meaning. Their significance is provided by their reader, and that reader is too often overwhelmed by the wealth of findings to make much use of them. One reason for this problem is that the "if . . . then" relationship is not established between community data and library response. When published community surveys are examined, the connection between community findings and resulting recommendations is difficult or impossible to discern. Even the rightfully respected Martin study of the Chicago Public Library does not have a clear linkage between findings and recommendations.[10] A second reason for the problem is that the relationship between descriptors of community residents and their information needs and behaviors is not well known. The information about the population that can be obtained from census data will not allow clear inferences about the information behaviors of the population.

This is not to say that the library cannot use community data to improve programming, but there are no guidelines for doing so. The use of community analysis data is a creative act, and one who expects findings to clearly suggest action will be disappointed. A part of the difficulty is identified by Evans.[11] He describes the problem as one of expecting descriptive research (the study of what is) to provide answers to what should be. He correctly points out that, in order to determine how patrons will react to changes in service, ex-

8. Thomas Childers, *The Information Poor in America* (Metuchen, N.J.: Scarecrow, 1975).

9. Brenda Dervin et al., "The Development of Strategies for Dealing with the Information Needs of Urban Residents: Phase I—Citizen Study" (Final Report on Project #L0035JA, Grant #OEG-0-74-7308 to the Office of Libraries and Learning Resources, U.S. Office of Education, Department of Health, Education, and Welfare, April 1976). ERIC #ED 125 640.

10. Lowell Martin, *Library Response to Urban Change: A Study of the Chicago Public Library* (Chicago: ALA, 1969).

11. Evans, "History of Community Analysis."

perimental research is required. Such research is beyond the scope of community analysis as presently conceived.

Recommendations

Plan for Reiteration

One of the dangers of performing community analysis is thinking of it as a one-time activity. Since the study is so complex and consumes so many resources, the library heaves a sigh of relief after the study and returns to business as usual. In fact, community study *should be* business as usual. A one-time study is of limited use; static pictures of the community provide very few meaningful comparisons that will indicate needed adjustments by the library. But repeated studies will provide dynamic pictures of community changes that should be responded to by the library. Of course, the library cannot be forever studying everything. The resources are just not there. For this reason, more modest studies are to be recommended. Those variables that are likely to be changing over the course of a year should be identified, and only those variables should be monitored. For example, the library may want to be sure that it responds to community organizations. It should design a way of inventorying such organizations that will allow annual repetition while building on previous study as much as possible. Patterns of change in the nature of community organizations may be a powerful indication of community interests and information needs.

Any single study by a library will be imperfect, but if studies are repeated, improvements will occur: the question being investigated will be phrased more sharply, the group being studied has had services targeted for them, a better way of collecting data has been developed. As these improvements cumulate, the studies will become both easier to do and more productive. By the third repetition, community study will be a routine function of a responsive library.

Ask Specific Questions

A crucial part of any community analysis is the plan for the study. A flaw in many efforts is that major attention is given to the methodology of the study, and insufficient attention is given to the objectives, the ends of the study. As a result, data are collected that have no utility for decision making. If the library will not change its programming on the basis of the occupational character of its community, then it should not spend much time collecting data relating to it.

In a similar fashion, decisions can be made in advance about the precision needed in the data, and therefore the effort necessary to gather the data. For example, if the library would not respond to changes in the community that made less than 5 percent difference, then less precision would be needed than if 2 percent differences were seen as crucial for service. The effort, after all, is not to establish scientific verities but to determine guides for decision making. So the key question is: What decisions are likely to be affected by this information? For *each* item inquired about, ask, "What will I do differently on the basis of the information I obtain?" If such test questions are applied to each item of data sought, the study will be greatly simplified.

Determine the Proportion of Resources to Be Committed

Community analysis should be done continuously by every public library. Of course, the resources committed to such an activity will differ for different libraries. Some observations should make the burden seem more manageable. Smaller libraries with less resources serve smaller communities and so have an easier task. And the library staff does not need to perform the data collection alone. Professionals from local colleges and universities, volunteers from the community, staff of other governmental agencies can all be used in this effort. The library staff should concentrate its efforts on determining the questions to be answered and on interpreting the data obtained. Even in these efforts, volunteers from the board or the community can share. Again, the important thing is that community analysis is continually being performed, not that every aspect of the community is being studied.

As part of the relations with the external environment and planning, community analysis is rightly the responsiblity of the chief administrative officer of the library. However, in larger public libraries—those with specialists in such areas as personnel, budgeting, children's services, etc.— the responsibility for community analysis should be permanently delegated so that its continual practice is assured and not dependent on the library director's personal energies. The community analysis office should, however, have the character of a coordinator rather than of a researcher. Only if the whole staff shares in community analysis activities can the analysis have the desired pervasive effect on planning. Up to now, community analysis has been only a sometime thing with no commitment to follow-up or iteration. For community analysis to be a useful tool, a permanent commitment is required.

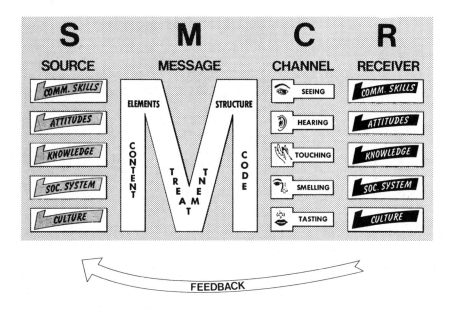

Fig. 4.2. SMCR model of the ingredients in communication

SOURCE: David Berlo, *The Process of Communication: An Introduction to Theory and Practice*, p. 72. Copyright ©1960 by Holt, Rinehart and Winston, Inc. Reprinted by permission of Holt, Rinehart and Winston.

Employ a Conceptual Model

One reason community analysis has used such a scattershot methodology is that there has been no conceptual frame to allow more precise aim. In the absence of an explicit model that lays out what will affect what, the librarian has no guide for what aspects of the community to study. And it has been the absence of such models that has made community analyses seem so loose. However, too little is known in the library field to allow the development of such a model yet. In the meantime, other fields have models that are justified by research or pragmatism and that can be used in the study.

For example, the library field is closely related to the communications field. We are in the business of making connections in the communications process, and, in providing our service, of being communicators as well. The communications field has a great variety of models that could be used to structure inquiries. David Berlo has proposed the SMCR (Source, Message, Channel, Receiver) model as presented in figure 4.2.[12] We may look at authors, for example, as senders and at readers as receivers. His model alerts us to the importance of the communications skills of the receiver. Unless

the receiver has adequate skills, the message cannot be transmitted. Thus, this model suggests that community analysis for libraries should include study of the proportion of a community that is deficient in communications skills in order to identify areas for special attention. The recent attention to the functionally illiterate is an example of that concern.

Another field that suggests useful models is that of marketing. Clearly, public libraries are in a situation analogous to the entrepeneur marketing a product. The question both have is how to increase the number of customers. Recently, the importance of marketing to nonprofit organizations has been recognized through works that explicitly make that application.[13] To take just one marketing approach: segmentation begins with the recognition that not all potential users are alike and that they should not all be served in the same way. The users are then segmented into subgroups in ways that will reflect on services. For example, the library users may be divided into geographical segments. One segment may be served with a central library, another by a bookmobile, another by a branch library. Other ways of segmenting an audience might be age, income,

12. David Berlo, *The Process of Communication* (New York: Holt, Rinehart and Winston, 1960).

13. See, for example, Philip Kotler, *Marketing for Non-Profit Organizations* (Englewood Cliffs, N.J.: Prentice-Hall, 1975).

education, volume of use, use of other media. An innovative segmentation approach described by Massey identifies the benefits different users attempt to gain through libraries and then groups the users by like benefits.[14] The market segmentation approach causes us to consider just what ways of segmenting will make a difference in service (i.e., what variables to examine) and leads us to think how we will respond differently to different segments. In sum, then, the library field has not provided conceptual models to "rationalize" the community analysis process, but other, analogous fields have many models that we can adapt for our purposes.

A conceptual model that we have been using holds that the distinction between a user and a nonuser is important. A great deal of study has been made of the characteristics of library users and in particular of nonusers. But several limitations of this model have become apparent. First, with all the attention this question has received, we have not learned as much as we thought we would. For example, several studies have used findings on a large set of variables to try to "explain" statistically an individual's amount of library use. The question asked is, What characteristics in terms of these variables will describe library users as opposed to nonusers? Even those studies that have used a wide variety of variables, such as demographics, personality variables, social roles, media use, general information behavior, and relationship to the library have only been able to "explain" one-third of the variation in amount of library use. Two-thirds of what distinguishes users from nonusers has not been dealt with in any study, and researchers have not been able to propose how we can reduce this large unknown area.

Second, when the user/nonuser distinction is studied for planning purposes, it is by no means clear what to do with the findings. If we discover that the user is characterized, in those areas we do know something about, by reading more books generally, being more open-minded, being more educated, using more information sources generally, being more involved in the community—if we know this, the resulting plan is not obvious. Should the library concentrate its energies on serving those users, as Berelson suggests,[15] or should it redouble its efforts to reach those who do not read books, the less open-minded, the less

educated, those who use fewer information sources, those isolated in their communities? The application of user/nonuser information is not intuitively obvious.

Third, recent research and conceptual work suggests that the user/nonuser distinction is one that looks at the community's residents from the viewpoint of the library and does not take a people-oriented perspective.[16] When we try to relate a number of fairly stable variables—for example, demographics, media use, community involvement—to users and nonusers, we are assuming that being a user or nonuser is a similarly stable characteristic of people. This assumption needs to be searchingly examined. Dervin found that information seeking is largely situational.[17] That is, people do not seek information for its own sake but because they are facing some situation in which information is needed in order to resolve a problem or to make progress in it or to live with its unsolvableness. From the person's view, then, information seeking will occur when a situation requires it but will not occur otherwise. This view would explain why people with the characteristics of users do not use the library and vice versa—and why a person may be offended if we suggest to him that the user/nonuser distinction is meaningful. The more meaningful question may be, Is our library helping people or not? In sum, the only utility of the user/nonuser distinction for an individual library may be for purposes of identifying that portion of the portential public that is actually reached by its services—the market penetration of the library.

Clarify Units of Analysis

It has gone unrecognized that community analysis concerns different units of analysis at different times. The units are the individual, the organization, the subgroup, and the community. For example, one of the basic dilemmas of community analysis is that, while we can study and describe the community we serve, we provide most of our services to individuals. And no amount of information about the community will tell us how to best serve the individual in front of us; for that we have to study that individual at that particular time. A whole different set of activities come into play, which might be termed "individual analysis" to distinguish them from community analysis. What, then, would community analysis have contributed

14. Morris E. Massey, "Market Analysis and Audience Research for Libraries," *Library Trends* 24:473–81 (Jan. 1976).

15. Bernard Berelson, *The Library's Public: A Report of the Public Library Inquiry* (New York: Columbia Univ. Pr., 1949).

16. Brenda Dervin, "Useful Theory for Librarianship: Communication, Not Information," *Drexel Library Quarterly* 13:16–32 (July 1977).

17. Dervin et al., "Phase I—Citizen Study."

to serving this individual? To the extent that this individual is a member of subgroups that were studied, we may be alerted to potential information needs, capacities, or preferences and be better prepared to respond to this individual inquiry. However, we must be clear about the distinction between preparing to serve a community and actually serving an individual patron. Each patron is a unique combination of community characteristics at a unique time and place and must be responded to uniquely.

The study of community organizations is much simpler for two reasons. First, the unit we study is the same as the unit we serve, for we can serve the organization as a patron. Second, organizations can be classified by topic: sports, political, cultural. This classification of organizational patrons by topic allows a direct match with library materials that are also classified by topic. The leap from study to service is much more direct than it is for individual patrons who cannot be so classified. In fact, as a recent study has shown, topic may be only one useful way to classify individual information needs, even though the library field has relied on it exclusively.[18]

A related problem of definition is that the delineation of a community is not straightforward. Communities may be defined by libraries as having political boundaries, but patrons may not see those boundaries as determining access. The "population served" notion is meaningful to the library but may not be to the public. The problem for community analysis becomes much more complicated when the library conducting the study is part of a library system. Here patrons have free access to the library and are served by the library even though they do not reside in the community being studied and so are not included in the population being described by the census data.

One recommendation here is that the library should be clear as to what unit of analysis is being used in each portion of the study and should not use data from one level of unit (community, organization, individual) to make inferences about another level. Second, the library should give explicit attention to the definition of the community to be used for the purposes of the study.

18. Ibid.

Use the Results

Finally, at the risk of belaboring the obvious, it is crucial that library planning and action should reflect the findings of the community analysis. Community expectation will be aroused by the study and should be met. The mental health of the library staff will require that the library respond to the reality it finds.

This point is made stridently in part because of the findings of a survey of libraries in northern New England.[19] Public libraries were asked to report the percentage of their populations that were French speaking or of French background and also to report the percentage of books and magazines that were in French or with a French-Canadian orientation. The results indicated that knowledge of the community does not necessarily lead to responsive programming. The article in which this survey is reported is worth reading because the results themselves are more impressive than any report of them and because the verbatim rationalizations of librarians for not acting on their knowledge may vaccinate the reader against the same disease.

This chapter has emphasized the hazards of conducting community analysis. The translation of community analysis findings to library service programs requires a high degree of professional insight. The notions of community diagnosis and information need contain many conceptual traps. Data are often collected that have no utility for decision making. Data collected in community analysis are not helpful in determining how to respond to individual client requests for service. Why, then, when all of its limitations are explored, should a public library expend the huge effort that community analysis involves? There may be no alternative for effective library planning. In this we may share the rationale of a Welsh shepherd. Dylan Thomas, in a note to his *Collected Poems*, tells of the shepherd who was asked why he danced in a fairy ring to protect his flock. "I'd be a damn fool if I didn't," he explained.

19. James G. Igoe, "The Sioux Are Silent, Boy General with Golden Locks," *Library Lit. 2—The Best of 1971*, ed. Bill Katz (Metuchen, N.J.: Scarecrow, 1972), pp. 450–58.

Bibliography

Bone, Larry Earl, ed. "Community Analysis and Libraries." *Library Trends* 24:429–643 (Jan. 1976).

Gotsick, Priscilla. *Assessing Community Information Service Needs. Library Service Guide, no. 2.* Morehead, Kentucky: Appalachian Adult Education Center, Morehead State Univ., 1974.

Warncke, Ruth. "Analyzing Your Community: Basis for Building Library Service." *Illinois Libraries* 57:64–76 (Feb. 1975).

Zweizig, Douglas, and Dervin, Brenda. "Public Library Use, Users, and Uses—Advances in Knowledge of the Characteristics and Needs of the Adult Clientele of American Public Libraries." *Advances in Librarianship* 7:231–55 (1977).

5 Public Relations—
Its Meaning and Benefits

ALICE NORTON

A sound public relations program is essential for good public library management. The practice of public relations, like personnel and other people-centered administrative functions, can trace its heritage through centuries of good human relations practices. As a well-defined field of administration, however, public relations is a newcomer. Most of its development has taken place since the end of World War II. And although younger than the century-old public library, public relations too is an American creation. Most of the world looks to the United States, and primarily to the corporate sector of the country, for leadership in public relations.

Although no one set of words has been accepted as a standard definition by all public relations specialists, the following description of this management function incorporates the ideas of today's leaders in the field: "Public relations is a planned program of policies and conduct that will build public confidence and increase public understanding."[1]

Several elements that are essential for an understanding of public relations by the library administrator are embedded in this deceptively simple definition. One is that the policies and services of the library are the foundation for its public relations. A second is that good public relations requires a *planned* program, including a mechanism for evaluation. The pre–World War II press agent who was the predecessor of the public relations specialist too often offered activity without sound planning. Finally, a continuous program of communication, based on knowledge of those with whom the library communicates, is essential for the development of confidence and understanding. Among the results of such a program should be more library users, wider general support, and an increased budget.

Because the basis for a library's public relations program is the variety of services it supplies, some administrators say that the public relations job is

shared by all the staff. This is only partially true. Certainly a good public relations program depends on the actions of every staff member. The functions, however, of overall planning, development of specific activities, communicating with various publics, and evaluation are distinct ones that must be assigned to staff with the required skills and the time and resources to carry them out.

Among most American corporations the name for this management function is *public relations* or *public affairs*. Government agencies and other not-for-profit organizations frequently use the term *public information*. A public library that serves a community whose residents equate public relations with publicity, and perhaps self-seeking publicity at that, may find it wise to call the function public information or community relations. This will help communicate the function's true meaning.

Public Relations—
Whose Job?

Although public relations is a distinct management function, its activities at various times involve almost every member of the staff. For this reason it is essential that responsibilities be well defined and understood by all. When the library's staff size or budget is too small to include a full-time public relations officer to direct the program, the need for skillful coordination is even more essential. For example, in a small library the announcements of the expansion of evening hours of public service should follow a plan probably created by the director. The plan must include: (1) a succinct statement on the new service, including benefits to the community and source of funds; (2) a list of the persons and groups to whom it is to be communicated, such as city officials, present library users, and working persons who are not library users; (3) an outline of methods of communication, such as posters, news releases, and printed bookmarks with hours; (4) a list of the persons responsible for each part of the plan; and (5) a timetable. Several staff members may share these responsibilities.

1. J. Handly Wright and Byron H. Christian, *Public Relations in Management* (New York: McGraw-Hill, 1949).

Every staff person should be informed about the new policy, communicate it person-to-person, and help the library administrator evaluate how effectively the message was communicated and what the effects of the new service are.

The Library Board

For the public library that has a policy-making board, the trustees, with the advice of the administration, formulate the basic policies on which the library's public relations program is based. Other library board responsibilities for public relations include assessing the understanding of public relations of candidates for the position of library director and requesting reports at every meeting, followed by board discussion, on the library's public relations activities. Library board members bring to these discussions their own experience with public relations programs in corporate and non-profit organizations.

The Library Director

As with all administrative functions, public relations is ultimately the responsibility of the library director. The director should have general knowledge about the field, but he or she will rely on staff or outside specialists for skills, that may range from planning an effective year-long public relations program to conducting an attitude survey in a neighborhood or producing a radio spot announcement.

The library director whose administrative style includes broad staff participation will have many vehicles through which staff can help plan the library's public relations program. But even in a more authoritarian library administration, the staff should be called on for advice and kept informed about the public relations program.

Public Relations Staff

The patterns of public relations programs vary, as they should, and the size and type of staff needed to carry them out reflect this. Among the factors that influence public relations staffing are:

1. The size and the extent of diversity of the population served
2. The number of library service outlets
3. The size and organization of the library staff
4. The importance placed on public relations by the board, administrators, and members of the community
5. Public relations services available from a library system or state library

6. The extent to which the library purchases such services as production of printed materials, radio/television spot announcements, and exhibits
7. The existence of Friends of the Library or other volunteer groups.

A factor that unfortunately often influences a library's public relations program is the publicity experience of the staff. Small- and medium-sized public libraries often divide public relations functions among a number of staff members without a strong central coordinating position. The result can be an expensive (in staff time), uneven program that fails to keep up with changing community needs and new methods of communication.

Just as staffing patterns vary, so does the cost of the public relations program. As yet, few libraries identify and analyze their total public relations expenditures. In the 1960's a book on public library administration suggested that from 1 to 2 percent of the total operating budget be spent on public relations.[2] In 1967 a library consultant who studied library public information throughout a Midwestern state wrote that, while 1 percent of the operating budgets of all public libraries could finance an effective statewide program, "5% so invested could potentially create a revolution in usage and understanding."[3] A successful public library administrator who served as president of the American Library Association recommended that 2 percent of every public library's budget be spent on public relations. A former editor of *American Libraries* suggested the percentage be 5.

Public relations departments in corporations and such not-for-profit organizations as museums and health agencies can supply information on the costs of such single activities as an annual report or a citywide information campaign. But their programs are too different from those in libraries to offer clear-cut guidance to libraries in overall budgeting. Public relations specialists have not devised budgeting formulas for this work, either in all organizations or for not-for-profit agencies.

The following guidelines are based on the writer's twenty years of work with public libraries throughout the country. From 3 to 7 percent would finance an adequate public relations program for most libraries, with the larger percentage required for libraries with smaller budgets. For example, a library operating on an annual budget of $150,000 would find it difficult to develop an

---

2. Joseph L. Wheeler and Herbert Goldhor, *Practical Administration of Public Libraries* (New York: Harper and Row, 1962).

3. William F. Summers, *Communications: A Survey of Ohio Libraries* (Columbus: State Library of Ohio, 1967).

effective program for an expenditure of 7 percent ($10,500) for staff time, materials, and purchased services. For a library budget of $1,500,000, perhaps for a population of 150,000 at $16 per capita, however, 4 percent allotment for public relations would provide $60,000. In 1978 this would support a public relations staff of two-and-a-half or three positions and allow enough money to purchase printing and art supplies and finance special events.

Library administrators who do not have well-coordinated public relations programs staffed with one or more specialists sometimes suggest that these percentages are too high for their libraries. The director and staff may learn that, although their present activities and materials fail to meet their own standards for professionalism, the cost actually approaches these percentages. A useful test is to identify the library's present costs, including staff time and fringe benefits, for the activities defined as public relations in the following section. Another test is to gather rough costs for promotional services and materials other community agencies offer and that the library staff believes would effectively communicate its professional library services.

As systems of public libraries continue to develop, their public relations services and materials can benefit the small member library immensely. One cooperative public library system in New York State formerly devoted 15 percent of its total budget to public relations; its thirty-eight member libraries received printed promotional pamphlets and posters, circulating exhibits, and public relations assistance through workshops and individual consultations.

Four Staffing Patterns

The size of the community and the size of the library budget dictate the library public relations staffing patterns.

The small library. (Population of less than 40,000; about 6 to 7 percent of operating budget for public relations.) Library director: Plans and coordinates public relations program; with staff assistance organizes library-sponsored special events and speaks before community groups; works with Friends of the Library. Part-time paid or volunteer specialist working under the direction of the library director: prepares library publicity for the press and radio; produces promotional materials with production by commercial printers; prepares library signs and displays. (Standards for volunteer work should be as high as if specialists were being paid for their work.)

The medium library. (About 40,000 population; about 5 percent of operating budget for pub-

lic relations.) Public relations officer, half-time: plans and coordinates public relations program, including preparation of publicity for newspapers, radio, and television; produces and distributes printed materials. Staff artist, half-time: prepares library signs and displays; designs library printed materials. Clerical assistant, half-time.

The medium-to-large library. (Population of about 100,000; about 4 percent of operating budget for public relations.) Public relations officer, full-time: coordinates and develops the public relations program. Staff artist, full-time: produces library signs, posters, and displays for use within the library and in the community; designs library publications. Clerical assistant, half-time.

The large library with branches and perhaps other service outlets. (About 500,000 population; 2.5 percent of operating budget for public relations.) Staff of eight: public relations officer; assistant for publications and newspaper publicity; assistant for radio/television and work with community groups; two staff artists; one publications assistant, clerical; one secretary; one clerk/page.

Outside Public Relations Specialists

As the four staffing patterns presented above suggest, outside specialists hired on a contract for a period of time or for special jobs are often useful for the library too small for regular public relations staff. Even larger libraries sometimes find outside specialists an effective way to secure services. These services might include:

1. Helping plan and develop a staffing pattern for a library's public relations program
2. Offering public relations consultant service to the staff person who is in charge of public relations, with regular conferences
3. Carrying out specific projects that require specialized skills or more manpower than the library staff can provide. Examples: production of a library annual report for general distribution; production and distribution of radio or television spot announcements; producing a library special event; preparing library exhibits to mark a special occasion; conducting a survey of community attitudes and opinions; conducting a campaign for a library bond issue election; and evaluating a library's public relations program.

Sources of outside public relations specialists include: public relations agencies, preferably small- or medium-size with some experience in not-for-profit clients; self-employed specialists or staff who work part-time for other agencies; and employed persons who want extra projects. The library administrator should examine samples of previous work that are similar to those the library requires, in order to evaluate their quality, and assess the person's judgment and reputation for completing work thoroughly and on time.

In addition to the time required for locating and selecting part-time specialists, staff must allocate time for informing them about the projects they are to work on and supervising or working with them on these projects. The collaboration can, if successful, not only reach the objectives for the project but also broaden the experience and expertise of the library staff. The pattern is one that is widely followed in corporate public relations.

The Library Public Relations Office

Staffing and equipment needs depend on the size and budget of the library and the extent to which the library seeks services from such outside sources as a library system, a free-lance artist, or a printer. It is unreasonable to expect a small library's administrator—for whom public relations is one of several major responsibilities—to have all the skills and experience of a full-time public relations specialist. Through ingenuity, however, the director can gain supplementary help from outside specialists, trustees, and a Friends of the Library group. Several neighboring libraries might profitably share the services of a public relations specialist as well as those of an artist for displays and publications.

Staff

The public relations officer. The full-time or, in the small library part-time, public relations officer should have the following minimum qualifications:

1. A B.A. degree, preferably in the liberal arts with courses in fields of communication such as writing, editing, speaking, and nonprint media
2. Experience in planning, conducting, and evaluating a public relations program
3. Knowledge about the production of printed publications; the methods of working with the press, radio, and television; the principles of graphic communication; and the coordinating of a special event
4. Ability to manage the public relations office and work with staff, outside specialists, and community organizations.

A library degree is not required. Unless the public relations officer has held a library position, however, his or her orientation should include the development of a plan for continuing education in the library field through reading of professional books and journals, participation in library associations activities, and attendance at library school institutes and workshops. If the new officer has had a library public relations position, all these educational activities should continue.

The library administrator can find candidates for the position of public relations or public information officer from such sources as: the national office or chapters of the Public Relations Society of America, a local publicity club, the placement service of a university or college that offers public relations or journalism courses, and administrators or public relations officers in local organizations, especially educational and nonprofit agencies. Advertisements in the library press may attract library public relations specialists who are seeking new positions. The salary offered should be competitive with the current ones paid in the region for similar work and at the scale for those paid to the library's personnel officer, the head of business operations, or the head of a major department.

Other public relations staff. In addition to clerical support, the public relations officer will need the services of one or more artists to plan and produce displays, exhibits, and signs and to design library publications. In a small library, one person, perhaps part-time, will probably do all the art work. In selecting a graphic designer, the procedures are similar to those suggested for hiring outside public relations specialists. Most graphic designers have a portfolio of past work and will probably accept a free-lance assignment to demonstrate their skill. In larger libraries or library systems, public relations staffs can divide the work among specialists in writing and editing, radio and television, and library-sponsored programs and special events. Purchase of photographic services from a skilled commercial photographer usually brings the library a higher quality of pictures at less cost than if a staff member takes publicity pictures.

Space and Equipment

The minimum space requirements include a private office for the public relations officer and an exhibit preparation room with drafting table, sink, and extensive storage space for display materials and displays. For medium and large libraries, a signmaking machine of the type used by department stores is a good investment. (Many library systems offer signmaking services.) A library page can make signs and posters following the specifications and layouts prepared by the library artist.

If the library operates offset printing equipment for administrative purposes, it may be economical and convenient to produce public information pamphlets and fliers within the library. If the only use for such equipment is the production of public information materials, however, the library should utilize commercial printers or develop cooperative printing facilities with other libraries. Any printer will give quotations of prices for potential work. The library staff can use these to plan the production of printed materials and a budget.

Operations

As part of management, the public relations officer participates in administrative planning meetings, attends library board meetings as an observer, and works closely with the staffs of all library departments. The public relations officer should base all plans and activities on the goals of the library and function both as a service unit to the public service departments and as a supportive part of the library's central administration. Although the public relations officer will often be seeking the newsworthy, dramatic elements in any event or service, this will be for the purpose of attracting attention and users, not to change or create a service.

The public relations officer should keep others in the P.R. office well informed about library activities, involve them in planning, and encourage them to contribute ideas about all the office's work. Two-way communication is also vital for work with free-lance staff and volunteers such as Friends of the Library.

Friends of the Library

Many public libraries, both large and small, benefit from the energy and enthusiasm of a local Friends of the Library group. Members are men and women who believe in the importance of their local public library and show it by giving time, and often money. Friends' funds are most effective when they finance additional library activities. They should not replace tax support for essential, ongoing operating expenses. The Friends of the Library, as the name indicates, work with the library administration to carry out the policies that the trustees or other governing body has formulated. As a citizen group, the Friends can play a major role in presenting the library's financial needs to the appropriating body or to the voters when the library is on the ballot.

The library's public relations program is of primary importance to most Friends of the Library groups. The public relations officer is an appropriate person to provide liaison with the Friends.

Examples of Friends activities are: sponsorship of film programs, book discussions, and seminars on subjects ranging from investments to rare books; presentation of major cultural events, sometimes combined with fund raising; organizing and providing volunteers for new services, such as the lending of original art and sculpture, that later may become part of the library's ongoing program.

Good publicity is needed to attract members to a Friends group and to stimulate interest in Friends' activities. This publicity should be carefully coordinated with the library's own publicity. To avoid dual library spokes-persons it may be useful to have the library staff member who handles relations with the press, radio, and television also coordinate the announcements the Friends of the Library make to these media. Similar procedures may be useful when a library has other volunteers assisting the library programs or when it co-sponsors activities with community service clubs or similar organizations.

Research—The Base for a Public Relations Program

The library's public relations program must be based on a foundation of facts about the library and about the library's publics. Most of this information, which must be updated continuously, is important for the library's overall administration and service programs. The staff member responsible for public relations, however, needs to be familiar with the information and able to acquire it quickly.

Information about the Library

What facts must be known about the library? These include: the library's objectives, both the official ones adopted by the policy-making body and service objectives of various staff units; the library's total resources, including staff, library materials of all kinds, and physical facilities; services of the library; and administrative information, such as the legal base of operation, sources of funding, and current budget. Although most of this information will concern present operations, data must also be gathered about the library's history and plans for the future. It is important to have a clear concept of the library's strengths and specialities and of its weaknesses and needs. Most of this information can be found in written form in such documents as annual reports and the staff reports that are used to compile them, minutes of meetings, official library publications, newspaper articles, and memoranda.

Information about the Library's Publics

Public relations specialists use the word *public* to refer to a group of persons with a common characteristic who are important to an institution. Two of the library's most important publics are the trustees, or members of whatever policy-making body the library has, and the staff. Information about their work for the library is part of the library profile described above.

Two important publics relate to the library's funding. These are the government agencies that supply tax funds to support the library, and any private sources of support the library may have. Organizations with a commitment to library development include the Friends of the Library, if one has been organized, and those educational and community agencies and organizations with close library ties.

The groups named above are easily identified, and information about them consists of the names and addresses of organizations and officers and descriptions of activities, with emphasis on library relations. Three additional publics are broader and more difficult to define.

The first of these publics is composed of present library users. Circulation and registration records, staff reports, and observation will yield valuable information about characteristics of users. A second broad public is composed of those nonusers who, because of their needs, interests, and activities, are the most likely to become library users. Finally, the entire population in the geographical area served by the library can be considered a public. For both the potential library users and the general population, the types of information that should be sought are age, educational level, ethnic background and languages used, occupations, patterns of daily life, hobbies, and interests. All of this information—whether found in printed sources such as census data, supplied by researchers in such other agencies as schools and universities or corporations, or gleaned from newspaper articles and the staff's daily work—will have a dual use. It provides the essential basis for the library's own public relations program, and it also is a valuable resource that the library can use in serving as a purveyor of community information.

Library Surveys of Opinions and Attitudes

Occasionally a library needs to supplement the ongoing information-gathering process with a survey that will supply the answers to specific ques-

tions. More and more libraries are sponsoring opinion and attitude surveys. Major steps in conducting a survey are:

1. Formulating goals for the survey
2. Selecting the sample to be surveyed (libraries frequently fail to do this properly)
3. Creating the survey instruments, such as questionnaires
4. Developing survey procedures and timetables
5. Training the persons who will conduct the survey
6. Testing the instruments
7. Conducting the survey
8. Tabulating, interpreting, and communicating the results.

Sources of help for conducting surveys are readily available to libraries. A college or university may agree to carry out a survey, with or without a fee, or the library may ask a research firm to do the job. The staff of marketing research firms or research departments in business firms will often supply advice, without charge, to a library that wishes to conduct its own survey. The selection of the sample and the preparation of the questionnaires or other instruments are areas in which it is wise to seek help. If, for example, the League of Women Voters or another service club cosponsors the survey, the library not only receives valuable hours of work but also avoids the dangers of distortion that can occur when a library representative conducts a phone or in-person interview.

Before launching ambitious plans for its own survey, a library might investigate a statewide library survey or a regional survey. Colorado and Pennsylvania are among the states that have done this. The Maryland Library Association conducted a survey in that state. The nationwide study of attitudes and behavior concerning the use of public libraries that The Gallup Organization conducted in 1975 provides information of value to every public library administrator. Gallup also conducted state surveys for some of the sixteen state library agencies that with the American Library Association sponsored the national survey. A public library in an area in which marketing firms or corporate researchers conduct surveys might suggest they add a few library questions to commercial surveys.

For most library surveys, extreme accuracy—which may be expensive to achieve—is not required. A library that receives general data about community interests and opinions can then experiment with new services and test their acceptance. For example, a library might conduct a survey in which a sample of library users and potential users is asked about adding a new service. If the results show general interest in using the service, the library can initiate it on an experimental basis. It is not necessary to find out exactly what percentage of the community believe they would use the service.

One town's survey. Even a small library with a limited staff can conduct its own survey. The library in one Connecticut town with a population of twenty thousand conducted a telephone opinion and attitude survey in cooperation with the League of Women Voters. The research department from a nearby business organization supplied valuable advice on the selection of the sample and the contents of the questionnaire. The random sample of 147 persons was larger than the number required for statistically valid results and showed close correlation in age, sex, etc., with the general population. Because the primary goals of the survey were to find out how much nonusers knew about the library and to assess their interests, opinions, and attitudes, separate tabulations of results were made for users and nonusers. The survey's results did not bring startling new information, but it provided guidance to the trustees.[4] And, like all surveys, it demonstrated to the community the library's desire to be responsive to community interests and needs.

Planning a Continuous Public Relations Program

A key word in the definition for public relations used in this chapter is *planned.* Unfortunately this vital function is often pushed to the background by the pressures of the day. Planning requires time and may appear to offer no immediate, tangible results. But it is an essential basis for action and for the evaluation of a program's success.

The library's public relations staff should contribute to the formulation of the library's overall goals; the public relations program then is planned to help achieve these goals. One library that had as a major goal increasing service to the city's large Mexican-American population planned a three-month-long "Spotlight on Mexico" that included lectures, film and dance programs, exhibitions of crafts, books, and art prints, and a pamphlet with an essay and reading lists. The festival, which had a community planning committee, attracted large audiences of both Mexican-Americans and others. By using this theme for almost every library program, display, and publication produced during

the three-month period, the staff had time to produce this major event. And in addition to achieving the library's major goal—increased awareness of the library among a major part of the population—the event also dramatically publicized materials and services from almost every department. The key to success was careful planning.

Even the smallest library should have a plan for its public relations program with clearly stated objectives. Such a plan should incorporate: identification of potential disasters; information about the library's policies and practices that relate to that disaster; and procedures for handling the disaster including responsibilities of various staff members and channels of communication within the staff and through the mass media. Library administrators should prepare the plan, but all staff should know their roles and have lists with the home telephone numbers of key staff.

Probably the most difficult part of the preparation of the public relations plan is allocating the amount of staff time that will be spent for various functions. No such schedule can be followed rigidly, but one should be prepared. The person in charge of public relations should be able at year's end to give approximate estimates of the percentages of time the staff devotes to such major activities as press relations, exhibits and displays, and work with community organizations.

Money, of course, also plays a part in public relations planning. Although the major cost of a library's public relations program is used for staff salaries or purchased services, funds for the latter and for materials should be allocated for the major activities. When services, such as printing of promotional materials, are supplied by other library staff units, an estimate of their cost should be made. This makes it possible to determine when and in what circumstances the library should purchase services and materials rather than calling on staff to produce them.

Communicating with the Library's Publics

As a central function of management, public relations requires the involvement of many staff members for sound planning. But for the day-to-day implementation of these plans, the administrator should assign responsibility to the public relations staff. Other staff members and outside specialists, including volunteers, may share in the work, but unless one person coordinates the program, it will not have its full impact. In fact an uncoordinated program may even impede the library's progress toward its goals. For example, if communication to the press is not channeled

---

4. *The Ridgefield Library: Self-Survey Report,* Alice Norton, Library Consultant (Ridgefield, Conn.: Ridgefield Library and Historical Association, 1973).

through one office, the result will probably be confusion or distortion of the facts.

Communication is only one of the public relations activities in a public library, but is the one on which the staff usually spends most of its time. Although communication skills cannot replace the ability to plan and execute a program, their possession is essential for the public relations staff. Tradition, budget restrictions, and lack of staff expertise have combined to keep library communication in most libraries print oriented and conservative in approach. For this reason it is important that libraries have access to specialists who will choose from the wide range of contemporary media in communicating the library's many messages. As an illustration, summer reading programs for children, which are traditional in many communities, usually rate a feature newspaper article but are rarely thought of as major news. An imaginative public relations officer with political campaign experience created media news events to promote a summer reading program by using a frogman in rubber diving suit and mask as the program's spokesman. His school appearances enthralled the children, but the stunt also gave the library high visibility when he appeared in film clips on prime-time evening television newscasts. In this case publicity needs dictated the method of promotion, but the basic goal of the program, to promote reading, was unchanged.

Internal communication. Although internal communication among library staff and trustees is necessarily the responsibility of many persons, the public relations staff should be considered a resource to help plan the most effective communications program, assess current attitudes, select the best media, and advise in their use. A posted staff memorandum, minutes of a board meeting sent by mail, the personnel manual for new staff, a staff meeting discussion that incorporates videotape— these are among the many media that carry messages within the library organization. The public relations staff should have some skill in each. The library staff and trustees also should feel free to seek help from the public relations specialist when they are preparing articles for library professional journals or speeches for library conferences.

Publications. A pamphlet or bookmark is probably the most versatile medium for carrying a library message. It is easy to produce and distribute, and the cost can be kept low. Economy should not exclude the purchase of writing and design services, however, when the library staff lacks these skills. Every library needs an attractive, readable pamphlet that describes its basic services and is produced in sufficient quantity to reach every household. A publication is also a good way

to report to the community annually on the preceding year's accomplishments and, equally important, the goals for the future. One public library launched a new quarterly newsletter by using its first issue for a brief annual report and look to the future, a calendar of library events, and, as a separate insert, a brief guide to the library's resources and services. Using the low-cost bulk mailing rate, the library sent a copy to every household and business. The library produced extra copies of the library guide for distribution within the library, at other community centers, at meetings of community organizations, and by the Welcome Wagon greeters.

Other messages are carried by newsletters, fliers, bookmarks, brochures, and forms such as notices requesting the return of books. Whether a library produces one publication a year or hundreds, at least as much thought and energy should be devoted to distribution of a publication as to its production. Methods can include convenient pick-up points at the library and other community centers, direct mail by the library or other organizations, and promotion at meetings, in the press, and over radio and television.

Signs and posters. A coordinated, well-designed signage system attracts users to library outlets, guides the user within the library to services and materials, and identifies the library as a contemporary, progressive institution. The best department stores offer useful models for effective signs and displays. A library building program should include specifications for:

1. Exterior signs with night lighting, to direct the driver or pedestrian to the library, identify the library, and give hours of service
2. Exterior display areas or inviting views of library interiors
3. An interior signage system
4. Building directories
5. Display boards and exhibition cases for library materials, borrowed display items, and community announcements.

Every library should use professionally produced signs, either made by the staff, requested through a library system or state library, or purchased.

Posters and portable displays. Posters on library services stimulate use when exhibited in shopping centers, banks, and other community centers. Every library can afford to purchase the professionally designed and produced posters provided by the American Library Association through the National Library Week program, state and regional associations, and commercial suppliers. These are most effective when displayed throughout the community to attract new users and only secondarily used inside the library building. Within the library, slide-sound units that operate on request or continuously, cassettes with taped messages, phones offering recorded explanations or services, such as the library catalog—these are among the ways libraries can publicize and interpret services and save staff time.

Newspapers and magazines. Daily and weekly newspapers and local or regional magazines offer good opportunities for continuous reporting of library news. The library should regularly supply the press with accurate news releases, article suggestions, and photographs or picture ideas, and should respond promptly and openly to requests from the press for information. One library, working with a newspaper writer, developed an entertaining feature story that told, with names and pictures, how six or seven persons used the library. Library materials and services had helped them start a thriving business, plan an unusual vacation, continue to read through talking books after eyes failed, and care for an unusual pet. Another library that invites the press to cover board meetings demonstrates in this way the administration's interest in communication. The result is good coverage of the library's operation—which is important when budget time arrives—and occasional support through editorials.

Public relations staff from a group of libraries in a major urban region worked for two years on plans for a newspaper feature on library services. Their efforts paid off in a major Sunday newspaper supplement, 4 million copies, which contained a variety of professionally written articles and appealing photographs on all types of libraries. Libraries *are* news if their staffs have the skill and determination to identify and promote their newsworthy services.

Close working bonds between the public library and the press are forged when the library staff capitalizes on its unique opportunities to offer information and research materials to journalists. Foreign language newspapers, organization bulletins, and corporate employee publications are all good outlets for library news.

Regular analysis of library press clippings and radio and television coverage will tell the staff what facts and impressions about the library a nonuser is gaining through these media. Articles and programs that describe and interpret services and goals take time to develop, but they communicate a message that announcements of film programs and new books never can.

A newspaper article on the library can have a long life and serve multiple purposes. Reproduced by economical offset, it can be distributed like a flier or sent by mail. Enlarged photographically, it can become a dramatic poster.

The library should keep the library profession informed about its activities, especially innovative services, through announcements, articles, and pictures sent to regional and national professional periodicals. The American Library Association's public information staff welcome news of library services and activities from all libraries. They combine these into features for submission to newspaper wire services, national magazines, and network radio and television programs.

The public library's public relations staff should inform all employees about news that is going to the press and should post articles that have appeared and announcements of radio and television programs on the library. The public relations staff should offer other staff members assistance in preparing professional articles and submitting them to editors.

Radio and television. A radio or television station usually reaches an audience in an area that is beyond the boundaries of any one library. A number of libraries can effectively join to produce television film spot announcements and slides, recorded or written radio messages, and segments for ongoing programs. By sharing the costs, libraries can afford high-quality, imaginative production, which is essential to gain free radio and television time.

For five years the public libraries of one state cooperated to produce and distribute to every station in the state lively radio and television spot announcements. In another state, the state library and the state library association pooled resources, including federal funds, to commission a leading advertising/public relations firm to produce television spot announcements. These public library promotional messages were as universal as advertising for nationally distributed products. Therefore the producer sold them to other libraries for successful local adaptation at a modest cost. When libraries combine forces in this way, they can achieve a professionalism in radio and television production that is impossible for any one library to finance.

Educational radio and television stations and cable television offer good communication opportunities to libraries in many communities. Here, too, cooperation among libraries usually benefits all.

Community Organizations

An active library cooperates with community organizations in a variety of ways such as offering services to members, cosponsoring programs, and receiving materials or other support. Library staff and trustees can take the library message to members through talks, slide-sound presentations, exhibits, library pamphlets, and articles in organization newsletters. When the library cosponsors an activity with a community organization, both agencies can multiply their publicity activities. Often the other agency or organization will have a public relations program with staff and resources beyond that of the library.

For almost every service the library offers, a number of community organizations have a special interest. For business books and periodicals, the chamber of commerce, investment groups, and special-interest groups like personnel or accounting associations are obvious outlets. A special service, such as large-print or talking books, can be publicized through groups that serve the target audience—in this case opthalmologists, senior citizen groups, hospitals, and service clubs. In fact the opportunities for publicity through organizations and groups are so vast that the library must continuously evaluate its activities in terms of changing goals and community needs.

A library special event can dramatically introduce a new library service, mark an anniversary, pay tribute to a donor, or focus attention on a subject of current interest. One suburban library captured the interest of the community when it celebrated its sixteenth anniversary with a "Sweet Sixteen Love In." Hundreds came to the library to play games built on library services, see films made by the town's teenagers, record answers on cassette recorders to questions asked by young people, eat birthday cake, and take home booklists and a cookbook of staff recipes. The questions they were asked were: "What do you love?" and "What do you love about the library?" A metropolitan library system filled a void in its community by sponsoring monthly art shows that attracted thousands of visitors. Libraries can help residents cope with inflation through supplying consumer information and find work by offering guidance in resumé writing and job seeking. In fact, a library that is attuned to local concerns and events and is in close touch with community organizations can become the scene for almost any event from a series of programs on local political issues to a celebration of a sports victory.

Other publics—other media. The public relations staff should be aware of all forms of communication even though the administration may assign responsibility for these to other staff. Examples are: orientation of new trustees and new staff; recorded phone messages that operate when the library is closed; listings in the phone directory; postage meter slugs; printed guides to community resources that include library references; and slides or other visuals used by staff or trustees to illustrate talks.

Cooperative Public Relations Activities

Cooperation with other agencies in developing and conducting public relations programs brings multiple benefits to the local library. The library's public relations resources, both staff time and dollar expenditures, can go farther. The impact of a multi-agency program can be greater. And the library will become more involved in its local community, its region, and perhaps also with other libraries nationally.

Success in any cooperative effort must be based on shared interests and benefits for each agency. Because a local library has almost unlimited opportunities for cooperation with other agencies, the staff must evaluate every prospective partnership or project in relation to its current goals. Among the questions to be answered are: What library services and resources could a cooperative project publicize? What new publics could a cooperative project help the library reach? From what sources could the library gain understanding and support through a cooperative project? The staff also should analyze the probable cost to the library of a cooperative project in terms of staff time and actual expenses.

Local Community Agencies

With elementary and secondary schools, the public library can cosponsor such activities as a summer reading program, a film or concert series, a photography contest, a career clinic, and adult activities from auto repair to family life discussions. If the town or city has a college or unversity, the public library and the academic library can combine their efforts for educational events planned especially for students and faculty or for the entire community. Government agencies (such as a parks and recreation department), museums, service clubs, professional associations, and hobby groups are logical library allies. In the corporate world the growing emphasis on public affairs among business firms, often with staff assigned to community activities, offers new opportunities for library cosponsorship.

Library Systems and Networks

Public relations services are among the most important and useful ones a cooperative or consolidated public library system can offer its members. Promotional materials without cost or at cost, consultant services, training workshops, and coordination of systemwide public events—all can be of enormous help to the member library. Within systems that encompass a variety of types of libraries, the members' public relations needs may be diverse, but the systems can offer such useful services as coordinated public information campaigns directed toward specific publics, and staff-training seminars.

State Libraries

The state library is the most logical source from which the local public library might receive public relations services. The few states that have already launched programs have demonstrated the potential for statewide programs. More state libraries should move beyond public information programs for their own services to the development of activities for all the libraries in the state. In some states, permanent public relations staff publicize public library services through the mass media directly or by supplying releases and spot announcements to local libraries, coordinate statewide special events, and conduct staff-training workshops. In several states federal grants have financed the production of posters and promotional pamphlets. Wisconsin's former Coordinated Library Information Program, Inc. (CLIP) offered to public, academic, school, and special libraries: public relations advice and ideas through a newsletter; posters, pamphlets, radio spot announcements, and other materials, free or at cost; and staff-training workshops. Before CLIP ceased operations, libraries throughout the country could purchase its excellent materials.

Library Associations

Regional and state library associations generally lack the finances and staff to offer continuous public relations services, but a number have sponsored public information campaigns and conducted staff workshops. The Library Public Relations Council presents programs for its members in the New York City area, sends each member a packet of the year's best public relations pamphlets and posters, and sponsors awards for excellence in public relations. A continuous source of new public relations ideas is the John Cotton Dana Library Public Relations Award program, sponsored by *The Wilson Library Bulletin* in cooperation with the Public Relations Section of the American Library Association's Library Administration and Management Association. The goals of the awards are to identify and honor the best library programs each year and to share information

about them through lending the scrapbooks and audiovisual materials that serve as entries.

Many national professional and trade associations, such as those for teachers, bankers, or members of the oil and gas industry, conduct continuous public information campaigns nationally and offer public information services to local chapters and members. The American Library Association could play a similar role for the library profession. At this time ALA, through its small public information office and the help of a public relations firm, is playing a valuable but more limited role. Among ALA's current activities are: stimulating national newspaper, magazine, radio, and television media to report library news and develop library features; supplying a syndicated book column, which about 375 newspapers carry, and radio public service spot announcements for a national network; serving as a center of information on innovative library services and programs and offering guidance to librarians in the field of public relations; and directing and coordinating the National Library Week program, the only national program that promotes all types of libraries. NLW focuses on one week each April but produces materials that libraries can use all year.

Through ALA's Public Relations Section (Library Administration and Management Association), about two-thousand members sponsor a remarkable range of useful activities. Among these are: production of a series of practical pamphlets on such topics as press relations, promotional publications, and public speaking; sponsorship of "Swap and Shop" sessions at the annual conference, during which hundreds of librarians and trustees visit exhibits, watch library audiovisual presentations, and seek advice from public relations specialists; service as a clearinghouse for information about Friends of the Library groups; and sponsorship of occasional two-day preconferences on public relations.

The Children's Book Council, Inc., sponsors Children's Book Week and supplies posters and other promotional materials designed by leading artists. The council also produces materials for other library reading programs.

Other Sources

Upstart, a commercial firm, produces a variety of library promotional materials from posters to T-shirts. The *New York Times* on occasion supplies to libraries its imaginative posters produced for display by bookstores. Library supply firms also offer some publicity materials. As more and more libraries add skilled public relations specialists to their staffs, the interest in and market for high-quality promotional materials should grow.

Evaluation of the Public Relations Program

Pubic relations evaluation can take one of three major forms. The first is a comprehensive study of the entire program, sometimes called a public relations audit. This audit may appropriately take place when a library hires its first professional public relations staff person. It may then be repeated periodically. Outside specialists often make these audits, in cooperation with the library staff. The second form of public relations evaluation is a regular review of the library's entire program as part of the administrative schedule. An annual evaluation at the end of the library's reporting year is usual. Finally, the third form is the evaluation of every public relations activity, from the production of a printed pamphlet to the publicizing of a new service.

In planning any evaluation two main concerns should be, What are the goals of the program or activity? and, What aspects can be measured? One public library director evaluated the communications media the library used by placing two questions about publicity in a general library survey conducted among a sample of library users. Most of those who answered identified the monthly newsletter as their main source of information. From this the director was able to justify the money needed to produce and mail the newsletter and, if necessary, reducing his reliance on other means to reach this audience.

If the purpose of an activity is to stimulate action, such as use of phone reference service, the library must measure such action before and after the publicity campaign. If the purpose is to change attitudes and opinions about some aspect of library service, the library must sample attitudes, also before and after the campaign.

Much of the information needed for evaluation is already available in library records or can easily be collected. Informal sharing of observations and results at library staff meetings and board of trustees meetings can gather useful information and increase awareness of evaluation methods.

In evaluating the library's communications program such methods can be used as: studying the number and costs of the printed pieces that the library produces and the results of each in attitude, actions, questions, and comments; collecting press clippings to evaluate the amount of coverage the library gets in newspapers and other publications and the messages that the articles contain; and estimating the use by radio and television stations of library spot announcements and news items, and soliciting the opinions of radio and television staff regarding the quality of the library's material.

If the library board of trustees includes as members public relations specialists or representatives from the communications media, they can offer continuous evaluations of the library's public relations program. On occasion the library may want to hire an outside specialist for help in evaluation. In addition, public relations staff from the state library or library system may agree to help with periodic evaluation.

Evaluation is probably the most difficult and perhaps the most neglected aspect of library public relations. If, however, the library's public relations staff builds evaluation into their program, they will be able to collect and interpret information that will both justify the expense of the operation and also guide them in their future allocation of time and resources.

What's Ahead for Library Public Relations?

In three decades, public relations has evolved from press agentry and publicity into a major corporate management function. The nonprofit world of universities and hospitals, museums and government agencies is not far behind the business world in its recognition of the role of public relations. These nonprofit organizations, including libraries, sometimes even lead the way in the development of responsive, effective public relations programs. Today the best library administrators understand the public relations function. It will not be long before this creative new function in the administrative world will be as well understood in libraries as are sound business practices and criteria for selecting books and films.

The impetus for the growth of the role of library public relations will probably come primarily from the increase in management expertise among library administrators and other staff. Other support will come in varying degrees from library trustees, government officials, Friends of the Library, and individuals and groups who in increasing numbers are pushing tax-supported agencies to be more effectively run and more responsive to community needs. Another important factor in the growth of the library public relations function is the increasing interdependence of libraries. Through regional systems and statewide networks, the local library finds its operations compared to and measured against those of other libraries. The growing reliance on the principles of accountability is subjecting library public relations programs to a scrutiny that can reveal both strengths and weaknesses.

Measurement of library public relations programs has too seldom been the subject of research studies. In one 1972 study of the promotional aspect of library public relations, however, researchers learned that vigorous selling appears to attract more than users. The researchers studied thiry-eight California public libraries and concluded, "Libraries using certain basic sales promotion devices and techniques tend to receive a larger share of the tax dollar than do libraries not using such devices and techniques."[5] Certainly a

---

5. Elizabeth Oakes, "Libraries and Sales Promotion," *California Librarian* (July 1972), p. 163.

sound public relations program cannot guarantee that a library will have no financial problems. But since in the long run a community buys what it wants, either through individual purchases or through taxes, every local public library should find that a strong public relations program not only helps it serve the community better but also helps it attract the support needed to assure future vitality.

Some Public Relations Books, Journals, and Associations

GENERAL PUBLIC RELATIONS

Cutlip, Scott, and Center, Allen. *Effective Public Relations.* 5th ed. Englewood Cliffs, N.J.: Prentice-Hall, 1978. The basic guide to the field.

Norton, Alice. *Public Relations: Guide to Information Sources.* Detroit: Gale Research Co., 1970. Still the basic bibliography in the field.

Public Relations Review. College of Journalism, Univ. of Maryland, College Park, MD 20742. Quarterly. An annual issue includes a comprehensive bibliography.

Public Relations Society of America. 845 Third Avenue, 12th Floor, New York, NY 10022. Phone: (212) 826-1776. PRSA is the major, national public relations association in the country. Its publications include the monthly *Public Relations Journal.* The Information Center publishes annually an excellent, free, six-page bibliography of books and journals. Use of the center's voluminous collection of current materials is available to all.

Public Relations Society of America. *Public Relations Guides for Nonprofit Organizations*: 1. *Planning/Setting Objectives.* 2. *Using Publicity to Best Advantage.* 3. *Working with Volunteers.* 4. *Making the Most of Special Events.* 5. *Measuring Potential/Evaluating Results* by Alice Norton. 6. *Using Standards to Strengthen Public Relations.* New York: The Society, 1977.

LIBRARY PUBLIC RELATIONS

Angoff, Allan, ed. *Public Relations for Libraries: Essays in Communication Techniques.* Westport, Conn.: Greenwood, 1973. 246 pp.

Baeckler, Virginia, and Larson, Linda. *GO, PEP, and POP! or 250 Tested Ideas for Lively Libraries.* The U*N*A*B*A*S*H*E*D Librarian (G.P.O., Box 2631, New York, NY 10001), 1976.

Ellis, Vivienne. *Lively Libraries.* 55 pp. Paperback. Illustration. Order from: Australian Library Promotion Council, c/o State Library of Victoria, 328 Swanston St., Melbourne, Vic. 3000 Australia. Excellent as a source of ideas and information.

Fontaine, Sue. *PR Tick Click.* Chicago: ALA, 1976. 30 minutes. Slide tape production about public library public relations; interviews with library administrators and PR specialists.

Gilbert, William H., ed. *Public Relations in Local Government.* Washington: ICMA, 1975. 266 pp.

Kies, Cosette. *Problems in Library Public Relations.* New York: R.R. Bowker, 1974. 179 pp.

Prepare! The Library Public Relations Recipe Book. Chicago: Public Relations Section of the Library Administration Division, ALA, 1978. 83 pp.

"Public Relations." In *The ALA Yearbook: A Review of Library Events.* Chicago: ALA, annual.

Rice, Betty. *Public Relations for Public Libraries: Creative Problem Solving.* New York: H. W. Wilson, 1972. 133 pp.

Sherman, Steve. *ABC's of Library Promotion.* Metuchen, N.J.: Scarecrow, 1971. 182 pp.

LIBRARY PERIODICAL

"Library PR News." P.O. Box 687, Bloomfield, NJ 07003. Bimonthly newsletter. Articles on library publicity, how-to information about exhibits and graphics with tips about free or inexpensive materials to order, and an exchange of successful public relations ideas and activities from all types of libraries. Special bulk rates for state and regional agencies.

SOURCES OF IDEAS AND MATERIALS FOR LIBRARIES

American Library Association's Public Relations Section of the Library Administration Division presents public relations programs and exhibits at the annual conference. This section has an active Friends of the Library Committee. Through ALA's Publishing Department, the Public Relations Section distributes practical pamphlets on such topics as library publications, broadcast publicity, and special events.

The Children's Book Council, Inc., 67 Irving Place, New York, NY 10003. Source of excellent posters and other promotional materials for Children's Book Week and all-year use.

John Cotton Dana Library Public Relations Awards. Printed portions of award-winning entries may be borrowed from the Headquarters Library, American Library Association, 50 E. Huron St., Chicago, IL 60611. Standard ALA interlibrary forms should be used; the borrowing library pays transportation both ways.

Library Public Relations Council. Each participating member receives an annual packet of the best library publications produced during the preceding year. The council sponsors an annual awards program and four meetings a year in New York City. Write: Membership Chairman, Library Public Relations Council, Suite 1242, 60 East 42 Street, New York, NY 10017.

National Library Week. Annual campaign sponsored by the American Library Association for promotion of all types of libraries. ALA sells posters, pamphlets, buttons, and radio and TV materials for distribution by libraries, and from ALA headquarters supplies public-ity material to the national media. ALA, 50 E. Huron St., Chicago, IL 60611.

Upstart Library Promotionals, Box 889, Hagerstown, MD 21740. Phone: (301) 797-9689. Diversified library promotion items from balloons and table displays to book bags and unusual wearing apparel. Themes include National Library Week, Children's Book Week, and year-around promotions.

6 The Administrator: Characteristics and Skills

ELLEN ALTMAN

In twenty-eight states there are no legal certification requirements for a person to be appointed as chief librarian. In the twenty-two states where certification laws are "on the books," three states have never enforced their statutes, and four require certification of county library directors only. The remaining states generally require a master's degree in library science only for directors of libraries in the largest cities.[1]

The 8,000-plus public libraries in the United States cover a broad spectrum in terms of collection, budget, facilities, and staff. At one end of this continuum are small rooms containing a few thousand books, open only a limited number of hours per week, and operating on budgets of less than $10,000 per year. At the other end are highly complex organizations with multimillion-dollar budgets, hundreds of employees, and huge collections. Yet, all of these are called public libraries, and each is directed by a chief librarian. Obviously, the personal characteristics and the library and administrative skills of these directors will tend to vary with the size of the institution.

Background Characteristics

Since nearly all research on public library directors has concentrated on people in larger organizations, our knowledge of administrators of very small libraries is limited and is generally based on personal observation and impressionistic judgments. The consensus of these observations and impressions leads to the conclusion that directors of small public libraries are for the most part married women, native to the area served by the library. Many work only part-time. Their educational backgrounds range from high school graduation to completion of the bachelor's degree. Few have had any formal library school training, and fewer still have the M.L.S. degree. In 1974 only 15 percent of "professionals" in libraries serving communities under 10,000 had a graduate degree in any subject.[2]

Some of these libraries are one-woman operations. If the library employs other staff members, they are also likely to be married women with little or no formal library training or high school students who work as pages or circulation assistants. In these libraries the director is likely to perform many of the same tasks as other members of the staff and to have more direct and personal contact with the library's patrons. Administration in these small libraries is generally informal and performed on an ad hoc basis. For the most part, directors of very small libraries can be characterized as having a local orientation; their professional concerns are confined to the boundaries of their own institutions and communities. Except for occasional attendance at state library meetings or workshops, they are generally isolated from the mainstream of the profession's thinking, writing, and influence.

The type of individual pictured above represents the overwhelming proportion of public library directors in the United States. The Bureau of Labor Statistics study in 1975 identified 7,105 public libraries serving populations under 25,000. However, three-fourths of public librarians are employed in the 1,664 libraries serving larger communities, and a majority of these work in the 100 largest libraries.[3]

In recent years a number of studies have been published that give demographic information about librarians as an occupational group or about administrators in larger libraries, almost all of whom have master's degrees in library science.[4] Ideally, one should be able to construct a matrix

1. American Library Association, Library Administration Division, Certification Committee, *Certification of Public Librarians in the United States*, 2d ed. (Chicago: ALA, 1972).

2. Robert D. Little, "Public Library Statistics: Analysis of NCES Survey," *Bowker Annual*, 23d ed. (New York: R. R. Bowker, 1978), p. 249.

3. U.S., Bureau of Labor Statistics, *Library Manpower*, bull. 1,852 (Washington, D.C.: Govt. Print. Off., 1975), p. 2.

4. Examples of these kinds of studies from which the profile has ben extrapolated are: Henry T. Drennan and Richard Darling, *Library Manpower: Occupational Characteristics of Public and School Libraries*, U.S.

showing the findings on each characteristic for each study, thus giving a comparative profile. However, the way that data are reported does not allow such comparison. Not all studies report the same variables. Where the variables are the same, they are not reported in a uniform manner. For example, some studies classify undergraduate degrees in history and government with humanities; in others these are lumped under social sciences. In some cases, education and social sciences are grouped together; in others, education is considered separately. The categories on fathers' occupations overlap to such an extent that comparisons are impossible. In some studies, age and experience are reported in year intervals; other studies give only the mean. Since the data are so fragmented, the following descriptive profile has necessarily been extrapolated from a number of studies reporting information on the background characteristics of library administrators.

Although one can cite specific atypical cases, the age, experience, and sex of the chief librarian generally correlate with the size of the library. Most directors of libraries are over age fifty, which is not surprising in view of the fact that considerable experience is usually requisite for appointment to such a position. The typical rise up the administrative ladder can be divided into two tracks: successive directorships in increasingly large libraries, or a series of increasingly senior administrative positions within one or several libraries. Almost all directors responding in studies published to date have been former assistant directors in other libraries, usually smaller in size.

The proportion of males directing libraries increases dramatically as one moves from small to large institutions. A study by the U.S. National Center for Educational Statistics estimated that men represent only 16 percent of all public librarians but fill a disproportionate number of large

library directorships.[5] In 1975, 98.4 percent of chief librarians serving populations over 400,000 were males. Sixty-two percent of those serving populations of over 100,000 in 1970 were males; by 1975 their proportion had increased to 72 percent.[6] The publicity generated in recent years by women's liberation appears to have had little or no impact on influencing the appointment of women directors. On the contrary, four studies done since 1970 reported that a number of incumbent male directors had been appointed to jobs formerly held by women.[7] The most recent studies found that, between 1950 and 1975, the number of women public library directors declined 12 percent in Kentucky, 19 percent in Michigan, 32 percent in Indiana, and 47 percent in Ohio. The total loss in these four states amounts to 27 percent. The survey further notes that males are directors in the majority of the largest public libraries in these states.[8] Nationwide the proportion of women directors in libraries serving populations of over 100,000 declined from 34 to 28 percent between 1973 and 1975. Even when women hold directorships in larger libraries, they receive salaries an average of 28 percent lower than those of their male counterparts.[9]

One explanation commonly cited to explain the low percentage of women administrators is that women who are married are usually assumed to be geographically restricted by their husbands' employment and thus have fewer opportunities for advancement than their male colleagues. However, Taylor, who did a study of mobility and professional involvement, found that only 20 percent of women characterized as immobile were married and that "the proportion of all married women who are immobile (19%) differs very little from the proportion who are highly mobile (22%)."[10]

Other factors beyond the obvious one of sex discrimination may have influenced this trend. From the end of World War II up to the early 1960s, American women were bombarded by the media with the idea that female "success" meant a

Office of Education (Washington, D.C.: Govt. Print. Off., 1966); William V. Nash, "Characteristics of Administrative Heads of Public Libraries in Various Communication Categories" (Ph.D. diss., Univ. of Illinois, 1964); Richard Alan Farley, "The American Library Executive: An Inquiry into His Concepts of the Function of His Office" (Ph.D. diss., Univ. of Illinois, 1967); Mary Lee Bundy and Paul Wasserman, *The Public Library Administrator and His Situation* (College Park, Md.: School of Library and Information Services, Univ. of Maryland, 1970); Ray L. Carpenter, *The Public Library Executive: An Exploration of the Role of an Emerging Profession* (Chapel Hill: Univ. of North Carolina Pr., 1967); Robert S. Alvarez, "Profile of Public Library Chiefs: A Serious Survey with Some Comic Relief," *Wilson Library Bulletin* 47: 578–83 (March 1973); Ruth Kay Maloney, "The Average Director of a Large Public Library," *Library Journal* 96:443–45 (Feb. 1, 1971).

5. Little, "Public Library Statistics."

6. Kenneth Shearer and Ray L. Carpenter, "Public Library Support and Salaries in the Seventies," *Library Journal* 100:777–83 (March 15, 1976).

7. Alvarez, "Profile of Public Library Chiefs"; Shearer and Carpenter, "Public Library Support"; Maloney, "the Average Director."

8. "A Comparative Analysis of Library Directorship in Four Midwestern States," *Focus on Indiana Libraries* 29:4–5 (Fall/Winter 1975).

9. Shearer and Carpenter, "Public Library Support."

10. Marian R. Taylor, "Mobility and Professional Involvement in Librarianship" (Ph.D. diss., Rutgers—the State University, 1973), p. 166.

home in the suburbs, a station wagon, and a houseful of children. This occurred during the period when most women who would now be potential director material were in the process of choosing a career. That most opted for home and motherhood is reflected in national statistics showing that the proportion of women receiving bachelor's and "first professional" degrees declined by 16.1 percent between 1940 and 1950. The percentage increased by only 9.5 percent during the following decade. Despite all the emphasis on expanding career aspirations for women, by 1975 the proportion of degrees mentioned previously was only 2.7 percent above the 1940 figure.[11]

The qualifications of women for top administrative positions in public libraries have been mentioned in both a positive and a negative context in a number of studies. Farley found no evidence to support the contention that women are less effective administrators than men or that women administrators tend to be over emotional. He characterized women directors as taking a more personal approach to their staffs than did men, which may be a positive factor since studies of employee attitudes in a variety of occupations emphasize the desire for personal interactions with supervisors.[12]

On the other hand, the women directors in Carpenter's study indicated that they did not enjoy the administrative aspects of the job as did their male counterparts. Also, the women felt that they had lower status than the male government officials in their communities.[13] Harvey's studies of characteristics related to career advancement categorized the less successful as younger, less experienced, unmarried, and female. In the group that he called "Fast-Advancers," those holding high-level positions at a relatively young age, there were no women.[14]

All studies on the educational background of librarians including administrators show that the majority chose undergraduate majors in humanities. Majors in the social sciences, including education, ranked second, with the natural sciences trailing far behind. No study specifically mentioned business administration as an undergraduate major or an area of formal study after completion of the bachelor's or the library degree. These findings indicate that most administrators learn about budgeting, management, and supervision in a few library school courses and from their own on-the-job experiences.

For the most part, the decision to enter librarianship is not made until some time after completion of the undergraduate degree. Administrators do not appear to have made this decision any earlier than their colleagues who have no supervisory responsibilities. The most frequently cited reasons for choosing librarianship are a liking for the activities and atmosphere of the library; desire for public service work; influence of relatives, librarians, employers, or vocational counselors; and "just drifting" into the field.

However, the overwhelming majority of chief administrators are well satisfied with their choice of librarianship as a career. The degree of satisfaction appears to correlate with position in the hierarchy of the organization. This is not surprising in view of the fact that salary, status, autonomy, and decision-making power are directly related to supervisory responsibilities.

Involvement in professional activities and top administrative position seem to go hand in hand. Chief administrators are not only likely to belong to state, regional, and national library associations, but they are also more likely to serve as committee chairmen or elected officers than those librarians further down the career ladder. The degree to which position influences professional involvement, or professional involvement influences position, cannot be accurately determined, but in all probability each exerts an influence on the other. A considerable number of administrators engage in other types of professional activities such as consulting, teaching, and writing for the library press.

Professional involvement and external mobility are also significantly related. Taylor found that those individuals who changed jobs frequently were more likely to engage in library association activities, publish on library topics, pursue formal continuing education, and supervise more staff than their less-mobile colleagues. She concluded that those who have strong career aspirations engage in professional pursuits as a means of gaining recognition and thus obtain better jobs through the collegial system that influences a candidate's selection.[15]

Psychological Characteristics

Evidence from psychological research indicates that an individual's personality needs and characteristics exercise considerable influence on career

11. U.S., Bureau of the Census, *Statistical Abstract of the U.S.*, 98th annual ed. (Washington, D.C.: Govt. Print. Off., 1977).

12. Farley, "American Library Executive."

13. Carpenter, *Public Library Executive.*

14. John Harvey, "Advancement in the Library Profession," *Wilson Library Bulletin* 36:144–47 (Oct. 1961).

15. Taylor, "Mobility and Professional Involvement."

choice. Thus, most individuals who elect careers in a particular field evince similar personality traits, in part because of the factor of occupational self-selection and in part due to environmental shaping forces.[16]

Although there has been no research on the personality characteristics of public library administrators as a distinct group, there are several personality and attitudinal studies of librarians in the following categories: library school students, librarians as an occupational group, and librarians in particular types of libraries. Since public library administrators are generally chosen from these groups, it seems reasonable to assume that administrators in the aggregate evince personality characteristics similar to those of the population from which they are selected.

Table 6.1 shows a matrix that Evelyn H. Daniel developed to compare the findings from the personality studies. A "yes" indicates a positive finding; "no" indicates a negative. A dash means that data for those traits were not available.[17]

A trait is considered significant if the score obtained differs significantly from that of the control group. Significance is determined by applying statistical tests to the scores of the groups being compared. If the number obtained exceeds the expected probability of occurrence, that trait is considered significant. However, the deviance from the norm on these traits need not be extreme. In most cases the scores for the librarians fell within the normal range, but were weighted heavily on one side or the other. Also, group scores tend to average out those individuals who differ from the pattern of the group.

The personality profile that emerges from these studies indicates that librarians as a group are intelligent and self-sufficient and generally relaxed, though both Bryan and McMahon found women to be more tense than men. On the other hand, every one of these studies discloses traits reflecting low self-confidence, passivity, submissiveness, shyness, and feelings of inferiority—although certain individuals display characteristics different from this pattern.

Even though research on the personality of librarians is limited and the number of people studied thus far is relatively small, there is evidence to suggest that, in the aggregate, librarians tend to respond to certain types of questions on personality tests in a similar fashion, indicating that people with certain characteristics are drawn toward librarianship as a career.

Although there is no published research on the personality characteristics of public library directors per se, there is no reason to believe that their personalities are atypical of those reported in the other studies mentioned. Stone found that 78.8 percent of her sample of 1956 library school graduates and 67.4 percent of the 1961 class became administrators.[18] Since these represent the majority of her sample, it seems apparent that studies of students and working librarians have validity for hypothesizing about the personalities of administrators.

These profiles of librarian personalities are in almost direct contrast to the popular stereotype of the aggressive, decisive, dynamic American business executive. Generally, researchers who have written about librarians' personalities and backgrounds have implied that entrepreneurial and charismatic qualities are an asset and the lack of them a liability in administering an organization. However, there is considerable debate among experts on management as to whether administrative success can be predicted by analyzing personal traits. Campbell and others compiled a list of desirable personality traits for administrators as reported in the literature of management science and concluded that they "seem to include every human value," and are "based on little more than personal experiences or opinions about traits possessed by 'good' managers . . . ."[19] In reality, there is really little evidence to link psychological characteristics with administrative effectiveness in business and no evidence to positively correlate the two in librarianship.

However, there are certain qualities that should be considered vital to the success of the chief administrator in any organization. These are: compatibility between the director and the staff, the technical and managerial skills of the director, and the behavior patterns the director evinces. How these factors influence administrative success is discussed below.

Essential Qualities

Compatibility

In every organization a symbiotic relationship exists between the administrator and the staff.

16. Samuel H. Osipow, *Theories of Career Development* (New York: Appleton-Century-Crofts, 1968).

17. Evelyn Hope Daniel, "An Analysis of the Organizational Position of School Media Centers and the Relationship of This Position to Communication Patterns and Personality Characteristics of School Librarians" (Ph.D. diss., Univ. of Maryland, 1973).

18. Elizabeth W. Stone, *Factors Related to the Professional Development of Librarians* (Metuchen, N.J.: Scarecrow, 1969).

19. John P. Campbell, *Managerial Behavior, Performance and Effectiveness* (New York: McGraw-Hill, 1970), pp. 7, 15.

Table 6.1 Comparison of Personality Studies

	Bryan (1952)	Douglas (1957)	Rainwater (1960)	Morrison (1961)	McMahon (1965)	Segal (1970)	Sladen (1972)	Clayton (1967)
n =	1808	525	94	707	30	320	98	150
library type[a] =	P	Stu	Stu	A	PAS	All	U	Stu
Traits								
Passivity[b]	Yes	....	Yes	....	....	Yes	....	....
Submissiveness[c]	Yes	Yes	Yes	Yes	Yes	Yes	....	Yes
Lack of Self-Assurance	Yes	....	....	No	Yes	Yes	....	No
Self-Sufficiency[d]	....	Yes	Yes	....	Yes	....	Yes	....
Intelligence	....	....	....	Yes	....	Yes	Yes	....
Introversion	....	Yes	....	....	....	....	Yes	....
Tension	No	No	....	....	Yes	....	....	....
Heterosexuality	Yes	....	Yes	....	....	....	....	....
Orderliness	....	Yes	Yes	....	....	....	....	....
Conservatism	....	Yes	....	....	....	Yes	....	....
Reserve	....	....	....	....	....	....	Yes	....
Shyness	....	....	....	....	....	....	Yes	....

a. P = public, Stu = student, A = academic, U = unknown, S = special.

b. Bryan calls this dimension "pressure for overt activity"; Morrison calls it "initiative"; Rainwater measures "need aggression."

c. Morrison calls this dimension "supervisory qualities"; McMahon "leadership"; Rainwater measures "need dominance"; Clayton "lack of ascendency."

d. Rainwater measures "need affiliation."

SOURCES: Bryan, *The Public Librarian,* p. 41; Douglas, "The Personality of the Librarian"; Rainwater, "A Study of Personality Traits"; Morrison, *Career of the Academic Librarian*; McMahon, *Personality of the Librarian*; Segal, "Personality and Ability Patterns"; Sladen, "The Personality of the Librarian"; Clayton, "An Investigation of Personality Characteristics."

Generally, no administrator, however dynamic in personality, can successfully function independent of the staff and their support in working toward organizational goals. Because of positional authority and its associated status, all administrators, whether they realize it or not, serve as role models for their staff and must satisfy staff expectations regarding how the director should fill that role. The behavior displayed by the director projects an image to the staff about desirable norms and values in the library. If that image is not congruent with norms and values deemed appropriate by the staff, or if the norms and values are radically different than those the staff had come to expect from previous directors, conflict is usually the result. If librarianship attracts people with similar personalities as the research to date indicates, an entrepreneurial administrator might have difficulty in relating to and motivating the staff.

In fact, the librarian respondents in Walters's study were somewhat "turned off" by entrepreneurship.[20] " . . . professionally employed librarians moderately reject the general stated American entrepreneurial value of enjoying directing the work of others, nor do they think getting recognition for their work is terribly important."[21] He goes on to say that the librarians' "aspirations seem to diverge somewhat from the supposedly competitive, achievement orientation that is generally thought to be characteristic of upward mobile Americans." This attitude is not surprising since the profession these people have selected is generally considered genteel, cultural, intellectual, and conservative.

20. Jay Hart Walters, "Image and Status of the Library and Information Field," U.S. Office of Education, Bureau of Research, A Program of Research into the Identification of Manpower Requirements, the Educational Preparation and Utilization of Manpower in the Library and Information Profession (Washington, D.C.: Govt. Print. Office, 1970), p. 17.

21. Ibid., p. 19.

Wasserman and Bundy recognize the mutuality of organizational relationships: " . . . ultimately human beings get the kind of leadership they seek. This may nowhere be more true than in the library profession where the leadership class so accurately reflects the prevailing attitudes and values of the majority of librarians. For one key to holding a leadership post . . . is the ability to satisfy the rank and file."[22] The astute director, therefore, realizes that compatibility with the staff is vital for successful performance in the organization and therefore tries to develop and maintain system compatibility by the implementation of technical and managerial skills.

Skills

There has been considerable question in the literature about the dichotomous role of the library director—ideally should one be a book specialist, a technocrat, or a leader with vision? The assumption is that these are mutually exclusive roles. However, a diversity of roles with their associated skills is not limited to librarianship. Both educational institutions and businesses that rely heavily on scientific research—for example, pharamaceutical, chemical, and computer manufacturers—all require administrators with technical as well as administrative competencies. Furthermore, the formal training of these administrators for the most part has emphasized a discipline other than administration.

Directors in all but the smallest public libraries have obtained the basic library degree and hence are familiar with functional operations. However, as one rises on the administrative ladder one's knowledge of the technical aspects of librarianship is likely to become outdated, since less and less time is spent on technical operations even though more and more technological advances are introduced. In order to make decisions on complex technical problems, it is imperative that the administrator have sufficient technical knowledge to understand reports and recommendations submitted by department heads and staff specialists and to base adoption of such recommendations on probable optimization of services.

One of the most serious weaknesses of librarians as a group is their nonanalytic approach in deciding operational issues. A great many technical decisions can and should be based on quantification and/or systems analysis. Because of their basically humanistic educational backgrounds,

most librarians are seriously handicapped in formulating, directing, or even fully comprehending analytical studies that could be helpful in solving their administrative problems. As a result, too many decisions are based on little more than impressions of the situation or a sense of what appears to be appropriate in given circumstances.

Despite the dramatic increase in the number of doctoral degrees awarded in library science since the late 1960s, it is puzzling that neither the number of doctoral degree recipients nor the research from their dissertations has had any noticeable impact on the administration of major public libraries. The recipients of these degrees have moved in large numbers into academic but not public library administrative positions. Of the thirty largest public libraries, only one is directed by a Ph.D. in library science.

Although public libraries were chosen as the topic of 115 doctoral dissertations done between 1930 and 1978, reports of any application of the findings of such research in public library settings is conspicuous by its absence in library literature. Since it is apparent that people trained in data gathering and analysis are seldom found in public libraries, and since reports of research conducted by or applied in public libraries by the staff as an aid in making technical decisions are virtually nonexistent, the logical conclusion is that many technical decisions are made without objective data as a guide.

Writers on library administration have almost unanimously advocated that library administrators adopt the methods and theories developed by experts on management science for internal operation of the library. Yet, what most administrators know about management skills they learn from job experience and self-education, not from library school.

Basic library education has always concentrated on technical functions—cataloging, reference, bibliography, and specific kinds of literatures. Furthermore, most library school students see themselves working in technical, not administrative roles.

This role identification is further reinforced by early employment experiences. The typical new graduate is hired to perform functional, not administrative, tasks. The crunch comes a few years later when the employee correctly perceives that rising on the career ladder depends on gaining an administrative position, which he usually has few readily identifiable credentials to assume. Expanding the master of library science program to two years seems unrealistic in terms of present beginning salary levels and the limited number of advanced administration courses in most library school curricula. However, public libraries them-

22. Paul Wasserman and Mary Lee Bundy, eds., *Reader in Library Administration*, Reader Series in Library and Information Science (Washington, D.C.: NCR Microcard Editions, 1968), p. 325.

selves could provide staff with in-house training and development programs emphasizing those topics of most concern in that library. In addition, staff should be encouraged to pursue self-education in management.

Administration theories have been filtering down to local pubic library administrators for some years. De Prospo and Huang found that the directors in their 1969 study were generally familiar with the writings of such "big names" in management as Herbert Simon.[23] The library press now regularly features discussions of such newer management techniques as program budgeting, sociotechnical analysis of library jobs, and concepts from public administration. However, the authors of these papers are overwhelmingly academic librarians or library educators. Therefore, what impact their papers are having on public library administration is not discernible. The Management Review and Analysis Program that was developed for and implemented in major academic libraries since the early 1970s has not been picked up and applied in any major public library, although many of the areas in the MRAP package are directly applicable to public library administration.

The personal example set by the director is a factor frequently ignored in the management literature, yet it is of paramount importance for the continuing viability and progress of the organization. The crux of the issue is whether the director is what Robert Hutchins calls the administrator or the office holder. The administrator is responsible for the "discovery, clarification, definition and proclamation of the end." By this he means the mission of the organization.

> The administrator's responsibility is to get others to join him in the search for the end and to try to teach all his constituency to see and accept it when it has been found. He must conceive of himself as presiding over a continuous discussion of the mission and destiny of the institution.[24]

The office holder busies himself with routine tasks and shrinks from making decisions which might have unpopular consequences. One might characterize this as maintenance management or figureheadship.

The true leader considers the welfare of the organization and the staff over his own self-interest. "One will not be able to motivate others for any length of time if such motivation is being used for personal or selfish reasons."[25] In essence, the prime requisites for any administrator are old-fashioned virtues called integrity and character, plus a strong sense of commitment to the organization. Warren Bennis says the best tool an administrator has is himself. He likens administrators to physicians because

> . . . like the physician it is important that the leader heed the injunction 'heal thyself' so that he does not create pernicious effects unwittingly. Unless the leader understands his actions and effects on others, he may be a 'carrier' rather than a solver of problems.[26]

If the director sincerely is interested in the quality of service the library provides, the staff will emulate his interest. A director who is genuinely concerned about employee morale, challenging work assignments, adequate salaries, and quality job performance will gain loyalty, respect, and cooperation from the staff. The administrator who is honest and honorable in dealing with the staff will create a climate of trust and confidence in leadership. To ensure high productivity, the director must convince the staff that he is working at least as hard as they are. This means not overcommitting oneself by taking on consulting or teaching assignments that require long or frequent absences from the library. Also, the director should have a commitment to learning new ideas and innovations. The director's personal example will stimulate the staff to continue their own learning and to suggest improvements. The characteristics outlined here reflect the attitudes that the successful administrator, by personal example, sets as a model for the staff to emulate.

23. Ernest R. De Prospo and Theodore Huang, "Continuing Education for the Library Administrator," in *Administration and Change; Continuing Education in Library Administration*, ed. Rutgers—The State University, Graduate School of Library Service (New Brunswick, N.J.: Rutgers Univ. Pr., 1969).

24. Robert M. Hutchins, "The Administrator," in *The Works of the Mind*, ed. Robert B. Heywood, University of Chicago, Committee on Social Thought (Chicago: Univ. of Chicago Pr., 1947), p. 151.

25. Charles H. Goodman, "Employee Motivation," *Library Trends* 20:39–47 (July 1971), p. 44.

26. Warren G. Bennis, "The Leader of the Future," *Public Management* 52:13–19 (March 1970), p. 18.

Bibliography

Bryan, Alice. *The Public Librarian.* New York: Columbia
Univ. Pr., 1952.

Clayton, Howard. "An Investigation of Personality
Characteristics among Library Students at One Midwestern University." U.S. Office of Education, Bureau
of Research. Washington, D.C.: Govt. Print. Office,
July, 1968.

Douglas, Robert R. "The Personality of the Librarian."
Ph.D. diss. Univ. of Chicago, 1957.

McMahon, Anne. *The Personality of the Librarian: Prevalent Social Values and Attitudes towards the Profession.* Occasional Papers in Librarianship 5. Adelaide:
Librarians Board of South Australia, 1967.

Morrison, Perry. *The Career of the Academic Librarian:
A Study of the Social Origins, Educational Attain-
ments, Vocational Experience and Personality Characteristics of a Group of American Academic Librarians.* ACRL Monograph 29. Chicago: American Library Assn., 1969.

Rainwater, Nancy Jane. "A Study of Personality Traits of
Ninety-Four Library School Students as Shown by the
Edwards Personal Preference Schedule." M.L.S.
thesis. Univ. of Texas, 1962.

Segal, Stanley J. "Personality and Ability Patterns of
Librarians." Final Report, Part of a Program of Re-
search into the Identification of Manpower Require-
ments, the Educational Preparation and Utilization of
Manpower in the Library and Information Profession.
U.S. Office of Education, Bureau of Research.
Washington, D.C.: Govt. Print. Office, 1970.

Sladen, David. "The Personality of the Librarian: An
Investigation." *Library Association Record* 74:118–
19 (July 1972).

7   Leadership Styles, Strategies, and Tactics

MELVIN J. LEBARON and MARSHALL FELS

The library administrator has a variety of leadership styles from which to choose. Since leadership style is a means of expression and an extension of one's personality, values, and strengths, it is important to explore the many philosophical and operational variables in order to better understand the relationship between personal characteristics and available options. Once a leadership style has been identified, a person is in a position to employ strategies and tactics that are the behavioral game plans for making the most effective use of a style in human relationships.

History has provided us with numerous philosophies toward leadership. With respect to effective administrative leadership, each philosophy assumes a somewhat different point of view—a point of view that usually is a product of its author's background, personal values, and individual experience. Unfortunately, no one philosophy has been encompassing enough so as to be universally accepted as the final set of guidelines for the leadership styles, strategies, and tactics—or in other words, the approach—to be practiced by library administrators.

So many scholars have been fascinated by organizational leadership that no aspect of the topic has been left unexplored—often to the confusion of the working public administrator. The extensive research on leadership occupies a central place in the human-work-relations literature. Mayo's work at Hawthorne was a study of major importance that stimulated other studies of leadership and the relationship of leadership style to workers' attitude and performance.[1] Many of those studies found that a leader with a permissive style created a cooperative group atmosphere with a subsequent increase in workers' performance. Authoritarian leadership, on the other hand, was repeatedly found to be associated with poor productivity.[2] As a result, permissive leadership was considered, by writers of management textbooks, to be the remedy for all industrial ills.

However, further research undertaken during the so-called human relations period of the 1940s to 1960s began to indicate no significant correlation between leadership and morale. Relationships between leadership, productivity, and morale tended to be highly dependent on conditional variables—those having to do with one's orientation toward people and task.[3]

Abraham Maslow, in one of his last publications, said that he was dissatisfied with the material on leadership in the management literature.[4] He saw a tendency to be pious about the democratic dogma as opposed to an approach that recognizes the objective requirements of the situation as the centering point for leadership. This insight is extremely important to the librarian and to the success of the library. Leadership is more complex than the idea that "in a management sense, leadership means the guidance or direction given by the chief executive."[5] It is more correctly defined, we feel, as *interpersonal influence directed toward the attainment of a specified goal*. This definition is not part of the democratic dogma referred to by Maslow, but rather is a recognition of the realities of the attendant dynamics of library administration.

Leadership, then, may be a more complex topic than what one is led to believe when reading the

1. See F. J. Rothlisberger and W. J. Dickson, *Management and the Worker* (Cambridge, Mass.: Harvard University Press, 1939), and Henry A. Lansberg, *Hawthorne Revised* (Ithica, N.Y. Cornell Univ. Pr., 1958).

2. For a general review see Saul W. Gellerman, *Motivation and Productivity* (New York: American Management Association, 1963).

3. Among many sources, one of the more interesting is C.W. Mills, *The Contributions of Sociology to Studies of Industrial Relations*, Proceedings of the First Annual Meeting, Industrial Relations Research Association, vol. 2, 1948.

4. During the summer of 1962, Maslow visited Non-Linear Systems, Inc., in Del Mar, Calif. A result of that visit was a series of notes, published as Abraham H. Maslow, *Eupsycian Management* (Homewood, Ill.: Richard D. Irwin, 1965).

5. Roberta Bowler, ed., *Local Public Library Administration* (Chicago: The International City Manager's Association, 1964).

work of an author who has briefly included the topic in a broader exploration of administration of the work organization, be it library, school, or manufacturing plant. By looking at leadership in terms of *leadership responsibility*, the complexity of leadership may be more easily understood. The responsibility of the leader is, primarily, not to provide directives, but to maintain a system of adaptation and involvement. This would include responsibility for keeping the goal in sight, for creating an atmosphere in which others are encouraged to participate, for stimulating consensus, and for helping persons find their place in a cooperative effort.

This point of view does not deny a leader's responsibilities for such traditional functions as controlling and directing, but it does suggest that simply ordering things to be done does not necessarily ensure goal attainment. This approach seems to fit the library situation quite well in view of the care with which librarians are trained and selected—and their pride in professional status.

Library administrators must thus be prepared to consider more than a simple how-to-do-it approach to leadership in the library. They must be willing to examine their own personal skills in relationship to providing leadership. The best way to begin might be to look at some of the theories of leadership found in the general literature of administration and management.

Leadership Theory

Management techniques are essential to getting the job done, but leadership tends to be the more pertinent ingredient. Though the word *leadership* may have fallen into disrepute, especially during the human-relations-in-management period, management science theories or applications of techniques are no substitute for personal character and sound leadership. A person of courage, vision, and experience is an absolute necessity (if you can forgive our slip in suggesting these as the basic qualities required of a leader). The power of good leadership is, of course, a fact. It is difficult, however, to measure the value of leadership and assess the process whereby it becomes powerful.

Charisma

Charismatic power is one widely discussed explanation of leadership. It is a theory that suggests that there are people who have natural qualities of leadership. It is said of Florence Nightingale that her voice and her countenance were of such quali-

ty that, once she had given some direction, only obedience could follow.[6]

The general view of charisma is that, when a person "has charisma," that person has been given the gift of leadership qualities, and no matter what group that person is in, he or she will be recognized as being charismatic and others will accept the person's authority. Popular examples of charismatic leaders include Adolph Hitler and Winston Churchill, but the list for such organizations as libraries, departments of social welfare, highway departments, and so on, is not extensive—at least not in the textbooks that quote the more popular examples.

Thus, the notion of charismatic leadership may not be of much use to the working library administrator, except that it does suggest that status and/or esteem may be important leadership qualities. Too, there are documented instances of superior results that have been achieved through inspiring leadership.

Trait Theory

Our brief discussion of charisma seems to lead naturally to the suggestion that leaders possess some number of a list of leadership traits. These traits may add up to a natural leadership ability that has variously been seen as characterized by a wide variety of traits ranging all the way from "neatness" to "nobility."[7] This avenue has not been a fruitful one for the researcher, however, for no matter how carefully traits are described, there seems to be very little consistent match between sets of traits and various persons who are seen as successful leaders.

Jay makes the point that Churchill could be a totally unacceptable leader of Britain in 1935 and yet be the very best of possible choices in 1940.[8] Perhaps the same set of traits does not fit any two situations or any two time periods; perhaps we are better served by a colorless leader in one period, while best served by brilliance in another.

As Dale suggests, there may be three traits essential to leadership.[9] The first is intelligence— not as an absolute, but rather as relative to the intelligence of the followers. Another is self-confidence, or the ability to appear self-confident.

6. From a portion of the discussion of leadership in Ernest Dale, *Management: Theory and Practice* (New York: McGraw-Hill, 1973).

7. Charles Bird, *Social Psychology* (New York: Appleton-Century-Crofts, 1940).

8. Antony Jay, *Management and Machiavelli* (New York: Holt, Rinehart and Winston, 1967).

9. Ernest Dale, *Management: Theory and Practice* (New York: McGraw-Hill, 1965).

The third essential trait may be initiative, for one might assume that a leader must initiate ideas and/or action. These suggested leadership characteristics do indeed merit consideration as they might relate to administration of the library—though accepting the idea that the traits are essential may be of little help to the person already administering a library.

Situational Theory

Today the more generally accepted theory of leadership is referred to as the situational theory. This theory simply suggests that leadership is specific to the particular situation under investigation. The relationships between leadership, productivity, and morale are only valid under certain conditions, such as personality distribution of the group being led or the type of job to be done.[10]

We agree that this approach does little to provide simplistic answers to the questions we all have about leadership, but submit that it constitutes a necessary broadening of scope. Leadership is not to be simply described, nor is it to be universally prescribed. In fact, if the situational theory is acceptable, one should probably envision the dynamic library as having a rather shifting leadership pattern. This does not suggest the replacement of the librarian on a ninety-day schedule but may well suggest that the top administrator find ways of sharing leadership as the situation changes.

Cartwright and Zander report that empirical findings on shared leadership are available, though the studies seem inconclusive.[11] They report that in several specific experiments with groups on which leaders were externally imposed, those leaders who tended to distribute the functions of leadership more widely obtained group performance generally regarded as "better" in our society. When production was measured, it was higher, and when cohesiveness was measured, it was stronger.

Leader Behavior

The topic of leader behavior is included in the general discussion of leadership theory because the topic needs to be dealt with in a theoretical framework, at least at this introductory point.

One aspect of leader behavior is the way in which decisions or actions stem from the leader's basic assumptions about human behavior. McGregor's Theory X and Theory Y are perhaps the best-known descriptions of this aspect of behavior.[12] Theory X is the more traditional view; it assumes, in part, that the average human being has a dislike for work and must therefore be coerced, controlled, directed, or threatened with punishment to extract performance. Theory Y, on the other hand, looks to integration of individual and organizational goals; it assumes, for example, that the expenditure of energy in work is as natural as in play, and that the avearage human being not only learns to accept responsibility but actively seeks it.

The point is, not to polarize types of leadership choices, but to stress that library leaders must begin their exploration of leadership by looking at themselves. Do you make Theory X or Theory Y assumptions—or do you make still other assumptions that are not as definitive—perhaps not known even to yourself?

Blake and Mouton popularized the task and relationship dimensions of leadership by developing the managerial grid.[13] It addresses leadership style and behavior by identifying five different types of leadership based upon two basic dimensions: concern for production or task and concern for relationships or people. The grid based on these two dimensions has a leadership style located in each of four quadrants and a fifth in the center. The style with high concern for people and low concern for production is called "country club." High concern for task and low concern for people is simply labeled "task," and little concern for either is referred to as "impoverished." Concern for both is appropriately called "middle road." The fifth style emphasizes high concern for both people and accomplishment.

If we look further into leadership behavior as it is manifested in various styles of leadership, we run into many descriptions, including these, in a list with literally no end:

1. Leadership behavior, or style, in which the leader behaves in a parentlike manner
2. Leadership behavior of accumulating and dispensing power so as to manipulate individuals
3. Leadership behavior that trades on expertise as a way to command power and status
4. Leadership behavior that abundantly ex-

10. Mouzelis covers a wide variety of organization and administration topics of interest to the library administrator. See Nicos P. Mouzelis, *Organization and Bureaucracy* (Chicago: Aldine, 1967).

11. See Dorwin Cartwright and Alvin Zander, eds., *Group Dynamics: Research and Theory* (Evanston, Ill.: Row, Peterson, 1962).

12. Douglas McGregor, *The Human Side of Enterprise* (New York: McGraw-Hill, 1960).

13. Robert R. Blake and Jane S. Mouton, *The Managerial Grid* (Houston: Gulf, 1964).

hibits convictions about the essential quality of all human beings
5. Leadership exercised by allowing groups to make decisions within prescribed limits
6. Leadership through selling decisions to subordinates
7. Leadership exercised through doing; being the administrator who is the dynamic doer.

Leadership in the Library

This exploration does not necessarily provide the library administrator with a compendium of how-to-do-its of leadership. Of course, this is a lack with purpose. We have already begun to address the facts that there are variables in the leadership situation and that an all-important variable is the leader's insights into his own beliefs and behavior.

Whether in a library or a business organization, a person is a many-faceted, complex being. Leadership must recognize that human makeup does not consist of mechanically fitted parts, well lubricated to follow the predictable rules of physics or mathematics. Each person is unique, and this uniqueness is the focal point of leadership. In this respect, library organizations face the same human challenges as all other organizations. The library administrator must be as concerned with the efficieny and effectiveness of people as is the manager of a small manufacturing plant or a department store. In all instances of leadership, there is need for a clear sense of purpose and an intense dedication to a function not always broadly understood.

Accepting this uniqueness of individuals and not the organization suggests that the training of library administrators should include a great deal of learning about ways for gaining confidence and respect from followers, regardless of the theory used or the methods by which goals are achieved. It further suggests that one of the criteria for selecting library administrators be adaptiveness, to support the necessary dedication to a somewhat ambigious role and set of circumstances. One can say however, without fear of contradiction, that the work setting within a library is different from any other in many aspects; the staffing patterns, the physical arrangement, the nature of the product all suggest a certain uniqueness.

Those conditions do not mean that a library needs a unique style of leadership. We suggest that they do lead to strong consideration of leadership approaches that vary with the situation.

No Normative Leadership Style

A number of investigators conclude that there is no one best style of leadership—that is, there is no single, all-purpose leadership style that is broadly successful.[14] The evidence indicates that directive leaders, leaders oriented to the human-relations approaches, and task-oriented leaders have all been successful under some conditions. The evidence further tends to show that successful leaders are those who can adapt their administrative leadership approach to meet the needs of those they lead and the particular situations.

To be an effective leader, one must be able to diagnose one's own behavior in light of the environment. For example, one needs to consider one's assumptions about the needs of people; one's attitudes and perceptions regarding the differences among people; one's ability to communicate and act effectively; and one's ability to utilize input from others for evaluation and personal growth. The particular job demands in the library setting should be given due weight, but the complexity or uniqueness of the task must not be allowed to become an excuse for leadership behavior that emphasizes the leader's needs more than those of organizational members and clients.

The Client and Library Leadership

To this point, there has been only one mention of the library client. The reference immediately above suggests that the client is a variable who has to be taken into account when deciding upon leadership style. In *Local Public Library Administration*, clients are seen as potential users who live and work within the community to be served.[15] The library's purpose is to make books and other library materials readily accessible to this client system.

A library's "livelihood" is dependent upon its capacity to meet and schedule its clients' needs. Some organizations can actually mold and create clientele needs, but the library's effectiveness ultimately depends on its capacity to modify functions whenever its public's needs change, grow, or extend themselves. Therefore, one of a library's serious requirements is to research and measure—or at least probe—the community and its tastes and interests.

---

14. For additional insight into the idea that different situations require different leadership styles, see the following works: A. K. Korman, "Consideration, 'Initiating Structure,' and Organization—A Review," *Personnel Psychology* 19 (Winter 1966); Fred E. Fielder, *A Theory of Leadership Effectiveness* (New York: McGraw-Hill, 1967); and C. A. Gibb, "Leadership," in *Handbook of Small Group Research*, ed. A. P. Hare (New York: Wiley 1965).

15. Bowler, ed., *Local Public Library Administration*.

In meeting the needs of the client system, library administrators must concern themselves with effectively organizing their physical resources and personnel to meet two sets of objectives. One is to meet the needs of active library users, and the other is to promote the library's services to nonpatrons and work to meet their potential needs. To work effectively toward both sets of objectives, a library leader must determine the nature and characteristics of the client system and diagnose and predict future problems and trends that will influence client needs. An effective library administrator is one who is tuned in—and able to get the staff tuned in—to basic social, economic, and political factors that underlie the library's utility. These factors are not static; they impel change and have their genesis in population shifts, economic conditions, emphasis on research and training, level and type of education, social awareness, national priorities, new technology, communication patterns, and emerging life-styles.

All members of a library organization need to have a keen sense of the priorities with which people in their community regard these issues, and the staff should regard the service of these needs as the basic purpose of the library operation. To promote alertness and sensitivity to these emerging forces, the library administrator must give leadership to the development of a well-trained, well-staffed, communicative, and motivated personnel system in which the clients' needs and concerns become the primary criteria for effectiveness. The development of a staff that is anticipative and responsive toward outside forces is an important priority. Another is the building of personal and organizational mechanisms for sensing and measuring change and clientele needs for library services. These are not easy tasks. They require the library administrator to do more to look ahead and plan, and to do less to sit back and react.

The sensing and diagnosing of clientele needs should focus on:

1. Trends in personal growth and cultural enrichment
2. The increasing awareness of special groups at the upper and lower age and economic brackets of our society
3. The increasing demands for variety and depth of library services that result when library users become better educated, more cultured, and in general more purposeful in using the library's services

4. The development of new communities and the type of migration in and out of these communities
5. The impact of new technology on life-styles, the job market, and professional specializations
6. The need of increasingly specialized users for more constant and immediate communication flow, coordination, and integration among professional fields
7. National priorities that are shaping future employment potentials
8. The exploitation of such mass media as paperbacks, film, tapes, television and microfilm.

Very often the fulfillment of clientele needs is not simply one of monitoring and then meeting. Rather, libraries may need to work toward expediting the sheer availability of resources within and without the library. Thus, in many cases it is necessary to promote the concept of cooperative systems among public libraries because so many lack the funds to meet their objectives and needs by themselves. An important strategy may be to consolidate to exchange and share multiple resources and superior administration, counseling, and planning centers.[17]

Such systems range from small and informal to areawide and interstate compacts. They extend to rural and metropolitan libraries and transcend geographical and political bounds. They combine the talents and resources of independent libraries to obtain better performance for present and potential users.

In summary, then, the sensitive observation of needs and trends, correlated with effective administrative preparation—within the individual library and cooperative regionwide—should lead to better service of patrons.

Besides presenting needs to be met, clients should be a major determinant of the leadership style chosen. Unfortunately, too often library processes tend not to change from year to year. Administrative leaders in libraries tend to focus more on accommodating the mechanics of their internal operations and less on determining the needs of present and prospective clients, for which they are ultimately responsible.

In terms of systems analysis, objectives for library service need to result from input to the library leadership as to (1) the money available to purchase library materials, (2) buildings in which to house the library materials, and (3) needs of clientele and/or the general public. The output for the library is best measured in terms of how well

16. Ruth W. Gregory and Lester L. Stoffel, *Public Libraries in Cooperative Systems: Administrative Patterns for Service* (Chicago: ALA, 1971).

17. Ibid.

the leadership meets the objectives determined by the input. For many, many years the library processes or functions have not basically changed, in great part because client needs have not been a regularized input in library operations. Today, those needs should be frequently determined and considered one of the variables determining library objectives. This requires that the library administrator give leadership to the external as well as the internal parts of the organization.

Styles, Strategies, and Tactics

The probability that the question of leadership has a simplistic answer is beyond the realm of statistical reasoning. As negative as that may sound, it is reality. One illustration of complexity is the view that persons have of work. At one time, the organizational leader could be very secure in the knowledge that those in the work force accepted the admonitions that work is good. This acceptance gave great power to the leader.

Today, it seems people—and especially young people—no longer accept the idea that work is ipso facto good. They are demanding better working conditions and more meaningful work. In relationship to the question of whether "hard work always pays off," Van Kelovick found that from 1968 to 1971 student opinion dropped from 69 percent affirmative to 39 percent affirmative.[18] People are beginning to protest dull jobs, to question all the old values about work and jobs. This is another fact that must be taken into account in a discussion of leadership for the library.

The issue of employee and organizational values is extremely important to the discussion of leadership styles. Today, organizational values have shifted toward a value system of adaptation to and involvement with others. Basic human needs and desires are receiving more attention than in the past, and efforts are being made to meet these needs and desires within an organization setting. Power tends to rest on the concepts of collaboration and reason, rather than on the traditional basis of threat and coercion. Organizational values based on humanistic and democratic values are replacing mechanistic ones. Perhaps the most important shift is one that recognizes that work should encourage personal growth as well as achieve organizational goals.

This condition of values in transition has generated many conflicts within library organizations and a new set of leadership challenges for library administrators. Some of the conflicts that are outgrowths of new and emerging concepts regarding organizational life-styles are: professionalism versus bureaucracy, technology versus established procedures and operations, and employee unions versus management. Leadership in a modern library organization must certainly have a substance different from that required to run the town library of fifty years ago.

Both the organization and the individual have changed. Technological advances have brought about new ways of doing things and require tasks which were never before necessary. Personnel are becoming more mobile and have less loyalty to a particular organization—which, without effective leadership, will result in an unstable and unproductive work force.

Many library administrators are in trouble because they have sets of values that are typically held in traditional management. These are basically pragmatic in the sense that they place reliance on what has been tried and seems to have worked. But such administrators hold on to traditional approaches even when there is evidence that other approaches might work better in the same situation. Traditional values are much like the previously mentioned Theory X of McGregor.

In order to move out of being unnecessarily traditional and toward coping more effectively with new organizational values and behaviors, new knowledge and skills must be developed by the library administrator. Particular attention needs to be given to increasing one's skill in dealing with people and to understanding that the "people movement" of today emphasizes human growth and distrusts structure and authority.[19]

The Leader's Values

The processes that accomplish high output for an organization, it seems, would be less related to the mechanics of organization than to fostering personal competence. Promoting the intellectual and emotional growth of the participants in the organization seems to be the appropriate strategy, as opposed to a strategy of continual improvement of the processes.

The library leader whose values are rather traditional and who thinks of employees as having to be controlled and motivated will almost certainly have a leadership style that reflect this. On the other hand, the leader who sees individuals as being strongly self-motivated will probably have a quite different style. Each person's "natural leadership style" is likely to reflect individual feel-

---

18. *Work in America*, A Report of a Special Task Force to the U. S. Secretary of Health, Education and Welfare (Washington, D.C.: Gov. Print. Off., 1972).

19. John M. Pfiffner and Marshall Fels, *Supervision of Personnel* (Englewood Cliffs, N. J.: Prentice-Hill, 1964).

ings, and those feelings are largely affected by the values that have become a part of the leader's personality. This then, to repeat, is the starting place for the library administrator in looking at the tasks of leadership. Leaders must either have or gain some insight into their basic value system, difficult as that may be. Armed with such insight, one can begin a search for a leadership style—or combinations of styles, strategies, and contacts can be sought out. Programs such as the Menninger program "Toward Understanding Human Behavior" are designed to elicit the values that unconsciously influence an administrator's choice of decisions. This suggests a certain flexibility in the leader, but we feel that a person who lacks such flexibility—or a situation where a rigid leader can survive—should probably consider alternatives to daily conflict with the demanding complexity of library administration.

Styles

Leadership styles have been discussed in brief, though the discussion did not specify a great number of specific styles. One might refer to a natural style or a style that suggests leader flexibility; charisma might be pointed out as a style. Others speak of a hard-hitting style, a manipulative style, or a conciliatory style. Though the term *leadership style* is frequently used and popularly accepted, the semantics become rather sticky when one tries seriously to discuss the matter of providing leadership to an organization such as a library.

Without a doubt, there are distinctive leadership styles, but perhaps more important, there are almost as many unique styles as there are leaders. Closer examination of the organizational environment of public libraries reveals that effective leadership is best achieved by integrating the style, whatever it is, with strategies and tactics, along with a value orientation toward change.

Leadership styles, of course, become exemplified in the behavior of the leader. It is likely that library administrators adopt one or more of the following behavior patterns as they give expression to their particular style.

The parent. The library administrator who uses this behavior pattern acts or behaves in a parent-like manner. The leader expects to be treated like a parent and is expected by others to behave like a parent. This person is expected to know all the answers and to be able to control and direct the actions of subordinates.

The parental leader expects loyalty from employees, and employees expect protection and help from the leader. The primary functions of the parental leader are to guide, direct, and protect employees—whom this leader insists need help.

There are two main types of parental leaders. One is dominating, forbidding , punishing, evaluating, judging, and directing—the "father figure." The other is nourishing, supporting, defending, reassuring, and protecting—the "mother figure." It is likely that most parental library administrators combine these two kinds of qualities in varying degrees. Both kinds of library leaders are autocratic—that is, they consider their decisions to be superior to their subordinates'.

The manipulator. This is the library administrator who creates, accumulates, possesses, uses, and dispenses power by means of an ability to analyze persons and situations and to gain advantage by playing one individual off against another. Very often, the manipulative leader does not hold a position of official leadership but is a shadowy figure in the background—the power behind the throne.

The library administrator who is manipulative probably enjoys power for its own sake; that is, the leader enjoys controlling persons and situations by exploiting others through their weaknesses.

The chief characteristic of manipulative administrators is that they are "lone wolves." Even when they enlist the cooperation and collaboration of others, they actually play their own game. They exercise power, not because they have strength and prestige, but because they know more about how things work and use this knowledge to the disadvantage of others.

The expert. This kind of leader has authority by virtue of special knowledge, skill, and training; these attributes command power and status. This person is not interested in power for its own sake, or in taking power away from anyone else or accumulating it for selfish ends. The expert is interested in helping those who have power.

The expert library administrator is professional in every sense and operates on the basis of solid knowledge of how a library is put together and how it should run.

Expert library administrators often become the target of hostility because of their intellectual honesty, and because they will not say what others want them to say. It is not unusual to see the "alert expert" having little patience with traditional methods.

The humanist. The humanistic library administrator is one who respects the rights of subordinates to make decisions about matters that have to do with their function and responsibility. This person has deep convictions about the essential qualities of all human beings.

The humanistic library administrator often disturbs other types of library administrators, who feel the humanist is not dignified enough, allows others to take undue advantage, lets operations within the library get out of control, or shares too much power with supervisors and other subordinates.

As an "artist," the humanistic library administrator does not rely on techniques alone. Techniques—even novel ones—may be used to achieve certain goals, but the humanist's greatest strength is an ability to sense the feelings and needs of coworkers. This is basically an artistic ability, and it depends on a balance between sensitivity and humanistic values. It cannot be attained merely by practicing a set of techniques and maneuvers.

The humanistic library administrator is not immune from the hostility of others. One reason for hostility is that subordinates may be so accustomed to having an administrator make the major decisions for them that they resist and resent having to take responsibility on their own.

Some checkpoints whereby a library administrator can evaluate the effectiveness of his or her behavioral style are:

1. The amount of investment members of the organization are making toward the achievement of the organization's goals and objectives
2. The amount of time it takes to get results from communication and decision-making activities
3. The expediency with which conflict is handled and resolved
4. The amount of creativity on the part of staff members
5. The number of staff members' personal needs being met
6. The number of times a crisis ends with the solution of a problem rather than the distribution of blame
7. The number of people in the organization who feel supported rather than alone in their efforts to bring about change or carry out procedures
8. The number of people who have clarity and motivation regarding the organization's purpose and directions
9. The degree to which the organization is functioning in proportion to its capacity.

Strategies

Leadership strategies are designed to enable people to function in a manner different from their previous way of functioning. In other words, their purpose is to produce change. Library administrators should be perceived as agents of change, and they should make the effort to equip themselves with the tools necessary for dealing with continual change and adaptation. They should be able, not only to move from concepts to action, but to understand and use the proper methodology for perpetuating the process of change in the work environment.

The initial phase of most strategies for change is to create a state of readiness for change by exploring individual and organizational capacity and need for change. During this phase, employees can begin to identify their individual and organizational needs and to search for effective and meaningful methods for doing something about their problems. In other words, the employees begin to take some "ownership" of the organizational environment.

A change strategy must be structured to require action that creates desirable situations rather than simply preventing the undesirable. Leadership in library administration requires a disposition toward proactive rather than reactive approaches toward the job. Administration that is proactive sets targets and causes events to occur.

The facilitation of a change process depends on both research and feedback. Research is needed to gather authentic data, and constant feedback is necessary for evaluation. Strategies for changes in library operations should be developed after sensing and then actually identifying critical needs in the organizational environment, establishing the options available, and making nonemotional judgments as to the best course of action.

Systematic inquiry into the library's climate is needed in order to formulate and initiate developmental activities that will guide the employees toward change. The expected result of this process is to create situations in which employees can become instrumental in solving their own problems and be included in formulating the goals and objectives of the library.

The effectiveness of a librarian's leadership strategies for change is conditioned by the interpersonal climate within the library. Success rises according to the degree of mutual problem solving that exists, while worthwhile outcomes become less likely when library personnel avoid involvement or blame others for problems that arise. Library staff members must recognize the issues confronting the organization and themselves, and accept some responsibility toward resolution. It is the responsibility of the leader in this situation to develop an organizational climate of trust, directed toward participative interaction and cooperative effort so that this recognition and responsibility can occur.

Tactics

Library leadership must be viewed in terms of the power it releases in others and not in terms of power over others. Rewards must relate to growth in competence and not exclusively to measured production. In short, the leadership strategy must focus on intrinsic as well as extrinsic motivation. Human values need enhancement from within, not just control from without. This process requires a leader to free individuals from fear of risk, thus allowing them the freedom to approach problem situations with unrestrained determination. This movement from fear to trust is the dynamics of interpersonal and organizational growth within the library setting. Fear controls the accuracy of communication among library people. In climates of fear, library administrators receive only the information that others think is safe to give—which may or may not be related to real needs. Fear requires controls; and the more controls there are in a library organization, the more faking will go on. Respectful conformity is often hostility. Lack of creativity can often be considered rebellion. The essence of a library administrator's leadership challenge is to develop an organizational climate in which all individuals can find a work life that is self-rewarding and organizationally productive.

The following items are specific tactics that are crucial to the development of leadership that achieves both individual and organizational purposes.

Be objective. Too often the management of people in a library is handled on the basis of long-held assumptions that usually relate more to personal opinions than established facts. Instead of objectively analyzing all the information we can collect and then putting ourself in the other person's position, one has a human tendency to make quick, easy, and superficial conclusions that seems to have the right "feel." Whatever the tactic, it must be supported by objectivity.

Provide challenges for hidden potential. There is nothing that elates most library employees more than to discover they are better than they thought or better than someone else thought. Everyone has a deep reservoir of hidden potential that can be discovered though challenging responsibilities. Library employees do their best when continually given a greater opportunity to fulfill themselves.

Employees' goals must be understood. Goals, if properly set and understood, can create within the library worker intense desire for accomplishment. Such goals must be individually made but realistically designed. Regardless of the nature of the goals, they are no better than the commitment given them. Problems are complicated rather than solved when goals lack acceptance and attainment.

Freedom of expression is essential. One of the most powerful forms of intrinsic motivation is to satisfy the human need for individual expression. Human dignity is best fulfilled when the individual can put personal style into work duties, no matter how routine the job may be. This is not to suggest the abandonment of unity and design, but to indicate the need to work within the possible limits of the organizational framework of the library and to allow individuals to put something of themselves into each project.

Develop a pattern of flexibility. Rigidity is an enemy of creativity. Tactics are handicapped when problem situations are stereotyped. When past history of the library, or of libraries in general, is too heavily relied upon as a guide for future action, the library employee is left in a fixed position that provides little inspiration for trying new things. Unfortunately, individuals become bound by such a system and assume there is less chance for flexibility than there really is. The library employee needs to feel an environment of innovation that says it is safe to test ideas.

Encourage any evidence of problem solving. The more essential people feel, the better they work. This is another way of saying that the nearer people are to problem solving, the more problems will be solved. Any evidence of individual involvement in the process of solving a problem is a sign of self-development. Regardless of the significance of the problem, the mere investment of energy is likely to release unknown potential, which will give a library employee the confidence to pursue much more meaningful tasks.

Don't expect stupidity and failure. It is impossible to perform well in an atmosphere of negative expectations. Library employees who are perceived as being stupid and failure prone will usually behave in that manner. Tactics based on positive expectations, on the other hand, will motivate individuals to set and attain gratifying goals.

Take the creative approach. Creativity, which may be defined as the ability to generate new ideas, is the basic human faculty for leadership tactics. Creativity is the safeguard against rigidity and the foundation for continuous innovation. Originality of thought on the part of the leader will in turn assist library employees in becoming more resourceful and secure in solving their own problems. Creativity, to be effective, must have direction. It must be triggered by a specific problem and must result in work that helps to solve that problem. Only in this way does creativity evolve new ways of thinking about old problems—something essential for the library employee.

Conclusion

Leadership in a library therefore becomes a journey and not an event. There are no terminal points. Whatever leadership style, strategy, or tactic a library administrator may take today will need adaptation to survive tomorrow. Leadership will hold up only to the extent that those in charge of the library are flexible and developmentally oriented. This discussion has not been a series of how-tos but an attempt to broaden the horizon and illuminate the challenges within the library's human and organizational system. Library leadership cannot be built on answers—only alternatives!

8 Decision Making

JAMES M. BANOVETZ

In its simplest form, decision making is defined as the act of making up one's mind. It is thus an act in which everybody is engaged continuously every day. Like other similar, everyday acts, decision making is frequently taken for granted, performed subconsciously, and underestimated in importance. Yet, on other occasions such as the selection of a new car or the choice of a vacation, decision making can be filled with tension, fraught with complexity, and portentous in its implications.

In either context, decision making can readily be construed as a positive, deliberate act. Decision making, however, also occurs just as readily when there is a refusal or reluctance to act. General Mohammad Ayub Khan, who later became president of Pakistan, once described one of his superiors who disposed of important decisions by placing the file on a particular matter under a pile of other files and leaving it there until the matter lost its importance. Such deferment is, in fact, a decision—it is a decision to let matters take their course without action or effect by the decision maker. In library work, a decision *not* to offer computer-based reference service is as important, and has consequences just as serious, as the decision *to* offer such a service. And postponement of a decision to institute the service is, in fact, a decision not to start the service at the particular time.

In short, decision making is not an activity in which a person can choose to engage. It is an integral and unavoidable part of everyday activity. It is, furthermore, the real essence of administrative work, regardless of whether the administration occurs in city hall, in the librarian's office, at the circulation desk, or in the reference room. Decisions are the substance of administration; they must be made in executing routine tasks ("Where in the reference room is the best place to look for this information?"), in responding to periodic questions ("Can I leave work an hour earlier tomorrow?"), and in handling tough prob-

lems ("What would be the best location for a new branch library?").

Given its key role in everyday activities, then, decision making as a focus of study takes on important dimensions. Since decision making is the substance of administrative activity, improvements in decision-making processes should produce better decisions, which in turn should result in improved administration. Even more important, better decision making in the library should mean the delivery of improved public services. With this end in mind, this chapter will undertake a study of decision making, examining what is known about the subject and looking at ways to bring about improvements in decision-making processes.

Decision Making in General

Decision making, as a topic of study, has emerged in scholarly and administrative literature only within the last few decades—and then it quickly became a matter of importance to scholars from many different disciplines. Psychologists, for example, who focused on the factors that lead to a particular decision, view decision making as a thinking activity of the mind; they analyze a predecision, postdecision, and intradecision state of the individual engaged in decision making. Physiologists have studied the complex activities and transformation phenomena associated with the infinite numbers of neurons in the brain cells of human beings. Building upon this notion of decision making as a mechanical process, mathematicians and statisticians have contributed to a clearer understanding of the functional processes involved in decision making and have led the search for methods to arrive at a theoretically best solution for a given problem.

Taking still a different approach to the subject, philosophers have studied decision making from a concern with the conflicting principles of free will and determination in such activities. Economists have searched for methods that would facilitate a maximum achievement of goals or profits. Similarly, political scientists have been interested in the

The author wishes to acknowledge the assistance rendered by Jean Major, Director of Libraries, Northern Illinois University, in the preparation of this manuscript.

process because of their concern with the public policies that are the consequence of decision making.

Principally, however, the subject of decision making has been of interest to students of administrative sciences. Students and practitioners of administration, be it business or government, study decision making with a view to increasing the potency, rightness, and utility of executive decisions in order to increase the efficiency with which administrative functions are conducted. In the field of library science, interest in decision making centers upon the challenge of improving the processes of library administration so that, as a consequence, the quality of the services provided to the public will be constantly improved.

In its simplest form, decision making involves a situation in which an individual is presented with a problem of selecting one out of several alternative courses of action. Indeed, decision making is sometimes regarded as an exercise in the scientific method, and, systematically practiced, it does bear much resemblance to it. Systematic decision making follows a prescribed series of steps, attempts to rely on total objectivity in analysis, and seeks a better understanding of interacting phenomena.

From a related perspective, Edwards and Tversky have explained that decision theory is an attempt to describe in an orderly way which variables influence the ultimate selection or choice from among the various alternatives. In most cases, according to Edwards and Tversky, two classes of variables come into play: the first class is concerned with the relative attractiveness or utility of each of the alternatives, and the second is the individual's evaluation of the likelihood or chance that each alternative will produce the desired outcome from the decision.[1] This likelihood or chance is called *probability* in the technical language of decision-making theory. These two variables structure the key questions that underlie decision-making theory. These questions are:

1. How do persons make judgments on the utility or attractiveness of various alternatives, and how can these utilities be measured?
2. How do persons judge the probabilities of events that control what happens to them, and how can these judgments of probability be measured?
3. How are judged probabilities changed by the arrival of new information?
4. How are probabilities and utilities combined to control decisions?

5. How should psychologists account for, or think about, the fact that the same person, put in the same situation twice, will often not make the same decision?[2]

By seeking the answers to questions such as these, decision theory seeks to gain deeper insight into the nature of decision making and, as a result, to discover ways to improve the quality of the decisions that are made.

Decision Making in the Library

Just as every person is regularly involved each day in decision making, so too is every member of the typical library staff involved at some level of decision making for the library. To be sure, different members of the library staff have different responsibilities, some members of the staff have more responsibility for more decision making than others, and some have more responsibility for nonprogrammed or policy decisions than do others. Nevertheless, all share in decision making to some extent. It is easy to visualize the goal of the head librarian in decision making, but harder to do so for the person who works part-time at the circulation desk. Even part-time people, through actions such as deciding which comments made by library users should be passed on to supervisory personnel, help to formulate policy decisions.

Participation in decision making has always been a widely shared staff function in libraries. In part, this has been due to the small size of most library staffs. In general, small staffs tend to be characterized by much more frequent and effective interaction and communication between members, and tend to involve all staff members, informally if not formally, in discussion of pending decisions. Reginald Northwood Lock has commented upon this tendency in library administration:

> The medium and smaller units tend much more to be multipurpose organisms, with all staff requiring and using all skills . . . the burden really being transformed into the human problem of finding among comparatively few, all the necessary skills, training them, and insuring that due balance is maintained.[3]

In part, too, widespread participation in decision making within libraries can be traced to the diffi-

---

1. Ward Edwards and Amos Tversky, *Decision-Making* (Baltimore: Penguin Books, 1967), p. 7.

2. Ibid.
3. Reginald Northwood Lock, *Library Administration* (New York: Philosophic Library, 1962), p. 42.

culty in distinguishing between executive and routine functions. As Lock noted,

> Within the library profession, it is not always easy to see the distinction between what should be "executive" or "routine" tasks, parts of "management" and "administration," establishment of objectives, broad policies of operation, and standards of achievement.[4]

Finally, widespread staff participation in library decision making can also be traced to the response of library administrators to the general societal demand for greater worker participation in organizational management. Ruth Gregory and Lester Stoffel described this trend toward "participatory management" in library administration in the following terms:

> Evolving management theories point to an administrative obligation to create a climate conducive to broadening the basic staff involvement in the improvement of work productivity. This responsibility involves an old-fashioned concept of morale. Defined in contemporary terms as a "mode of participation" this term is translated to mean a process of effective or ineffective participation. Sustaining a productive mode of participation means the application of such motivators as the stimulation of challenging new relationships between the staff as members of a working group and increased opportunities for achievement through the organization of the creative and analytic abilities of all the members of the staff. Participatory administration requires learning new terminology for leadership skills. . . . The philosophy of sharing the responsibility of the administrative function within the organizational structure of the library has changed the role of the chief administrator from that of a "boss" to that of a stimulator, a trainer, coordinator, and an enabler. In the average library, this change does not lessen the accountability of the head librarian for decision-making or for the effectiveness of the overall library program. Shared responsibilities serve to multiply leadership capabilities and promote a high sense of personal and professional responsibility at key points in the library service programs.[5]

Decision making, then, is often considered synonymous with administration, and an administrator's success is seen to lie in finding opportunities for decision making, making the right decisions, and implementing them.[6] Decision making and administration, however, are not the sole province of supervisory personnel. In all organizations, and particularly in libraries, all staff members share in the daily work and information exchanges that involve and are intrinsic to decision-making activities. The influence of informal interactions among the library's staff are ever more important to decision making as shared responsibility and participatory management become more common characteristics of library administration. Thus decision making can literally and increasingly be called a general library staff activity.

The Process of Decision Making

As a process, decision making is both technological and psychological in nature. It is technological in the sense that it is a process that can be subdivided into its component parts, which can then be arranged in a formulalike relationship to each other; the careful and considered execution of each part can lead to an improvement in both process and outcome. Since, then, decision making is partly a matter of proper execution of each part, or step, of the process, potential decision makers can be trained to perform more effectively or efficiently in the decision-making task.

Decision-making, however, is also a psychological process. Each step in the process is affected by the human, behavioral characteristics of the decision makers and by the environment in which they are operating. Decision making is affected by organizational considerations, but it is also affected by the attitudes, values, experience, and personality of the decision maker and by the interactions among decision makers when the decision is being made collectively by several persons. The human influence on the decision-making process will be treated at length later in this chapter.

As a technological process, decision making has four discrete steps: recognition of a problem that requires a decision, establishing the method that will be used to make the decision, making the actual decision—a process that itself involves several discrete steps—and, finally, implementing the decision (i.e., putting the decision into effect and seeing that it is carried out).

Recognizing the Need for Decision

The recognition of the need to make a decision is so self-evident that it would appear almost redundant to make mention of it. To be sure, some

---

4. Ibid.
5. Ruth W. Gregory and Lester L. Stoffel, *Public Libraries in Comparative Systems* (Chicago: ALA, 1971), pp. 129–30.

6. Lawrence A. Welsch and Richard M. Cyert, eds., *Management Decision-Making* (Baltimore: Penguin Books, 1970), p. 7.

problems requiring decisions are readily apparent and could not be missed by even the most careless observer—the resignation of an employee, for instance, requires a whole series of decisions about a replacement.

Other problems, however, are not so apparent, and failure to recognize them could be costly. Failure to recognize change in the use patterns of a library, for example, may mean that a needed evaluation of existing resource allocation policies within the library would not be undertaken and a chance to increase the attractiveness of library services might be missed.

Equally dangerous is the failure to recognize the problem in all of its dimensions. Even the best decision-making procedures will not produce a desirable outcome if the problem has been incorrectly recognized and diagnosed. An attempt to improve the morale of an unhappy employee through a salary adjustment, for example, will fail if the cause of the employee's unhappiness stems from personality conflicts with other employees. Further, such a misguided decision might well exacerbate the problem, since the salary adjustment might well increase the antagonism toward that employee by those with whom he has the conflicts.

More common, however, is the situation in which decisions are made in a repetitive and routine manner with too little attention or concern given to long-run consequences. As David S. Brown has noted,

> One of the major impediments to sound decision-making is the obliviousness of many individuals and groups to the critical relationship between what they are doing, or not doing, and later events.[7]

Clues to the existence of problems or potential problems can be found by the sensitive librarian in many places: in the casual remarks made by library staff and patrons, in statements by public leaders, in routine operations reports, in the professional literature, and in dialogue with other professionals. Librarians alert for existing or potential problems will—

1. Maintain an open door policy for library staff so that subordinates will feel free to discuss their perceptions of current or forthcoming library problems. The library staff will typically be the best source of information about

internal operating problems, and the staff will communicate this information if given encouragement to do so.
2. Be sensitive to socioeconomic and political trends that may affect library operations or the demand for library services. Information on political trends can best be obtained through the maintenance of a continuing dialogue with local political leaders and especially with the leadership of the city or county in which the library is located. Socioeconomic trend information can usually be best secured from state, regional, and local planning offices and through dialogue with local educational officials.
3. Scan operations reports closely, compare them with similar reports from the past, and treat them as an internal diagnostic tool.
4. Be alert to detect unhappiness or interpersonal friction among library staff and patrons. Such conditions are usually indicative of real or forthcoming problems.
5. Schedule a time, on a regular basis, when routine administrative work is set aside and creative energy is devoted to reflection about library operations, planning, and searching for weaknesses in existing activities. Perhaps the major failing of administrators today is their tendency to become so dominated by routine work that they allow themselves no time for reflective and creative thinking about the organization they serve.

The first step in decision making, then, is the recognition, first, that a problem exists; second, of the nature of the problem; and, third, of the future consequences of the problem and any decisions made regarding it.

Deciding How to Make the Decision

Basic to any decision making situation is the establishment of policies governing the manner in which decisions are to be made. In many situations, the manner is of far greater consequence than the actual decision itself. Employees, for example, are likely to be highly critical of decisions made regarding working rules—sometimes even when the substance of those decisions is consistent with their personal preferences—if they feel that they were not appropriately consulted beforehand. Yehezkel Dror has stressed the importance of this facet of the decision-making process in a

7. David S. Brown, "Making Decisions," in *Managing the Modern City*, ed. James M. Banovetz (Washington, D.C.: International City Management Association, 1971), pp. 134–50.

public policy context, calling it the "metapolicy making stage."[8]

This stage of the decision-making process seeks to determine, either for an individual decision or for different categories of decisions, who will participate in the decision-making process, the nature such participation will take, what rules are to be followed in making the decision, when different kinds of decisions are to be made, and the kind of agreement that must be secured for any particular kind of decision.

Many of the aspects of the decision-making process are, of course, prescribed in law. State laws, local ordinances, and the rules and regulations established by the library board of trustees itself will largely determine, at least in a formal sense, the who, where, when, and how of decision making in the library. Nevertheless, within these formal prescriptions, considerable latitude for the administrative officer often exists. The administrator can encourage or discourage widespread consultation on an impending issue, recommend specific adjustments in standard procedures for particular circumstances, and otherwise play a consequential role in setting the informal "stage" for the decision-making act. Decisions about the location for a new branch municipal library, for example, are often made by the local legislative body, but the librarian can seek to affect the decision-making process by recommending the employment of consultants, urging that the legislators hear presentations by library staff members, encouraging library supporters in the community to become interested in the matter, and making judgments about the kinds of information that should be considered.

Setting the stage for decision making is important. The way in which those affected by a decision respond to it after it has been made will depend, in large part, upon how legitimate the decision-making process was perceived to be. Decisions viewed as having been made in an inappropriate manner are likely to be resisted or accepted only half-heartedly and reluctantly. Further, the substance of the decision itself is likely to be affected by the stage setting. A decision by a city council to cut the library's proposed budget, without consultation with the head librarian, is apt to result in a different curtailment of services than would have been the case if the head librarian had been consulted. It might be different still if public hearings on the proposed budget had been held and principal library users had had an opportunity to express their views. The way in which a decision is made, then, will affect both the substance of that decision and the reception accorded it by those who must abide by it.

Making the Decision

Once a problem needing a decision has been recognized and policies governing the decision-making process have been determined, the actual task of making the decision begins. Most observers describe the decision-making task as one involving some variation of the following steps: definition of problem and objectives, identification of alternative courses of action, evolution of alternatives, and selection of an alternative.[9]

Definition of problem and objectives. This first stage really requires two discrete actions. First, the problem to be resolved must be stated in operational terms. This means that the problem must be defined in terms of its specific, distinguishable aspects on which action needs to be taken, a statement of the reasons why action needs to be taken, a description of the forces that have given rise to the situation, and a definition of all potentially complicating or delimiting factors that might restrict the kinds of decisions that can be made. Second, there must be a precise statement of what the decision must accomplish: what are the objectives being sought through the decision-making process?

These tasks are complex; the way in which they are handled can predetermine the kinds of decisions that will be made and, in any event, will ultimately determine how successful any decision can be in achieving satisfactory, if not optimum, results. For example, if the librarian responsible for the children's collection and programs has resigned, a decision regarding either a replacement or a reassignment of duties must be made. Such a decision should be preceded by a statement of the problem and a statement of the objectives to be attained. The problem might be stated in terms such as:

> Should the vacated position be filled with another appointment, or should the position be phased out, with its duties assigned to other members of the library staff? The decision would have to be made soon enough to permit its timely execution, and it should include budgetary, personnel, organizational, and client service considerations (ideally these considerations should be specified).

---

8. Yehezkel Dror, *Public Policymaking Reexamined* (San Francisco: Chandler, 1968).

9. See, for instance, Joseph W. Newman, *Management Applications of Decision Theory* (New York: Harper and Row, 1971).

Objectives might be stated in terms such as:

The decision should seek to reduce total personnel costs of the library as much as possible, improve or at least sustain staff morale, and maintain existing library service levels.

Such a problem statement clearly suggests the kinds of action that need to be taken, and the objectives present a set of criteria by which alternative decisions can be evaluated. Note that these objectives are not the only ones that might be used, nor need these necessarily be used. Faced with such a decision, for example, a library might see it as an opportunity to hire an additional librarian, regardless of budgetary considerations. It might also be seen as an opportunity to split the position and hire two additional people. Whatever the objectives are, they should be so stated.

Identification and development of alternate courses of action. Once the problem and objectives have been identified, the next task of the decision maker is to identify as many alternative courses of action as possible that might resolve the problem. A major weakness of most decision makers is their failure to consider more than two or three possible alternatives. In point of fact, however, Herbert Simon has pointed out that, at any time, there are many courses possible for a decision maker.[10] Even problems that appear to have but two solutions can usually be found, upon rethinking and redefinition of the problem, to have multiple alternatives. The most successful administrators are typically those who are adept at developing a long list of alternatives from which a decision can ultimately be made, thereby creating a number and range of optional courses of action. Even typical dilemmas, which are usually posed in terms of two alternatives, can frequently be avoided by extending the list of options.

Alternatives for the above example involving the resignation of the children's librarian might be listed as follows:

A. Fill the position with a newly hired person possessing the same approximate training and background as the resigned librarian.
B. Fill the position with a person of lesser background but with some relevant training or experience.
C. Promote an existing employee who lacks relevant library science training but whose

experience in the library equips him or her for the position.
D. Consolidate positions, transferring responsibility for the children's programs to the coordinator of young adult services, creating thereby the position of coordinator of children's and young adult services.
E. Fill the position by promotion of the assistant to the children's room librarian, leaving the latter position vacant.

Any similar situation might have even more alternatives; this list is illustrative but restricted by space considerations.

Evaluation of the alternatives. For each of the alternatives listed, there are any number of possible consequences. A cut in the library's budget, for instance, might pose the alternatives of reducing bookmobile services or curtailing library hours. Reducing bookmobile services would reduce library services to patrons in outlying areas, reduce circulation, and adversely affect public support for the library. Curtailing library hours might cause a decline in library usage by the public, inconvenience patrons, reduce circulation, force curtailments of some programs, and force a cutback in staff salaries as the number of hours worked decreased. Secondary consequences also occur and must be anticipated. A curtailment of library hours leading to a reduction in salaries might undermine staff morale and result in resignations by key staff members. All such possible consequences, and their resulting effects, must be anticipated.

A major weakness of the American culture is a tendency to give too little consideration to the consequences of alternative courses of action. This is sometimes due to a failure to distinguish between important and unimportant decisions, i.e., between those with meaningful consequences and those without. It is sometimes due to the human tendency to be lazy—to consider problems only in their most simplistic terms and ignore complicating considerations. Sometimes it is due to an overemphasis upon fast action, or to excessive work pressures that allow too little time for deliberation. Then, too, it is partly attributable to the contemporary political style of viewing only the symbolic aspects of decisions and ignoring real life considerations; increasingly, decisions have been viewed in terms of their ideological "rightness" rather than in terms of their consequences for the problem to be solved. Much of the nation's failure to resolve its race and poverty-related problems in recent decades can be attributed largely to this latter consideration.

Failure to anticipate consequences can not only lead to poorer decisions, but it can have other adverse consequences as well. It can, for example,

10. Herbert A. Simon, *Administrative Behavior*, 2d ed. (New York: Macmillan, 1957), p. 34. See also, A. Newell, J. C. Shaw, and H. A. Simon, "The Process of Creative Thinking," in *Contemporary Approaches to Creative Thinking*, ed. H. E. Gruber, G. Terrell, and M. Wertheimer (New York: Atherton, 1962), pp. 63–119.

Table 8.1 Evaluation of Five Alternatives in Terms of Three Criteria

Alternative	Personnel Costs*	Staff Morale	Library Services
A	Save $ 500	Lower — 15% Same — 75% Higher — 10%	Sustained — 50% Improved — 25% Lower — 25%
B	Save $ 1,500	Lower—100%	Sustained — 25% Lower — 70% Higher — 5%
C	Save $ 1,500	Higher — 50% Same — 25% Lower — 25%	Sustained — 30% Lower — 60% Higher — 10%
D	Save $ 8,000	Mixed, but on balance: Same — 40% Lower — 40% Higher — 20%	Lower—100%
E	Save $11,500	Sustained — 90% Lower — 5% Higher — 5%	Lower—100%

*Since salary levels are fixed by the organization, these can be known in advance with relative certainty. Probabilities are listed for the other criteria.

lead to decisions that will exacerbate rather than resolve problems. It can lead to the generation of new and wholly unnecessary problems, such as the staff morale and retention problem in the example used above, and it can result in commitments that restrict future alternatives and make later problem-solving efforts less effective. In short, failure to anticipate the possible consequences of alternative courses of action can result in decisions that worsen rather than alleviate the problems to which they are addressed. Consequences that must be taken into account include immediate, short-run results of the decision; long-run effects of the decision; primary or direct effects of the decision upon the situation to which the decision is directed; secondary or indirect effects—the effects upon others who are not directly related to the decision itself; and the symbolic or political interpretation that will be placed upon the decision by interested parties.

Not only must consequences be anticipated, but the probability that each consequence will occur must also be estimated. A consequence that has only a 10 percent likelihood of occurring must not be given the same concern or attention as a consequence that has a 90 percent probability. These two actions—anticipating consequences and estimating the probabilities of each consequence—together constitute the evalutation of each alternative.

To be sure, the estimation of probabilities is a highly speculative venture. There is no known means for assessing with precision the likelihood that a future event will occur. Nevertheless, such estimation, rough as it may be, is indispensable in the evaluation of decision alternatives. Further, an informed or considered estimate is better than no estimate at all. Thus, it behooves decision makers to make estimates of probability in as thoughtful and deliberate a fashion as possible.

In terms of listed criteria—reduced personnel costs, sustained or improved staff morale, and sustained library services—the five alternatives regarding replacement of the children's librarian in the previous example might be evaluated as shown in table 8.1.

In addition to the listed criteria, other primary and secondary consequences must also be anticipated. For example, in alternative D, the administrator should consider how the coordinator of young adult services may react to the increased workload. The effect of potentially lower-quality services on the probability of future private gifts to the library should be considered. The morale of some members of the staff will be affected more than others, and the nature of these effects should be considered along with the importance to the library of the individual, affected staff persons. The effects, too, on future library appropriations should be considered. Public support for the library may also be affected. In short, a well-considered decision will take a great many factors into account, and the consequences of the occurrence should be estimated.

Selection of an alternative. Once the alternative courses of action have been identified and evaluated, the ultimate moment of decision making has arrived: the point at which an actual decision must be made upon a particular course of action. As indicated in the introduction to this chapter, a decision at this point can be avoided: failure to make a decision is in itself a decision—albeit a decison by default—to let the course of events proceed unaffected by action of the decision maker.

Assuming, however, a positive decision has to be made, that task can then be identified, essentially, as one of selecting the best of the alternatives that have been identified and evaluated. Alternately, of course, a decision might be made to select portions of several alternatives. This, of course, would constitute a new and separate alternative. James D. Thompson and Arthur Tuden have identified four different techniques that can be used in selecting among alternatives: (1) a decision can be made by computation; (2) a decision can be rendered by majority judgment; (3) a selection can be made on the basis of compromise among competitive viewpoints; and (4) a decision can be based on the inspiration or judgment of an individual decision maker.[11] These strategies, of course, are not mutually exclusive.

From a systematic point of view, the process of selecting a particular alternative involves three steps. First, those alternatives that are impractical or not feasible should be eliminated. Second, the remaining alternatives should be compared in terms of: (1) the extent or manner in which each would accomplish the stated goals or objectives to be achieved from the decision, (2) the probability that each alternative would achieve the desired outcome, and (3) the decision maker's own propensity to assume risk. Some decision makers are, by nature, gamblers and are more willing to select alternatives with a low probability of success if the potential benefits are sufficiently great. Other decision makers are much more conservative and will prefer to choose an alternative with limited benefits but with a high probability of success. Depending upon the subject matter, different persons might choose to behave differently in different situations, being willing to undertake higher risks in some situations and little or no risk in others. Ultimately, however, the alternative is usually chosen that promises to provide maximum benefits within tolerable limits of probability or risk.

In mathematical terms, the above procedure can be expressed in the following sequence of steps:

1. Identify the objectives towards which the decision making should be directed.
2. Identify the alternative courses of action that should be considered.
3. Identify the possible events (environmental conditions) that would influence the payoff of each course of action.
4. Assign a numerical weight to the payoff to each course of action, given each possible event.
5. Assign a numerical weight (probability) to the occurrence of each possible event.
6. Using the weights (probabilities), compute the weighted averages (expected value) of the payoffs assigned to each course of action.
7. Assess the exposure to both gain and loss associated with each course of action.
8. Choose among the alternative courses of action on the basis of a combination of (a) expected value and (b) exposure to gain and loss that is most consistent with the decision maker's objectives and attitude toward risk.[12]

In the example under consideration, of course, the alternative ultimately selected would depend upon the method used and persons involved in making the decision, upon the extent (as well as the probability) of projected changes in morale and services, upon the evaluation of secondary consequences, upon the nature of risk the decision makers are willing to assume, and upon the weighting given to each of the several criteria and considerations. If all criteria are weighted equally and secondary considerations balance out, then alternative C might be chosen; if, on the other hand, budgetary considerations turn out to be paramount, then alternative E promises a better outcome than alternative D on cost as well as on morale considerations.

Alternately, if the decision in the example is based upon calculation, it may turn out that alternative C would be chosen. If, however, it is made by the head librarian in consultation with department heads, alternative D might be preferred because it would involve a substantial pay increment for the department head who would assume additional responsibilities. If the decision is made by a library advisory board, alternative A might be preferred because it offers the best probability of maintaining high service levels, while a decision

---

11. James D. Thompson and Arthur Tuden, "Strategies, Structure, and Process of Organizational Decision," in *Comparative Studies in Administration,* ed. J. D. Thompson et al. (Pittsburgh: Univ. of Pittsburgh Pr., 1959).

---

12. Newman, *Management Applications,* pp. 6–7.

made by a local governing board might favor alternative E because of its cost savings. Thus, different persons or groups of persons will decide a matter differently because their values, motivations, and willingness to deal with uncertainty are different.

Implementing the Decision: Control

Ultimately, of course, the effectiveness of any administrative decision or policy depends upon the implementation of that decision or policy. It is one thing to make a decision—to employ an OCLC service to streamline cataloging operations—and quite another thing to see that the decision's purpose—processing materials faster and less expensively—is actually accomplished. Assuring such accomplishment on management's part requires effective control systems that both measure and promote a desired correlation between the intention of administrative action and the results of that action.

Administrative control, historically, has been viewed negatively as a system or several systems designed to assure that employees have been and are performing their jobs properly. Admittedly, this is one of the objectives of any control system, but it is only one of the objectives. Effective control systems depend more upon positive actions—employee motivation and encouragement—than upon "controls" such as work appraisal and sanctions. The more closely an employee identifies with the organization and its objectives, the greater can be the organization's reliance upon positive control mechanism.

Feedback. Employee motivation and supervision is only one of the functions of any control system. A second and equally important function is the generation of information about the consequences or results of administrative actions. Called feedback, such information becomes an important basis for the formulation of decisions in the future.

Feedback is the ultimate stage in any decision-making process. It is the stage that occurs after the decision has been made and implemented; the information it provides enables the decision maker to appraise the consequences of the decision and ascertain whether or not the decision will achieve the intended consequences. This, in turn, can lead to any necessary modifications, either in the initial decision or in the provisions for its implementation, that might promote greater goal achievement. For the smart decision maker, such information also builds an experiential base upon which future decisions of a similar kind can be based, so that the quality of such decisions can if possible be improved. Feedback can be both formal and in-

formal. Formal feedback is that provided by information gained through staff conferences, reports, and performance appraisals. Informal feedback is that which comes by word of mouth, directly or indirectly, from those affected by the decision, including colleagues, employees, clients, and friends or associates of any of these persons. Both kinds of feedback should be systematically gathered, evaluated, and utilized.

Implementation controls. There are three distinct processes through which management implements—controls—organizational decisions. These are preparation processes, motivational processes, and oversight processes.

The first and often overlooked phase of managerial control is employee preparation. Preparation involves the selection of employees for a particular task and the provision of adequate training to provide them with both the skills necessary for the tasks to be assigned and the attitudes most appropriate in any control system. Employees with the appropriate attitude and training can be given greater latitude and freedom to do the jobs assigned to them and will require much less supervision while they are performing those tasks. In short, proper selection and training of persons to undertake particular tasks has the effect of minimizing the effort required in other control activities.

The second control process is that of motivation. The purpose here is twofold: (1) to provide the organizational context—guidelines, rules, job descriptions, and role relationships—necessary to inform the employees both of what they are to do and of the kinds of actions that are or are not permitted in doing so; and (2) to provide an incentive structure that will encourage employees to do the tasks assigned and to devote to the work an optimum level of creative energy.[13]

The third control process is employee oversight. This is the process of supervision designed to maintain continuing surveillance and supervision of employees' behavior, ensuring both that they are working in the desired manner and that their efforts are having the desired consequences. As is true with other kinds of control, oversight involves the collection of information, which may be collected in a number of ways, including reports, production charts, and periodic inspections. Such formally procured information can and should also be supplemented with informal feedback on

---

13. The subject of employee direction and motivation lies at the very heart of the study of organization theory. One of the best single treatments is James G. March and Herbert A. Simon, *Organizations* (New York: John Wiley & Sons, 1959), especially chapters 3 and 4.

employee performance, though care must be taken to assess the veracity of such informally derived information.[14]

In assessing such control processes, however, several caveats are in order. First, as noted in an earlier edition of this text, "As a first step in achieving control, the librarian should review all basic management principles as they apply to the library, beginning with the objectives including policies, plans, organization structure, and management processes."[15] In short, control is not a separate and distinct administrative process but one that is intrinsically related to all aspects of organization and library management. "Control is not something that is applied after all else is done. It is an integral part of all managerial effort."[16]

Second, any administrative control "is most effective where it is least obvious."[17] Positive inducements and motivations are typically far more effective in securing employee compliance with rules and regulations and in encouraging employee promotion of organizational objectives than are reports, regulations, and the ultimate threat of sanctions.

Third, as March and Simon have noted, organizational controls "have the consequences anticipated by the organizational leaders, but [they] also have other, unanticipated, consequences."[18] Thus, before instituting any control system, it is essential that, as in making any other kind of decision, consequences of proposed courses of action—intended and unintended—be accurately assessed. The development of work rules, for instance, gives employees clear clues about what it is they are to do, and thus reduces the level of tension involved in job performance. On the other hand, work rules, by defining unacceptable behavior, also increase employee knowledge about minimum acceptable behavior and consequently can have the effect of encouraging such behavior.[19] Those control systems that focus principally upon informing and motivating employees will typically be more effective than those that rely principally on scrutiny and potential threat.

To emphasize the former, a new concept of management, termed *management by objective,*

or MBO, has evolved; it is future oriented and predicated upon subordinate employee involvement in the planning processes. Its purpose is to produce a more constructive relationship between organizational leader and subordinates—a relationship that seeks, by subordinate involvement, to intensify subordinate identification with organizational goals and commitment to the tasks required to achieve those goals.

Although its operational characteristics differ widely from organization to organization, MBO typically embraces most or all of the following characteristics:

1. MBO employs a collegial process, involving the organizational leader and subordinates, in the establishment of organizational goals, and in the formulation and assignment of tasks necessary to achieve those goals. It is a participatory management process, in which subordinates and leaders collectively participate, through group discussions, in these tasks.

2. The deliberative process must deal with reality. By itself, the process cannot enable an organization to achieve objectives that would otherwise be beyond its capabilities. Therefore, the discussion must deal with questions regarding the capabilities of organizational manpower and the availability of funds, equipment, and skills necessary to fulfill suggested objectives.

3. MBO requires the achievement of consensus between leaders and subordinates. Without consensus, the commitment sought through the deliberative process will not be produced.

4. Leadership role and style is somewhat different in an organization run with MBO. Under such a system, the leader cannot be the lone decision maker in the organization; his task, rather, is to be that of convener, discussion leader, motivator, and resource person. It is the job of the leader, in such discussions, to raise issues and alternatives; clarify attitudes, ideas, and responsibilities; guide discussion toward consensus; and coodinate the efforts ultimately chosen for pursuit of the stipulated objectives. In such a setting, the leader is not purely a director, but a manager in partnership with his subordinates, attempting to fulfill the organization's objectives.

5. MBO emphasizes the establishment of objectives and programs to deal with future opportunities as well as present problems. In this respect, it is future oriented; it provides a format in which organizations can take the

---

14. For a fuller treatment of this topic see Wallace H. Best and Frank P. Sherwood, *Supervisory Methods in Municipal Administration* (Washington, D.C.: International City Management Association, 1958), especially pp. 105–12.

15. Roberta Bowler, ed., *Local Public Library Administration* (Chicago: ALA, 1964), p. 108.

16. Dalton E. McFarland, *Management Principles and Practices* (New York: Macmillan, 1958), p. 305.

17. Ibid., p. 306.

18. March and Simon, *Organizations*, p. 37.

19. Ibid., p. 44.

initiative for making changes and improvements, rather than just responding to crises and problems as they occur.

MBO was conceived for, and works best in, organizations such as libraries in which most of the employees are educated and competent people in their own right, persons who possess a high degree of professional skill and technical expertise. Such persons frequently are as familiar with the technical aspects of their assignments as are the organization's leaders, and thus they become uncomfortable with the traditional hierarchical patterns of organization—especially leadership that is perceived as arbitrary or nonconsultative. For such employees, and organizations with a high percentage of such employees, the collegial nature of administration provided by the MBO format tends to produce higher morale and greater productivity. Since it utilizes collective wisdom, the probability is high that it also produces a better-quality decision. Because of the nature of their employees, libraries have a particularly strong potential to benefit from the implementation of MBO techniques.

Human Factors and Decision Making

While the decision-making process can be studied in its technical aspect and can be analyzed through the method and logic of mathematics, it remains fundamentally a human process. This is true even of decisions made with the aid of sophisticated computer programs and information processes. It is even more true of the decisions made in the conduct of daily business by a small staff, such as those characteristic of most libraries.

This section of the chapter will explore the human factors of decision making, looking at the role played by human rationality and psychology in the process. It will also explore the way people make decisions when acting by themselves and when acting as members of a decision-making group.

The Role of Rationality and Values

"Rational" decisions have traditionally been considered one of the benchmarks of "good" administration, and all administrators were charged, at least theoretically, with the goal of maximizing "rationality" in their decision making. Rationality, in turn, required a detailed description of the problem to be solved; a clear understanding of the objectives to be pursued; complete information on alternatives, consequences, and probabil-

ity; and the application of the principles of logic in an attempt to "maximize" the achievement of the stated objectives.

While such a definition of rationality may serve to function as a model or ideal to be pursued, it obviously can never be achieved in the real world. Herbert A. Simon, in his classic *Administration Behavior*, offered the first insightful analysis of the concept of rationality as practiced in administrative decision-making situations, and described the inevitable limitations on rationality in such situations.[20] Simon argued, for instance, that actual behavior departs from the model of objective rationality because it is impossible for any human to know all the alternatives in a given situation, all their consequences, and all of the probabilities involved. As a result, he argued, administrative behavior is not rational in a pure sense, but rather purposive

> insofar as it is guided by general goals or objectives; it is rational insofar as it selects alternatives which are conducive to the achievement of the previously selected goals. . . . In an important sense, all decision is a matter of compromise. The alternative that is finally selected never permits a complete or perfect achievement of objectives, but is merely the best solution that is available under the circumstances.[21]

Factors other than limited knowledge also serve to qualify the degree of rationality that exists in decision-making situations. The most important such constraint is the role played by human values. Value judgment plays a role in *every* decision-making situation. Values affect the way people perceive problems, the priority they attach to different objectives, the degree of importance attached to different information inputs, the assessment of probabilities about what is likely to happen in the future, and the degree of risk people are willing to assume in choosing between alternative courses of action. In deciding whether to keep open a branch library in an inner-city neighborhood where usage and circulation is very low, for example, different librarians will reach different conclusions because they attach different degrees of importance to the relative value of keeping library services accessible to poorly educated, low-income persons who have demonstrated very little interest in, or appreciation for, such services.

Various persons will typically make different value judgments about any topic that cannot be subjected to empirical verification. For instance, it is impossible to verify empirically how a library

---

20. Simon, *Administrative Behavior.*
21. Ibid., pp. 5–6. See also March and Simon, *Organizations,* especially chapter 6.

should divide its resources among fiction and nonfiction works. To be sure, professional guidelines are available, but these guidelines must be modified in the light of a considerable number of indigenous variables. These variables include the nature of the existing holdings of the library in question, the purpose of the particular library (e.g., a university library will have a different division of its holdings than will a branch library in a residential neighborhood), library use, book market variables, and a host of other considerations. While empirical decision-making methods permit greater scientific objectivity in rendering decisions about such matters, they cannot eliminate entirely the factor of human judgment, and, where human judgment occurs, human values will enter the decision-making process.[22]

Different decisions, furthermore, demand different degrees of fact and value input. Some decisions, especially routine ones such as determining the fine owed on an overdue book, can be handled with very little judgment on the part of the decision maker. Other decisions, particularly those made on major policy by top levels of management, are heavily judgmental in nature, and value judgment plays a major role in such situations. Since human values themselves cannot be empirically verified or tested, the part played by value judgment in any given decision-making process necessarily qualifies the role that rationality can play in the process.

Another limiting factor is the tendency of decision makers to restrict the number of alternatives to be considered in any given decision. The more alternatives are considered, the greater is the likelihood of finding one that is clearly superior in terms of its acceptability, feasibility, and effectiveness in achieving stated goals. On the other hand, each additional alternative renders the decision-making process more complex: each alternative, for example, requires the gathering of additional information, the projection of another set of consequences, the estimation of additional probabilities, and, in essence, the processing of more information by the decision maker. A tendency to limit alternatives, then, is born out of a need or desire on the part of the decision maker to simplify the decision-making situation, at least to keep the situation manageable. Simon has attributed this tendency to the desire to reduce anxiety, whereas Kenneth Boulding sees it as a desire to prevent

"information overload."[23] Many librarians, for example, receive such voluminous statistics on the operation of individual departments that they are unable to integrate the data into a systematic framework that would be useful for future decision making. As a result, the effort expended on data collection is underutilized, and decisions are based more on impressions than need be.

Finally, time is also a factor that serves to qualify rationality in decision making. For many decisions, particularly routine decisions, the marginal benefit to be derived from increased rationality in decision making may simply not be worth the added expenditure of time and effort required to achieve it. A decision about whether or not to restrict a particular book to a seven-day loan period is clearly not worth a market survey to determine potential demand for the book. On the other hand, the decision to change the hours during which the library will be open may, because of its considerable cost factor in wages and salaries, be well worth the time and cost involved in making a sophisticated analysis of real and potential library demand at different times of the day and week.

In any decision-making situation, some judgment has to be used to determine how much information must be collected about the problem at hand, and about the various alternatives to be considered. Joseph Newman, for example, has suggested that the following questions be posited in determining the cutoff point for information. Should an attempt be made to obtain any additional information before making the final decision on the course of action? If so, what expenditure of funds would be needed? How should alternative proposals for the acquisition of additional information be evaluated? How should information be combined with management judgment so that both may have an appropriate influence on the alternate decision?[24]

The Role of Psychological Factors

Because it is a process involving individual human behavior, decision making obviously is affected by a great many psychological factors and variables. It is therefore not surprising that a great deal of literature in the field of psychology deals with decision-making situations and the reactions of individuals to such situations. On the basis of this literature, it is possible to describe the effects of some of the crucial human variables influencing decision making. For example, human thinking processes in decision making have been ex-

22. Kenneth E. Boulding, "The Ethics of Rational Decision," in *Management: A Decision-Making Approach*, ed. Stanley Young (Belmont, Cal.: Dickenson, 1968), pp. 93–103. See also Simon's discussion of values in *Administrative Behavior*.

23. Boulding, "Ethics of Rational Decision."
24. Newman, *Management Applications*.

plored,[25] time constraints and their effects have been analyzed,[26] and the relationship between thinking and choice behavior has been investigated.[27] Practical experiments have reported the process of human thinking[28] and have shown that decision making is affected by several active forces, some generated by the decision-making process itself and others already existing in the environment of the decision maker.[29] Personality attributes associated with management team decision making have been explored,[30] as have the effects of participation in decision making on personality.[31] Other studies have found correlations among confidence, caution, and speed in a decision-making situation[32] and between certain personality traits and propensity to take risk in specified decision-making situations.[33] Finally, Festinger's work in comparing the predecision and postdecision periods is worthy of note.[34] The remainder of this section of the chapter will describe in some detail the psychological and sociological factors that affect human behavior in decision-making situations.

Behavioral Factors in Individual Decision Making

Individual behavior in decision-making situations, as in all administrative situations, reflects personal motivations and psychological needs, the influence of fellow workers, the impact of organizational rules, and the effectiveness with which the organization communicates its rules, guidelines, and expectations to the worker.

Historically, the earliest organizational theory held that behavior could be prescribed by organizational rules—that such rules could determine the specific tasks to be performed by each individual, establish a predetermined method by which the task would be performed, and require that all decisions be made in accordance with well-established "rules of the organization."[35] Obviously, there is considerable validity in this point of view. Organizations can prescribe rules that govern the behavior of their organizations and can expect that these rules will be carried out. Thus, for example, libraries establish policies governing the circulation of books and reasonably and appropriately expect that the librarians staffing the circulation desk will make decisions consistent with these rules. Equally obvious, however, is the fact that not all human behavior in any organization can be so prescribed; it is particularly difficult to prescribe and routinize behavior that is very discretionary in nature. Further, even organizational rules and prescriptions themselves are frequently modified by the reaction of employees to them. For example, while the formal library closing time may be set at 9:00 P.M., staff may be reluctant to admit persons to the library stacks after 8:45 P.M., so that the librarians themselves will have an easier time closing the library promptly at 9:00 P.M.

A great many of these exceptions or variations in employee response to organization rules can be traced to the norms and values of the informal social groups that exist among the organization's workers. Persons who work together inevitably develop informal social relationships among themselves in addition to the formal, organizationally prescribed work relationships. Like any other social group, these informal work groups tend to develop shared attitudes and values among the

25. N. R. F. Maier, "Reasoning in Humans I: On Direction," *Journal of Comparative Psychology* 12:181–84 (1931), and N. R. F. Maier, "Reasoning in Humans III: The Mechanism of Equivalent Stimulus of Reasoning," *Journal of Experimental Psychology* 35:349–60 (1945).

26. D. Cartwright, "Decision Time in Relation to Differentiation of the Phenomenal Field," *Psychology Review* 48:425–42 (1941); L. Festinger, "Studies in Decision I: Decision Time, Relative Frequency of Judgment, and Subjective Confidence as Related to Physical Stimulus Differences," *Journal of Experimental Psychology* 32:291–306 (1943); and L. Festinger, "Studies in Decision II: An Empirical Test of a Quantitative Theory of Decision," *Journal of Experimental Psychology* 32:411–23 (1943).

27. J. S. Bruner, J. J. Goodnow, and G. A. Austin, *A Study of the Thinking Process* (New York: John Wiley and Sons, 1960); and R. D. Luce, *Individual Choice Behavior* (New York: John Wiley and Sons, 1959).

28. See, for example, J. Davidson, P. Supper, and S. Siegel, *Decision-Making: An Experimental Approach* (Stanford, Cal.: Stanford Univ. Pr., 1957).

29. See the section on mathematical applications in decision making later in this chapter.

30. S. W. Bither, *Personality as a Factor in Management Team Decision-Making* (College Park, Pa.: Pennsylvania State Univ., Center for Research of the College of Business Administration, 1971).

31. V. H. Vroom, *Some Personality Determinants of the Effects of Participation* (Englewood Cliffs, N.J.: Prentice-Hall, 1960).

32. J. Block and P. Peterson, "Some Personality Correlates of Confidence, Caution, and Speed in a Decision Situation," *Journal of Abnormal Psychology* 5:34–41 (1959).

33. A. Scodel, P. Ratoosh, and J. S. Winer, "Some Personality Correlates of Decision-Making Under Conditions of Risk," *Behavioral Science* 4:19–28 (1959).

34. L. Festinger et al., *Conflict, Decision, and Dissonance* (Stanford, Cal.: Stanford Univ. Pr., 1964).

35. The so-called principles of administration were enunciated in *Papers on the Science of Administration*, ed. Luther Gulick and Lyndall Urwick, (New York: Institute of Public Administration, Columbia Univ., 1937).

group members; some of these attitudes and values will tend to reinforce organizational norms and prescriptions, while others will lead toward deviations from them.

The historic Hawthorne experiments amply demonstrated the existence of informal cliques within formal organizations and the effects, that the shared attitudes and values of such cliques can have upon worker output, morale, and response to organizational rules.[36] Of particular interest from the standpoint of decision making was the finding that individuals tend to subordinate their thinking to that of the group and compromise to some extent the obligations placed upon them by the organization. Sometimes these compromises stem from informal norms and pressures developed by the work group, norms and pressures that conflict with the rules or expectations of the organization. Tension results when such conflict occurs, and behavior and decision making are then affected, usually adversely, by the influence of stress. Typically, too, such stress leads to decisions that compromise the competing demands of the organization and peer groups—compromises that may adversely affect both rationality and the achievement of organizational objectives.

In addition to peer group influences, individual behavior in decision-making situations is also affected by the individual's own psychological needs and motivations. Psychological needs, first cataloged by A. H. Maslow, range on a continuum from the lowest-level physiological needs to the higher needs for prestige, esteem, and personal intellectual development. According to Maslow, individuals are motivated toward particular actions by their desire to satisfy these needs. People seek first to satisfy the basic physiological needs and work to satisfy the higher-level psychological and intellectual needs only when lower-level needs are fulfilled.[37] Other writers, such as Chris Argyris, build upon Maslow's theories by focusing on the impact of the individual's felt need to "self-actualize."[38] Self-actualization refers to the motivational structure of the individual—the personal goals and satisfactions that each individual sets for himself or herself. Some individuals seek to self-actualize by adopting the organization's goals and values as their own, subsequently seeking to rise

as high as possible within that organizational structure. Other individuals, however, seek employment simply for the purpose of earning money and seek to self-actualize through other organizations, such as the family, the church, or social and civic groups. Still others seek to self-actualize within the organization but find themselves unable to adjust their behavior to the goals and values of the organization, a situation that leads to tension and frustration. Robert Presthus has labeled the first group "upward mobiles," the second group "indifferents," and the third group "ambivalents." He has extensively described the behavior of each kind of person in the organizational setting.[39]

Finally, individual behavior in decision-making situations is also affected by the individual's perception of organizational goals and expectations. Such perceptions are modified by the behavioral factors discussed above—by the individual's psychological needs, personal motivations, and peer group pressures—but to a considerable extent it is also a function of the effectiveness with which the organization has communicated its goals and expectations to its members. In making decisions, individuals are prisoners of the information at their disposal, and their decisions will reinforce organizational values and objectives only to the extent that the individual decision maker is familiar with, and comprehends, those goals and expectations. In point of fact, the type, speed, and mode of decision making within an organization by an individual will be dependent upon the nature of the communication system within the organization. Simon places organizational communication on a parity with employee training as an important determinant of individual behavior in administrative situations, thinking that either is sufficiently important to compensate for deficiencies in the other.[40]

Behavioral Factors in Group Decision Making

Decision making is, in many respects, similar whether the decisions are being made by individuals or by groups of persons. In either case the same basic steps are followed, and the same objectives are pursued. Group decision making differs, however, in that several persons collectively share in the decision-making process. This adds a dimension of human interaction to the process and thus necessarily changes the process's be-

36. F. J. Roethlisberger and William Dickson, *Management and the Worker* (Cambridge, Mass.: Harvard Univ. Pr., 1959).

37. Abraham H. Maslow, "A Theory of Human Motivation," *Psychological Review* 50:370–96 (1943), recently reprinted in *Readings in Managerial Psychology*, ed. Harold Leavitt and L. R. Pondy (Chicago: Univ. of Chicago Pr., 1964), pp. 6–24.

38. Chris Argyris, *Personality and Organization* (New York: Harper and Row, 1957).

39. Robert Presthus, *The Organizational Society* (New York: Vintage Books, 1964).

40. Simon, *Administrative Behavior*, chapter 8, see also Harold J. Leavitt, *Managerial Psychology*, 3d ed. (Chicago: Univ. of Chicago Pr., 1972), pp. 189–207.

havioral context. Leavitt has suggested that group decision making differs from individual decision making in the manner in which decisions are made, kinds of decisions made, problems faced by the group, and the evaluation of the decisions.[41] Such differences are reviewed in the following paragraphs, which focus on the advantages, disadvantages, and procedures of group decision making.

Advantages of Group Decision Making

Decision making by committee has been the object of many jokes in American society, but the fact remains that such decision making does offer several distinct advantages. Not the least of these—particularly in this era of emphasis upon participatory management and diverse representation—is the simple arithmetic fact that group decision making includes more people. Group decision making typically requires discussions of the problem under consideration ranging over some period of time and involves, formally and informally, a number of different persons. This broadened participation is likely to produce a higher level of involvement and satisfaction on the part of the participants and a wider acceptance for the ultimate decision itself among the affected persons. The broader the level of participation in decision making, the higher is the degree of legitimacy likely to be attached to the decision on the part of those who are affected by it.

Second, groups typically have a greater capacity to carry out all the different steps in the decision-making process. As the number of persons added to the decision-making group increases, so too does the range of available perspectives, attitudes, and expertise. Three persons, for instance, are likely to produce a longer list of alternative courses of action than could a single person. Further, the more persons there are involved, the more hands there are to gather and process the necessary information. Finally, the benefits of division of labor and specialization are also more available in group decision-making processes.[42]

Perhaps most important, however, is the probability that the broader blend of backgrounds, experiences, aptitudes, and values available to decision-making groups is likely, at least over time, to produce better decisions. Although most experimental research on decision making has found that individuals are better than groups in terms of speed, efficiency, and accuracy, it has also been found that groups offer a collective judgment that is more likely to arrive at correct decisions (as measured by results), thus supporting the common adage that two heads are better than one.[43]

Anthony Downs, in his study of bureaucracy, has concluded that organizational decision making is distinguished by the greater capacity of an organization to carry out all the major steps in the decision-making process, extensive internal specialization, and the availability of a variety of viewpoints and opinions.[44] Compared to individual decision making, the group process is more likely to produce a decision that is acceptable to more people, and to avoid many of the errors of oversight and omission to which individual judgment is prone.

Finally, group decision making acquires added significance in crisis situations when decisions are required within a relatively short period of time. Most individuals, in fact, seek wide consultation, if not assistance, in decision making when crises occur, not only seeking reinforcement and support for such decisions, but also apparently instinctively seeking the greater reliability of consensus decisions. Further, crises typically produce increased interaction among group members and a decrease in the frictional behavior typically involved in such interaction. Thus, crisis situations tend to reduce some of the dysfunctions of group decision making, such as slowness and difficulty of achieving agreement, while accentuating the importance of its higher reliability.

Disadvantages of Group Decision Making

As might be expected, the advantages of group decision making are not obtained without certain costs. Some of these are quite obvious and have been noted—the process is slower and more costly than individual decision making. Deliberative processes take time and, consequently, involve a commitment of more personnel dollars. Even

41. Leavitt and Pondy, eds., *Managerial Psychology*, p. 279.

42. N. R. F. Maier, "Assets and Liabilities in Group Problem Solving: The Need for an Integrative Function," *Psychological Review* 74 (1967).

43. The following are typical of studies supporting this point of view: M. E. Shaw, "A Comparison of Individuals and Small Groups in the Rational Solution of Complex Problems," *American Journal of Psychology* 44 (1932); R. A. Webber, *Time and Management* (New York: Van Nostrand Reinhold, 1972); I. D. Lorge, J. D. Fox, and M. Brenner, "A Survey of Studies Contrasting the Quality of Group Performance and Individual Performance, 1920–1957," *Psychological Bulletin* 55 (1958).

44. Anthony Downs, *Inside Bureaucracy* (Boston: Little, Brown, 1967), p. 178.

when the group members involved in decision making are salaried officials, there is still a cost involved because the time committed to decision making is time that, alternately, might have been spent on other organizational activities. Related to the time and cost factors, of course, is a commensurate effect on organizational efficiency.

Of more consequence, however, are three other distinct costs related to group or organizational decision making. The first of these is a repression of individual creativity that is likely to occur in response to the inevitable pressures for conformity that are an intrinsic part of any group activity. Group pressures for conformity, furthermore, are most assertive during times of uncertainty and tension, and uncertainty and tension, in some degree, are customarily found in decision-making situations.

Group decision making, moreover, typically requires the development of some kind of a consensus, i.e., a decision can be made only when the members of the group reach agreement on a course of action. Collective agreement, or consensus, is usually based upon compromise. Compromise, in turn, has negative side effects, including:

1. Contentious arguments, problems, questions, and alternatives must be avoided because they raise tension levels and threaten group harmony. Thus, important considerations may be deleted from the decision-making process altogether.
2. Any point of view strongly presented by any member is likely to be accommodated, again to sustain group harmony. This is likely to be true regardless of the relevance or utility of the point of view.
3. The process of compromise increases the possibility that decisions will be made that promote the goals and values of the individual members of the organization rather than those of the organization itself. Certainly the group process of decision making and the inevitable emphasis upon compromise which it entails increase organizational exposure to the values of objectives of the individual members of the organization.
4. Finally, the process of compromise increases the likelihood that decisions will be made that promote the welfare of the organization itself, rather than that of the community being served. In the library, for example, group decision making is likely to lead to decisions that promote the interests of the library staff rather than the interests of library patrons. For instance, group involvement in decisions regarding library hours might produce results that give greater weight to the personal working hour preferences of the staff members than to the convenience of patrons.

Finally, the process of group decision making, emphasizing as it does the need for compromise and harmony, may well substitute satisfaction for rationality as the principal criterion on which decisions are rendered. To the degree that optimum satisfaction and harmony within the group become the principal standard of decision making, the degree of rationality involved in the process will be constrained, with the expected consequent effects upon the overall quality of decision making.

In short, group decision making offers the advantage of producing, on the average, decisions with a greater perceived legitimacy and a better performance record because such decisions encompass a greater range of perspectives and expertise. On the other hand, while such decisions are less prone to be wrong, they are also less likely to achieve excellence because, almost inevitably, they involve elements of compromise and lowered levels of rationality.

Procedures for Group Decision Making

Group decision making typically follows a fairly standardized series of stages. These are:

1. Perception or recognition and interpretation of the problem to be solved. As is the case in any decision-making situation, the manner in which any problem is described and defined sets the tenor of the resulting discussion. This is particularly true in group decision making which, even more than individual decision making, tends to be aggregative and cumulative, with each action building upon the actions that preceded it.
2. Information dissemination—a stage in which the various participants in the decision-making activity share with others the information about the problem at their disposal.
3. A struggle for power typically occurs, in which some or all of the members of the decision-making group seek, consciously or subconsciously, to increase their influence in shaping the ultimate decision.
4. A consensus-building stage in which attempts are made to narrow differences of opinion, produce new alternatives that compromise competing points of view, and identify as many areas of agreement as possible.
5. A control phase, in which efforts are made to promote the acceptance of particular alter-

natives, and pressure is brought to bear upon decision-making participants. This is the point of greatest tension in the process. Attempts at pressure may be overt, or they may merely be tactfully applied. In any event, the conformist tendencies of the group, peer pressure, and the need for collegial harmony all play a most decisive role at this stage of the process.

6. The final stage is the formalization of the decision. Sometimes this takes the form of a motion, formally made and approved by vote. At other times, agreement is noted by the absence of any further dissent.

Needless to say, most of these steps need not be followed in sequential manner, and many of them may be conducted simultaneously.

There are several methods by which individual members of the group may exert power and influence during the course of the decision-making process. Five are worth particular note. First, the person who presents or defines the problem can, by the method of definition, structure subsequent deliberation. Second, information is power, and those who present it, by determining which information to present at what point in time, can substantially affect the course of the decision-making process. Further, special expertise is frequently attributed to those who possess information, and expertise is a frequent basis for influence. Third, skills in intergroup relations can bestow power on their possessors, particularly skill in discussion and debate. Fourth, the person who chairs the decision-making meeting has a substantial potential for influence by virtue of the capacity to guide and direct the discussion and, in the process thereof, to lead the group toward particular kinds of consensus. Finally, a key position of influence goes to the person who, by virtue of sensitivity to evolving attitudes and feelings and with an appropriate sense of timing, can advance compromise suggestions and solutions for group consideration.[45]

Conclusion

Decision making is an administrative activity that requires a blend of technical, behavioral, and political characteristics. Good decisions are central to good administration, but good decisions, in turn, require good information, good leadership, and a cooperative staff as well as sound decision-making methods. Thus, the quality of decision making in an organization is dependent upon many other administrative activities as well. Other sections of this book, and especially those dealing with leadership, communications, and information systems, should be read in light of their impact upon decision-making processes.

Ultimately, the quality of the decisions that are made, including decisions of major consequence as well as the myriad of routine decisions, will determine the quality of a library's services, and that, in turn, plays a major role in setting the level of public support for the library itself.

---

45. For a further discussion of aspects of group decision making, see William J. Gore, "Administrative Decision-Making in Federal Field Offices," *Public Administration Review* 16:281–91 (Autumn 1956). See also R. F. Boles and F. L. Stradlbeck, "Phases in Group Problem Solving," *Journal of Abnormal and Social Psychology* 46:485–95 (1951).

9   Communications

RODERICK G. SWARTZ

Commending. Cajoling. Coaxing. Conversing. But is it communicating? Any administrator spends a large percentage of the day either receiving or imparting information in these various ways. Yet faulty communications are a serious problem in most organizations because the administrator does not understand the communication process. How you document the assertion that administrators do not understand the communication process is important. If the administrators do not understand communication it is because 74 percent feel that they are not controlling adequately or that it is not a problem but only a potential problem.[1]

Any public library administrator responsible for the organization and flow of information services should be expert at the art of communication. But, here also, there is an obvious lack of understanding of what managerial communication is, how this communication network should be organized, what information or data should be communicated and when, and what the responsibilities are for communication at different administrative levels. This chapter will address these questions.

What Is Organizational Communication?

Communication Requires Structure

Managerial communication has been defined in three different ways by management philosophers.[2] The first theory looks at the most effective framework for transmitting information and concerns itself with communication patterns in the organization. The emphasis is on the construction of a communication structure that can carry messages up, down, and throughout the organization. There is interest in how this network changes over a period of time, and how individuals in the organization react to and use the system.

Perhaps because of the librarian's concern with cataloging, networking, and other efforts to organize information flow, library administrators understand this need for a framework or structure. These directors design and maintain an internal communications framework that is well thought out, well publicized, and well organized. It follows the textbook diagrams and involves all oral and written communication, but it fails to take into account the difficulties of the human involvement and the complexities of the messages the human being sends over the framework. These are addressed by theory two.

Communication Is a Function Involving People and Messages

Organizational communication, according to the second theory, is a series of written, oral, and hidden messages, both created by and affecting individuals in the organization.

The important factor is not just a framework, but a *common* framework for communication. One attempts to make some fact, thought, or feeling common to another person or group of persons, but there must be some common background or framework for this communication.

The problem of a common framework based on words is boldly emphasized in Alice's conversation with Humpty Dumpty in *Through the Looking Glass*. Humpty Dumpty explains:

> "There's glory for you!"
> "I don't know what you mean by glory," Alice said.
> Humpty Dumpty smiled contemptuously. "Of course you don't—till I tell you. I meant 'there's a nice knockdown argument for you.'"
> "But glory doesn't mean a nice knockdown argument," Alice objected.

1. R. R. Blake and Jane S. Mouton, *Corporate Excellence through Grid Organization* (Houston: Gulf Publishing, 1968).
2. Richard Farace and Donald McDonald, "New Directions in the Study of Organization Communications," *Personnel Psychology* 17:1–19 (Spring 1974).

"When I use a word," Humpty Dumpty said, in rather a scornful tone, "it means just what I choose it to mean—neither more nor less."[3]

Both participants or groups of participants require some common framework in which to operate. With words as the medium, this may prove very difficult. Even the three-letter slang expression *hey* carries different meanings in different parts of the United States. In the South it serves as a warm form of greeting, whereas in the northern locations it many times precedes a threat or scolding.

Peter Drucker, in his book *Management*, insists there is no communication until the recipient "perceives" what is being communicated. To have a full perception of the communication is to have a *common* frame of understanding.[4]

Organizational communication, to the proponents of the second theory, involves and affects the entire human being. Not only the intellect, but also the emotions, prejudices, fears, and peculiarities are involved. This leads to research into such areas as clarity of message by the sender, the importance of listening, the response of the sender, and other levels of communication besides oral and written. Communication occurs on various levels, and the traditional oral or written communiqué is only a small portion of what is communicated. Gestures, facial expressions, and the manner of sitting or standing project more meaning than words.

Yet many still find this approach lacking. It assumes that the subordinate will feel free to communicate, that the subordinate will know what and when to communicate, and that the administrator will understand what is being communicated.

Communication Develops out of the Proper Climate

A third approach recognizes the common framework and the peculiarities of the sender and the receiver but then goes on to emphasize the very environment in which that communication occurs. Writers who favor this interpretation of organizational communication closely relate the effectiveness of the communication system with the leadership style of the top executive. It is the very climate of the organization that is important.

The "information-sharing" level in an institution is a barometer of management's effectiveness with the staff. The cry of "bad communications" comes only when the administrator is out of touch with the organization.

Administrators who see the importance of the climate of communication are aware of four principles that affect this environment:

1. The library is an artificial social organization made up of a variety of human beings.
2. There are a multiplicity of communication channels in that organization.
3. Information is power, even within the organization.
4. A good communications climate depends on an atmosphere of mutual trust.

The library is a contrived social organization. As such, it is made up of human beings, who are unpredictable souls at best. To make such a tenuous situation work at all, the librarian must be extremely sensitive to the individual human being. The administrator must be aware of the employee's need for making a contribution to the library program, and the resultant need for information about the library. The administrator must also recognize the need for involvement in the social organization, and thus the urge for involvement in the communication process.

The administrator should then be aware that this artificial social organization has a multiplicity of channels for communicating. The administrator may be most at home with downward communications: relaying information, instructions, and ideas to the subordinates in the organization. Three other channels must also be recognized and properly used. (1) Upward communication is the sending of information and attitudes from the firing line up to the top administration. (2) Horizontal communication occurs at all levels below the administrator. It is one administrative level— e.g. middle management—circulating information at its own level in both a formal and an informal manner. (3) Informal communications networks are the most intriguing and are best known by the nickname that grew out of the chaotic Civil War telegraph systems, the grapevine. Each of these channels should be understood and used effectively at the right time.

The director should sense the effect that access to organizational information has on the staff. Librarians are aware that, for a patron, the right information given at the right time in the right manner enhances that patron's power. Studies of information needs of the disadvantaged show that consumer information improves buyer power,

3. Lewis Carroll, *The Annotated Alice: Alice's Adventures in Wonderland and Through the Looking Glass* (London: Harmondsworth and Ringwood, 1966).

4. Peter F. Drucker, *Management: Management, Tasks, Responsibilities, Practices* (New York: Harper and Row, 1974).

and data on government help people control their own future. Yet the same library administrators who are sensitive to these user requirements for information sometimes ignore the information needs of their own employees. Access to information on the job also means power. Being involved within the communication process of the organization means even more power. It means the power to contribute to the organization and to assist one's own personal and professional goals.

Many library administrators are reluctant to release this power to others in the library organization, perhaps fearing a loss in their own influence and effectiveness. The result would actually be the opposite. By enabling individuals at all levels to participate in the organizational thought, the library administration would strengthen the library program. Such involvement not only would allow the employees to control their own individual and professional interests more completely but also would enable them to make a greater impact within the library program.

Studies indicate that the major component needed for a good climate of communication is interpersonal or mutual trust. Each member of the library staff has to be assured that his or her ideas are accepted and that no punishment will occur if these thoughts are out of step with the general thinking in the library.[5]

One recent study looked at the impact of various factors on organizational communication patterns and climate. Above all else, the importance of trust was stressed as a necessary condition to a good communication system. The employee has to believe that an opinion can be freely expressed and that the superior will listen—regardless of whether the superior agrees or not.

This third communication theory—stressing the critical nature of a climate for communications—is the most comprehensive and includes elements of both previous theories. It provides the most complete results, but it is most difficult to initiate and maintain. In developing a communication climate, the administrator must look at the communication problems at the administrative level, at the middle-management level, and at the firing-line level.

The Administrator as Communicator

Any public library administrator, regardless of the size of library, spends more time in communi-

cation than any other person within the organization. The higher one moves in the administrative hierarchy, the less one actually practices librarianship and the more one tends to communicate how the profession ought to be practiced. The director does not give direct reference service at all but discusses with the reference staff how such service should be given, negotiates between reference and technical services on interdepartmental difficulties, and plans new reference services for the future.

Communication about the profession has become more important to the administrator than the actual practice of librarianship. The director may spend 80 to 90 percent of each day in some type of communication mode. Communication becomes the major tool of his professional life. To succeed, he must learn to use the communication system within the library.

The library director's main contacts with the communication system within the library are at three points:

1. Individual contact, mainly with middle management, but periodically with the entire staff
2. Group contact with departments or divisions, temporary groupings such as committees and task forces, and other representatives from the staff
3. Contact with the organization as a whole through written communication, as well as with formal and informal oral statements and contacts.

Contact with Individuals

As with any social organization, there are a multiplicity of communication pathways within the library. The administrator needs to understand the proper use of all these channels, but the first to be perfected should be the upward channel.

Upward communication. Much lip service is given to the upward channel in the communication manuals; yet even in recently published materials, upward communication is still considered largely as feedback. Feedback is certainly important as the final link in the chain of downward communication, but it does not constitute the major function of upward communication.

What does constitute upward communication? What is important enough to flow over these upward channels? What do employees want to say?

They want you to know about their role in the library as they see it, what is satisfactory about this and what needs to be changed. They want to talk about their relationships to others in the organiza-

---

5. Karlene Roberts and Charles A. O'Reilly, "Failures in Upward Communication in Organizations: Three Possible Culprits," *Academy of Management Journal* 17:205–15 (June 1974).

tion. They want you to be aware of how their work interrelates with other jobs in their area of the library. Problems in making the group process work are of special concern to them.

Finally, they want to talk about the library, what it is and what it could be. They want you to be aware of the problems with current library policies and procedures and what is wrong for the library system. They also want to tell you what is going well regarding the policies and procedures outlined. They want to make suggestions about the library's future, what they feel can be accomplished, not only in their own department, but with reference to the library as a whole. They want an involvement with the job and with the work, knowledge of the overall operation, and a sense of "being in on things."[6]

Good news is always readily accepted by the director's office, but what about unpleasant or bad news? When the director hears that the latest policies on interlibrary loan are not working, or that there are personality conflicts in the reference department, or that the recently installed circulation control equipment is not satisfactory, these are most unwelcome facts. How does the administration adjust the climate so that upward communication is stimulated under good *or* bad conditions?

The library director has to understand the individual superior-subordinate relationship with each staff member. This is a complex matter and involves questions of perception, role behavior, listening techniques, and action plans after communication. It requires looking at the situation both from the viewpoint of the employee and from the administration's point of view.

In understanding the employee's attempts at upward communication, the director has to be aware of the employee's motivational traits. What are this person's reasons for being with your particular library? Or, why is this person associated with a library at all? Does he or she agree with your library's philosophy, or is the person simply working there because of geographic restraints or a lack of initiative to move elsewhere? The employer has to attempt to understand the employee's reasons for remaining with the library program, what there is about the job that entices this person to stay rather than to go on to another library or into another field.

The employer has to know what motivates the individual to improve communication. Given weak rapport with the boss and strong incentive to move up in the organization, honest communication may be extremely limited. Given low aspirations, but open rapport with the boss, conversa-

tions may be affable, but not very productive. Given well-directed growth tendencies, plus an open, productive communication link, the results may be phenomenal.

Third, the director has to understand the perception the subordinate has of the library, of colleagues, even of the library director. This perception is influenced by the person's beliefs, prejudices, cultural and personal background, emotions, and other factors. What actually happens is less important in this context than how the employee perceives the situation. How does the employee perceive the director's reaction to problems, difficult situations, mistakes, or even major failures? If the reaction is perceived as punishing, the employee will tend to protect the director from bad news. The upward communication flow is then inhibited. The impact of imparting information, especially bad news, is carefully weighed.

Open upward communication also depends on how employees perceive their role in the organization and the relative amount of knowledge they possess in comparison with colleagues. If the head of acquistions feels fairly secure in the field of computer applications, he or she will be more outspoken with the superior in topics of this nature. If an employee has some background in human relations, then that employee will be more open in deliberations on personnel matters within the department.

These same questions of motivation, role behavior, and perception have to be answered by the library director, too. What factors motivate the administrator on the job? Why did the public library administrator select this occupation? How does the administrator perceive this role in relation to the staff, to the board of trustees, to the city or county administration? One must understand oneself and one's own communication difficulties.

The director may feel an open communication climate is being created when in essence just the opposite is occurring. Argyris points out that "what executives say and how they behave" are many times in conflict and thus create a climate of tension rather than trust. While they talk open communication and input from the ranks, in actual practice they exhibit a style that does everything but encourage a healthy climate for upward communication.[7]

Continuing the self-analysis, the administrator needs to be sure he or she is actually listening to what is being communicated. If the administrator spends four-fifths of the time in communication, a healthy percentage of that time is in listening. In

6. Daniel Katz and Robert Kahn, *Social Psychology of Organizations* (New York: Wiley, 1966).

7. Chris Argyris, "Interpersonal Barriers to Decision Making," *Harvard Business Review* 44:3–15 (March–April 1966).

any interview with an employee, the librarian needs to be sure all aspects of the problem are made clear. The director listens for feelings and emotions as well as for facts and data. Proposed solutions are as important as facets of the problems. One method of maintaining listening interest and ensuring comprehension is to interject a series of questions and summary statements at appropriate intervals. Direct questions can be interspersed with reflective summaries. "Do you really mean...?" or "Do I hear you saying...?" are ways to keep listening and comprehension levels high.

A reliable standard the employee uses to evaluate the administrator's listening ability is to observe whether there is any action or reaction to what is communicated. If there is a problem between departments, the department head who informs the division head of the difficulty wants corrective action; or if the department head recommends recognition for a particular employee, he expects some response from the division head. Listening without any type of follow-up action is worse than not listening at all. It results in a lack of faith in the administration and a jaundiced view of the communication process.

Downward communication. The administrator may generate downward communication as a response to individual upward communication or group discussion, as a follow-up to meetings of policy-making bodies, or as a self-initiated action.

In all of these efforts at downward communication with individuals in the organization, the administrator will use a number of written and oral techniques: appointments, interoffice memoranda, telephone calls, reports, informal visits, and formal letters. To use these skillfully and to best advantage, the library director should be aware that, in most downward communication situations, the most effective technique is oral communication with a written follow-up.[8] On a sensitive personnel matter, an informal visit with the person or persons involved followed by a memorandum to the parties concerned should be most effective. On a matter involving a change in the computer system that affects both internal departments and outside concerns, a telephone call followed by a formal letter would be most effective.

Communication research has also shown that, as the numbers of errors in spelling, punctuation, and grammar in written communication increase, the understanding of the communication and the value attributed to the document and its sender

decrease. Similar results have been found for oral communication.[9]

Individual communication. There will also be times when the director needs to talk individually with persons on a job level that does not usually communicate with the administrator directly. On an informal basis these contacts can be quite pleasant: congratulations on a job well done, a brief visit on avocational matters of mutual interest. On a formal basis, these contacts can be delicate and require the administrator's best skills as a communicator. A major error by a firing-line employee, resulting in bad service or poor public relations, sometimes requires direct discussion between that individual and top administration. Such discussions could be handled on a group or an individual basis, but it is important that everyone in the particular communication line be informed of the results of the discussion.

Communication with Groups

Even if the administrator has developed good communication channels with individuals in the library organization, little or no attention may be given to communication with groups. Such communication extends to the team of middle managers directly below the administrator, to committees, to task forces, and even to experimentation with the process of participatory administration.

Group communication in libraries has become increasingly important for several reasons. First, as libraries have grown more complex, time has dictated that more of the administrator's day be spent with groups rather than with individuals. Second, smart administrators have discovered that the contributions of many minds to a problem or decision result in a stronger program for the library. As an illustration, the clerical staff member working in audiovisual services sees things from quite a different vantage point than the director and therefore makes a different contribution to the solution. Third, management authorities, such as Herzberg, Likert, and Argyris,[10] have repeatedly pointed out that employees who are involved in the communi-

---

8. Dale A. Level, "Communication Effectiveness, Method and Situation," *Journal of Business Communication* 10:19–25 (Fall 1972).

9. B. S. Greenberg and E. Razinsky, "Some Effects of Variations in Message Quality," *Journalism Quarterly* 43:486–92 (1966). See also G. Miller and M. Hewgill, "The Effect of Variations in Non-fluency on Audience Ratings of Source Credibility," *Quarterly Journal of Speech* 50:36–44 (1964).

10. See Chris Argyris, *Integrating the Individual and the Organization* (New York: Wiley, 1964); Frederick Herzberg, *Work and the Nature of Man* (Cleveland: World Publishing, 1966); and Rensis Likert, *The Human Organization: Its Management and Value* (New York: McGraw-Hill, 1967).

cation process, especially as it affects their own job, are more highly motivated and generally happier employees. Fourth, with more sophisticated service patterns caused by pressures such as new client demands and new technological advances, it becomes less and less likely that the administrator will have all of the answers. The director will need to rely more and more on groups of specialists on the staff.

The group process. Perhaps one reason the group communication process is so difficult for the average American administrator is that it is alien to the administrative process traditional in the United States. In the American tradition, decisions are made and solutions are found on a quick, decisive one-to-one basis. To involve more people only means more time consumed, the danger of personality conflicts, and confusion over who is responsible for what.

Japan, on the other hand, has proven the importance of group process in administration. There the emphasis is upon defining the question rather than securing an immediate answer. Hours may be spent in the group process where the problem is thoroughly analyzed and attention is focused on various approaches and alternatives. When a decision is reached, those who will help execute that decision have been involved in the process and have communicated their thinking on the issue.[11]

U.S. management philosophers now point to the importance of group communication as a major component in effective leadership patterns. Writers from the human relations school of management, such as Likert and Argyris, stress that successful group interchange strengthens the organization's program and the individual's participation in that program.[12]

Administrators who are adept at communicating with employees on an individual basis are many times at a loss when working with staff groups. The various techniques discussed for successful group work can be summarized in a simple set of rules. Following are five steps that outline an effective approach to group communication.

1. Understand the problem or topic for discussion. Make sure that everyone present understands all ramifications and has all questions clarified and that the group is agreed in its interpretation of the problem.

2. Analyze the problem or topic. Find the documentation needed to begin to form alternative solutions. If these facts are not available within the group, immediate attempts should be made to secure expertise from outside the group.

3. Formulate different solutions. Here different answers should be outlined and dissent encouraged rather than discouraged.

4. Select the best solution.

5. Follow up to implement the decision. A firm understanding is required about who does what when to implement the results of the group process. Many times the first four steps are followed, but this last crucial step is omitted.

The key to the group process is dissent, and this is probably the reason many administrators shy away from this process as a communication technique. Too many times dissent is viewed by an administrator as a destructive force used outside of the formal communication channels. However, dissent in group communication actually strengthens the library system by allowing a greater diversity of solutions to its various problems. It strengthens the individuals involved by stimulating their creative ability and their belief in their own power to contribute to the organization and to understand the thought processes of coworkers. When constructive dissent is encouraged within the communication system of the library, and especially via the group process, the result is a more vibrant, healthy library atmosphere.

The administrator and the management team. The first group the administrator has to communicate with is the management team. This is the group of department or division heads who, along with the director and perhaps the assistant or associate director, form the management in most public libraries. As a group, the management team presents certain communication problems to the administrator that individual communication with these same people does not.

The administrator must be aware of many of the problems of perception, role behavior, job motivation, and other factors that are important in one-to-one communication. In addition, the leader must also be aware of the communication interrelationships within the group and top management's particular relationship to the group as a whole.

To understand the communication potential of the management team, the librarian must know how long this group has worked together, to what degree mutual trust is offset by interdepartmental or interdivisional rivalries, and what the level of

11. Richard Tanner Johnson and William G. Ouchi, "Management in America—Japanese Style," *Washington Post*, November 3, 1974.

12. Argyris, *Integrating the Individual*, and Likert, *Human Organization*.

group support is when agreement is reached. The director also needs to be cognizant of how the group responds during periods of difference and dissent. Each of these factors will tell the administrator how willingly the group will communicate on any issue.

The administrator must be sensitive to the special relationship of the leader to the group. When all communication tends to flow through the leadership position, the communication pattern is what communication theorists call a "wheel." The department or division heads are spokes of the wheel who communicate through the hub of the wheel, the director. It is a communication system where each person's role is clear and matters are dispatched with speed and accuracy—but the group's creativity and ability to change things are not given high priority.[13]

Satisfaction within the group is minimal with the exception of the hub of the communication system, the library director. Here satisfaction is quite high. However, the library director should be aware that a communication pattern that may be highly satisfactory to the leader is not necessarily satisfying to other individuals within the group.

Some administrators have realized this situation and looked to a more participatory type of communication pattern with their management teams. In this case, decisions are made on a group basis, and the discussions that precede the decision also involve more group interchange and involvement. From a communication standpoint, this type of administrative pattern has both strengths and weaknesses. Its success depends on attributes of both director and group, including personality, patience, and understanding of the communications process. The management team, where decisions are reached by the participatory or group process, forms a "circle" system of communication. That is, as a decision is reached or a topic discussed, communication moves rather freely throughout the entire group without the direct control of the administrator. Studies have shown that this type of communication system produces high creativity within the group, a strong feeling of being able to contribute to the solution, and therefore, a high level of individual and group satisfaction. From the viewpoint of speed and accuracy, this type of process is much more inefficient than the "wheel." The public library director, therefore, has to weigh the advantages and to determine which communication technique to use with the management team.

---

13. G. K. Ready, *The Administrator's Job: Issues and Dilemmas* (New York: McGraw-Hill, 1957).

Beyond that, the director needs to decide when to use the group process and when to stay with individual communication. For subjects that require quick decisions, involve substantial expertise beyond that available in the group, or involve factors that cannot be controlled by the group or sometimes even the administrator, the one-to-one communication is still more desirable. Problems of an interdivisional nature or long-range fulfillment of program objectives are subjects more appropriate to the group process.

The administrator and teams throughout the organization. Two temporary group communication systems that have been used frequently by administrators are the committee and the task force. The committee uses a more traditional communication system than the task force, which involves elements of a participatory communication system.

The committee is a group communication process whereby several employees are assigned investigatory or fact-finding responsibility on a well-defined issue. They usually report the findings to the director or someone else designated by the administration. From a communications viewpoint, this is a temporary "wheel" network controlled to a great extent by the individual to whom it is responsible. It allows formal group communications to function within the library, but with well-defined restrictions.

The task force provides another example of formal group communications below the management level. In this sistuation, a task force is given an assignment, assured of the expertise to do the job, and then given some responsibility for implementing the decision or solution it generates. For the time being, the task force becomes a semiautonomous communication system with the organization. The task force is an example of diagonal communication because it draws expertise from all levels within the organization. It is a temporary communications group that cuts through all hierarchies in the library.

In a progressive public library, a task force might be called together to examine the impact of telecommunications on public library service. The group could consist of representatives from audiovisual service, extension service, the business office and the administration, together with outside experts. This type of temporary, semiautonomous communication network is strongly recommended by management theoreticians for organizations facing rapid change in such areas as new technology and changing client requirements. Its use as a temporary communication system in the public library should therefore be explored.

Contact with the Total Organization

Beyond the individuals and groups within the library, the director has to be consistently in touch with the library staff on a systemwide basis. The staff must recognize that the administration is aware of and concerned with activities in their area of the library and that the director keeps in contact with the problems and progress within each area. However, it is harder to keep in touch with the total organization than to maintain individual or group contacts. As the library grows larger, the administration becomes more and more isolated. Both director and staff begin to feel this isolation unless the library administrator takes steps to correct the situation. This can be accomplished through a variety of written and oral communication techniques and, in many cases, simple nonverbal devices.

The procedure of staying in touch with a total organization is a difficult one that becomes even more awkward as the organization grows larger. In the smaller library it is possible to keep these contacts informal, depending mainly on oral contacts. In the larger metropolitan library such communication must depend to a larger extent on such written contact as memoranda and newsletters.

Conciseness and consistency are two important criteria for written communication meant for the entire staff. Time is limited throughout the organization, and written notices, memoranda, and newsletters should make their point in one or two pages. Patterns of written communication should remain consistent. If the director chooses to send a memo after each board meeting, these should be issued regularly. The staff adjusts to a pattern of communication, and deviations from that pattern cause apprehension and rumor.

Continuing oral and visual contact with even a large public library system should be maintained. Without the appearance of the librarian in parts of the library other than the administrative area, or without the opportunity to visit from time to time with the director on a face-to-face basis, the staff begins to feel the "people upstairs" are simply not in touch with the real activities of the library. This means being in the various divisions, holding some staff sessions there instead of always in the director's area. It means making the opportunity to visit with staff members on an informal basis. It means the scheduling of regular, librarywide staff meetings on a yearly or half-yearly basis to air current issues and problems. The director of the larger library must not become wrapped in a paper communication system that allows no personal contact with the total organization.

In keeping this oral contact with the total organization, the director often overlooks one of the major channels within the library: the grapevine. This informal communication system is the fastest information network in the library, even if it is not the most accurate.

The grapevine is very difficult to trace since it does not follow any official lines. And, because each person in the chain tells several other persons, you have a cluster effect that is difficult to follow. To further complicate matters, one person may be involved in several of these clusters, and at various levels from the center of the cluster. A typical grapevine is shown in figure 9.1.

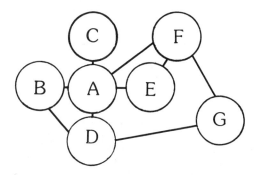

Fig. 9.1. A typical grapevine communication system

The grapevine should not be ignored by the administration but should be considered a major communication link. Researchers have found the presence of grapevine activity to be an indication of the library's vigor as an organization. In fact, a library director should be concerned if a grapevine is absent or excludes the director. Top management should even use the grapevine.

To use grapevines (there may be several distinct vines in the library), the director needs to identify those persons who are near the center of the cluster. These people may or may not have an influential place in offical communication channels. They are usually individuals who, because of their personality and nature, become the hub of a grapevine cluster.

If connected properly, the informal channel is an excellent means to obtain honest feedback. If incorrect rumors are circulated, they can be quickly clarified through regular channels. The grapevine can also be used by the administration to send information throughout the organization on an informal basis. For example, if there is general laxity on a policy or rule in an area in the library, corrective suggestions can be put out on the grapevine, perhaps eliminating the need for more severe measures of a more formal nature.

What to communicate on formal channels is sometimes as difficult to decide as what to send on the grapevine. Generally, staff want to be aware of all policy decisions, new or revised, made by the board of trustees and the administration. Special attention is given to all types of personnel decisions. The staff are concerned how these decisions will affect their jobs. A high regard is held for rumors picked up on the grapevine, and personnel are anxious for a confirmation or denial from the librarian's office.

The administration meanwhile tends to view organizational communication with a different perception and loads the channels with information of high relevance to it, but of relatively low importance to staff members. The administration ignores, at the same time, information of high interest to the staff. The fact that the Friends of the Library has secured a nationally known author for its annual banquet is of less concern to staff than that the same group is recognizing a well-liked staff member of twenty years' service.

By the use of feedback, the administrator begins to understand the priorities that need to be placed on this downward channel to the total organization. In a good communication climate, securing feedback from the library is no problem. It comes to the director in upward communication through individual conversations and group sessions. Additional feedback is gathered through the grapevine.

The director may also tend to confuse priorities other than those of content. The relative importance of internal and external communication is an illustration. All policy-making sessions of the governing body are generally attended by the press. Many times press communication networks are more effective than the one within the library. As a result, personnel appointments, pay raises, new buildings, or exciting program developments reach the general public prior to announcement to the staff. Such news must reach the staff first. Many library administrators use a series of group meetings or one-page memoranda to counter this problem. Nothing is more demoralizing to a staff, or more detrimental to internal communications, than for library personnel to obtain library news from TV or the newspaper.

The problem also arises of how much to communicate with the total staff on questions of a delicate nature. In the case of a patron questioning certain books and magazines in the library collection, how much should the staff know? This is a question of a totally open communication system versus a "need-to-know" system. The former relays practically all delicate information to the staff, with the exception of personnel matters where

someone would be harmed or embarrassed by the release of such information. Directors who firmly believe in the "need-to-know" theory feel information flow is adequate when the various staff members have enough data to accomplish their jobs. Proponents of a good climate for communication stress the importance, not only of open upward communication, but also of total downward communication and would encourage open communication, even on delicate issues.

Another crucial content problem is the communication of change to the total library organization. Administrators who are responding to new service demands and patterns may find that the staff have a great investment in the past and are reluctant to give up the more traditional methods. For example, a sociologist interviewed the staff of one library about new service trends. The staff insisted that these new programs took them away from the "real work."[14]

When trying to introduce new forms of "real work" to the library, the administrator may encounter severe difficulty. The lack of information about some new innovation makes the staff uncertain. Yet, an attempt to provide such facts may meet severe communication blocks, so that the data are relayed in limited form or not at all. Staff members tend to process familiar parts of the message immediately but to delay the unfamiliar, and this filtering process plays havoc with the introduction of change.

To overcome this roadblock, the administrator has to understand who are more receptive to change in the organization and how their enthusiasm can envelop the entire group. Early converts to innovation tend to be younger, less dogmatic and rigid, involved in more specialized operations, or have status within the organization. In other words, they could come from any area in the library. While these people often depend on regional and national sources for information, they tend to become opinion leaders for later converts who depend more on local, personal sources of information.[15]

This should indicate to the director the types of communication patterns important when the message is one of change. First, the group process would be excellent. It would involve early adopters with laggards in the planning and communicating of change. Next, the informal channel is impor-

---

14. Nancy G. Feldman, "Pride in Heritage, or Resentment? A Sociologist Analyzes Library Staff Reaction," *Wilson Library Bulletin* 46:436–40 (January 1972).

15. Everett M. Rogers, *Diffusion of Innovations* (New York: Free Press, 1962).

tant here, because the opinions of peers are important to those late to adapt to new ideas. Finally, because of the importance of personal influence, face-to-face two-way communication throughout the organization is important. Instead of using old-fashioned communication techniques to relay new ideas, the director needs to update his communication patterns as well.

Middle Management in Communication

The administration of any public library needs to be aware of the frustrating position in which middle management is placed with regard to the library's communication system. Middle management is at the switching point in the network where the upward channel crosses the downward channel. Studies have shown that the most frustrating position in any communication network is the middle position in a chain; as shown in figure 9.2.

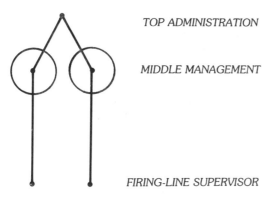

TOP ADMINISTRATION

MIDDLE MANAGEMENT

FIRING-LINE SUPERVISOR

Fig. 9.2. A typical communication chain

Unfortunately this is the most typical communication system in public libraries. The administrator therefore needs to be extremely sensitive to these pressures in order to secure an open climate of communication at all levels.

Besides the position in which middle management finds itself, several other factors could serve as potential barriers to the communication flow through this level. These include problems of physical distance, distortion (especially through personal conflict with the program), and communication overload.

Geographic distance is a continuing communication problem in any public library system that consists of a central facility plus an extension net-

work scattered throughout the jurisdiction served. Branch librarians in charge of their buildings tend to acknowledge their distance from the central library, making decisions and taking actions a department head within the central facility would not think of doing independently. In such cases, both up and down channels are not used effectively either by the extension personnel or by the administration to whom they are responsible.

Another type of distance problem may be encountered by the middle manager regardless of location because of the type of work habits of the administration or middle management. If either party tends to be hard to contact, is inaccessible during work hours, or makes appointments and cancels them, the communication flow gradually dries up. The information system may start as an excellent combination of oral followed by written communication, proceed to written communication of decreasing quality, and then deteriorate into no communication.

To overcome this distance factor, the director and middle management have to be sure that accessibility is assured. This means the director must respond to messages at some point during the day of receipt, even though involved in community activities outside the building. Or, if the system is large enough, such communication may be handled by an assistant director for day-to-day operations. One way or another, day-to-day contact must be kept between middle management and the administration despite the distance factor.

As messages are passed from person to person up and down the network, their content tends to become altered. This is called distortion. Part of the distortion factor is unintentional, another portion is probably subconscious, and sometimes a minor part may be intentional. Unintentional distortion results because it is virtually impossible to relay information from one individual to another without slightly changing the content. The result of the game of whispering stories through a line of children illustrates this factor.

More serious is the subconscious distortion of fact. Usually this occurs when the relaying party would like to cast an incident in a more favorable personal light. In describing an incident between the reference department and the technical services department, the head of the reference department may subconsciously distort the incident to cast that department in a more favorable light. Less frequent, though extremely serious, is the deliberate changing of facts to give a different interpretation to an incident or a problem. If this type of communication problem occurs in a library on a continuing basis, it warrants disciplinary action.

The more frequent problems of unintentional and subconscious distortion require correction by the use of good communication practices. These types of distortion can be lessened by the use of oral followed by written communications, the availability and use of multiple channels, and the awareness of where distortion might occur on a particular subject.

Many times the reason for poor communication is the clogging of the network with too much information. This type of log jam is heightened by the continued release of information from various units and levels within the library. This results in overloading the system with messages, and the system collapses of its own weight, usually at a sensitive switching point such as middle management. When the load becomes too much to bear, errors of various types begin to appear. There are delays in the transmission of important information, which when it is transferred includes errors of fact or unintentional deletion of certain material.

The combined efforts of the administration and the middle management are required to correct such a situation. Top administration needs to be sure that information sent from the top is high priority and is delivered in a succinct form. Memoranda should be kept to two pages maximum, while appointments and group sessions should be properly scheduled. Middle management, in turn, should see that information moving up and throughout the system has high priority for the well-being of the library program and of the individuals developing that program.

In summary, middle managers are situated at a key location in the communication system. They are responsible for relaying information both up and down the network. Because of their importance as switching points, problems such as communication overload, distortion, and physical distance are extremely troublesome at this administrative level. To overcome these difficulties, the library administration and middle management need to:

1. Be aware of the individual's subconscious effort to color the message to his benefit.
2. Develop a communication schedule that allows for regular and frequent communication contacts between levels within the library, and includes a mechanism for emergency contacts.
3. See that the size of oral and written message units is kept manageable and that the correct priority is given to those units.
4. Use multiple formats in communication, remembering that in most cases oral followed by written is the most effective.

The Firing-Line Staff and Communication

The staff who work on the firing line give service to the public, process information for delivery, and also present unique challenges in creating a good climate for communication. These challenges need to be recognized and met.

The communication process at the firing line is perhaps the most difficult for the library director because of the following factors. This group is the most distant from the director in both the organizational hierarchy and physical distance. In modern and large-sized public libraries, it is a much larger group than middle management and consists of several hierarchical layers in itself. One area in a large library might have a professional supervisor, professional staff, library assistants and/or technicians, as well as clerical personnel. It is at this level that the formal and informal communication systems are most frequently in competition with each other. In libraries with poor communication patterns, it is difficult for the firing line to sort out the true, false, and partly correct messages coming from the grapevine and a poor downward channel.

The librarian must look at the various communication channels and see how they operate at this level. Upward communication again is of prime importance. This level of staff many times consists of young professionals recently graduated from library school as well as library assistants and clericals who are either interested in the field or working in the library while securing an education in a related field. They are overflowing with ideas about service programs, bibliographical control techniques, extension patterns, and administrative practices. These are innovative, creative, or sometimes impractical ideas. Nevertheless, an honest appraisal of these contributions would strengthen the system, and their exposure upward through the formal communication system would certainly improve human relationships within the library.

All previous problems discussed come into play at this level in the hierarchy, and it requires real skill by the administration to keep upward channels open. As an illustration, the beginning professional many find his or her supervisor or middle manager unimpressed with such contributions. These managers may see such contributions as a threat to their position, and either distort or altogether "forget" such communication. Either the staff member blames the administration as nonresponsive, or the middle manager is recognized as the culprit. Then the young quietly withdraw in resentment or turn their communication toward a supervisor in another division or department who is responsive to new ideas. While this releases the pressure on the young firing-line professional, the message—when and if it is communicated upward—more than likely becomes even more distorted than if it had come from the professional's direct supervisor. Or the young professional leaves the library system. In any of these cases, the library system "loses" a good employee.

Communication blockage between staff and supervisor will always exist in an organization, because of personality differences if for no other reason. The administrator's concern is to keep it to a minimum and encourage the use of formal upward paths. This can be done by building self-assured middle managers with good communications practices. Diagonal communication, such as the task force, also allows an outlet for this type of communication. Finally, the administrator needs to know intimately the organization's communication network to see where bottlenecks are developing and correct the situations before they become problems.

The downward flow can be equally as troublesome when extended over this many levels in the organization. Communication is again filtered, distorted, and sometimes not relayed at all. Each level within the library judges that less and less is of importance and/or interest to subordinates. Therefore, the administrator is never sure if the message reached the firing line, and if it did, what reactions to the message were.

A feedback program is therefore important to the administration. If such a program is not instigated by the top level administration, unrest and confusion can simmer for weeks before it erupts and is called forcefully to the administration's attention. The following feedback techniques might be utilized:

1. Written feedback on statements by the administration
2. The maintenance of oral contact throughout the entire operation
3. A proper connection with the informal network
4. An established pattern that allows direct access to the administration by anyone in the organization if other channels have been blocked.

All of these methods allow the librarian to assess the depth to which information has penetrated in the organization, and what the reactions are.

Many harried administrators sum up the above feedback process with the old adage, my door is always open. While the door may be open, the administrator is usually gone, out in the community, or off to a statewide meeting. If the office is occupied, it is a steady whirl of appointments, meetings, and dictation. Even in the best of climates, it takes a fairly sturdy soul to make the break into that busy schedule. An open door policy is only one minor approach to feedback and a rather ineffectual one at that. It must be buttressed by the many other approaches discussed in order to have a true climate for communication.

Another communication network is most active at this level: the horizontal chain or network. From the middle management on down to the clerical, there is communication of both a professional and a social nature among colleagues at each administrative level. At each level, but more so at the firing level, this horizontal system is liable to become overbalanced in favor of informal communication and to become just a cluster within the grapevine rather than another informal communication network. It is the administrator's responsibility that the formal portion of this chain is maintained. Groups at various levels should be charged with communication functions relating to the operations within that area: problem solving, scheduling, coordination, and evaluation.

Horizontal communication networks exist in a library without the sanction of the administration. Unless they are channeled to constructive tasks, they become a communication defect.

The Perfect Communication System

The library administration can be almost baffled by the challenge of constructing a workable network of interconnecting channels marked upward, downward, and horizontal. The director then envisions these wavelengths being constantly scrambled by distortion, overload, role behavior, and perception; he questions whether the perfect communication system can ever be attained.

More to the point is whether the perfect communication network exists, and if it does, would the library director want it installed in the public library? Both questions must be answered in the negative. Because the components in the network are human, there is little chance for perfection. Nor would it be desirable, even if possible. Even in the most personal of relationships, complete, continuing open communication would destroy that relationship.

The best to hope for is a system that is 90-percent effective. While not perfect, it is a system that recognizes the need for a climate of communication. To create this climate, upward, horizontal,

and informal channels are given as much importance as the downward channel. Group communication is given as much attention as one-to-one
interchanges. Communication roadblocks are recognized as inevitable challenges that occur in any
social organization made up of human beings. It is
a system that allows for change within its own
structure and lets messages of change flow freely
through its network. It is a system that depends on
the best communication and interpersonal skills of
the top administration.

10 Personnel Procedures and Practices

BYRON COOPER

Thomas G. Spates, a former vice-president of General Foods Corporation, defined personnel administration as

> organizing and treating individuals at work so that they will get the greatest possible realization of their intrinsic abilities, thus attaining maximum efficiency for themselves and their group, and thereby giving to the enterprise of which they are part its determining competitive advantage and its optimum results.[1]

The public library is no different from General Foods in this respect. If nothing else, they have in common the fact that they both employ people, and the success of the organization is dependent upon the performance of its employees. The public library should be looked upon as a competitive organization. Even if it is the only agency in town providing library service, it must compete for the time of its patrons. A library with declining circulation figures may find it difficult to compete with other governmental agencies for public funds. The well-run organization will have the competitive advantage, and sound personnel policies and procedures will foster the success of the organization.

Selection

Although it is assumed that the library is a going concern, the first logical step in developing the organization is staffing. Staffing is a two-step process—recruitment and selection—that requires somewhat different standards for professional and clerical staffs.

In a sense, much of the work in recruiting professionals has already been done for the library. State and national library associations, schools, guidance counselors, and other librarians have already directed people into the profession. The individual library plays a more subtle role in the recruitment effort. It must show the prospective librarian that the profession offers rewarding career opportunities and that a library is a good place to work.

Assuming that the minimum educational requirement for a professional librarian is a graduate degree in library science, the available labor force is well-defined. Frequently, with state or local regulations requiring that the librarian's graduate degree be from a program accredited by the American Library Association, the labor force is even more narrowly defined. It is logical, then, that the first source for recruiting professional librarians would be the library schools.

Virtually all library school students have access to a professional placement service, either within the library school itself or as part of a general placement service in the university. These placement services make job openings known to students currently enrolled in the school or, in some cases, to alumni via placement bulletins. They frequently operate as a clearinghouse, making available resumés, transcripts, and letters of recommendation. A library school placement director will probably make some attempt to know personally the students using the service. Such a person can be in a better position than a general placement service to direct the recruiter to specific individuals rather than to a file of resumés.

In addition to the placement services offered by the library schools, there are a number of other such services throughout the country, all with varying degrees of competency. The largest placement service for professional librarians is the National Registry for Librarians, a service administered by the Illinois State Employment Service under the direction of the U.S. Department of Labor. The registry receives notices of job openings from libraries throughout the United States and matches them with applications from librarians. Information about the applicant is then sent to the library, which has the responsibility for making the initial contact with the applicant. The registry prescreens the applicants according to certain selection criteria as instructed by the library. These criteria include geographic preference, educational background, years of experience, minimum sal-

---

1. Thomas G. Spates, *An Objective Scrutiny of Personnel Administration*, Personnel Series, no. 75 (New York: American Management Association, 1944), p. 9.

109

ary requested, and type of library and type of position preferred. This service is free to both the applicant and the library. In addition to this full-time placement activity, the registry operates a placement service at the annual and midwinter meetings of the American Library Association, where it allows applicants to browse through listings of available positions and helps recruiters arrange interviews with interested applicants.

Other free placement services are available through many state libraries or state library associations. The former are generally restricted to filling positions in public or school libraries within the state. They are not full-time operations and are not commonly known to job hunters. For these reasons, they are not an effective means of recruiting, except as a supplement to some other source. State library associations have developed "hotline" telephone job information services. Callers listen to a recorded message that describes jobs available within the state and gives information about application procedures. The success of such ventures depends upon the support each receives from libraries within the state.

In addition to the above services, librarians are frequently placed through private employment agencies. These agencies require that a fee be paid, generally 10 percent of the starting annual salary, when an applicant is hired. Because public libraries are generally prohibited from spending funds for employment agencies, it is up to the applicant to pay the fee. This will definitely discourage many qualified applicants from using the service. In choosing a private employment agency, care should be taken to determine that the agency is capable of recruiting and selecting qualified applicants. There are some private agencies that deal exclusively with librarians; they frequently advertise in the professional journals. These agencies also have the advantage of being known to a wide number of interested individuals. Reliable private employment agencies are desirable because they free the recruiter from all the preliminary steps of selection. The agency carries out all recruitment activities and screens out all unqualified applicants. In most states, employment agencies are regulated by statutes and required to be licensed by an office of the state department of labor. That office should be consulted if there are any questions about the reliability or integrity of the employment agency.

Because, for a number of reasons, many professional librarians do not use placement services, it is necessary to inform them of job openings in another manner. All the major library journals

carry classified advertising, and for a few dollars the library could place a description of the job before thousands of librarians. When advertising a vacancy in the professional journals, it is important to describe the job with great accuracy. Minimum qualifications should be clearly spelled out. This practice will tend to spare the administrator from poring through applications from underqualified or overqualified individuals. It is important that the advertisement not overglamorize the position or make promises that cannot be kept. Such practices will later result in bad feelings among staff.

A commonly used method of recruiting is the grapevine. When a position falls vacant, the recruiter notifies his friends and colleagues who either may be interested in the position themselves or may know of people who are interested. Although the library may consistently obtain good people through such a method, it will never know if there are better-qualified individuals who have not been considered because they do not know about the position.

Recruitment procedures, however, must comply with the requirements of Title VII of the Civil Rights Act of 1964, as amended by the Equal Employment Opportunity Act of 1972, which makes illegal discrimination in employment because of race, color, religion, sex, or national origin[2] (although in some instances, religion, sex or national origin may be a bona fide occupational qualification where justified by strict business necessity). The Equal Employment Opportunity Commission (EEOC) was established to ensure compliance with Title VII and to investigate complaints of employment discrimination. Title VII covers all private employers, state and local governments, educational institutions, labor organizations, and public and private employment agencies with fifteen or more employees or members.

Under the requirements of Title VII, recruitment cannot be undertaken in such a manner as to perpetuate past discriminatory practices. A notice or advertisement relating to employment opportunities cannot indicate a preference based on race, color, religion, sex, or national origin except in those cases where religion, sex, or national origin is a bona fide occupational qualification.[3] Word-of-mouth recruitment has been condemned by the courts as tending to perpetuate the characteristics of the existing work force,[4] although

---

2. 42 U.S.C. §2000e (Supp. V 1975).

3. See 29 C.F.R. §1604.5 (1976); Hailes v. United Air Lines, 464 F.2d 1006 (5th Cir. 1972).

4. EEOC v. Detroit Edison Co., 515 F.2d 301, 313 (6th Cir. 1975); Long v. Sapp, 502 F.2d 34 (5th Cir. 1974); Rowe v. General Motors Corp., 457 F.2d 348, 359 (5th Cir. 1972); Parham v. Southwestern Bell Tel. Co., 433 F.2d 421, 427 (8th Cir. 1970).

such practices have been held valid in the absence of a showing of previous discrimination.[5]

It has been shown that, because the professional librarian job market is national in scope, it is necessary to carry on recruitment activities on a national level. The nonprofessional labor market, on the other hand, is local in nature. Hence recruitment activities must be adjusted. Unless the position is exceptionally difficult to fill, it is not normally necessary to work through a private employment agency. State employment service offices are frequently in a position to refer qualified applicants. A second approach, which is more desirable for broad coverage, is to advertise in the local newspaper. Again, it is necessary to state the minimum qualifications for the position. Perhaps the only position that rarely needs to be recruited is that of page. High school students frequently look to the library as a source of employment after school hours and during the summer. Applicants will commonly be students who spend much time in the library and are known to the library staff. Should it become difficult to fill a page position, it would be advisable to contact the librarian or guidance counselor at the neighboring high schools.

Recruitment

Given the current excess supply of labor within the library profession,[6] it is probable that there will be many qualified applicants for each open position. The administrator must then, through some method or combination of methods, select the applicant best suited for the position. The selection decision is generally based upon the administrator's prediction of the applicant's success on the job. Each prediction may result in one of two kinds of errors. A *false positive* error results when an individual placed on a job later fails; in this case, a positive outcome (success) was predicted and failed to materialize. A *false negative* error results when an inaccurate prediction of a negative outcome (failure) prevents the job placement of an individual who could have been successful.[7]

The most widely used method of selection is the employment interview. The usefulness of the interview as a selection tool depends solely upon the skill of the interviewer. An interview must be planned so that the interviewer can obtain sufficient information in three areas that are basic to

selection. The interviewer must assess the qualifications of the applicant in greater depth than they appear on the application blank or resumé. Using the application blank as a guide, the interviewer may mentally develop a chronology of the applicant's education and work experience. He may ask the applicant about minor periods of unemployment, reasons for leaving previous employers, and details about previous work experience.

Secondly, the interviewer may assess the appearance and expression of the applicant and note those characteristics that are related to job success. The applicant being interviewed for a public service job should have good physical appearance, a pleasing voice, proper diction, a broad vocabulary, and a general ability to communicate orally. It may be necessary for the institution to develop standards and judge each applicant by the same standards.

The third aspect of the interview is the deportment of the interviewee. The interviewer should note the applicant's poise, self-assurance, manner, and other traits that will allow the interviewer to infer whether the applicant is outgoing, respectful, considerate, and so forth. It is obvious that these inferences will be based on first impressions, but improving the skill of the interviewer will result in increasing the reliability of these impressions.

An interview is a two-sided exchange of information. The interviewer must remember that the job, in turn, must be sold to the ideal candidate. The interviewer's own appearance and deportment have a bearing on this aspect of the process, and the applicant needs enough information to make an intelligent decision about the job.[8]

There are two basic interview techniques that have been used in selection interviewing. The structured or directive interview requires the interviewer to plan specific questions prior to the actual interview. Often the interviewer will ask questions from a printed form and note the applicant's responses directly on the form, either during the interview or immediately following. Other structured interviews allow the interviewer to word the questions spontaneously, but the areas to be covered are established in advance. The structured interview has the advantage of lending standardization to interviews where more than one interviewer is meeting with different candidates. On the other hand, this method has the disadvantage of

5. Taylor v. Safeway Stores, Inc., 524 F.2d 263, 272 (10th Cir. 1975).

6. See, for example, Carol L. Learmont and Richard L. Darling, "Placements and Salaries," *Library Journal* 102:1345 (June 15, 1977).

7. Marvin D. Dunnette, *Personnel Selection and Placement*, Behavior Science in Industry Series (Belmont, Cal.: Wadsworth, 1966), p. 7.

8. Felix M. Lopez, Jr., *Personnel Interviewing: Theory and Practice* (New York: McGraw-Hill, 1965), pp. 240–42.

not transmitting all the necessary information because of its lack of flexibility.[9] The structured interview is frequently used by civil service systems where an oral examination is used as a selection criterion.

The nondirective interview is a device originally used in psychotherapy and counseling. This approach allows the candidate to control the interview with the interviewer reacting to the statements of the candidate. It enables the interviewer to explore areas in the candidate's background not known to the interviewer prior to their meeting. Much of this information, however, may be irrelevant to the employment decision. For this reason, the interviewer should combine structured techniques with the nondirective techniques so as to explore the candidate's background but at the same time obtain the necessary information for an employment decision.[10]

A technique successful in private industry, particularly in the selection of administrative personnel, is the group interview, also known as the group oral performance test. After all other selection criteria are used, the top candidates are assembled to solve a problem presented to the group. The interviewer acts as a moderator and observer, providing as little direction as possible. A skillful interviewer can observe leadership traits in the group situation that may not be evident in an individual interview situation. One common exercise in such a performance test is to have the candidates each assume the role of a different department head and defend a budget request based upon known facts about the department and the institution. This technique has the advantage of allowing the interviewer to make comparisons more readily among the candidates. It should not, however, be used by persons without experience or training in areas such as group dynamics.

For the library, the application form is as much a record-keeping device as it is an information-gathering tool. For each applicant, the library should have certain information that describes the applicant, and this information should be collected on a standardized form so that the same information is available for all applicants. The application form should present in an outline format the same basic information that is provided in the candidate's resumé. It may be divided into sections for personal data, education, experience, and references. It should not ask questions that are not related to the position for which the applicant is applying. For this reason, it may be advisable to have separate application forms for professional and nonprofessional positions.

One must avoid certain questions that could be used to discriminate against a candidate on the basis of race, religion, sex, or national origin, intentionally or not. These include questions regarding the birthplace of the candidate; native language; military service other than with the U.S. armed forces; or organizational affiliations that indicate race, religion, or national origin. The library may be required to obtain information about the candidate's race, religion, and national origin for evidence of compliance with the Equal Employment Opportunity Act, but this information should not be available with information that may be used in determining whether an applicant should be hired, transferred, promoted, or terminated.[11] Likewise, a second form should be used for soliciting information needed for health insurance or pension purposes.

On the application form, then, the library should not seek any information that is not used in making the employment decision and should be prepared to defend information that is used. Such a defense must rest on "business necessity," that is, a showing that the information sought is essential to the safe and efficient operation of the business. This justification is required of all policies that have the *effect* of promoting past discriminatory practices, whether intentionally or not. Thus, for example, the policy of denying employment to persons with arrest records has been found to perpetuate racial discrimination.[12] Before any information is sought on the application form, the need for it should be analyzed carefully.

Federal legislation also protects applicants from discrimination because of their age or because of a handicap. Discrimination in employment practices on the basis of age is prohibited by the Age Discrimination in Employment Act of 1967.[13] The 1974 amendment of this act extended coverage to political subdivisions of the states, which include public libraries. This law protects employees and applicants for employment between the ages of forty and sixty-five from refusal to hire, promote, or retain employment when the sole reason is age. Under this law, mandatory retirement ages of less than sixty-five are illegal unless age is a bona fide occupational qualification. In 1978 Congress passed legislation extending protection to age

9. John B. Miner, *Personnel Psychology* (Toronto: MacMillan, 1969), pp. 144–45.

10. Robert E. Carlson, et al., "Improvements in the Selection Interview," *Personnel Journal* 50:268–75 (April 1971).

11. 29 C.F.R. §§1602.7-.14 (1976).

12. Gregory v. Litton Systems, Inc., 472 F.2d 631 (9th Cir. 1972).

13. 29 U.S.C. §§621-34 (1970).

seventy, except for tenured school and college teachers and highly paid executives.[14] Several states have supplemented the federal law by expanding coverage; some have abolished mandatory retirement completely.[15]

The Rehabilitation Act of 1973 states that

. . . no otherwise qualified handicapped individual . . . shall, solely by the reason of his handicap, be excluded from participation in, be denied the benefits of, or otherwise be subjected to discrimination under any program or activity receiving federal financial assistance.[16]

Public libraries receiving federal funds, under such programs as the Library Services and Construction Act, will have to comply with the requirements of the Rehabilitation Act. In 1977 the Department of Health, Education, and Welfare issued regulations implementing this law. Recipients of federal funds must establish grievance procedures to handle complaints of bias against handicapped persons. Employers must make "reasonable accommodation" to the physical and mental handicaps of job applicants who are otherwise qualified, unless such accommodation would impose "undue hardship." The nature and cost of the accommodations would be among the factors weighed to determine what constitutes undue hardship.[17]

The courts have added another category of prohibited discrimination for the library as a public institution. The United States Supreme Court has ruled that public employers may not discriminate against potential employees on the grounds that they are not citizens, unless there is some compelling justification. Such discrimination was found to be a denial of the Fourteenth Amendment's guarantee of equal protection of the laws for all "persons."[18]

In addition to this myriad of federal laws, the administrator must be familiar with state and local laws dealing with discrimination. Several states go beyond the requirements of the federal government, especially in the areas of discrimination on the basis of age and handicaps. Some states have prohibited other forms of discrimination, such as those based on arrest records or marital status. The administrator should make certain that the

application form solicits no information that could be used for prohibited discrimination.

The completed application form eventually becomes part of the employee's permanent personnel file. It should be reviewed periodically with the employee to determine if there are any changes in personal data, education, or other areas that may affect the employment relationship in the library. It is also necessary to retain application forms from candidates who are not hired. The primary purpose for retaining these records is to show compliance with the Equal Employment Opportunity Act.[19] In addition, they give the library information about potential candidates for future positions.

The application blank can also be used as an effective tool in the selection process, through weighing the possible responses to certain questions and scoring each application. Such a technique is most commonly used in predicting turnover. The library searches its files of applications for those of staff, past and present, and determines which responses seem to be associated with a short period of employment. Such a procedure must, however, conform to the requirements of the Equal Employment Opportunity Act and other antidiscrimination legislation. The same questions must be asked of all candidates, and no inquiry should be made that has the effect of perpetuating prohibited forms of discrimination. It is important that the assumptions on which the criteria are based be validated for the individual library and that cross-validations be conducted at periodic intervals, especially if any major changes in the jobs involved or in the labor market have occurred since the weights were originally established.[20]

A third method of selection is testing. Since the 1880s, the federal government and many state and local governments have used civil service testing to reduce political patronage, to promote the efficiency and effectiveness of government, and to eliminate sources of conflict between executive and legislative branches of the state and federal governments. The basic concept of a civil service system is uniformity of treatment of public employees based on merit. The system is usually administered by a civil service commission. In some states and localities, employees of the public libraries are part of the civil service, although even then certain positions may be exempted. Common exemptions are for part-time or seasonal employees, professional or consultant employees, student trainees, and positions involving policymaking. Civil service personnel policies rely extensively on examinations, but contrary to popular

14. Age Discrimination in Employment Act Amendments of 1978, Pub. L. No. 95-256, 92 Stat. 189.

15. See, for example, Mr. Rev. Stat. tit. 5 §1006 (1977).

16. 29 U.S.C. §794 Supp. V. (1975).

17. 42 Fed. Reg. 22,677, 22,888 (1977) (to be codified at 45 C.F.R. §84).

18. Sugarman v. Dougall, 413 U.S. 634 (1973).

19. 29 C.F.R. §1602.14 (1976).

20. Miner, *Personnel Psychology*, pp. 147–49.

belief not all civil service examinations are written. Some examinations test only job skills, such as typing ability; others, which are often called "un-assembled examinations," involve no testing at all, but consist of an evaluation of education and experience.

Testing is not limited to the civil service. Selection testing has, in fact, become extremely popular since World War II. At the beginning of the war, the armed forces realized that, if they were to make optimum use of a limited supply of man-power, they must place people in positions best suited for them. Obviously, because of the great manpower demand of the war, this did not always work out. The greatest success, though, was in the placing of individuals with mechanical abilities in jobs that required such skills. Employers in the private sector later found that they, too, could optimize their labor force by using selection testing.

Selection testing can take many forms. The best predictor of employment success is the test that requires the applicant to perform tasks that are actually part of the job. One of the most popular is the basic typing test. The applicant is given printed copy to be typed and is evaluated on the number of words typed in a given time period and the number of errors.

A second type of test employs the same skills that are required on the job but is more abstract in nature. A test for a file clerk or page, for example, may require the applicant to put items in alpha-betical or numerical order. As with the typing test, a standard may be set for the minimum number of items placed in order and the maximum number of allowable errors.

A third kind of test, which is even more abstract, measures psychomotor skills required for the job. An example is the O'Connor finger and tweezer dexterity test. This test requires a board with one hundred small holes in roles of ten and a shallow tray in which a number of pins are placed. The applicant is to fill the holes with the pins using either his fingers or tweezers. The score is the amount of time required to complete the task. This is the traditional measure of finger dexterity. Similar pegboards with screws, nuts, bolts, and so on provide a measure of more comprehensive psychomotor skills. The O'Connor measures have proved valid as predictors of success among power sewing machine operators and dental stu-dents, and on a variety of other manipulative tasks. Such a test may be useful in screening appli-cants for positions that require the incumbent to work with and repair AV materials.[21]

A test that has had questionable results within the past couple of years is the general intelligence test. Tests of this nature are heavily weighted with material of the kind that is normally learned in school. A majority of the items on such tests tends to be verbal in nature, dealing with subjects such as spelling, vocabulary, and reading. Some tests also examine basic mathematical skills. These tests have declined in popularity because of a recent U.S. Supreme Court decision requiring that all employment tests be related to the job for which the applicant is applying.[22]

The Equal Employment Opportunity Commis-sion has issued "Guidelines on Employee Selec-tion Procedures," which require that if a prima facie case of discrimination has been made against an employer, the employer has the burden of demonstrating the validity of any test and of show-ing that alternative procedures are not available.[23] The *Guidelines* provide standards for validation. Empirical validity will be shown where there is a high correlation between test scores and criteria that have been found to indicate success in a particular job. Content validity requires that the test closely approximate the tasks the job involves. Construct validity requires that the test evaluate traits that have been found important in successful performance of a particular job.[24] Any combina-tion of these validation procedures may be used, though the courts have shown a preference for empirical validation.[25]

In *Griggs* v. *Duke Power Company*, the United States Supreme Court determined that one intelli-gence test in particular—the Wonderlic Personnel Test—violated the Civil Rights Act because it was demonstrated that whites had fared far better than blacks on this test, and this consequence could be directly attributable to race. The Court stated that "basic intelligence must have the means of articu-lation to manifest itself fairly in a testing process."[26]

It seems, then, from the decisions of the Su-preme Court and the guidelines of the Equal Em-ployment Opportunity Commission that, before a test is utilized for employee selection, it is vital that the institution identify those characteristics that can accurately predict success in the particular job to which the test will be applied. A test may then be developed that would accurately measure those characteristics inherent in the job. If, through some

---

21. Ibid., p. 165.

22. Griggs v. Duke Power Co., 401 U.S. 424 (1971).
23. 29 C.F.R. §1607.3 (1976).
24. Ibid., §1607.5.
25. Douglas v. Hampton, 512 F.2d 976, 985 (D.C. Cir. 1975).
26. 401 U.S. 424, 430 (1971).

error, the test screens out applicants for a characteristic that was not inherent in the job, the test may not be used.

In *Griggs* the Court also attacked "paper credentials" that are not related to job success. The requirement of a high school diploma for employment was held to be a violation of Title VII because the requirement "disqualif[ied] Negroes at a substantially higher rate than white applicants" and was not "shown to be significantly related to successful job performance."[27] The Equal Employment Opportunity Commission's guidelines define "test" to include "personal history or background requirements, specific educational or work history requirements, scored interviews, biographical information blanks, interviewers' rating scales, scored application forms, etc."[28] Consequently, such qualifications when required of applicants must be validated by the same techniques used to validate objective scored tests.

As for affirmative action programs in general in public libraries, the controversial decision of the United States Supreme Court in *Regents of the University of California* v. *Bakke*[29] will probably have little impact. Alan Bakke had been denied admission to the Medical School of the University of California at Davis, which reserved a number of places in each entering class for members of certain specified ethnic and racial minorities. Maintaining that the school's refusal to admit him was the result of the special admissions program, Bakke brought a lawsuit claiming that the Davis program violated the equal protection clause of the Fourteenth Amendment to the United States Constitution and Title VI of the Civil Rights Act of 1964,[30] as well as the constitution of California. Title VI governs any program or activity receiving federal financial assistance and prohibits racial discrimination in such programs.

The decision of the United States Supreme Court in *Bakke* is very complex. Four justices concluded that the Davis program violated Title VI,[31] while four other justices believed that Title VI was only intended to prohibit such discrimination as was prohibited by the Fourteenth Amendment to the Constitution and that the Davis program did not violate either.[32] Justice Lewis Powell filed a

separate opinion; each of the other groups of justices concurred in different parts of the opinion. The result was that Davis was ordered to admit Bakke, but other educational institutions were allowed by the Court to use race as one—but not the only—criterion in admission programs. The major difficulty presented by this case is that there is no majority opinion explaining the reasoning behind the Court's action, since no opinions are written in cases of four-four decisions.

One effect of *Bakke* on public libraries does, however, appear fairly clear: a library that receives federal funds and uses strict racial preferences would be held by at least a majority of the justices to violate Title VI of the Civil Rights Act even if it had not previously been found guilty of discrimination by a court or administrative agency. In Justice Powell's opinion, affirmative action programs required by law are not relevant to the *Bakke* situation since such programs are ordered only after a judicial or administrative finding of prior racial discrimination. Furthermore, the Court has "recognized the special competence of Congress to make findings with respect to the effects of identified past discrimination and its discretionary authority to take appropriate remedial measures."[33] Hence the constitutionality of an affirmative action program required by a court or administrative agency in a public library found guilty of past discrimination is not in doubt.

Job Evaluation

A continuing problem of all employers is the task of placing a monetary value on the services of employees. In this aspect of personnel management, the administration of a public agency differs from that of a private business concern. Manufacturers consider several factors when establishing a wage-and-salary program. They must estimate the amount of labor required to produce the product, their share of the market for the finished product, the price of the finished product, and the desired profit. In addition, they must consider the supply and demand for labor.

The public employer, on the other hand, is frequently given a definite budget by some administrative body. The level of library service provided to the community is then determined by the level of financial support. In some communities, funds are specifically allocated for items such as wages and salaries. In other communities, the library receives a budget that it must allocate on its

---

27. Ibid. at 426.

28. 29 C.F.R. §1607.2 (1976).

29. 98 S. Ct. 2733 (1978).

30. 42 U.S.C. §2000d et seq. (Supp. V 1975).

31. 98 S. Ct. at 2815 (Stevens, Rehnquist, Stewart, & Burger, concurring in the judgment in part and dissenting in part).

32. 98 S. Ct. at 2767 (Brennan, Marshall, Blackmun & White, concurring in the judgment in part and dissenting in part).

---

33. 98 S. Ct. at 2755 n. 41.

own. In most cases, personnel represents more than half of the total budget.[34]

The first step in filling this task is to evaluate each position in the library. Job evaluation is a method of assigning a monetary value to each job by appraising that job in relation to others in the library in terms of its difficulty and importance.

The process of job evaluation includes studies, interviews and/or questionnaires that aim at: (1) objectifying job content and evaluating such things as manual, technical, or professional know-how; (2) measuring problem solving as either routine, standardized or abstract; and (3) assessing the job impact or accountability. The building of a rational and equitable salary structure is thus advanced.[35]

By assigning relative weights to the requirements of the job, it is possible to develop a ranking of all jobs. The first element of the job evaluation program is the analysis of the jobs, or the preparation of job descriptions. A job analysis entails the study of the work performed by the incumbent, often over a relatively long period of time. This information is then prepared as part of the job description, which also states the qualifications and responsibilities for each job. It is important that the job be analyzed, and not the individual filling the position.

Once all the jobs in the institution are properly described, the job evaluation may proceed as follows:

1. The rater reads the job description and job specification, taking one job at a time. Some or all jobs in a department are examined to get an overall picture of the job activities and review at first hand the relationships among various jobs under study.
2. The rater begins assigning actual ratings to the various factors of jobs—e.g. mental requirements, skill requirements, physical requirements, responsibility, and working conditions. Second, the definition of the factor is compared with the performance shown for that factor.
3. The rater selects the appropriate level for each factor. In some job evaluation systems, the rater has to decide on a specific point of value within the assigned range of a particu-

lar level. This gives the rater greater flexibility in deciding borderline cases; but it calls for fine discrimination resting on judgment rather than on scientifically measurable job differences.
4. Ratings are recorded on job specification sheets. If more than one rater prepares ratings for each job, individual ratings are noted on a worksheet. Averaged or finally agreed-upon ratings are then entered on the permanent record.[36]

When all the jobs in the library are evaluated, it is possible to place them in some order. Job levels, pay rates, or ranges are techniques for grouping different jobs with approximately the same level of difficulty or value to the library. By grouping several jobs into a range, the need for individually pricing each job is avoided. Ranges rather than single rates also minimize inequities resulting from job analysis. The next step in the process is the determination of the salary to be paid for each job level.

Compensation

Determining salary range poses several problems. Ranges can be too broad, too narrow, too many, or too few. Too much spread between minimum and maximum salaries within a range, or too few ranges, usually means that either beginning salaries are low or employees at the top of the range are overpaid.

Each salary range normally has at least three steps. The maximum rate is that paid only to outstanding employees, usually with top seniority. The midpoint between these two rates is the standard salary paid to experienced employees with satisfactory performance. There can be any number of steps between the minimum and maximum rates. The rates within a range may also be unstructured, allowing the administrator to pay the employee any salary between the minimum and maximum rates.

Assigning salary figures to each range first involves the determination of a base salary. This may be at any grade, but is usually either the lowest grade or the highest grade. It is then necessary to determine a percentage of differential between grades. For example, if grade 1 has a midpoint salary of $9,000 and there is to be a 10-percent differential between grades, grade 2 will have a midpoint salary of $9,900. Once the

34. Helen M. Eckard, *Survey of Public Libraries, LIBGIS I, 1974*, U.S. Department of Health, Education and Welfare, National Center for Education Statistics, (Washington, D.C.: Gov. Print. Off., 1978), p. 48.

35. Barbara Manchak and Barry Simon, "Wage and Salary Administration," *The Protean* 2:18 (Summer 1972).

36. *Personnel Management: Policies and Practices* (Englewood Cliffs, N.J.: Prentice-Hall, 1966), pp. 15, 316.

midpoint salaries are determined for each grade, the administrator determines the spread from minimum to maximum. If, for example, it is determined that the maximum salary will be 35-percent greater than the minimum salary, the minimum figure is found by dividing the midpoint salary by 1.162 (the square root of 1.35) and the maximum salary is found by multiplying the midpoint salary by 1.162.

Frequently when jobs are reevaluated a few employees will be earning more than the top rate established for their grade. Because it is poor policy to lower employees' salary, it is common to "red circle" such over-grade salaries. Then the employees' rates may be frozen until natural turnover or general pay increases eliminate the problem. If civil service regulations, the employment contract, or the union agreement permit, it may also be possible to remove the employees temporarily from the job evaluation structure and assign a personal rate to the employees rather than the job.

Fringe Benefits

Fringe benefits are looked upon by employers and employees in a number of ways. The employer tends to look at a fringe benefit package as a means of improving staff morale. Employees sometimes look at benefits as gifts from a benevolent employer. A paid leave of absence, be it a vacation, holiday, or sabbatical, is viewed as merely a welcome break in the daily routine of work. Employers look at their pension plans as evidence of their social responsibility.

These views may be true to some extent, but the fringe benefit package is primarily compensation for services rendered, the same as salaries and wages. The total fringe benefit package may cost the library as much as one-third of the employee's salary. To the employee, most fringe benefits represent a tax-free increase in spendable income. The wise job seeker will weigh the fringe benefits when making a decision between two comparable job offers.

It follows that the library should evaluate its fringe benefit package to determine its competitiveness with neighboring or comparable employers. Fringe benefits for nonprofessional employees should be competitive with businesses in the community employing people with similar skills. Likewise, the benefits of professional staff members should be competitive with other libraries.

This is not to say that the fringe benefit should be offered simply because it is offered at other institutions. No benefit should be offered unless:

(1) it is to the long-term advantage of both management and employees; (2) it is defensible on economic grounds; and (3) employees can and will have a share both in planning the benefits and in the cost of upkeep by expending their time, money, or skill, especially in the administration of benefits when this is feasible.

The most common form of fringe benefits comprises those that fall within a class known as leaves of absence. This includes all periods of time when the employee is authorized to be away from the library, either with or without continuation of pay. One such leave of absence is vacation. The library should recognize that its purpose in offering vacation is to afford employees an opportunity to change environment temporarily and spend additional time with their family. The library benefits because the employees return to work more refreshed, which improves efficiency. Just as the efficiency of an employee varies during the day with relation to lunch and quitting time, so does the efficiency through the year in relation to holidays and vacation. It is very common for libraries to grant different lengths of vacation for different levels of employees. Professional employees are frequently given one month of vacation per year. The way this amount is expressed in the personnel manual often varies; the allowance may also be two days of vacation accumulated for every month of employment.

Nonprofessional and paraprofessional employees frequently are allowed less vacation than professional employees. It is not uncommon to grant ten working days to nonprofessional employees and increase the allowance to four weeks as the employee gains seniority. The Library Administration Division of the American Library Association recommends that all "full-time staff members in the professional and supporting staff services, except pages, receive 22 working days" of vacation per year. It is recommended that pages and maintenance employees be allowed ten working days in each of the first three years of service and fifteen working days thereafter. Part-time employees working on a regular schedule would receive the same proportionate vacation allowance as is given full-time staff members in the same service and with corresponding years of employment.[37]

Another common form of leave of absence is sick leave. Sick leave is the granting of time off with pay for reasons of the employee's illness, medical appointments that cannot be made after work

37. American Library Association, Personnel Publications Committee, *Personnel Organization and Procedure: A Manual Suggested for Use in Public Libraries*, 2d ed. (Chicago: ALA, 1968), pp. 18–19.

hours, or serious illness in the employee's immediate family. The length of the allowance for sick leave is generally between 2 and 15 days per year. In virtually all institutions, sick leave is cumulative to between 90 and 150 days. In a significant number of institutions, the accumulation of sick leave is unlimited.

In April 1972, the Equal Employment Opportunity Commission issued guidelines relating to pregnancy and childbirth. The Commission stated that

. . . disabilities caused or contributed to by pregnancy, miscarriage, abortion, childbirth, and recovery therefrom are, for all job-related purposes, temporary disabilities and should be treated as such under any health or temporary disability insurance or sick leave plan available in connection with employment. Written and unwritten employment policies and practices involving matters such as the commencement and duration of leave, the availability of extensions, the accrual of seniority and other benefits and privileges, reinstatement, and payment under any health or temporary disability insurance or sick leave plan, formal or informal, shall be applied to disability due to pregnancy or childbirth on the same terms and conditions as they are applied to other temporary disabilities. Where the termination of an employee who is temporarily disabled is caused by an employment policy under which insufficient or no leave is available, such a termination violates the Act if it has a disparate impact on employees of one sex and is not justified by business necessity.[38]

In 1976, the United States Supreme Court ruled that an employer with an otherwise comprehensive disability or health benefit plan is not in violation of Title VII if benefits for disabilities arising from pregnancy are excluded from the plan.[39] Legislation has been introduced in Congress that would require that disabilities related to pregnancy be treated like any other temporary disability.[40] The proposed legislation differs from the EEOC guidelines in that an employer would be able to choose to exclude disabilities relating to abortion except where the life of the mother is in danger.

As for maternity leave, the basic principle upheld by the courts is that physical disabilities related to pregnancy are temporary in nature and that pregnant female employees must be treated on the basis of their individual physical condition in relation to their ability to perform a specific job. An employer cannot require pregnant employees to commence maternity leave at a specific time. Pregnant employees are entitled to individual treatment, and generally the time when a woman becomes physically unable to work due to pregnancy is a matter to be determined by the employee and her physician. A company may require that a pregnant employee present a certificate indicating her doctor's opinion as to the time when she should commence her leave and when she may safely return to work if the employer has similar requirements for other employees who request leave for sickness or temporary disability. An employee's request for leave to nurse or rear children will depend on the employer's general policies for leaves for reasons other than physical disability, unless the woman is physically unable to work. Where an employer does permit leave that may be used for child care, male employees may be entitled to paternity leave under Title VII. An employer may wish to consult with legal counsel regarding a waiver of liability for pregnant employees.

Some employers have tried to avoid the problem of granting maternity leaves by either refusing to hire pregnant employees or requiring a minimum length of employment before granting maternity leave. EEOC guidelines bar any blanket prohibition against hiring pregnant women, but it would not be a violation of Title VII if the employer refused to hire a pregnant woman for valid job-related reasons. The policy of requiring a minimum length of employment before granting maternity leave may be permissible if the waiting period is no longer than the period required for any other leave for temporary disability.

The Vietnam Era Veterans's Readjustment Assistance Act of 1974 requires employers to grant a leave of absence to employees entering the military.[41] The law does not require the continuation of compensation, but it does guarantee reinstatement and rights to some fringe benefits.

Persons entering a reserve or National Guard program geneally have a six-year obligation.[42] At least four months of this term must be spent in active duty for training, usually during the first year in the program. Depending on the type of training, the active duty period may extend to a year or longer. The remainder of the six years is spent in the ready reserve. The obligation then consists of forty-eight four-hour drills per year, plus fifteen days of annual active duty for training ("summer camp"). Drills may be held weekly or combined as monthly weekend drills.

---

38. 29 C.F.R. §1604.10 (1976).
39. General Electric Co. v. Gilbert, 429 U.S. 125 (1976).
40. H.R. 6075, 95th Cong., 1st Sess. (1977).

41. 38 U.S.C. §2021 et seq. (Supp. V 1975).
42. See 32 C.F.R. §132.3(b) (1976).

Reservists are not excused from drills or summer camp because of employment obligations. Therefore, employers must cooperate in scheduling such personnel.

An employee must be granted a leave of absence upon entering the initial act of duty and must be reinstated if he:

1. Was not a temporary employee upon induction
2. Left his job to enter military service
3. Satisfactorily completes his training duty
4. Applies for reinstatement within thirty-one days after his release from training duty
5. Is qualified to perform the duties of his former position.

Employees are reinstated to:

1. The seniority status they would have attained if they had not been absent in service
2. The pay rate they would have attained, except for their absence, including all general increases or raises applicable to their seniority classification
3. The equivalent status they would have acquired if they had not been absent in service
4. The same fringe benefits as are granted to employees on nonmilitary leaves.

A reservist or guardsman is protected from discharge, except for cause, for six months following his reinstatement.

The same rules apply when the reservist goes on annual active duty for training. Leave of absence must be granted. The employer may not require the employee to use vacation time for this training period. The reservist, however, may at his option use earned vacation time.

It is not uncommon for employers to continue some level of compensation while the reservist is at summer camp. Most employers will pay the difference between the reservist's regular salary and military pay. Others will continue the employee's regular salary. Institutions that pay the difference generally only consider the reservist's base military pay, excluding travel and quarters allowances.

There are two additional points to remember when drafting a military leave policy. Reservists and national guardsmen are subject to emergency call-up during civil disturbances, national emergencies, and disasters. Policies should cover these possibilities. Also, "summer camp" is not always during the summer; many units train during the winter months.

A type of leave of absence that is almost unique to educational institutions is the sabbatical. Originally, the sabbatical year was a year of rest for the farmland, observed every seventh year in ancient Judea. This sabbatical helped the land regain its natural level of minerals. The employer now grants a sabbatical leave to certain employees to allow them to replenish their resources— that is, to return to school for further advanced education, to travel, or to do research. The granting of a sabbatical leave is important to the institution primarily because it results in a more knowledgeable staff. It is also an important tool in reducing turnover in that the employee, after three or four years of employment, looks forward to the sabbatical leave. Most institutions granting sabbatical leave require that the employee continue his employment for at least one year beyond the conclusion of the leave. In institutions of higher education, employees on sabbatical are usually entitled to full or partial compensation during the sabbatical period. In public libraries, however, true sabbaticals are very rare. Much more common is the practice of granting leaves of absence to nonprofessional employees to return to school, especially to fulfill requirements for a degree in library science. Policies governing such leaves vary greatly and are usually determined by the local library authority.

Every institution will grant various other miscellaneous leaves, such as leave for attending the funeral of a member of the employee's immediate family, for jury and for witness duty. Because jurors and witnesses normally receive a stipend from the court, the library should consider drafting policies regarding continuation of compensation just as they would for military leave. It is important to take notice of local statutes and ordinances that may require continuation of full salary for employees summoned for court duty.

A fringe benefit that is equal in importance to leaves of absence is insurance protection for employees. Insurance is considered a valuable fringe benefit because it is considerably more economical for an employee to participate in a group insurance plan than to attempt to secure comparable insurance individually. The benefit is even more attractive if the employer assumes some or all of the responsibility for the insurance premium.

The most common form of insurance protection available to employees is the medical and hospitalization plan. A hospitalization plan offers employees protection against expenses of hospitalization as a result of nonoccupational accidents or illness. Benefits usually are limited, and the employee must pay all costs over and above the stipulated maximum benefits. Medical care plans provide for surgical expense and/or medical (nonsurgical) costs. An employer may provide either a cash indemnity plan, which provides benefits in cash in accordance with a schedule of indemnities, or a service plan, which pays for physicians' services, when needed, without additional cost to the employee. An important addition to the medical and hospitalization plan is the major medical plan, which provides coverage for major medical expenses as a result of protracted illness or severe injuries. Such a policy would pay a fixed percentage of the employee's long-term medical expenses with a deductible amount paid by the employee, up to a fixed maximum benefit. Another form of medical plan, that is gaining popularity is dental insurance, although it is still rarely found in public libraries.

Two major decisions must be made whenever the institution considers any type of health care plan. It must be determined which employees will be eligible for benefits and who will pay the costs of the insurance. Many institutions pay the entire cost of the plan, while others require contributions by the employee. A third option is for the institution to pay the entire cost of the employee's coverage, but require the employee to pay all or part of the costs of coverage for his dependents.

The second most popular form of insurance is life insurance. In addition to determining the group of eligible employees and the responsibility for the premium, the institution must also determine the amount of insurance to be available to the employees. Insurance carriers' rules and state laws restrict the amount of term life insurance available to each employee. Within these limits, it is possible to determine a level of coverage in several ways. One method provides for a fixed amount of insurance for all employees. A second method gears the level of coverage to the annual salary of the employee. This method gives recognition to the employee's worth, but is more expensive because the higher-paid employees generally are older than those in lower salary brackets. A third method gears the amount of coverage to the seniority of the employee, with more insurance being available the longer the employee has been with the institution.

It is possible to create variations on the standard term life policy by adding a conversion privilege, which allows an employee who has terminated his employment to convert his group plan to an individual whole life plan. It is also possible to provide insurance for employees after they retire, but because of the increased premium for older insureds, the amount of insurance is usually reduced. Accidental death or dismemberment insurance is frequently added for protection against these perils.

In recent years, a new form of group insurance has become popular as a fringe benefit. The group prepaid legal service plan is a means for providing access to legal counsel to all employees within an institution. This plan works in the same manner as a medical insurance plan and pays scheduled benefits on specified services. A local bar association should be able to provide specific information about the availability for prepaid legal service plans in a particular community.

A third major form of fringe benefit is the monetary payment made to an employee after his retirement. Pension plans are probably the most frequently misunderstood of all employee benefits and are generally not appreciated until the employee approaches retirement age. Before any pension program can be developed, it is necessary for the library to establish a policy on retirement. Many institutions set a mandatory retirement age, which must comply with federal and state age discrimination laws.

The establishment of a mandatory retirement age, where permitted by law, will eliminate the need for making subjective decisions regarding retirement. It helps provide definite information to younger employees about the future availability of positions. On the other hand, it does not take into consideration the fact that many employees will be fully capable of performing their jobs past the mandatory retirement age, and the loss of these employees can deprive the institution of many years of valuable service.

There are three major forms of retirement income plans: the pension plan, the deferred compensation plan, and Social Security. A pension plan generally requires that the employee contribute a fixed percentage of his salary to the pension program. This percentage is frequently matched by the employer. The method for determining benefits under the pension plan is related to the determination of the contribution of the employer and employee.

There are basically three types of pension plans. Under a "money purchase" plan, a specified percentage of the employee's salary rate will be contributed and allocated to the participant. Whatever he has in his account balance at retirement or termination will be his benefit. A "fixed benefit" plan pays the employee a fixed monthly dollar amount multiplied by years of service. The third type is a "target benefit" plan, which is a hybrid between a money purchase pension and a fixed benefit pension plan. Like the fixed benefit, the funding of the target benefit plan is based on a certain promised level of benefits at retirement. The plan is like a money purchase plan in that the assumptions established initially are not substantially varied.

When an employee resigns before reaching retirement age, he or she may have a right to some of the money in the pension account. Any money contributed by the employee is invariably returned, except that a small service charge is sometimes deducted. Some plans pay interest on the employee's contribution. The employee may also receive a portion of the employer's contribution, depending on policy on vesting rights.

The deferred compensation plan allows employees to reduce their salary each pay period by an amount that they may determine, up to a legal limit. This amount may be matched by the employer and placed in an insurance-type account called an annuity account. The organization holding the funds, most likely an insurance company, will pay out benefits to the employee upon retirement for the rest of the employee's life. The amount of payment is determined by the total value of the employee's contribution and life expectancy at retirement. Some plans allow an employee to "retire" at any age, receiving a reduced monthly benefit. Annuity plans frequently have provisions to allow a surviving spouse to receive all monies in the account that have not been paid out as benefits.

The major advantage of a deferred compensation plan is that the employee is reducing taxable income during working years by the amount of the contribution. Under the standard pension plan, income taxes are paid on total income computed before deductions for pension. In the deferred compensation plan, the employee's taxable salary does not include the portion of income that is "deferred" until the employee's retirement. This money becomes taxable once the employee retires and begins to receive benefits, but at this time the employee will probably be in a lower tax bracket because of reduced earnings. Under a deferred compensation plan, the money withheld from the employee is owned by the employer until the employee elects to retire. This distinguishes such a plan from the tax-sheltered annutiy plan available in many educational and nonprofit institutions. In the latter plan, the employee owns the money, even though it is paid to the annuity plan. The latter plan is much more desirable for employees but needs the approval of the Internal Revenue Service, which must determine if the employer is a nonprofit organization under the definition established in the Internal Revenue Code. To date, few libraries have qualified.

Library employees who are not covered by employer-sponsored pension plans may establish tax-sheltered individual retirement accounts under the provisions of the Employee Retirement Income Security Act of 1974.[43] The employee may deduct from gross income any amount deposited in the account up to a maximum of 15 percent of compensation includible in gross income for that year, or $1,500, whichever is less. The library may contribute to the employee's retirement account, but any contribution will be regarded as compensation for tax purposes. Information about such accounts may be obtained from banks, insurance companies, or the Internal Revenue Service.

Every state today has established by legislation one or more retirement systems for public employees. Large cities in some cases have their own systems. These plans vary greatly. State pension plans may cover all public employees, or there may be separate systems for state and local employees. In some states all local governments are required to cover their employees within the state system or within a state-administered system for local employees, while in other states participation in the state plan is optional. The structure and functioning of these plans differs greatly from state to state.

Social Security, a federal program administered by the Department of Health, Education, and Welfare, is actually more than just a pension program. In addition to retirement benefits, Social Security provides unemployment compensation, aid to dependent children, maternal and child welfare, vocational rehabilitation, public health work, and aid to the blind. Its most popular program, though, is Old Age, Survivors, and Disability Insurance (OASDI). The purpose of OASDI is to provide a basic monthly income to workers and/or their families when the worker retires, dies, or becomes disabled. Both employers and employees fund this program by taxes collected under the Federal Insurance Contributions Act (FICA).[44]

When the Social Security Act was passed in 1935, it excluded coverage of state and local government employees, largely because of the constitution barrier to federal taxation of the states. Subsequent amendments to the act gave the Department of Health, Education, and Welfare the authority to enter into agreements with any state for the extension of Social Security coverage to certain groups of its employees or those of its local governments. Once an agreement is signed, the federal government receives an equal tax from employees and employers who are covered by the agreement. The agreement between the state and HEW may be modified in its coverage or abandoned altogether, but once an agreement is abandoned, that group of employees may never again be covered by Social Security.[45]

43. I.R.C. §219.

44. Barry Simon, "A Pension Primer," *American Libraries* 4:114 (Feb. 1973).
45. Ibid.

A fringe benefit especially important to professional employees is the financial support of the employee's participation in professional organizations. Professional growth is fostered through membership in national, regional, state, and local library organizations. Individual members benefit through association publications, workshops, and meetings. Associations are also capable of providing benefits to the library profession as a whole by developing standards of library service, conducting research in library science, and working for legislation that would be beneficial to libraries.

A library may provide this benefit to its employees in three ways. One approach is to provide a leave of absence with pay to participate in the meetings and workshops of professional associations. To further encourage membership in library associations, the library may choose to pay annual dues to one or several associations. The library may also choose to pay expenses to allow staff members to participate in association meetings. If the library is paying meeting expenses and not paying dues, it must face the problem of whether or not it will pay expenses for those employees who are not members of the professional association. In either case, the library administration should communicate its purpose in making this subsidy to the staff.

Staff Development

A library that intends to be dynamic and maintain a highly motivated staff must institute some program of staff development. Staff development is nothing more than the teaching of new skills so that the employee may assume new responsibilities. These skills may be technical in nature, such as bookmending or card catalog filing, or they may be theoretical, such as leadership skills for department heads. In any case, the library administration should first determine its objective in developing the staff. The staff development program should be tailored to the objectives rather than adopted from another institution simply because it was proven successful in another setting.

The most frequently used method of staff development is in-service training. This is a formal effort at training within the library facilities during normal working hours. In-service training is usually applied when the library introduces new equipment or operating procedures. It is also used in the training of new staff.

Programmed instruction is a form of training that might lend itself to several areas of the library.[46] Programmed instruction presents the material to be learned in a logical series of steps. The instructional material provides information and then asks questions about the information presented. Each trainee works at an individual speed and does not progress until mastering all the previous concepts. One method of programmed instruction, the linear method, breaks the subject matter down into simple statements requiring a word or two for completion. These statements logically lead the trainee to answer correctly. In addition, the same idea is repeated several times in differently worded statements to reinforce correct answers. Each step is based on the one preceding it and provides background for subsequent steps. Because the linear method presents information in very simplified form and gives many hints at correct responses, learners seldom make mistakes.

More complex material may be presented in a second method, the branching method, which presents larger amounts of material in the form of multiple-choice questions. This method anticipates that a learner will occasionally select the wrong response. When this happens, the trainee is led to an auxiliary series of steps showing where and why the error occurred. The learner must respond correctly to these steps before returning to the main track of instruction.

Programmed instruction is valuable in areas where there is a high turnover in jobs requiring many trained employees, an overburdened training staff, a need to give everyone on a certain job exactly the same training, and a need for a continual training program in which only a few people at a time are enrolled. Student pages would probably be the best subjects for programmed instruction. The same materials presented to the student pages may also be used in a program for user orientation.

A second method of in-service training is job rotation, a variation of which is job enrichment. Job rotation involves the actual transfer of an employee to another position in the institution, to perform tasks different from those performed in the first position. The employee gains additional skills, and the institution benefits because employees are then able to cover positions for absent or vacationing employees more effectively. Employees are also given a better understanding of the structure of the total organization, which in-

---

46. See Henry M. Yaple, *Programmed Instruction in Librarianship: A Classified Bibliography of Programmed Texts and Other Materials*, Graduate School of Library Science Occasional Paper No. 124 (Champaign: Univ. of Illinois, 1976).

creases their involvement in their jobs. Employees must have an understanding of the intent of a job rotation program; otherwise they may get the impression that they are merely pawns on the library chessboard. Rotation periods should be long enough to provide the employee with ample experience in the new position. Management personnel should also be given sufficient time to develop subordinates effectively before they are transferred to another unit.

Job enrichment involves the addition of more challenging tasks or responsibilities to present job descriptions without transferring personnel. The intent of such a training program is to develop the employee to a point where he or she may be eligible for promotion. Job enrichment gives the employee an opportunity to gradually adapt to the increased responsibilities of a new position. It also gives the library management an opportunity to evaluate the employee's performance under these new conditions. Again, it is important to communicate the intent of a job enrichment program to the employee involved. A failure to do so would merely suggest to the employee that the library is expecting more work without providing additional compensation.

A third type of in-house training is the professional seminar. Groups of employees periodically meet to discuss topics of concern to the library. These topics may include instruction in the use of new equipment, new processes, management skills, etc. A leader using a seminar approach should be careful not to allow the meeting to develop into a classroom lecture. A seminar should be structured to allow the free flow of communication from all participants, who should be encouraged to share the knowledge they possess.

The library should not overlook outside opportunities for training staff. One such opportunity, mentioned earlier, is the professional association meeting. In addition to the regular programs and meetings of these associations, they frequently conduct workshops directed at staff development. The Library Administration and Management Association has conducted staff development workshops for several years at the annual meeting of the American Library Association. Some of these workshops have focused on methods of training, such as the use of educational technology in staff development; others have been directed at the development of the participants—for example, a workshop on the role of the middle manager in a library.

The library should also be aware of continuing education programs at library schools and schools of business or public administration. Some of these programs are directed at the development of administrative skills of librarians. A typical program is the seven-day Executive Development Program for Library Administration conducted by the School of Business Administration at Miami University in Ohio. Similar programs for librarians are conducted by the University of Maryland and Washington University in Saint Louis, to name a few. Such programs vary in subject matter and quality, and it would be best for the library to obtain an outline of any continuing education program to determine if the subject matter corresponds with the objectives of the library training program. A more costly approach is the use of private management consultant firms. These firms frequently conduct training programs on specific areas of management at various locations across the country. These programs are also available on an in-house basis. It should be remembered that such programs are general in nature and should only be attended by individuals who can relate general principles to the library setting.

In the past ten years, we have seen a significant increase in the use of psychological training techniques in organizations. These techniques strive to develop the employee on a personal basis rather than on a professional basis. The objective of most of these programs is to develop a better understanding of interpersonal relationships and how one fits into the organization. To accomplish this objective, trainers employ various verbal and non-verbal exercises. This type of training is frequently called sensitivity training because it attempts to develop the individual's sensitivity to the needs of self and others.

The success of such a program is frequently dependent upon the ability of the staff to communicate freely and honestly. This often requires the use of exercises to break down any existing barriers of communication. The trainer may also employ exercises to create a sense of trust within the group. Once the group is able to communicate on an acceptable level, the trainer will switch to other exercises, taking advantage of this free flow of communication.

A T-group is a leaderless, unstructured group that purports to teach its members more about themselves and how they operate in groups so that they can increase their effectiveness as group members. The method employed is analysis of the interaction within the T-group. The participants become sensitive to the roles played by the others within the group and to their own feelings in the roles they themselves play.

In using sensitivity training in an institution, it is important that the institution recognize the necessity of having a professional trainer. The trainer should be aware of the training objective of the institution so as to structure the program to meet these objectives. It is not always necessary for the trainees to be aware of the training objective prior to the training session. The skilled trainer can conduct the sessions in such a way that these objectives will become clear to the participants during the course of the training.

Administrators frequently overlook an obvious tool of staff development. Performance appraisal is generally considered only a means for determining merit increases in compensation. But a library that recognizes the need for management by objectives will receive the full value that performance appraisal can provide. An institution that is managed by objectives will set objectives for individuals as well as for the organization. The setting of objectives, however, is senseless without an evaluation of how well the employee has met them. Evaluation should be regular and frequent. Employees failing to meet objectives should be informed of this fact and instructed on alternative methods of meeting them. The library should also evaluate the objectives set by the employee to make certain that they are not too simple or unrealistic. Performance evaluation should be carried out in face-to-face communication with the employee to be evaluated. Only through this two-way communication is the evaluator able to obtain feedback from the employee. To foster personal growth, employees should also be able to evaluate themselves and make recommendations for their own personal development.

Employee Regulation

Virtually all employment organizations have various rules and regulations for employees. These rules generally cover attendance and work hour requirements, safety, production, administrative and operational matters, and personal conduct. Rules are frequently stated positively as standards or objectives, which is psychologically preferable to listing prohibitions. Because these rules represent standards of performance, they must be communicated to the affected employees.

The library can make and enforce any reasonable rules that are necessary to the conduct of its own operation. These rules, however, must not violate a law or conflict with a union contract. If the library deals with a certified bargaining agent, it is generally necessary to consult with the union when making new rules or changing existing rules. The library administration should be aware of any laws that affect personnel regulations. These laws are not always found in general employment stat-

utes. The Federal Truth in Lending Law, for example, prohibits discharging an employee whose earnings have been garnisheed for indebtedness, regardless of the number of levies made or the number of procedures brought for collection. Individual states also have laws restricting the discipline allowed for garnishment. The library administration should also take care not to set rules or standards that are in conflict with the Library Bill of Rights.

The setting of standards or the creating of rules is meaningless unless the employer can impose sanctions upon those employees who fail to meet standards or who violate written rules. Penalties for violation of work rules can vary from oral warnings to immediate discharge. The severity of the penalty should be dependent upon the seriousness of the violation and the employee's prior record. Because of variations in circumstances, it is frequently recommended that the employer establish maximum penalties for violations rather than perscribe a definite penalty for all cases of violation of the same rule.

The oral warning is usually the first step in any disciplinary process. The purposes of the warning are to inform the employee that a violation has occurred, to explain the personnel policies, to attempt to determine the reason for the violation, and to inform the employee of future penalties for the same violation. Records should be kept of oral warnings and should include a description of the event, the date, and a summary of the discussion with the employee. It is important that the employee understand that the warning is a disciplinary measure and that a record is being kept for future reference. A written warning generally has a stronger impact than an oral warning. Again, the employee is informed of the violation and the policy and is reminded of the disciplinary actions that will be necessitated by future violation. The employee should acknowledge receipt of a copy of the written warning, and the acknowledgement should be placed in the employee's personnel file. Sending a written warning does not eliminate the necessity of having a meeting with the employee to discuss the violation.

If oral and written warnings prove to be ineffective, or if the misconduct is serious enough, the library may choose to suspend the employee. Suspension is a compulsory leave of absence without pay for a specified period of time. It is more effective than warnings because the employee is hurt financially and because the misconduct becomes known to fellow workers. If the employee continually fails to meet the library's standards of behavior or performance, or if the employee commits a serious infraction of library rules, the library may choose to terminate that person's employment. Dismissal is a last resort and should not be decided upon lightly. The basis for dismissal and the procedure to be followed in the event that an employee must be discharged should be set forth explicitly. Procedures vary somewhat according to the legal structure or governance of the institution and its personnel. Employees covered by a civil service act, for instance, have certain measures of job security established by law. The act will probably outline dismissal procedures that supersede those of the library.

Whenever an adverse action (including the denial of a salary increase) is taken against an employee for failure to meet certain standards, the employee should have the opportunity to contest the action. A formal grievance procedure will give the employee this opportunity. The grievance procedure is a system by which the employee may appeal an adverse action up the chain of supervision to the body having ultimate authority, generally the library board. According to Barry Simon,

> The structure of the appeals procedure should state explicitly: (a) types of actions that may be appealed; (b) who is eligible to appeal (probationary employees are sometimes denied appeal of dismissal); (c) time within which appeal must be made; (d) steps of appeal, i.e., to whom the employee appeals first, higher appeal if action is affirmed, persons on board with final authority; (e) composition of any appeals board or community; (f) status of the employee during the appeal; (g) time within [which] appeal must be answered.[47]

In a grievance hearing, the grievant should be assured of due process. This may be required by state public employee labor relations acts or by civil service regulations. Whether it is required by the due process requirements of the United States Constitution is a complex matter. As a public institution, the public library when it dismisses an employee must provide the protections required by the Fourteenth Amendment to the Constitution in circumstances involving a "property interest" such as a justified expectation of continued employment.[48] A tenured employee, for example, has such an interest, but this is not necessarily true of all nonprobationary employees. Whether the employee has a right to continued employment depends on applicable local law.

The Supreme Court has not decided whether due process is required for lesser sanctions such as transfers or demotions. The lower courts have not developed a clear standard. One federal district court required a hearing for an adverse performance evaluation,[49] while another did not require due process even for a suspension, where the public welfare was involved.[50] The extent to which due process is required depends on a number of factors, including the severity of the sanction, the presence of an affected property interest, and the needs of the institution.

Procedural due process guarantees that the grievant shall have proper notice of the action against him and an opportunity to be heard and to defend himself in an orderly proceeding adapted to the nature of the case. This opportunity to be heard may include the right to counsel and the right to call witnesses. The board hearing the grievance should decide the matter only on the basis of the facts presented at the grievance hearing. Given the same fact situation, the board's decision should be the same for all employees.

Should the grievance procedure reach an impasse, the parties may consent to submit the grievance to mediation or arbitration. Under such a procedure, the grievances are heard by an impartial arbitrator, who then renders a final decision. Under mediation, the decision of the mediator is only advisory to the parties. Under arbitration, the parties agree in advance to be bound by the arbitrator's decision. Under compulsory arbitration provisions, a grievance must be submitted to arbitration as soon as an impasse is reached.

Staff Associations and Unions

Library employees organize into groups for a number of reasons. Two main kinds of employee groups are staff associations and employee unions. The former are generally an outgrowth of the desire to pool the talents of the individual staff members for the benefit of the entire staff. The latter are usually the result of the employees' desire to negotiate with the library administration on an equal footing in matters of wages, hours, and working conditions.

The ability of library employees to organize into unions and bargain with a library administration is governed by state and local laws. The National Labor Relations Act exempts states and political subdivisions of states from coverage by the act.[51] While the National Labor Relations Board has

47. Barry Simon, "Developing Termination Policies and Procedures," *American Libraries* 4:47 (Jan. 1973).

48. Board of Regents v. Roth, 408 U.S. 564 (1972); Perry v. Sindermann, 408 U.S. 593 (1972).

49. Bottcher v. Florida Department of Agriculture and Consumer Services, 361 F. Supp. 1123, 1129 (N.D. Fla. 1973).

50. McIntyre v. New York City Department of Corrections, 411 F. Supp. 1257 (S.D.N.Y. 1976).

51. 29 U.S.C. §152 (2) (1970).

declined to rule that public libraries are exempt, it has consistently refused to exercise jurisdiction over public libraries on the grounds that the purposes of the act would not be served if jurisdiction were asserted, because of the close relationship between public libraries and state and city governments.[52] If, however, a public library were independent of state and municipal control and received a large percentage of its funding from private or internal sources, such as donations, fines, user fees, and investments, the National Labor Relations Board might well assert jurisdiction.[53] The federal courts have, however, recognized that the right of public employees to form and join unions is protected by the First and Fourteenth Amendments to the United States Constitution.[54] Despite these guarantees, some restrictions on a public employee's freedom of association may be permissible, but such restrictions must be justified by overwhelming public interest. Such a justification would probably seldom be found in the case of public librarians.

The staff association is the most common form of organization of library employees. The staff organization may consist of all employees on the library's staff or may exclude the library director and department heads. Many staff organizations exist only to provide recreational benefits that cannot be furnished by the library administration. Out of its dues and monies collected from activities, the staff organization may sponsor seasonal and retirement parties. It may also be responsible for sending cards and flowers to employees who are hospitalized or who have suffered the loss of a family member. This association may also sponsor a newsletter providing information about staff members and an opportunity for staff to display their literary talent.

Frequently, in addition to providing social benefits, the staff organization will assume responsibilities similar to those assumed by unions. Representatives of the staff association may meet regularly with the library administration to discuss personnel policies before they are implemented or changed. A staff organization that is truly representative of the library staff can provide the library director with excellent insight into the acceptance of new personnel policies. It is not uncommon for recommendations or changes in existing policies to originate with a staff organization. The staff organization may also provide an informal stage in the grievance procedure by attempting to mediate grievances between employees and the administration.

A union is an organization of employees organized with the expressed intent of engaging in collective bargaining with the library administration on matters of wages, hours, and conditions of employment. Increasingly, state public sector labor relations legislation is making the refusal of public employers to bargain collectively an unfair labor practice. Even in the absence of such legislation, a public library administration may choose to bargain voluntarily in order to avoid bitter confrontation or perhaps to reduce the need for a public employee bargaining act that might further restrict the employer's freedom of action. In the absence of such statutes in some states, however, the public employer may not have the authority under the common law to engage in collective bargaining. Where they exist, public sector labor relations statutes generally specify those activities of either the employer or the union that are prohibited or permitted. If such a statute is in effect, it is advisable for the library administration to obtain adequate legal counsel at the earliest stage of union organization in order that the administration may protect itself from committing prohibited activities.

Once the employees have decided that they wish to have a bargaining agent, it is necessary to determine which employees will be represented by that agent. Where there is a collective bargaining statute, it is necessary to look to the law to determine which employees are eligible to be in the bargaining unit. Generally, the eligible employees are those who are not supervisors, guards, or confidential employees. The remaining employees with similar work interests may constitute an appropriate bargaining unit. Following the pattern of the Taft-Hartley Act, some public labor relations statutes provide that professionals and nonprofessionals shall not be members of the same bargaining unit unless the professional employees agree to such a unit by majority vote. The authority to determine the bargaining unit is usually placed in a state public employment labor relations board or commission.

Once the appropriate bargaining unit is determined and an election has been held to certify a bargaining agent, the parties will come to the bargaining table to negotiate the employment contract. A contract may be negotiated for any length of time but rarely exceeds three years. The three-

52. Nassau Library System, 196 N.L.R.B. 864 (1972); Queens Borough Public Library, 195 N.L.R.B. 974 (1972).

53. Cf. 195 N.L.R.B. 974, 975 n. 6.

54. American Federation of State, County and Municipal Employees v. Woodward 406 F.2d 137 (8th Cir. 1969); McLaughlin v. Tildenis, 398 F.2d 287 (7th Cir. 1968).

year period is a spillover from the private sector; where the Labor-Management Relations Act protects incumbent unions from the organizing activities of other unions for the first three years of a valid contract. During times of economic uncertainty, most unions attempt to negotiate a shorter contract.

There are differing opinions as to how soon before a contract expires the parties should commence negotiations. Some employers prefer to open negotiations as much as six months prior to expiration, under the assumption that this will allow time enough to come to agreement on all issues. The incentive here is to avoid a strike. Other employers, however, prefer to delay negotiations as long as possible. They feel that "crisis bargaining" under threat of a strike will result in greater concessions by the union. Contrary to popular belief, few unions like to strike. The losses incurred during a work stoppage are rarely recouped by any increases in the contract.

The negotiating team for the library generally consists of representatives of the library board, the library director, the personnel officer if there is one, and legal counsel. The union will generally be represented by a business agent from the international union, the president or representatives of the local, and the union's legal counsel. Bargaining in good faith over a contract involves the parties coming to the table with the intent of reaching an agreement. It does not necessarily mean that the parties must make concessions to attain agreement. If the parties are unable to reach an agreement through normal negotiations, several options may facilitate negotiations. The parties may agree to ask a mediator, an impartial third party, to participate in the bargaining and to make recommendations to both parties. A mediator only makes recommendations from an objective point of view; they are not binding on the parties. The parties may, on the other hand, choose to submit items in dispute to an arbitrator. An arbitrator is an impartial third party who listens to both sides of the argument and renders a binding decision. The parties must agree prior to submitting the dispute to arbitration that it will be binding. The courts will uphold as enforceable any reasonable decision by an arbitrator.

Where such activity is not barred by law, the parties may use various economic powers to force each other to agreement. These powers include a strike by the union or a lockout by the library. In spite of laws prohibiting strikes by public employees, unions occasionally resort to this activity. In such instances, the library may retaliate by obtaining a court injunction ordering the employees to return to work. The reader should, at

this point, clearly see the need for legal counsel in all union affairs.

There are three classes of issues for collective bargaining purposes. Mandatory issues are those concerns that, when raised by either party, must be bargained. This does not mean that mandatory issues must be in the final contract, but rather, if one party raises such an issue, the other party may not refuse to discuss it. Frequently, when mandatory issues are raised but do not appear in the final contract, a concession has been made. Mandatory issues are generally classed as anything related to wages, hours, or conditions of employment. Some issues obviously fall into one of these three classes, but an individual experienced in collective bargaining can easily rationalize the mandatory nature of any bargaining item. Where strikes are permitted, it is customary that a strike may only be held on a mandatory bargaining issue.

A permissive issue is any nonmandatory item raised for bargaining. Such an issue need not be bargained upon when raised by one of the parties, and it may not be carried to impasse. A prohibited issue is a bargaining item that is prohibited by law. Such items include closed-shop agreements that require union membership prior to employment and hot cargo clauses that require the employer to refrain from doing business with another specified employer.

Public employment relations statutes often specify that certain matters are "employer rights," which the employer is not required to negotiate. Such laws spring from the belief that the policies and services of a public agency should not be controlled by the employees of the agency. Commonly stipulated employer rights include the functions and programs of the public institution, its budget, the utilization of technology, the organizational structure, and the selection, direction, assignment, or number of personnel.

In the private sector, the strike is a means of showing force through economic power. When labor and management fail to come to an agreement at the bargaining table, it is common for the union to pull its members from the workplace. The employer, being unable to meet production needs, suffers an increasing economic loss during the term of the strike and is forced to make further concessions at the bargaining table. The employees also suffer economic loss because they are deprived of wages during the term of the strike. Such a loss makes them more likely to make concessions.

In the public sector, however, the government does not suffer economic loss through a strike. Rather, it is through the deprivation of vital public services that the union can hope to bring public pressure to bear upon the government negotiating team. Because of the vital nature of government services and because these services are not provided in the private sector, it is common for a state to prohibit strikes by public employees. Where strikes are permitted by law, they are sometimes restricted to those cases where there is no threat to health, safety, or welfare. When a strike is called by a union, it is not necessary for the employer to close down operations. The institution may continue to be run by administrative personnel, or by individuals hired during the strike. In many cases, people hired during the strike may permanently replace strikers terminated during the work stoppage.

Many unions feel that, in order to be successful, they must have some guarantee of membership among the employees. It is for this reason that a union will attempt to negotiate a union security clause into the contract. As mentioned above, the strongest such clause is the closed shop clause, which requires union membership prior to attaining employment. This form of union security has been universally declared against public policy and illegal. The strongest clause available today is the union shop clause. Such an agreement requires an employee to become a union member after a specified period of time on the job. Failure to become a union member is grounds for discharge. Under such an agreement, the union is guaranteed initiation fees, regular dues, and assessments from all employees. Further, in the event of a strike, the union has the power to discipline all employees who fail to participate.

The agency shop is a slight modification of the union shop. Although it does not require that all employees join the union after an initial period, it does require that employees not joining the union tender an amount equal to regular dues to the union. Nonmembers who pay this fee are entitled to the protection of the union contract and to representation by the union, on an equal basis with members, in grievance hearings. They are not, however, allowed any of the other benefits of the union, such as the right to vote, to hold office, or to participate in any union insurance or pension programs.

From the union's standpoint, the least desirable form of union security is the open shop. The absence of any union security clause in a contract will result in an open shop. Under such an agreement, neither membership nor the tendering of any fee to the union is required of any employees. Failing to obtain any other form of union security, the union faced with an open-shop agreement will generally attempt to get a dues check off agreement whereby the employer regularly deducts un-

ion dues from the payroll. This relieves the union of the responsibility of having to collect dues from its members regularly.

Employment Security

In the absence of any employment security afforded by union contracts or civil service, employees will seek alternative forms of security. One such method is the granting of tenure or permanent appointment. According to an ALA policy statement,

> Security of employment means that following the satisfactory completion of a probationary period, the employment of a librarian under pemanent appointment carries with it an institutional commitment to continuous employment. Professional competence, in accordance with the aims and objectives of librarianship and the official policies of the library's governing board, should be the criteria for acceptable performance for a librarian with permanent appointment, who shall not be terminated without adequate cause, and then only after being accorded due process.[55]

Tenure provisions frequently specify for what grounds an employee may be terminated and what channels of appeal may be followed.

Seniority is another method of job security. When a library with a seniority system reduces its work force, the last employee to be hired is the first laid off. Obviously, this is not an easy system to administer. It usually necessitates a staff reorganization so that vital positions remain filled. A distinction may also have to be made between professional and support staffs. A seniority system may also be used to determine eligibility for promotion. A general rule is that a more senior employee gets promoted when an opportunity is available unless the junior employee is "head and shoulders" above the senior in ability and performance. Seniority is a mixed blessing for the administrator. While it simplifies difficult decisions (which usually present awkward situations), it removes much discretionary authority.

A common form of employment security in libraries, particularly for professional employees, is the employment contract. Contracts between employees and the library board usually run for one year. More senior employees may be eligible for two- or three-year contracts. A contract should

---

55. "Security of Employment in Libraries: A Statement of Policy of the American Library Association," *American Libraries* 7:449 (July/Aug. 1976).

specify the job to be performed, the salary to be paid, fringe benefits, other conditions of employment, and the procedure for renewal. In the absence of any provision to the contrary, the employment relationship is terminated at the completion of the contract. Some contracts require the library board to give notice of intent not to renew no later than three months prior to the expiration of the contract. If no notice is given by the deadline, the contract is automatically renewed. Some contracts are automatically renewed unless a terminal contract is given.

Contracts are almost always binding on the employer and rarely on the employee. An employee terminated during the course of the contract may be able to continue receiving pay as long as the contract runs. As with any other contract, an employment contract should be drafted by an attorney.

Perhaps the most common form of employment security for public library employees, particularly support staff, is the civil service system. A civil service system is designed to protect employees and applicants for employment from political considerations so that they may be judged on merit alone. The system is usually administered centrally by a commission that has full authority to make regulations. Such regulations would likely take precedence over library regulations.

Further protections for many workers are found in the provisions of the Fair Labor Standards Act of 1938, which has been amended frequently.[56] The act regulates such matters as minimum wages and overtime pay. In 1963, the Equal Pay Act amended the Fair Labor Standards Act to prohibit discrimination in compensation on the basis of sex.[57] The 1974 amendments to the act for the first time made the act applicable to employees of the federal, state, and local governments and their agencies. In 1976, however, the United States Supreme Court invalidated the amendment.[58] Thus it is doubtful that any of the provisions of the act extend to public librarians.

Conclusion

The multitude of considerations that govern personnel procedure strongly suggests the need for a comprehensive policy statement. The formulation of such a policy will require management to analyze its practices, not only to improve the efficiency and effectiveness of the public library, but also to assure that such practices conform to federal and state legal requirements. A comprehensive statement that carefully outlines personnel policy should provide for uniformity and continuity in the treatment of employees. This should reduce personnel problems and the likelihood of lawsuits. A personnel policy statement protects the interests of both the library and its employees. It should be put in writing and widely circulated so that employees know what to expect. A sound and comprehensive personnel policy will help to maximize the performance of the employees, on whom the success of the public library ultimately depends.

---

56. 29 U.S.C. §§201 et seq. (1970 & Supp. V 1975).

57. Ibid., §204(d) (1).

58. National League of Cities v. Usery, 426 U.S. 833 (1976).

11   Finance and Budget

F. WILLIAM SUMMERS

Library finance for the most part is not an isolated activity but is rather a part of the highly complex and increasingly specialized process of governmental budgeting, financial administration, and accounting.

There may be a few libraries that receive public dollars on a lump-sum basis without governmental review processes, but these are increasingly anomalies. The great majority, at least 95 percent, of the public libraries in the United States request and receive support through a more-or-less-formal budget procedure.

Development of Governmental Budgeting

Professional administration in local government is a relatively new process if one considers that the spoils system prevailed into the twentieth century, indeed, still exists in some local governments. Professionally trained administrators are a twentieth century product. In a much shorter period of time, mainly since the end of World War II, the entire purpose and process of budgeting has also altered.

Originally because of widespread scandals in local government in the latter nineteenth and early twentieth century, budgeting developed as a control device—an instrument for checking excessive and improper action by presumably venal public officials.

In the post–World War II era, budgeting came to be seen as not only a control device but as a management tool for making improved decisions. This transition resulted in large part from the work of the federal government's Hoover Commission. Many of the recommendations of the commission were addressed to strengthening the relationship between the budget and policy. The commission also made strong recommendations leading to the reorganization and expansion of the U. S. Bureau of the Budget.

One important outcome of this activity was the linking of budgeting with economic forecasting to provide revenue and cost estimates and with planning functions to provide more cogent evaluations of alternative courses of activity. A parallel process occurred at the state level and to a degree at the local level, at least in the major cities.

Accompanying these changes has been a dramatic professionalization of the budget process. Local governments now employ a wide variety of highly trained fiscal experts whose primary functions are the development and administration of local budgets.

For the most part, library budgeting has not kept pace with these developments, except in the largest institutions. Often the librarian and a secretary/bookkeeper are the only resource persons available to develop the library budget and attempt as best they can to translate the library's program into whatever budget system may be employed in the local government unit.

The Budget as a Policy Document

Ideally the budget is not divorced from other aspects of the library program but serves, in simplest terms, as translation of the library's policies and programs into dollars. It is much simpler to state this axiom than actually to put it into practice. At its best, library service is a response to community needs, which manifest themselves at various times and in a variety of settings. There is an atmosphere of serendipity in providing library service programs that is not always consistent with the precise planning and anticipation that accompany many other governmental activities. Many library users are not able to be precise about their needs, and the processes of assisting them are frequently not easily articulated.

In recent years governments have focused upon establishing a very close relationship between objectives of services and budgeting. Libraries have experienced difficulty with this process for several reasons. Public libraries tend to have rather broad general objectives involving service to the total community. The library, unlike the garbage service, has a multiplicity of objectives, most of which are intangible in nature and for which the degree of accomplishment can only be measured over a long period of time. For example, one of the objectives of children's library service is to produce effective adult library users. The degree of accomplishment cannot be measured until long after the service is provided.[2]

However, many public libraries have given serious study to the problem of developing precise measurable objectives, and generally with good results. Libraries have been able to project service loads at branches, for example, with reasonable accuracy and to extrapolate increases in various kinds of programs from demographic data and specific user study. For example, beginning in 1968 the Vigo County (Indiana) Public Library attempted to relate priorities and objectives in service.[1] The library budget was organized around eight major service missions—self-service; lending service; individual service; alerting service; outreach service; contract service; group service; and research service. For each service input, costs, outputs totals, and cost per unit of output were calculated.

The American Library Association conducted an extensive study designed to develop performance measures for public libraries. This study developed and tested a number of performance-based measures, such as a test that measures the probability that a library owns a book published within the last five years and further the probability that a given user would be able to obtain that book from the library.[2]

A great deal more work remains to be done in this regard. But it is also apparent that the library will likely never be in the position to state its objectives with the precision and degree of measurability that is the case in some other municipal functions that have a single purpose or a relatively limited range of purposes.

The Relationship of Budgeting to Funding

The public library since its inception has been almost totally a local activity. Unlike some European countries, the United States has not developed a system of public libraries having state or national support.

As a unit of local government, the public library has been dependent upon local tax sources. In large part this has meant the local property tax.

The inadequacies of this tax source to support the multiplicity of modern government functions have been amply documented and fully discussed in numerous places and need not be described here. The scarcity of local resources has contributed to a number of movements in library finance worthy of note.

The Search for Larger Units of Service

Recognizing that a modern library program is costly, and usually beyond the resources of all but the largest or most affluent communities, library leaders have in the past quarter century been seeking the development of administrative units large enough to benefit from economies of scale in their operation. The result has been cooperative efforts involving cities and counties and in many cases several counties joining together to form a regional library. These efforts have been generally successful in reducing the number of small autonomous libraries attempting to exist only on local resources.

Related to the search for larger units has been the development of state assistance programs. Initially begun in the depression era, state aid plans have never been a significant part of local library funding except in a few states. The notable example is New York State in which the state expenditure is very large and the result approaches a library system with joint state and local funding. Nationally the percentage of library support coming from state sources is 12 percent.[3]

Public library support has not yet reached the point that the question of state assumption of funding responsibility has been raised, as is currently the case with education in a number of states. Where state funds have been made available in any significant degree, it has been for the purpose of fostering some plan of library development in which the state has an interest. Typically this has been the development of county and regional library units. Recently state funds have been used to sponsor cooperative networks of libraries for interlibrary loan and for cooperative cataloging ventures. At the local level the most common form of cost sharing has been a cooperative or contractual relationship between a city with an older, well-established library system and the surrounding county area in which suburbs have developed.

Private funding has not played a significant part in local libraries for many years. Great fortunes

---

1. Edward N. Howard, "Toward PPBS in the Public Library."

2. Ernest R. DeProspo et al., *Performance Measures for Public Libraries.*

3. Government Studies and Systems, Inc., *Alternatives for Financing the Public Library.*

that could build a large building or endow a library have either disappeared or have been channeled into foundations, which are generally chary of funding operational services, preferring to use their funds for research-and-development purposes. This is not to say that there are not instances in which a local person of means either directly or through a foundation assists substantially in a library capital funds drive, but private funding has accounted for a decreasing percentage of total public library support.

Most public libraries are supported by direct appropriations from the general funds of local government. In some states the people must vote on the millages to be appropriated for various functions, in which case the library has a specified millage rate. Libraries as a general rule do not have access to earmarked tax sources, a notable exception being Ohio, where libraries are funded from a portion of the proceeds of the intangible property tax, to which they have first claim. Most state and local governments have moved away from earmarked tax sources, finding it better administration to fund all government services except the most specialized or limited from general funds appropriated through an executive-type budget.

Types of Budgets and Their Preparation

Before proceeding to a discussion of the specific types of budgets used in libraries and a discussion of their preparation, it is important to focus upon several general matters.

Libraries do not usually establish unilaterally the type of budget that will be used or the details of budget preparation. Most libraries are part of some local governmental structure, and the format of the budget prepared by the library is mandated by the system of budgeting adopted by the local government unit. This may create either a constraint or an opportunity for the library. In some situations the library program could better be presented through a budget document other than that used by local government. In others, the library does not adapt its budget presentation to the format of local government but uses its own format. This is especially the case when the connection between the library and local government is tenuous or limited; for example, when the library is entirely independent of the local government structure. If the library has not seen itself as a part of local government, it may not present its budget in the same detail as do other departments and thus may not fare as well in the consideration process.

Lump-Sum Budget

In this type of budget a single lump sum is requested for the operation of the library for a single year, and the appropriation is granted as a single sum. This is the earliest budgetary form, but it is little used today. Some administrators may favor this type of budget because it gives the administering agency maximum flexibility allocating appropriated funds in transferring monies between various types of expenditures. Of all budget types it provides the appropriating body with the least amount of fiscal control over the operations receiving the funds. However, lump-sum budgets are used to fund operating budgets in only a few isolated and specialized situations, e.g., where a municipality contracts with a nonprofit corporation library to provide library services to the municipality. Lump-sum budgets are used with relative frequency to fund capital outlay projects, such as the construction of a new library building or the funding of a group of branch library facilities. In such a case a single sum is appropriated to cover the total estimated cost. Occasionally lump-sum budgets are used to fund new operating activities where there is no clear basis for estimating the initial costs; for example, extension of library services to a new jurisdiction that has previously been without such services.

Object-of-Expenditure Budget

The object-of-expenditure budget, also called the line-item budget, is the second-oldest and still the most common form of budgeting. The line-item budget has its origins in the reform movements of the late nineteenth and early twentieth centuries in which the object was to control and limit the excesses of public officials. The primary feature of this type of budget is a system of classification of accounts into which all anticipated expenditures must be grouped.

The classification systems used range from the most simple—Salaries, Expenses, Operating Capital Outlay—to the most complex system embracing several hundred individual accounts, each with a unique account number. In general, the smaller the unit of government involved, the simpler the classification system used, although this is not universally the case. An example of a simple account system used in libraries is shown in figure 11.1.

The line-item budget has endured because it has some advantages that recommend it to appropriating authorities. Among the advantages are the following:

1. It is an easy budget to understand. Commonly the amounts appropriated and spent in previous years are shown along with the estimates of expenditures for the current year and the requested amounts for the coming year. Increases and shifts in expenditure categories are readily discernible.
2. The same accounts are used for all departments. This permits quick, although sometimes inappropriate and misleading, comparison between departments.
3. It is relatively easy to relate to income. Across-the-board reductions or increases can then be made to bring budgets into line with income. For example, the 10-percent salary increase or decrease is relatively easy to effect in a line-item budget.
4. The budget relates easily to a cash-flow or transaction audit. This is turn permits ready determination of violations of applicable laws and regulations in purchasing goods and services. Control is also exerted over shifts within the budget by the latitude or rigidity with which agencies are constrained from transferring funds among budget categories. For example, limiting or prohibiting transfers of funds budgeted for personnel to other budget categories is a common control.

In the case of public libraries, the line-item budget has some additional strong points. The number of budget categories that a library may need to utilize fits reasonably well within most line-item systems. The second-largest item in a library budget, after personnel, is customarily library materials. These two items alone normally account for 80 to 90 percent of the library's expenditures. The remaining 10 percent is spread over the other accounts, most of which obviously tend to be relatively small and easy to understand.

As with any budget system, the line-item budget offers some distinct disadvantages, and it has been felt in recent years that the disadvantages outweigh the advantages.

Among the chief disadvantages are the following:

1. The line-item budget becomes incremental in nature. The budget of last year becomes the base for the budget for the coming year, and the budget system does not demand any review of the activities funded.
2. The budget reveals what is being purchased without indicating why. To know that the library spent X dollars on books means very little unless one knows a great deal more about the trends in book costs, increases in publishing volume, and loss and deterioration in the library's present collection than is apt to be known by most persons examining budgets.
3. It is impossible to examine the *specific* purposes of the expenditures. Line-item budgets may state such general purposes as "the provision of library services," but the preparation and presentation of the budget neither raises nor answers such questions as, Which library services? For whom? To what end?
4. Priorities within the operation are not revealed by the line-item budget. Does the library give primacy to staff or materials? Is an adequate amount being expended to maintain the collections, or are these rapidly becoming obsolete? Such questions cannot be answered by object-of-expenditure budgets.

The line-item budget, by virtue of its division into particular objects of expenses, does not organize expenditures by areas of library performance or program. However, it is felt that the line-item budget provides a precise method for controlling costs and it must be used if only in memorandum form.

Account Number	Object	Amount
100	Personnel Salaries	$100,000
100.1	Professional Salaries	30,000
100.2	Staff Salaries	60,000
100.3	Janitorial Salaries	10,000
200	Materials	25,000
200.1	Books and Printed Material	15,000
200.2	Serials and Journals	5,000
200.3	Recordings, Films, etc.	5,000
300	Miscellaneous Accounts	14,500
300.1	Travel	5,000
300.2	Utilities	5,000
300.3	Office Supplies	2,500
300.4	Library Supplies	2,000

Fig. 11.1. Example of a line-item budget

Performance Budget

Performance budgeting has, as a primary objective, operational efficiency. It seeks to develop the budget in terms of unit costs for each of the activities to be carried out—for example, the cost per book circulated or reference query answered. Born of a variety of government efficiency studies, performance budgeting has not been widely used

Activity	Unit of Activity	Unit Cost	Projected No. Of Units	Annualized Costs
Lending Books to Readers	Loan Transaction	$.24	100,000	$24,000.00

Fig. 11.2. A typical performance budget item

at the municipal level. First, it is a difficult system to develop and operate because unit costs for each operation must be calculated and maintained. In times of rapidly rising costs, this can be a difficult and costly process. Second, experience has shown that efficiency from a dollars-and-cents point of view may not necessarily produce effec-tiveness in terms of the accomplishment of purposes and objectives. Conversely, the most effective course of action may be in the long run the least costly in terms of consumption of resources.

A typical performance-budget item for a single library activity might resemble figure 11.2.

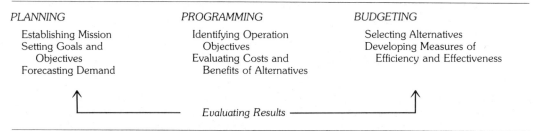

PLANNING	PROGRAMMING	BUDGETING
Establishing Mission Setting Goals and Objectives Forecasting Demand	Identifying Operation Objectives Evaluating Costs and Benefits of Alternatives	Selecting Alternatives Developing Measures of Efficiency and Effectiveness

Evaluating Results

Fig. 11.3. A simplified model of a planning-programming-budgeting system

Planning-Programming-Budgeting System

In the mid 1960s the concept of program budgeting was extended by the development of the Planning-Programming-Budgeting System (PPBS). The description of a PPBS process is very complex, but its basic objective is to link (1) planning—in terms of missions and objectives—with (2) programming the selection of operational alternatives and (3) budgeting in one coherent, interrelated system. A simplified model of this process is shown in figure 11.3.

In PPBS, great stress is placed upon the identification of program alternatives and the development of measurable program objectives.

The greatest utilization of PPBS has been at the federal and state levels. It has not had extensive impact at the local level except in a few relatively large cities. Major impediments to wider adoption of PPBS appear to be the following:

1. The systems are expensive to install and maintain, usually requiring the employment of specially trained staff or outside consultants.
2. For many government activities, the development of precise, measurable objectives is difficult if not impossible.

3. Appropriating bodies tend to prefer line-item budgets because the appearance of control is greater and the budget document is much less detailed.

One of the basic strengths of the PPBS approach is that it focuses on annual examination of the objectives and on the programs being utilized to meet these objectives. Also, to the extent that objectives are measurable, an element of accountability is injected into the process. Additionally, PPBS forces an examination of both the capital and operating costs, and it projects these costs over a planning period.

Zero-Base Budgeting

A natural outgrowth of PPBS is zero-base budgeting. The annual review of goals, objectives, and program alternatives involved in PPBS led to the concept that, in addition to projecting forward for an additional year in the planning cycle, the budget for the upcoming year should be returned to zero. That is, planners should assume that each program was not going to be funded and should annually rejustify it.

This assumption can certainly be challenged on the grounds of efficiency and logic. It can be argued that, so long as a library, for example, has a goal of making materials available for loan, there is little to be gained from an annual analysis of its circulation system. The zero-base approach would argue that there is a great deal to be gained from the forced annual examination of procedures and policies and consideration of alternative methods of accomplishing objectives.

Whatever its advantages or disadvantages, zero-base budgeting is certain to receive widespread attention over the next several years because of its endorsement by President Jimmy Carter. Zero-base approaches to budgeting are now in use in several states and being considered in many others.

Financial Administration

The Appropriations Process

Public libraries normally adapt their budgeting requests to the appropriations process of the local government of which they are a part. Many local libraries are not part of the executive budget process at the local level, because they function under policy-making boards. In these cases the budget is approved by the board and presented directly to the appropriating agency, usually the city or county council. In the cases where the library is administratively a responsibility of the local executive, the library budget is developed and submitted as part of the executive budget. Some librarians feel that the latter process works to the disadvantage of the library in that its budget is subject to the priorities of the local administration and often the appropriating body does not understand that the library budget as submitted has been altered by the executive budget process. City managers may issue budget instructions or guidelines that limit the requests that the library may submit—for example, "budget for no new positions," or "limit the budget to a fixed percentage increase." There is no hard evidence that libraries that develop and submit their budgets directly to the appropriating agencies fare better than those that submit their budgets as part of the local executive budget.

The channels through which the library budget must pass probably have far less to do with success than do such variables as skill in preparation, the political sensitivity of the librarian, and local attitudes toward library service. Even a hostile city manager and budget officer probably could not prevent a full and fair consideration of the library's financial needs in a community genuinely committed to excellent library service, and even the most supportive and forceful local executives will not be able to overcome local apathy or a low commitment to library service.

Normally the budget process requires the translation of the library's financial needs into a set of forms required of all governmental departments. These forms will, of course, vary depending upon the budget system utilized and the local traditions of budget review. All too often, libraries fail to present their budgets in the same form as other units of government. This is particularly the case where the library board has considerable autonomy and does not see the library as closely related to the local government structure. The library would be well advised to adapt its budget presentation to the format and process followed by other units. Budget submissions by libraries have sometimes consisted of only a letter from the board president to the mayor requesting a lump-sum appropriation. At the other extreme, some budget requests include a very detailed analysis using comparative data from cities of comparable size and complete documentation of all cost and salary increases, and relating accomplishments directly to previous expenditures. At minimum the budget should detail the expenditures in each category for the previous year, the estimated expenses for the current year, and the proposed expenditures for the coming fiscal year or budget period. A complete justification should be provided for each category in which there is an increase. Justification should be related to matters such as cost increases, increases in service or demand, and deteriorations of equipment or plant.

In recent years, cost increases for libraries have far exceeded those in other areas of government, particularly for materials. The budget should provide detailed and separate documentation of these increased costs because they are likely to be beyond the knowledge, and perhaps beyond the belief, of those who will have to review the budget. Costs for new programs or expansions of service should also be shown separately from other costs. A suggested format is shown in figure 11.4.[4]

Budget Review

Once the budget is prepared and approved by the library, it moves to the next level. Normally review is conducted by an appropriate administrative officer—budget officer, city manager—who has responsibility for making a recommendation to the appropriating body. In those cases where the budget is submitted directly to the appropriating body, a similar review may be conducted.

---

4. *Publishers Weekly* periodically provides information on book prices.

BUDGET CATEGORY: _____

Amount of funds needed to maintain current services	Include here cost increases for salaries, price increases, replacements of materials and equipment
Amount of funds needed to meet projected demand	Include here cost increases required by increased levels of current services
Amount of funds needed for expansion or improvement of services	Include here new programs or expansions of existing programs. Examples: expansion of hours of service, addition of a children's librarian, staff for a new branch, etc.

Fig. 11.4. Suggested format for library budget request

Except in the smallest of communities, the budget prepared by the library is almost certain to be reviewed by a professional person in the field of government finance. This review may take the form of formal hearing, or it may be no more than a brief person-to-person conference. The basic purpose remains the same: for some supposedly objective professional finance person to prepare recommendations to the appropriating agency on the library's budget. Librarians, and presumably other departmental administrators, have frequently felt some frustration with this procedure. It is difficult for budget review officers to remain completely objective, especially when they may be charged with responsibility for enforcing the policy decisions of the local executive relative to budget increases or decreases.

Once the financial review is completed, the budget moves to review by the appropriating body. This may take the form of a series of informal workshop-type meetings at which questions are raised and answered and the officials can examine the budget and gain a detailed knowledge of it. It is very important that the library have an opportunity to participate in such sessions when its budget is being considered. These work sessions are the substantive part of the budget process, and they are the point at which, for all practical purposes, decisions are made—although for legal reasons the actual adoption usually takes place in a formal meeting.

In addition to the work sessions, there is frequently a formal hearing on the total local government budget. Local practice varies as to how the library's budget is presented. In some cases the chairman or other appropriate officer of the library board may present the budget; in other cases the librarian presents, explains, and sometimes defends the budget. It is probably the wisest course for the budget to be presented by the person most knowledgeable about its contents and about the library program. In most cases that will, or should be, the librarian. It is equally important that members of the board be present to indicate their support for the budget. A good practice is for the chairman of the board formally to present the budget; briefly explain the process by which the board, as a group of responsible citizens, has reviewed it; indicate their strong endorsement of it; and then introduce the librarian, who actually explains and answers questions about the budget.

It should always be remembered that such hearings are frequently only the formal outward symbol of a much more intensive review and in many cases are window dressing designed to demonstrate that the city or county council is making a valiant effort to trim the budget. In the experience of many, budget hearings rarely result in any great benefit to the agencies, but they can result in harm if improperly handled or prepared.

Following the review process, there is normally a formal meeting at which the budget is legally adopted. In many cases, there are requirements for advertising and notices of the meeting at which the budget is to be adopted. From the library's point of view, the budget must be considered as only a proposed document until it is legally adopted. The wise and cautious librarian will plan to attend every public meeting pertaining to the budget and will get into as many private meetings as possible without being an irritant.

Obviously the budget review and adoption process is not an annual event occurring without reference to any other events. A great deal depends upon the kinds of relationships the librarian has developed, over the years and months preceding, with city officials and with various constituencies. The librarian whose only contact with the city council is a once-a-year appearance at the budget hearing cannot expect to fare well in the process. Budgeting is not a scientific-mathematical process; it is a political process and, like all processes, goes on continuously. Sensitivity toward the agencies, as described in chapter 2, is needed.

Budget Formalization

Depending upon the sophistication and thoroughness of the budget review process, there may be a need for formal revision once the total budget is adopted or at the time of adoption. If the review process has been thorough, there may be no "loose ends" in the budget. It is not uncommon, however, for there to be a need for budget revision after the total amount has been approved. For example, personnel may have been cut from the budget, but funds planned for their travel and new office equipment may not have been deleted. These amounts need to be altered. Also, following the budget review process the library may wish to revise its budget priorities and transfer funds from one area of the budget to another—for example, to provide some funds for areas that may have been eliminated or badly underfunded. Such adjustments are provided for in a number of ways. In some cases, only the total amount is actually appropriated, and the various agencies are then allowed to revise their budgets with the appropriated amount as a ceiling. In other jurisdications, the revision work goes on before adoption, the budget as adopted by the governing authority is considered relatively final, and all departures from it must be approved by the appropriating body. This latter arrangement is probably the most common. The budget is revised throughout its consideration and upon adoption is a final document with little or no administration discretion over shifting funds from one category of expense to another. It is rarely possible to transfer money budgeted for personnel to another category of expense or vice versa. It is sometimes possible to shift funds from expense to operating capital outlay, but rarely does the budget system permit the reverse type of transfer.

Budget Administration

Once the final budget for the fiscal period is established, it becomes an operating document against which operating expenses are charged. Formerly the budget was looked upon as a once-a-year event that remained relatively constant after approval. In recent years, however, budgeting processes have needed to provide greater flexibility. Various state and federal grant funds are not always known to be available at the time the budget is adopted. If, subsequent to the approval of the budget, the library qualifies for a state or federal grant, then the budget must be amended to reflect this additional income and to make provision for its expenditure under the terms of the grant.

Local governments make such budget amendments in a variety of ways. A typical, seemingly efficient method is the following. First the agency must obtain authorization from the appropriating agency to apply for the external funds. This step provides the appropriating body a review power over all such grant requests. Second, once the grant is approved, the agency submits a budget amendment reflecting the income to be received from the grant and altering the operating budget as required to expend the funds in the manner called for in the grant.

In the case of ongoing and relatively permanent grants-in-aid, typically state assistance to local libraries, the authorization to apply for the grant may be on a blanket basis, so that the library does not have to seek special authorization each year.

There have been occasional conflicts between local governments and state and federal officials over the ependiture of grant funds. Many state and federal grants have provisions that the locality must maintain its own financial effort and may not substitute grant funds for local funds. Local officials have sometimes wanted to treat such funds as reimbursement or additional support for the program already approved—hence the conflict. These conflicts have been persistent but not generally serious, principally because the state and federal grant funds available for libraries have not been substantial enough to cause a major problem.

A similar need for budget amendment occurs when the library receives a gift or donation. In the main, such private gifts to the library are channeled through some nonpublic agency such as the board of trustees or a Friends of the Library group to avoid mingling public and private funds and to provide the library the flexibility to expend the funds as specified by the donor. Gifts and contributions have never been a significant source of income for public libraries in general, although they may be substantial sources of income for some individual libraries.

Purchasing

In general, libraries can accommodate themselves well to most governmental fiscal systems with a few notable exceptions. The purchase and rebinding of library materials does not lend itself very well to the types of accounting systems used by many local governments.

Purchasing is done mostly from wholesalers and publishers and for the reasons to be discussed a blanket purchase authorization is needed by the library. Such purchases still remain subject to audit. Libraries frequently depend upon wholesalers or jobbers to obtain most of their materials. In dealing with the wholesaler the library negotiates over two matters, the discount from the list price that the jobber will provide and the service to be provided in terms of speed, comprehensiveness, and return policies. These matters are best negotiated directly by the library staff and do not fit well with central purchasing and with the bidding requirements of some governments. Bidding upon contracts by wholesalers is frequently not in the best interest of the library. There are no industry-wide standards for jobbers, and almost any company may submit a bid regardless of its ability to perform. The failure to perform will take place long after the contract is let, and the library services will suffer. Librarians spend a great deal of time discussing and evaluating the performance of the various jobbers serving a given area, and the preferred method is to permit the librarian to select the wholesaler or wholesalers that can best meet the needs of a given library.

In addition to wholesalers, libraries frequently find it advisable or necessary to purchase directly from some publishers. Some publishers do not deal through wholesalers, and their materials are available only by direct order. In other cases, where the library does a large volume of business with a single publisher, it may be to the library's economic advantage to deal directly with that publisher. Experience indicates that the library and the community will usually best be served by treating the purchase of materials and binding as areas in which the librarian is expected to exercise professional judgment, rather than activities that can be forced into whatever purchasing system the government may have adopted.

Accounting for materials purchases also causes the library some unique problems. The discounts that jobbers and publishers allow on materials vary, and frequently the library does not know at the time the order is placed whether a given title will receive the maximum, "long" discount or the minimum, "short" discount. Accrual accounting systems, which encumber the library's account for the list price, must constantly be adjusted when the items are actually received at discount. Similarly, purchase order systems that require that each purchase order be completed before the invoices are paid are not workable for the purchase of library materials. For any given order, some materials will be received promptly, some within a reasonable time, some much later, and some never, because the materials are out of print or otherwise unavailable. To delay payment until the entire purchase order is filled or otherwise cleared means that the vendor must wait a long time for reimbursement. Consequently the service to the library will deteriorate as the vendor loses incentive to fill the order promptly in order to be paid promptly.

Accounting

In some local accounting systems, library materials are treated as capital outlay items and are included in the value of plant and equipment. There is also frequently a requirement that some type of inventory record be maintained on such items. Library collections are usually too large and composed of too many individual items to make an actual site inventory record feasible. Also, adding the cash price of each item acquired to the value of the collection quickly produces a badly inflated value for the collection. Most of the books that the library adds will depreciate rapidly in value. A few books, a very few, will increase in value over time. Generally it is preferable to establish a cash value of the collection for insurance purposes, but not to carry it on the property inventory of the government at its actual cash value when acquired. For inventory purposes, library materials, except for the very few rare and unusual items, should be treated as expendable materials that will be worn out or become obsolete in fulfilling the information purposes for which they were acquired.

In order properly to administer the budget the library requires a financial system that will meet the following criteria:

1. The library should be able to decide which purchases are to be charged to which accounts. In most cases, the library will be purchasing items that no other government agency purchases. To allow the fiscal staff to allocate bills to the various accounts places an important decision in the hands of people who know little or nothing about the materials the library is purchasing and their use.

2. The reporting systems must be timely and full. Reports should identify the amount budgeted, the amount expended, the amounts committed, and the remaining balance for each account. These reports are needed at least monthly. Less-frequent reports will probably require the library to maintain its own records, which will be costly.

3. To the maximum extent, the library should be free to designate the vendors from whom purchases will be made. The anticipated economies of centralized purchasing are frequently more than offset by increased work in the library resulting from the purchase of materials that are not of the best quality and that increase the time spent in using them. For example, there is an enormous range in the price for which three-by-five-inch catalog cards can be purchased. The library staff should know the quality and brand of card that is most compatible with the duplicating system being used and that will be the best value in light of the fact that cards must be in the library catalog as long as the materials are present and must stand up under heavy use.

Receipts

Receiving amounts of cash is always a problem in governmental accounting, but it is especially difficult for libraries. Most governmental cash income is received as a result of some agency-generated billing, such as a water or sewer bill. But library cash transactions, principally in the form of fines for overdue books, arrive in an unpredictable manner and without billing documents being created by the library. Also the amounts involved in any one transaction may be relatively minor, frequently ten to fifteen cents and most rarely amounting to more than a dollar. In a small library, the amount involved is usually too small to make a cash register and receipt system economical; yet the security problems of receiving and accounting for cash remain. In a larger system the use of cash registers with symbols to record the various cash accounts is certainly worthwhile. In smaller systems a simple daily ledger sheet in which the various amounts received can be entered will suffice. It is common practice, long resented by librarians and library users alike, for fines received from the library to be treated as miscellaneous general revenue for the local government. A better system would be to credit these amounts to the book fund, which is always hard pressed, in the hope that provision of more books will tend to reduce overdues in the long run.

Insurance

Insuring the library, particularly its buildings, collections, and equipment, is a complicated problem. Most libraries today use a blanket type of policy that covers the general collection for an established value level. Most such policies require a minimum coinsurance by the library; the property must be insured to a specific percentage of its value. In addition, if the library possesses especially rare or unusual volumes, artworks, or papers, these must be scheduled separately. An ALA committee in collaboration with Gage Babcock Associates has developed a special policy for libraries, which is available through a number of insurance carriers and is referred to as the Hartford Library Policy.[5]

In insuring the library collection, care must be taken to include the value of replacing the card catalog. The cost of cataloging materials often equals or exceeds the materials' purchase price, and so a total loss to the card catalog would be almost as catastrophic as the complete loss of the collection.

Many localities do not insure buildings occupied for public purposes, preferring to be self-insurers. In the light of today's high building costs, this would appear to be poor economy, and such policies should clearly be reexamined. Like other government services, the library must continue to function even after a loss; so the policy should provide for paying the costs of temporary operations while the permanent quarters are being rebuilt or restored.

The question of liability coverage of library staff members and other governmental employees also needs to be reexamined. Many governmental units in the past have not carried such coverage on the theory that their employees in the performance of their duties were immune from liability suits. In recent years there has been a tendency for liability suits of all kinds to multiply and for damages to multiply correspondingly. No library employee can afford to be the test case that establishes that public agencies or employees of a particular governmental entity are liable for their actions or inactions while on duty. The locality should carefully consider securing blanket liability coverage that insures it and its employees at a high level. Similarly, librarians as individuals should also carry liability coverage in large amounts. In many cases such coverage could be arranged for on a group basis through professional organizations. No specific cases can be cited, but the exposure of the library to liability risks appears higher than one might at first assume, when it is recognized that many libraries operate vehicles and bookmobiles that can have accidents or upon which users may be injured. Libraries also operate elevators and other equipment that may injure persons or their property. Increasingly employees may claim damages for deprivation of civil and constitutional rights.

Since almost all library employees will at one time or another have access to various cash funds, and many of them will be responsible for verifying the receipt of goods or services prior to payment, all library employees should be covered by fidelity bond. The amount of such bond will vary from library to library. It is better to have a blanket bond covering all losses from employee infidelity than a position bond that covers the occupants of a particular position. In the former case it is only necessary to prove that a loss occurred through employee infidelity, while in the latter it may be necessary to establish that the loss is attributable to the occupant of particular position, tantamount in many cases to making a criminal accusation.

The number of library operations that may warrant insurance consideration are far too numerous

---

5. Gerald Myers and Associates, "An Insurance Manual for Illinois Public Libraries" (Author, processed, 1972), p. 19.

to list and will, of course, vary from state to state. A useful checklist is included in the manual prepared by Gerald Myers.[6]

Summary

Budgeting for library services, as a process, has followed patterns that parallel trends in governmental budgeting. In general, these trends have been away from a simple detailing of dollars and items to be purchased and toward an identification of the benefits to be obtained as a result of the expenditure.

Library funding continues to be dependent primarily upon local tax resources, which are severely strained. As a result, efforts have been directed toward creating larger, more efficient organizational units and toward state and federal sources of income.

The type of budget utilized by the library will normally be the type followed in the local government to which it is related. For the majority of libraries the line-item budget continues to be the predominant form, although there are increasing examples of program budgeting. PPBS has not yet been widely adopted at the local level, largely because programs are small and the system is complex and costly to install and administer.

---

6. Gerald Myers, *Insurance Manual for Libraries*, p. 60.

Processes for budget preparation and presentation vary widely from community to community. While no single method can guarantee success, it is likely that the political skill and sensitivity that the librarian and library board display throughout the year is a much more important variable than the specific events of the budgetary process.

Library purchasing can function well as part of most local government central purchasing systems, with the exception of purchases of books and materials. These are essentially "single-source" items vended through wholesalers. Libraries can best be served by keeping materials purchasing separate from centralized governmental purchasing systems.

Accounting systems that treat library materials as capital items pose difficulties because these items are difficult and costly to inventory and to value. It is preferable to treat books and materials as consumable items except for the few rare items in the collection.

Library insurance is a complex problem in which it is very important that the librarian and board have the assistance of qualified experts in the field. Current trends relating to liability suggest that many local libraries would be well advised to have substantial liability insurance coverage.

Bibliography

Burkhead, Jesse. *Governmental Budgeting*. New York: John Wiley, 1961.

Council of State Governments. *Budgeting by the States*. Chicago: The Council, 1967.

Davis, James W., ed. *Political Programs and Budgets*. Englewood Cliffs, N. J.: Prentice-Hall, 1969.

DeProspo, Ernest R.; Altman, Ellen; and Beasley, Kenneth E. *Performance Measures for Public Libraries*. Chicago: ALA, 1973.

Government Studies and Systems Inc. *Alternatives for Financing the Public Library*. Washington, D.C.: National Commission on Libraries and Information Science, 1974.

Howard, Edward N. "Toward PPBS in the Public Library." *American Libraries* 2:386–93 (April 1971).

Lee, Robert D., Jr., and Johnson, Ronald W. *Public Budgeting Systems*. Baltimore: University Park Press, 1973.

Lee, Sul H. *Planning-Programming-Budget System (PPBS): Implications for Library Management*. Ann Arbor, Mich.: Perion Press, 1973.

Loew, John H. "The Selling of the Budget." *Administrative Management* 33:71–72 (April 1972).

Moak, Lennox L., and Hillhouse, Albert M. *Concepts and Practices in Local Government Finance*. Chicago: Municipal Finance Officers Assn., 1975.

Myers, Gerald E. *Insurance Manual for Libraries*. Chicago: ALA, 1977.

Prentice, Ann E. *Public Library Finance*. Chicago: ALA, 1977.

Sharkansky, Ira. *The Politics of Taxing and Spending*. Indianapolis: Bobbs-Merrill, 1969.

Shields, Gerald R., and Burke, J. Gordon. *Budgeting for Accountability in Libraries*. Metuchen, N. J.: Scarecrow, 1974.

Summers, F. William. "Change in Budgetary Thinking." *American Libraries* 2:1174–80 (Dec. 1971).

Wildavsky, Aaron. *The Politics of the Budgetary Process*. Boston: Little, 1964.

12   Collections

Theoretical Basis

Public librarians do not bother much about theory. They are usually up to their ears in practical problems. There is, however, rough agreement on the theoretical basis for establishing and managing collections. In Mary V. Gaver's *Background Reading in Building Library Collections*, there is a variety of writing on selection theory.[1] The theory generally followed, although seldom spelled out, holds that access to the record of human activity and of the natural world is necessary to members of a society who are responsible for independent decisions about their government and their lives. The record is encompassed in print, pictures, audiovisual forms, computer banks, videotapes, and other media. The public library performs an essential role in ensuring citizens access to the record, but the public library is not the only agency providing such access. Newspapers, radio, television, other types of libraries, and other agencies share this function. However, the public library is the only general information source freely open to all. It serves and backs up the others; its collection is usually the most comprehensive in the community.

Selection Policies

So that the library may build up and maintain a current and useful collection in accordance with a plan, rather than catch-as-catch-can, a written selection policy is essential. It should focus on the needs of those the library aims to serve. It should also be consistent with the overall objectives of the library.

Needs of Users

Traditionally the public library has been a multi-purpose agency, trying to serve a public of all ages beyond infancy, ranging from the barely literate to the intellectually sophisticated. People come as gardeners, consumers, job seekers, students, business and professional workers, writers, researchers, civic leaders, curious citizens who want to satisfy some personal need for information, stimulation, or entertainment, or in any one of a thousand other life roles. So library collections are necessarily diverse in scope, form, and level of comprehension required. Discussion, sometimes reaching the heat of controversy, has been going on for a long time among librarians as to whether this general role of the library is too broad. Some think the library should focus on the intellectually alert, those best able to use its collections. However, the official position is that the public library has an urgent mission to reach out to all the people. *Minimum Standards for Public Libraries, 1966* presents the mission of the public library as intended for all people.[2]

Among accepted methods for identifying nonuser needs are the use of census and other statistical data, and studies and surveys made by the staff or consultants. Experienced librarians also pay close attention to the needs actually expressed by users.

Since regular library users are usually a minority of the population, the nonusers must be canvassed to find out how, if at all, the library can serve them. In one study, *Information Needs of Urban Residents*, questions were asked, not about reading and libraries, but about "problems/questions." The greatest concerns in order of importance had to do with the immediate neighborhood

---

1. Mary V. Gaver, ed., *Background Reading in Building Library Collections*, vol. 1 (Metuchen, N.J.: Scarecrow, 1969), pp. 9–45.

2. American Library Association, *Minimum Standards for Public Library Systems, 1966* (Chicago: ALA, 1967), p. 9.

(noisy children or dogs, trash pickups, rats, etc.), housing and household maintenance, and crime and safety. These concerns accounted for 52 percent of all problems/questions mentioned. They were followed by education, employment, transportation, health, discrimination, financial matters, legal problems, and public assistance.[3]

It becomes the task of the library to find the answers to problems such as were discovered in the study discussed above. As citizens and their advocates became more aware that there are answers to their problems, and as they gain experience in articulating their needs, libraries are feeling the pressure. They will be well advised to anticipate, as much as possible, public needs rather than to be forced, seemingly with reluctance, to satisfy them.

Objectives and Goals

Most public libraries, either in the law establishing them, in their budgets, or in other documents, have a statement of objectives and goals. *A Strategy for Public Library Change: Proposed Public Library Goals—Feasibility Study* brings together responses from librarians to the question, "What do you think the goals of the public library should be?" These are (1) to provide service to all (with stress on reaching the unserved); (2) to provide information services; (3) to provide adult and continuing education; (4) to collect and disseminate all kinds of informational, educational, and cultural materials, including nonprint resources; (5) to support education—formal and informal; and (6) to serve as a cultural center.[4]

Looking ahead, in *Response to Change: American Libraries in the Seventies*, Virginia H. Mathews and Dan Lacy, summarized major priorities and responsibilities:

1. To support and sustain formal education from kindergarten through graduate school, for which millions of students, widely diversified as to abilities and goals, will require access to a greater range of media than ever before.
2. To play an initiatory role, with other agencies and institutions, in developing in people an orderly acceptance of change and in helping them to adapt to it.

3. To serve as both the motivator and supplier of aspirations for the dispossessed and disorganized.
4. To support the increasingly complex operations of government, of science, and of the business sector of the country.
5. To provide support, with and through other agencies, for continuing self-education and training for people at all levels of work.
6. To accept the individual as an individual and to provide spiritual nourishment, intellectual stimulation, cultural enrichment, and information alternatives to him or her at the neighborhood or community level.[5]

How are collections to be developed to reach the goals and discharge the responsibilities laid out in these statements? By long-standing practice, public librarians, in providing "service to all," keep their eyes on two factors. First, they need to know who their particular "all" are. What are their interests—personal, business, professional, cultural? What is the range of their education? What ethnic groups are there? What is the structure and scope of the area's economy? Learning as much as possible about these complex matters, by means of the methods referred to earlier, the library must thoroughly master the scope of available materials in all media and then select those that bear on the community's individual and group interests and problems. If stress is to be placed on reaching the unserved, and it should be placed there—but not to the exclusion of the regular users—great care must be taken in selecting material within the comprehension of the less educated, who are the majority of the unserved.

Selection Policy Statement

The values of a selection policy statement are many. Without such a statement, a collection will be built up willy-nilly, based on the whims, enthusiasms, and hang-ups of successive generations of librarians and the public. Close study of collections often shows biases, or undue attention to some obscure subject. A collection will be balanced if it is based on a carefully drawn statement, in line with the library's objectives, taking into account the significant intellectual currents of the time and the known interests of the public, and open to dissenting, unorthodox, avant-garde points of view. A collection built on such a basis will increase in usefulness over the long pull.

3. Edward Warner and Ann D. Murray, *Information Needs of Urban Residents* (Baltimore: Regional Planning Council, 1973), pp. 96–97.

4. Allie Beth Martin, *A Strategy for Public Library Change: Proposed Public Library Goals—Feasibility Study* (Chicago: ALA, 1972), p. 46.

5. Virginia Mathews and Dan Lacy, *Response to Change: American Libraries in the Seventies* (Indianapolis: Indiana State Library, Indiana Library Studies, Report 1, 1970), pp. 41-42.

Another value of a selection policy statement is the opportunity it gives those who develop it to think broadly about the library's appropriate ends—service to the public that pays for the library and the protection of the individual's right to read what he or she wants.

A statement also has practical value to the staff responsible for selection. It gives them guidance in relating the library's goals and objectives to day-by-day collection building. Another value of a selection policy statement, officially adopted by the governing authority of the library, is that it can answer the public's questions about the collections, often forestalling painful confrontations and attempts at suppression.

What are the important elements of a useful materials selection policy? Although its length may vary from a few to a few dozen pages, it should cover several specific points. First, general matters should be set down. These include the overall library objectives, the detailed objectives of selection, and responsibility for selection. Policies should be spelled out on materials for adults, young adults, and children. The important questions of duplication and replacement should be covered. If the library is part of a system, consortium, or other cooperative arrangement, the relationships among the parts—central and branches, for example—and the responsibilities or limitations on selection in specific fields should be clearly set forth.

It will be useful, especially in a large library, to state selection principles by subject. Will the library try to develop a comprehensive collection in a field such as local history or a subject of great importance to the community—theater in New York, steel in Pittsburgh, oil in Houston? If the library has special collections acquired by gift or purchase or both, such as those on calligraphy in San Francisco or chess in Cleveland, how should these collections be augmented, if at all? Moreover, the sensitive problems of quasi-scientific or pseudo-scientific materials, religion, and sex should be covered with as much clarity as possible so that both staff and public are informed.

Also essential in a selection statement are principles of selection according to form as distinct from subject. Fiction—how many titles? All books by a Nobel Prize winner, even the bad ones? Pulitzer Prize winners? What about foreign languages? Classics in all? Only those likely to be read by the local public? What about significant research on a subject of local interest available only in a foreign language? The policy should also provide for newspapers, magazines, paperbacks, pamphlets, and documents. And the rapidly expanding and important micromaterials, films, recordings, tapes, and related materials should be provided for.

Selection policy statements, as has been suggested, are best drawn up by the staff serving the public. They know what is in the collections, what is in greatest demand, and what the gaps are. *How Baltimore Chooses: Selection Policies of the Enoch Pratt Free Library* is an example of a statement prepared by a staff committee after wide discussion involving professional staff and the administration.[6] This statement, in the 5th edition of 1973, took into account changes in the city, in the metropolitan area, and in the relationships among local, state, and federal governments as they affected library service, as well as the findings of studies and surveys. It was officially adopted by the board of trustees. As the product of careful work by experienced staff, revised every few years—an important consideration—it has been widely used throughout the library world. It has served well as a guide in the systematic building of the Pratt collections and in informing the public.

Selecting policies vary widely among libraries that have adopted them. Excerpts from a number of policy statements are given in *Building Library Collections*.[7]

The Administrator's Responsibilities for the Collection

Selection is among the most important responsibilities of the administrator. Without a collection there is no library. It is the principal asset of the institution—its capital. Most budgets are limited; so it is not possible to buy all desirable items. The administrator must see that the library stocks the most important and most needed items and that the collection is balanced. Since items not added when they are first issued are often unavailable later, or only at higher prices and at the cost of expensive searching, it is important that significant material be recognized and acquired promptly. The administrator cannot escape the ultimate responsibility for seeing that all this is done even though, in larger libraries, the actual selection work is usually delegated.

Most important, the administrator should assure that the materials budget is sufficient to meet basic needs, that the staff involved in the selection process are qualified and supported in their decisions,

6. *How Baltimore Chooses: Selection Policies of the Enoch Pratt Free Library*, 5th ed. (Baltimore: Enoch Pratt Free Library, 1973).

7. Mary Duncan Carter, Wallace Bonk, and Rose Mary Magrill, *Building Library Collections*, 4th ed. (Metuchen, N.J.: Scarecrow, 1974).

and that the proper administrative and physical arrangements are made for the selection process.

Funding

There is no rule of thumb on how much a library should spend on its collections. The range is from 10 percent to more than 20 percent of the total budget. New book titles published in the United States now number over thirty-thousand a year; new editions run to about ten-thousand. Important books published abroad in English-speaking and foreign-language countries, which must be considered in the selection process, add up to many tens of thousands more. The output of sixteen- and eight-millimeter films runs into thousands a year. The other media—recordings, cassettes, slides, etc.—are coming out in ever increasing streams. Out of his own judgment and consultations with the staff, the administrator must determine the amount of money needed for acquisitions and secure it through the budget process.

Figuring the funds needed for the materials budget is not an exact science and is worked out by different libraries in innumerable ways. Formulas based on circulation and the difference in prices—children's books cost less than adult books, reference volumes usually more than nonfiction—have their supporters and critics. Several factors to be kept in mind are the library's objectives on the degree of comprehensiveness in different fields, changing public needs and demands, gaps, replacements, and rising costs. In a field for which the library wants as complete a collection as possible—for example, local history, or foreign trade in a maritime city—the need can be calculated roughly by taking into account past experience and the kind of knowledge that comes from experts in the field who keep up on trends and advance announcements of publications. If the policy is to have multiple copies of Newbery and Caldecott award winners, past and current, in all branches, that can easily be figured. Filling in gaps and making needed replacements can be done by requiring the staff to pay special attention to these matters and report needs in time for inclusion in the budget. Prudent administrators set aside a reserve fund before the book budget is allocated to the departments and branches. Experience shows that unanticipated needs arise every year. It is less painful to meet them from a reserve fund than to raid funds assigned for specific purposes.

For many years inflation has been a serious problem for libraries as for all other public services. Overall, public library budgets have kept pace very well. *Bowker Annual . . . 1977* reported expenditures of $201,377,075 for public library acquisitions. This was an increase of 134 percent over the figure for 1965 of $85,746,000. During this same period, book prices went up by about 90 percent. Costs of other materials for the collections have also risen substantially. According to *National Inventory of Library Needs, 1975,*

> To give all [public] library patrons access to the indicated size of collections, by acquiring the materials to bring each collection up to indicated standards, would have required $1.5 billion in 1974 at 1974 prices, estimated conservatively.[8]

By 1978 the gap between library collections and needs had reached $2 billion or more; budgets for acquisitions must continue to keep ahead of inflation if our public libraries are to meet minimum standards.

The inflationary crunch has hit large urban libraries especially hard. They have adapted in various ways. Some have cut back drastically in acquisitions, thereby creating future catch-up problems. Some have cut branch services to protect the central collections. Almost all have reduced staff. The more fortunate urban libraries have received state funds in recognition of the fact that their collections are regional or even state resources.

The Selection Process

The selection process is crucial. It can greatly affect the quality of the collection. The steps in the process are: (1) examining bibliographical publications, publishers' catalogs, announcements, brochures, and other sources of bibliographical and other media information; (2) examining or reviewing, in many cases, the material itself; (3) making recommendations for purchasing or rejecting; (4) preparing annotations with recommendations; (5) preparing necessary forms for acquisitions.

The selection process takes time. It should be remembered that the selection of books and other material for public use is not the same as the purchase of items every one of which is identical, such as bricks, pencils, or typewriters of the same make. There is infinite variety in items considered for a library collection. In a large library, tens of thousands of individual decisions must be made. If

---

8. Boyd Ladd, *National Inventory of Library Needs, 1975* (Washington, D.C.: National Commission on Libraries and Information Science, 1977), p. 51.

the work is to be professionally done, the personnel involved must have the time to examine many items carefully. Each should be compared with similar material. The exercise of critical judgment is required. Finally, the decision of recommendation for selecting or rejecting must be recorded.

In addition to the familiar basic aids—*Publishers Weekly, Books in Print,* reviews, etc.—public libraries use dozens of other sources in selection. These include local newspaper book pages, historical society publications, specialized periodicals in which experts review important scholarly books, and the national bibliographic publications of countries in which significant publishing is carried on.

Staffing. Among the administrator's important responsibilities, in addition to securing an adequate acquisitions budget, is assigning the necessary staff for the selection function. There is no best method agreed upon and followed by all libraries. But somewhere in the organization, there should be a unit responsible for making selection decisions or recommendations, putting them in proper form, and passing them along to the acquisitions personnel so that, after necessary processing, material gets into the hands of the public as promptly as possible. This selection unit must have enough personnel to keep the flow of work moving. Two or more staff members are usually needed in a large library. But the size of the staff depends on the number of items examined and selected and the thoroughness of the process.

Facilities. The physical facilities for the selection process vary from library to library. But it is important to have a central place for handling selection decisions and for the staff to look over materials on which decisions must be made. Such a facility, sometimes called a book selection room, can be arranged with new items for each subject department brought together. In or adjacent to the book selection room there should be enough space for the staff who maintain the required files and other records. Recent issues of review journals and other selection aids should be at hand.

Staff Participation in Selection

Although there are several schools of thought on the subject, it seems obvious that many members of the staff should be involved in selection. It is, of course, possible for one person or a small group to make the selection decisions based on their own investigations, ideas, and knowledge. Selection has been done by checking publishers' announcements or by giving orders to salesmen on the basis of their recommendations. Time can be saved this way; the fewer people involved, the

speedier the process can be. However, in most library systems there is generally among the staff a broad spectrum of knowledge and experience that can effectively be brought to bear on the crucial selection process. Coming from varying backgrounds, probably from different regions, having majored in diverse subjects, with specialized interests in fields in which they may very well be collectors themselves, the whole range of staff should be active in developing the collection. Even staff members not especially trained may contribute. As examples, business office staff may be good judges of material in their special field; maintenance workers often have the capacity to determine the practicality of material in their areas, and some clericals may be sophisticated on unexpected but important subjects.

An advantage of wide staff participation in selection is that such participation not only draws on specialized knowledge but deepens that knowledge. The sharing of responsibility by those able and willing to accept it can also heighten their pride and give them more status as they contribute to the most important purpose of the library, bringing the best possible material to the public.

One good way to assure staff involvement in selection is to ask each new staff member to indicate on a card to be kept on file those fields in which he or she has special knowledge or interest. Then items can be assigned to those who are both interested and prepared to deal with them.

It should go without saying, but it needs to be said, that all who are involved in selection must be given time for critical reading. Not all books need word-by-word scrutiny. Experts get to be very good at scanning. But unless time is allowed, the staff and public are being shortchanged. Staff shortages in many libraries mean that almost all working hours of public service staff are spent on the floor with patrons. This, of course, cuts into time for selection reading on the job. Those who can and will spend their own time on this important task identify themselves as highly motivated professionals. They earn the respect of their fellow staff members and qualify themselves for advancement.

In addition to reading for the selection process, the writing of short reviews or annotations is often required. These annotations are helpful for other staff members, such as branch librarians, in choosing materials for their collections. Annotations should be concise, place the item in its field, and tell whether it is an original contribution, noteworthy in some special way, or journeyman work. The annotation should also indicate the potential age or special interest group most likely to be interested. Is it for sophisticates, for young people, for those who need material on an elementary level? The annotator should also point out comparable material already in the collection. Annotation writing is a special kind of writing. Those who master it have the ability to get to the heart of a book, film, or other item and put down its essence in a few words. Skill comes with practice. Those who have the skill are to be treasured.

Examples of annotation cards for nonfiction and fiction with instructions are shown in figures 12.1 and 12.2.

Branches and Subject Departments

In the past it was more or less accepted in a library system that at least one copy of every book acquired should be in the central collection. Now, however, the tendency is toward more freedom for branch librarians to tailor their collections to their own often differing clienteles. This makes sense. It assures that material is placed where it is most useful, and the central shelves will not be cluttered with deadwood. The branch staffs also benefit by having a chance to exercise their initiative and professional judgment.

Initiative should be encouraged among subject department heads in building their collections. If they do not have broad authority for selection in their special fields, the library and the public are not getting their money's worth. The subject department heads are in their positions presumably because they have the experience and knowledge to make independent decisions within the guidelines of the selection policy. The making of such decisions is the essence of professionalism.

Obviously decentralization and broad staff participation in selection make for a slower progress than if authority were more focused. However, the benefits to the public and to staff development should more than make up for the extra time taken in broadening the process. With careful planning and management, prompt supply of materials to the public need not be sacrificed. Speed in getting books on shelves is essential if the library is to satisfy its public, but the building up of a solid collection that will stand the test of time is also essential. It should be kept in mind that all the other communications media concentrate on the here and now. Newspapers, magazines, and radio and television programs are designed for today. After their reading, hearing, or viewing, they are generally physically and mentally discarded. Much of the material added to the library's collections will be useful and sought out in the future. Therefore the time spent by staff in careful selection is not a waste but an investment in the library's future.

Commercial Selection Services

Some libraries, in order to simplify and speed up the selection process, use commercial services. The McNaughton plan was initiated by an alert entrepreneur who spotted an opportunity that arose because many public libraries chronically fail to get their books processed and on the shelves anywhere near publication day. This brings on the number one gripe of the readers, "Why can't I ever find the book I want while it's still new?" To remedy this frustrating situation, McNaughton leases just-published popular books, already processed, ready to be put on the shelves at once. The library may return the books when the circulation drops off, or it may purchase at a big discount any titles wanted for retention in the collection. The advantages of the McNaughton lease-purchase plan are its assurance of prompt supply to the public of books in demand, clearing the shelves of multiple copies of titles no longer needed, and reduction of cataloging and processing work. Disadvantages are the cost, time, and effort involved in returns.

Another commercial service to simplify the selection process is offered by some book wholesalers. An agreement is made under which the vendor will supply automatically books that fit within a "profile" furnished by the library. The profile indicates the subjects, authors, and/or historical periods or geographical areas in which the library is interested. The profile can indicate whether the library wants all titles in a field, popular ones only, English language exclusively, etc. There are advantages in the profile method. One is that a large wholesaler with a comprehensive stock will send promptly titles of first importance to the library. Another advantage is the simplification of the selection process. There is also a potential saving of library time. The main disadvantage is that the employees of the vendor are not as likely as professional librarians to be able to identify all items called for by the profile. There is a chance, too, that marginal titles will be sent. In that case, time spent in examining and returning unwanted books can be costly.

In evaluating, for a specific library, the McNaughton plan, the profile system, or the Greenaway plan—under which publishers send all of their trade books automatically at a big discount—the relative costs, speed, and efficiency of each must be calculated. Each method has its advocates and critics. Before making any commitment, it is wise to examine carefully several libraries using the particular system and to ask probing questions about service, real costs, and benefits over the old method. Many libraries have been unhappy victims of unproven systems that have not delivered according to the sales pitch.

Participation by Outside Experts

Even a library with great range and depth of knowledge among its subject specialists will occasionally find it helpful to have the opinions of outside experts. Most libraries have among their patrons experts in a number of fields. Doctors, for example, can be helpful with popular medical books, where quackery is common.

Some might consider it an imposition to ask for free advice. However, in most cities there are experts ready to help as a public service. The designation of official consultants may be mutually beneficial, giving the library access to expertise and public recognition to the expert. In some cases it may be necessary to pay for a critical opinion. This should be the exception. Where does one find outside experts if they are not known individually to the staff? Most libraries have directories listing specialists and professional associations.

Retrospective Selection and Filling Gaps

Although libraries try to cast a wide net to catch all important items, some are bound to slip through. Or "sleepers," passed over, are later needed. If the staff does not spot a glaring omission, the best readers usually do. They are a good source of information. In libraries that are persistent in searching for missed materials, designated members of the staff will be constantly going through journals of the antiquarian book trade, catalogs, *Books in Print*, and other sources. The same publications will be used in filling gaps.

Gifts

Libraries are always potential targets for philanthropists. Often, generous citizens make bequests to favorite institutions. Many outright money gifts, large and small, come specifically for the purchase of additions to the collections. Well-administered libraries cultivate actual and potential donors, and in many cases collections have been created or enriched through gifts.

Potential donors can be identified in a number of ways. Alert staff members usually get to know those among their readers whose interests have led them to collect in some field. Their friendship to the library can be strengthened by tactful expressions of interest in their collections, by asking their advice, by inviting them to speak on their subject, by professional help in finding wanted titles, and by demonstrating through the skill and care devoted to the library collections that the institution would be an appropriate place for their books should they ever be available as a gift. There is no better way to encourage donors than by personal attention. Often, potential donors belong to bibliophiles' clubs or are members of Friends of the Library groups, where their goodwill can be cultivated in a convivial atmosphere.

The most welcome gifts are those with no strings attached. It should be made clear that gifts will be accepted only if they can be used in a way that is consistent with the library's general objectives and selection policy. Usually, if there is a chance for discussion with a donor who does not clearly understand the library's objectives and policies, a gift can be arranged to the satisfaction of both parties. Tact is essential, of course, in dealing with those who have both generous impulses and strong opinions.

It is the custom in some cities for money to be given for books as memorials to deceased relatives or friends. Or a gift may be made to add books or films on any of dozens of important subjects—art, gardening, management, or history.

These gifts, even some that bring problems, are usually to be preferred over the piles of books that are unloaded on libraries day after day. These piles generally assay 95 percent dross and 5 percent pay dirt. In order to avoid ill will and misunderstanding, it should be made clear to donors that, if the library cannot use all or any portion of a gift lot, the items not used will be disposed of. Figure 12.3 shows a modification of a form used to explain the library's practice to a donor.

On the other side of the form are directions to staff who receive gifts to make sure the donor reads the form and signs it. There is also a space for the donor's name and address so that the gift can be promptly acknowledged. Such acknowledgment is important but unfortunately too often overlooked.

Since the ability to recognize books of special value is gained only through experience and reading, it is good practice to assign to the screening of gifts a staff member or members who either have such experience or want to develop it. If the library has no qualified staff, it makes sense to set aside all items even suspected of having special value—early imprints, first editions, private press books, local history, handsome bindings, rich illustrations, etc.—and have them gone over carefully at intervals by experts.

Rarities have a way of showing up unexpectedly in the tiny amount of pay dirt. Donors have been deeply and properly offended when their trea-

```
Author                              Date
Title                               Reviewer
```

Underline appropriate words below; use reverse for further information if necessary

Author	Partisan, fair,	Permanent value	Pedestrian	Bibliography
Scholar	unfair	Current value	Involved	Notes
Specialist	Emotional		Light	Charts, Graphs
Popularizer	Objective	*Use*	Clear	Illustrations
Journalist	Questionable	As introduction	Too clever	Photographs
Unknown	Unsound	General reader	Sophisticated	
Standard	New; potentially	Requires some	Sentimental	*Format*
Occupation___	valuable	background	Humorous	Excellent
	Textbook	Self-educator		Standard
_____	Standard work	Specialist	*Scope* (use	Poor
	New ed; little	Student	reverse)	Paperbound
Treatment	new	Young adults	*Reference aids*	
Authoritative	New ed; revised	Children	+ outstanding	*Recommendations*
Thorough		Low reading level	✔ satisfactory	Central
Competent	*Topic*	Reference	--inadequate	Branches
Inadequate	Controversial		(use these sym-	Any
Superficial	Limited interest	*Style*	bols to check	Limited
Concise	Important	Effective	below)	Special interest
Practical	Unimportant	Suited to subject	Maps	Wait for authori-
	Little else pub.	Unusually good	Index	tative review

BETTER OR SIMILAR MATERIAL AVAILABLE, e.g.

```
To:

NONFICTION BOOK FOR REVIEW

Please read and annotate, returning book
to Book Selection Room by

     General Suggestions

1. Give your full name and agency in space
   provided.

2. Underline appropriate words on front of
   card.

3. Type annotation on back of card. In
   annotating, indicate:
     Subject matter and scope.
     Comparison with other books in the
     field, if possible.
     Reference use.
     Any specific viewpoint or approach,
     especially if controversial. Give
     examples.
     Special features that seem particular-
     ly useful.

4. Please use typewriter. Do not use pencil
   or make a carbon copy.

5. Do not refer to blurb or "Kirkus."
   Review is kept after blurb is gone. If
   you must cite Kirkus or other review,
   please include date and page in annotation.

6. Please keep review within limits of card.
   If more space is essential, use a 3 x 5 slip.
   Do not attach it to the card.

          THANK YOU

     ENOCH PRATT FREE LIBRARY
```

Fig. 12.1. Annotation card for nonfiction, with instructions. Reproduced by permission of the Enoch Pratt Free Library, Baltimore, Maryland.

Author

Title

    Underline descriptive words below and
    also in column of subjects

Effect: Dull, trivial, light, entertaining,
    unpleasant, inspirational, moralizing,
    depressing, wholesome, frank, unwholesome,
    thought-provoking, stimulating, controversial.

How Written: Very well, well, competently,
    adequately, poorly.

Appeal: Popular, average, limited, permanent,
    timely.

For Whom: All readers, men, women, young people.

Evaluation: Significant, good, adequate, useful,
    unimportant.

N.B. If possible, name some other book of similar
    appeal.

Reviewed in.....................................

Date....... Name & Agency.......................

Adolescents	Psychological
Adventure	Racial
Animals	Regional
Biographical	Religious
Career	Romance
Character	Science fict.
Children	Sea
Espionage	Short stories
Experimental	Social satire
Family life	Social signif.
Fantasy	Sports
Historical	Suspense
Humorous	Transl. from
Marriage	....
Mystery	War
Philosophical	Western
Political	

Place & time.................

....

          Consider for

Central.....................

Branches....................

ENOCH PRATT FREE LIBRARY

To:

FICTION BOOK FOR REVIEW

Please read and annotate, returning book to
Book Selection Room by

GENERAL SUGGESTIONS

1. Please fill in two cards for fiction. (One
   is filed in BSR, the other in Popular Library.)

2. Give your full name and agency in space provided.

3. Underline appropriate words on front of card
   and fill in other requested data.

4. *Type* annotation on back of card. In annotating,
   indicate:
       Brief outline of plot.
       Whether emphasis is on character, action,
         or setting.
       Special subject interest not covered by
         underlining.
       Any feature that might be objectionable to
         some readers. Would you consider objec-
         tion justifiable?
       Any particularly useful feature.
       Comparison with other books in the field,
         if possible.

5. Please use typewriter. Do not use pencil or
   make a *carbon* copy.

6. Do not refer to blurb or "Kirkus." Review is
   kept after blurb is gone. If you must cite
   Kirkus or other review, please include date
   and page in annotation.

7. Please keep review within limits of card. If
   more space is essential, use a 3 x 5 slip. Do
   not attach it to the card.

THANK YOU
ENOCH PRATT FREE LIBRARY

Fig. 12.2. Annotation card for fiction, with instructions. Reproduced by permission of the Enoch Pratt Free Library, Baltimore, Maryland.

READERVILLE CARNEGIE FREE LIBRARY

Gifts of Books and Other Materials

The library receives many gifts of books, periodicals, and other materials, for which we are always grateful. In order to avoid misunderstanding about the disposition of gifts, however, it is suggested that prospective donors read the following statement:

The Library adheres to a carefully planned policy in accepting gifts. It reserves the right of deciding whether or not the gift is to be added to the library. The book may be: (1) a duplicate of an item of which no more copies are needed; (2) outdated; (3) not of reference or circulation value; (4) in poor condition, such as would not justify the cost of repair.

Useful but unneeded gifts are sold, with the receipts added to the acquisition funds. Those not so used are disposed of.

The Library regrets that it cannot appraise gifts. As recipients our evaluations would be questioned by tax officials. On request, however, we will be glad to provide a statement describing the gift.

Fig. 12.3. Sample form used to explain library practices to a donor

sures were cast aside. In one instance, a library was given a number of indifferent-looking but very valuable type-foundry catalogs, that would have been recognized and protected for the future by a recently retired librarian who knew printing in all its phases. A new staff member threw the catalogs out, and they were rescued from incineration only because they caught the eye of another staff member who knew what they represented. The donor, who found out about it, understandably became reluctant to trust any other prized items to that library.

Weeding

Weeding the collections is actually selection in reverse. The same considerations apply as in the process that introduced the material into the library. There is no magic formula for weeding. But a few common-sense principles should be used. Multiple copies of once-popular books that seldom circulate should be thinned out to one or a few. A book that has never circulated, or last went out many years ago, should be eliminated if it is not of obvious value. With transaction-card or computer charging systems, it is not always easy to determine the last circulation date. But examination of the book will usually reveal its circulation history. Books in bad physical condition should be weeded, rebound, or replaced according to their condition and importance. The shabby state of many public library books turns fastidious people away. As with gifts, it is all too easy to weed and

discard valuable material. When one is in doubt, it is sound to hold off and call in other members of the staff or outside experts for an opinion.

Care should be taken in weeding to see that it does not become a covert form of book banning. One way to get rid of awkward material is to discard it. But intellectual honesty demands that the weeding process not be used in this way.

Disposal

Final disposition of unneeded items is a problem related to weeding. Sale of discards along with gifts not needed is a way to realize extra money for acquisitions, sometimes substantial amounts. The incentive to sell, which carries costs with it, is diminished when the money taken in must be turned over to the public treasury. With a little persuasion, the income can generally be salvaged for the library. The obvious way of disposing of absolutely useless material is to have it taken away and incinerated or gotten rid of by whatever other method is locally most convenient. Burning books has a bad connotation among librarians, but it is often the best method of destroying material that can't do anyone any good. To give away tattered, obsolete books to other libraries at home or abroad is a disservice. And it happens too often. Someone always asks, Why not sell old books as scrap paper? Such paper is usually a marginal commodity. It can be disposed of profitably only occasionally during times of national emergency.

Scope of the Collections

Twenty or thirty years ago, upon entering almost any public library, large or small, one would have had to look hard to find anything but print. A few pioneer libraries were already collecting and circulating phonograph records and motion picture films. However, the last several decades have of course brought an information explosion and the multiplication of the media of communication. Libraries have followed the trend—often at a snail's pace—and diversified their collections and services.

Print

Print is still the main stock-in-trade of public libraries. It will probably continue to be so for some time to come. It is easy to see why. The force of tradition is strong among librarians, many of whom are still leery of "nonbook" material. And it is true that there is a large public for whom printed material is the easiest means for study, information seeking, and satisfaction of personal needs and curiosity. The book is still civilization's greatest invention for storing and retrieving information without complicated and expensive electronic equipment. No other medium can match it in economy, compactness, portablity, simplicity of retrieval by means of table of contents and index, use at the reader's speed, and ease of going back to something not grasped the first time. As long as reading is a requirement for a successful life in a complicated, technological society, books and other printed material will be basic in public libraries. One of the key findings in *The Role of Libraries in America*, 1976, the result of a Gallup poll, was "printed materials are the information sources predominantly used by the public to answer questions or resolve problems."[9] In addition to books, the library's holdings in print include serials, pamphlets, pictures, and microprint in several forms.

Serials, a big part of the library's collection, include all publications issued at intervals—newspapers, periodicals, and annuals of many kinds. Newspapers are needed both for current information and as source material They are often the most important historical materials in a library. Every public library should hold all local newspapers, including those serving neighborhoods. Microfilmed files should be available with readers and printout equipment, along with the current issues on paper. Larger libraries will subscribe to the *New York Times* and its excellent indexes, as well as to the major newspapers of each geographical region of the country. In the largest libraries newspapers with national coverage from the most important foreign countries should also be available. Periodicals are a prime source of current information as well as useful in the long run, especially those included in the indexes to periodicals. Smaller libraries should have a good group of general magazines. Larger systems will want these and, in addition, many specialized journals, including those bearing on local business, commercial, and professional interests.

Pamphlets, brochures, flyers, broadsides, and other such occasional publications are constantly pouring from the presses of government at all levels and from organizations of all kinds. They also come from individuals exercising their right of freedom of expression. Many pamphlets on local history and neighborhood activities are the only source of information on their subject. Since pamphlets often come out in small printings, the staff responsible for selection should keep informed and be alert to acquire this elusive material during the fleeting time when it can be had.

Knowledge of ephemeral material comes only through constant effort. The library staff should be in touch with all local organizations—clubs, churches, schools, colleges, associations, printers, and publishers—and let them know repeatedly, because their officers and leaders change, that the library is interested in acquiring annual reports, membership lists, histories, newsletters, and other publications. Researchers will in future years bless the memories of librarians who have gathered a harvest of local information, most of which is usually irretrievably lost. The selection policy statement should give clear guidance on ephemera.

Pictures are to be found in most library collections. Advertisers, illustrators, teachers, and students are constantly searching for illustrations of famous people, buildings, flora, fauna, and countless other subjects. Many pictures are clipped from magazines. Such pictures, carefully selected and organized in vertical files, extend the scope and value of a library. Some libraries assemble and loan framed reproductions of works of art. Such pictures are appreciated by those who wish to vary the decor of homes or offices.

Microprint is one of the fastest-growing print media. Newspapers, periodicals, documents, books, and other kinds of publications are now available on microfilm, microcards, microfiche, and aperture cards. Since space is a problem in most libraries, the miniaturization achieved in microprint makes it attractive. In addition, some im-

---

9. Gallup Survey Organization, *The Role of Libraries in America* (Frankfort: Kentucky Department of Libraries and Archives, 1976), p. 6.

portant materials are available only in microform. The ease of making copies on reader-printers is another plus.

Audiovisual

Audiovisual materials most commonly acquired by public libraries are motion picture films, filmstrips, slides, and sound recordings. Videotape will become more important as the technology develops. Television sets with tape attachments are on the market, and soon many homes will be equipped with them.

Since motion pictures have gained recognition as important means of communication, with the film accepted as an art form, libraries that aim to provide access to all the media for the communication of information are building up extensive film collections. Films are among the most heavily used materials in many libraries. They are expensive and easily damaged; so special care must be taken in selection and lending. Content and technique are both important in evaluating films. As with books, criteria are significance of subject matter, lasting value, timeliness, imagination, and originality. Quality of photography, sound, and color and clarity of picture are technical qualities to be considered.

A comprehensive film collection should include outstanding documentaries, examples of the history and development of the medium, experimental films, literary and art subjects, and productions that stimulate the creative imaginations of children and offer them an aesthetic experience. Examples of the films of innovative producers, directors, cameramen, script writers, and composers of scores may very well be purchased for their technical excellence and to encourage critical study of the film. Examples of the performances of the best actors will enrich the collection. Kinescopes of significant television programs should be acquired, even when the technical quality is not outstanding. Films of local subjects should be added whenever possible.

Films usually are not bought by public libraries for classroom use or for teacher training. This has been considered to be the responsibility of the schools. However, with the trend toward more cooperation among different types of libraries, this practice may be modified. It should certainly be carefully studied with the view toward maximum usefulness of publicly owned materials and with care given to the conservation of films that are difficult or impossible to replace.

The library's policy on accepting sponsored films for loan or deposit should be consistent with its policy on gifts. Sponsored films that are little more than advertisements of commercial products or propaganda for special interest groups are usually not worth stocking, unless the library is building a collection of this kind of material, which can serve a useful purpose in the study of the influencing of behavior and opinion.

Films should be withdrawn because of poor condition or obsolescence. The projection of scratched, poorly spliced film with much footage cut out is a disservice to viewers and a discredit to the library. Because of the cost of films, there is a temptation to use films in a badly deteriorated condition. To keep the most important films in good condition, prints can be purchased specifically for archival purposes, shown only by library projectionists under conditions that will assure survival.

Other types of film materials that have both educational and recreational uses are filmstrips and slides. They have an advantage over motion pictures—they are easy to stop for leisurely study and discussion. Both film strips and slides can readily have sound added. Both forms lend themselves to travel and art presentations and to special programs on the library's services and activities.

Sound recordings have many library uses. Libraries started out with the old seventy-eight–rpm disks and have progressed through long-playing records of several kinds and speeds to the cassette tape, which seems to be the device that will dominate the field for the foreseeable future. Whatever the type, disk or cassette, the sound recording will carry a wide range of material basic in library collections. Music was the original output of recordings. Now there are recorded bird calls, speeches, plays, literary readings—sometimes by the writers of the material—and instruction in subjects such as languages and shorthand.

The videotape cassette is the hottest new entry among the communications media. With its capability of carrying the full array of music, speech, other sounds, and images of all kinds, the videotape will undoubtedly soon take a prominent place among the library's array of stock. As in the early years of disk recordings, videotape faces the problems of standardization and compatibility with different equipment. When that is resolved, progress will be impressive. The capability to record television programs opens many possibilities for adding to the library's holdings while at the same time raising serious copyright problems.

Newly Developing Media

Advances in other new media are so rapid and prolific it is impossible to keep track of them all. Four new means for assembling, storing, retrieving, and disseminating information that have significance for libraries are cable or community television (CATV), computerized data banks, and bibliographic data bases.

CATV has now progressed from experimentation to a practical means of communication. The great message-carrying capacity of cable systems, with fifty or more channels, and the competition for control, make it urgent that libraries make effective use of it. Otherwise they will be largely bypassed and ignored as in commercial television.

Kenneth E. Dowlin is one of the library pioneers in cable. His article, "Can a Library Find Happiness in the Big Cruel World of Television?", gives practical information on how the Natrona County Public Library of Wyoming got started. Dowlin made the sensible and obvious point that we cannot compete in the television entertainment field. Instead, we should "recognize our proper role and remain within the boundaries of that role." He also remarked that

> Other technological systems can be interfaced with a CTV system. Therefore, we must develop these interfaces in order to retain or build our position in the community as suppliers of rapid, accurate and useful information.[10]

Since Dowlin's article in 1973, much has happened in CATV. Brigitte L. Kenney, in "The Future of Cable Communications in Libraries," reviewed these developments.[11] The rapid growth in cable use among libraries is shown in table 12.1.

Table 12.1. Libraries Using Cable Television for Viewing and Broadcasting

	1973	1974	1975	1977
Libraries with Video Only;				
No Cable-Casting	100	185	293	250
Libraries with Video *and*				
Cable-Casting	43	60	76	61

SOURCES: Brigitte L. Kenney, "The Future of Cable Communications in Libraries," *Journal of Library Automation* 9:300 (Dec. 1976); B.K.L. Geneva, "Video, Cable Television and Public Libraries," *Catholic Library World* 49:324–27 (March 1978).

The number of public libraries among those in cable-casting does not show up in these figures, but a list of the kinds of programs presented makes

it obvious that some public libraries were represented. Cable programs of seventeen types were reported. These include information about library service, stories, educational programs, talk shows, book reviews, and local news.

Kenney believed that, although "video/cable activities in libraries have been many and varied," they are still in their infancy. She anticipated new uses for cable in fields where "information needs have been only partially met by librarians up to now." These new uses are "survival or 'daily coping' information," "leisure time activities and informal learning," "formal learning," and "job-related information needs."[12] Kenney concluded:

> We believe that cable can be a means of reaching a far larger constituency with specialized services, a means for sharing of scarce resources, and a technology through which support may be gained for libraries from people who have not in the past supported them.[13]

With the enormous expansion in the volume of information printed and otherwise sent out, the increasingly complicated problems of identifying, organizing for retrieval, and creating easy public access to the swelling mass have become critically urgent for libraries. Computers, originally made for highly specialized scientific and technical purposes, are now perceived as essential tools for public libraries. Well-known pioneers in library computer use are the National Library of Medicine, with its Medical Literature Analysis and Retrieval system (MEDLARS), and the Massachusetts Institute of Technology, with its Information Transfer Exchange project (INTREX). Other computerized information systems are operating in law, metallurgy, and other fields. Public libraries began with computers in cataloging, circulation control, business operations, and acquisitions. However, libraries have been slow to use them in public information services, and there are good reasons for this slowness. Computers work best in areas where there are a few repetitive tasks, such as in banking and payroll management. Libraries have had neither the money nor the skills to be freed to tackle the information job.

That is why libraries were beaten to the punch by a large and profitable organization such as the *New York Times*. Paul Doebler described "a milestone in the development of the information bank business" and suggested how the *New York Times* created a system in which

---

10. Kenneth E. Dowlin, "Can a Library Find Happiness in the Big Cruel World of Television?" *Wilson Library Bulletin* 47:763–67 (May 1973).

11. Brigitte L. Kenney, "The Future of Cable Communications in Libraries," *Journal of Library Automation* 9:300 (Dec. 1976).

12. Ibid., pp. 314–15.
13. Ibid., p. 316.

Materials available to users from the computer files include abstracted summaries of nearly half-a-million articles from more than 65 publications, including the *New York Times*, and a variety of business, professional, scientific and public affairs periodicals. Already one of the largest data bases in the world, it will continue to grow each year by about 100,000 articles from the *Times* and another 100,000 from other sources.[14]

Here for the first time was a big general store of information on important subjects from reputable sources. It was a reference librarian's dream. A number of libraries subscribed to the service. It was expensive, and like most complex systems getting started in a new field, technical and communication problems soon showed up, and the flaws were painfully obvious. There were bugs and a good deal of down time. Now the system has been improved, and the service is better; its potential is very great. If costs can be brought down as subscribers increase, librarians will have another information source to tap. It is to be regretted that a nonprofit system could not have been developed by the Library of Congress.

Library-Created Material

There is a role for libraries in the development of systems for organization, storage, and retrieval of local information needed for the "daily coping" Brigitte Kenney wrote about in connection with CATV. Mary Jo Lynch wrote in "Public Libraries" in *The ALA Yearbook, 1976*:

The increasing emphasis upon information led to a growing number of public library information and referral services on a regular basis. Detroit and Houston continued to report excellent results from their established I and R services. Memphis had a highly successful first year with its new service, reporting a file of more than 600 human service agencies and organizations and cooperation from all. Rochester's Monroe County Library System had its "Human Services Directory" data base chosen as the data base for Monroe County's I and R system. In Maryland, Baltimore County's AID service was working well, and Enoch Pratt began again with its INFER (Information for Every Resident) program. The Kentucky State Library reported I and R installed in four public libraries and informally in many more.[15]

These libraries have intensified and systematized services that have been given informally in the past. They have taken upon themselves the task of compiling practical information that did not exist in printed form. Such a service is susceptible to being expanded and computerized to cover a broad range of community information for which there is urgent, immediate need, often of an emergency nature, answering the distressed questions, "What do I do now?" or "Where do I go to get help right away?" The library becomes a crisis center and not just a purveyor of print.

In response to local needs, some libraries compile lists of organizations and speakers on various subjects. Staff-compiled indexes to local newspapers and other publications are also to be found in some libraries, where they speed up the searching for items not available elsewhere. Such homemade compilations are both useful and expensive. Their continuation with limited budgets and changes of staff often becomes a problem. When they are undertaken, there should be clear guidelines so successive compilers will be following the same ground rules. Some of these local productions have a use beyond the immediate community. Publishers have been known to request permission to make a printing for a wider distribution. In this way local work can have a broad usefulness at the same time that it is a credit to the institution, that has made a professional contribution to other collections.

Intellectual Freedom and Collections

So far this chapter has dealt with technical aspects of building collections—theory, policy, the administrator's role, the selection process itself, and the scope of the collections. Now to the spirit underlying all that. This spirit has been present among librarians for generations. It is expressed most explicitly in the Library Bill of Rights and the Freedom to Read statement. These two documents, landmarks in the long history of the struggle for human progress, deal with the opposing concepts of censorship and intellectual freedom.

Intellectual freedom is expansive and liberating, encouraging and defending minority and unorthodox expression, which censorship tries to smother and punish. Librarians, if they are true to the principles of the First Amendment to the Constitution, must stand with Thomas Jefferson in "eternal hostility against every form of tyranny over the mind of man." John Milton argued in the *Areopagitica*—still one of the timeliest writings on the subject, for all the rolling seventeenth-century rhetoric—as follows:

---

14. Paul Doebler, "New York Times Opens Its Information Bank to Commercial Clients," *Publishers Weekly* 203:60–61 (June 18, 1973).

15. Mary Jo Lynch, "Public Libraries," in *The ALA Yearbook, 1976* (Chicago: ALA, 1976), pp. 257–58.

Good and evil we know in the field of this world grow up together almost inseparably; and the knowledge of good is so involved and interwoven with the knowledge of evil, and in so many cunning resemblances hardly to be discerned, that those confused seeds which were imposed upon Psyche as an incessant labour to cull out, and sort asunder, were not more intermixed. . . .

I cannot praise a fugitive and cloistered virtue, unexercised and unbreathed, that never sallies out and sees her adversary. . . . Since . . . the knowledge and survey of vice is in this world so necessary to the constituting of human virtue, and the scanning of error to the confirmation of truth, how can we more safely, and with less danger, scout into the regions of sin and falsity than by reading all manner of tractates and hearing all manner of reason? And this is the benefit which may be had of books promiscuously read.[16]

Library Bill of Rights

It is against the background of Jefferson's hostility to tyranny over the mind, which is reflected in the First Amendment, and Milton's recognition that good and evil, truth and falsehood are intermingled, making careful consideration of all ideas necessary, that the Library Bill of Rights was conceived in the 1940s, when Americans were under attack for speaking out against repression. This document, in which librarians take pride, calls for the provision of all points of view in collections, for open challenge of censorship, for free access by all individuals, and for opening of the library's meeting rooms on equal terms to all groups whatever the affiliations of their members. It has been officially adopted by many libraries and included in their selection policy statements. Adoption and public display are helpful to the public and the staff as visible reminders of the great principles of freedom upon which the library's collections are assembled and maintained.

Freedom to Read

The other important defense of free inquiry, the Freedom to Read statement, was issued in 1953 by the ALA and the American Book Publishers Council. It was a courageous response to the reign of terror led by Sen. Joseph McCarthy. Revised in 1972, after the appearance of the Report of the Commission on Obscenity and Pornography, it

was endorsed by twenty-one national organizations in addition to the two originators.

After setting forth a powerful rationale for the freedom to read, the statement concludes:

We realize that the application of these propositions may mean the dissemination of ideas and manners of expression that are repugnant to many persons. We do not state these propositions in the comfortable belief that what people read is unimportant. We believe rather that what people read is deeply important; that ideas can be dangerous; but that the suppression of ideas is fatal to a democratic society. Freedom itself is a dangerous way of life, but it is ours.[17]

Repressive Atmosphere of the 1970s

It is unhappily true that the dangers of freedom continue to be glaringly obvious. If freedom is to be our way of life, all those concerned with ideas and their transmission have their work cut out for them in trying to minimize the attached dangers. After a long period in which there were many cases in the courts involving censorship, with decision rather consistently supporting the First Amendment, there was a shocking reversal in 1973. This came in a series of obscenity cases in which the Supreme Court voted five to four for chilling restrictions on the rights guaranteed by the Constitution. The new standards for defining what is obscene were:

1. Whether the average person, applying contemporary community standards, would find the work, taken as a whole, appeals to the prurient interest
2. Whether the work depicts or describes, in a patently offensive way, sexual conduct specifically defined by the applicable state law
3. Whether the work, taken as a whole, lacks serious literary, artistic, political, or scientific value.

Under the 1973 decision and the Supreme Court ruling in the 1977 *Smith* case, "community standards" are imprecise. Librarians or any others may be criminally prosecuted for distributing material that they could not have identified as violating community standards prior to prosecution.

Sexual conduct and attitudes have loosened drastically, at least for a vocal segment if not for a

---

16. John Milton, "Areopagitica," in *The Prose of John Milton* (New York: Doubleday, 1967), pp. 287–88.

17. "The Freedom to Read," in Carter, Bonk, and Magrill, *Building Library Collections*, pp. 329–34.

majority of the population. So much that is acceptable to some will be violently objectionable to others. Ahead, probably, is a time in which energy will be expended on controversies that were thought to have been settled. The always confusing question of what constitutes obscenity will become even murkier.

In turning away from the "utterly without redeeming social value" standard, and deciding that one determining factor is "whether the work, taken as a whole, lacks literary, artistic, political, or scientific value," the 1973 decision pulled the rug out from under a former constructive stand and flew in the face of the First Amendment, which says unequivocally, "Congress shall make no law . . . abridging the freedom of speech, or of the press. . . ."

Study of the history of the struggle between the forces of freedom and of repression shows the pendulum swings back and forth. The Elizabethan age, a period of uninhibited personal conduct, was followed by a reign of austere Puritans, who were succeeded in turn by the lusty rakes of the Restoration. In our time we have seen another abrupt turnabout. We inherited the strict moralistic outward values of the Victorian period, which now appear to have been hypocritical veneer over selfishness, sensuality, and cruelty. The avowed Victorian values have given way under the impact of Freudianism and scientific inquiry into sexual behavior. The result has been probably the greatest outburst in history of erotic literature, films, and art. Now not only do we have the works of our contemporaries vying with each other in exploring the limits of erotic sensation; we have the sum of all erotic literature of all the civilizations of the past that recorded the sensual side of their cultures.

In these circumstances it was not unexpected that Congress should find sex, and particularly traffic in its more uninhibited published materials, to be a matter of national concern. In 1968 Congress passed a law setting up a Commission on Obscenity and Pornography, which President Johnson appointed. Here for the first time was an approach to the problems of obscenity and pornography that was not only massive but backed up by the investigations and findings of experts and the statements of qualified specialists. The Report of the Commission on Obscenity and Pornography is the most thorough study of its kind ever made.

In spite of the congressional concern over erotic material, the commission found that only 2 percent of the population placed such concern among the two or three most serious problems facing the country. It was also found that antisocial behavior as a result of exposure to erotic materials could not be documented. Some persons exposed during the studies responded with revulsion. Others considered the erotic materials to be usefully informational.

Among the commission's most important recommendations was the repeal of federal, state, and local legislation prohibiting sale, exhibition, or distribution of erotic materials to consenting adults. It was also recommended that legislation prohibiting distribution to minors under seventeen or eighteen who do not have parental permission was appropriate.

By the time the commission report came out in 1970, Richard Nixon was in the White House. In the face of the commission statement, backed by the overwhelming majority of its members, that "public opinion in America does not support the imposition of legal prohibitions upon the right of adults to read or see explicit sexual materials," the president disdainfully disavowed the report. He announced self-righteously:

I have evaluated that report and categorically reject its morally bankrupt conclusions and major recommendations. . . . American morality is not to be trifled with. The Commission on Obscenity and Pornography has performed a disservice and I totally reject its report.[18]

During Nixon's years in office, he appointed four Supreme Court justices all of whom later led the Court in cutting back freedom of expression.

It was against the background of the Watergate scandals and the restrictive Supreme Court decisions that the ALA met in annual conference in June, 1973, just twenty years after President Eisenhower's "Don't join the book burners" statement in response to Senator McCarthy's rampage and the Freedom to Read statement. Having given strong support to the recommendations of the Commission on Obscenity and Pornography, and having taken an active part in the defense of freedom of expression for many years, the ALA reacted promptly and decisively to the Supreme Court decisions. The librarians assembled were alarmed by the prospect foreseen in the dissenting opinion of Justice William O. Douglas in *Paris Adult Theatre I* v. *Slayton*, District Attorney:[19]

What we do today is rather ominous as respects librarians. The net now designed by the Court is so finely meshed that taken literally it could result in raids on libraries. Libraries, I had always assumed were sacrosanct, representing

---

18. Statement by Richard M. Nixon, October 24, 1970, quoted in *Encyclopaedia Britannica*, 1973 ed., v. 5, p. 167.

19. Paris Adult Theatre I v. Slayton, 413 U.S. 49, 72 n. (1973) (Douglas, J., dissenting).

every part of the spectrum. If what is offensive to the most influential person or group in a community can be purged from a library, the library system would be destroyed.

The ALA filed a petition to the Supreme Court for a rehearing on the restrictive decisions. The petition was denied. So public libraries must be prepared for continuing activity in defense of intellectual freedom. To do this effectively, librarians and trustees will want to keep informed on all proposed legislation. Strong partners in this work are the ALA Intellectual Freedom Committee, the Office of Intellectual Freedom, the Freedom to Read Foundation, the state library associations and their intellectual freedom committees, the American Civil Liberties Union, and the press. Public libraries have been less in the news recently as victims of censor's attacks than school libraries. But that does not mean the public libraries are free of problems. Marjorie Fiske, in her scholarly *Book Selection and Censorship* (1959), found "an atmosphere of caution" among California public librarians.[20] They themselves were censors, reacting timidly if they heard there was a problem over a book in some other library. Caution undoubtedly still exists among some librarians. And the Supreme Court decisions tend to perpetuate it. Even in 1977 one public library was found to have restricted access to almost 900 books, including more than 40 novels. A visit to several libraries chosen at random, especially smaller ones, would probably turn up many such cases.

A Dilemma of Selection

Thoughtful librarians, with all their dedication to intellectual freedom that leads them to oppose unreasonable limitations on expression, still face a dilemma in building their collections. The dilemma has to do with the tension caused by the sense of social responsibility shared by many librarians as it comes up against the principles of the Library Bill of Rights. There appears to be a conflict here. It shows up most sharply when sexism and racism are involved, but the conflict is seen also in politics, religion, and other sensitive subjects. *Advocacy* is a term that is increasingly used in the communications professions, such as journalism and librarianship. If librarians become advocates of a cause and reflect this in their selection, what happens to the principles of impartiality of the Library Bill of Rights? Yet, social responsibility may inevitably involve librarians in advocacy.

In "Social Responsibility vs. the Library Bill of Rights," David Berninghausen attacked the application of the principles of social responsibility and advocacy to materials selection. Citing a number of authors whose findings are considered questionable from a scientific point of view or offensive to one ethnic group, and referring to the complete switch of thinking on the effect of cholesterol, Berninghausen pointed up the dangers of selection on the basis of current convictions on what is true and what is false. Most persuasively he wrote:

Books or other media expressing criticism of religion, or books alleged to foster hate, bigotry, or [feelings of] racial superiority exist. Some librarians hold that such material should be banned. When any librarian is tempted to include only what he considers "good" books in his collections, to promote the causes in which he believes, he then cuts the ground out from beneath his feet. He has destroyed his basis for resisting censorship when his opposite number violates the principles of the Library Bill of Rights in the opposite direction. The librarian who puts himself in this position has no defense for his conduct when a citizen of a different persuasion challenges his decision. This argument is no more valid as a guide to library practice when it is advanced by a civil libertarian than when it is made by a Daughter of the American Revolution or a John Bircher.

Those Librarians who understand the principles of intellectual freedom, as expressed in the Library Bill of Rights, will accept the statement: It is unethical for a librarian in a publicly supported library to suppress statements he does not like, or to exclude expressions of ideas that are objectionable to any religious, political, or other organization to which he belongs. A professional librarian's first commitment must be to preserve intellectual freedom for everyone.[21]

It is easy to see how, when traditional values are under the most aggressive challenge, the old question of distinguishing between knowledge and ignorance becomes more difficult. In *The Republic*, Plato held that the domain of opinion lies between knowledge of what really exists and ignorance of what does not exist. Opinion is more obscure than knowledge, but clearer than ignorance. Public libraries must continue to assemble both knowledge and opinion, recognizing that the distinction between them will not always be clear. They must then deal with the consequences of that confusion. It comes down to the fact that selection of public library collections is a sensitive

---

20. Marjorie Fiske, *Book Selection and Censorship: A Study of School and Public Libraries in California* (Berkeley: University of California Press, 1959).

21. David Berninghausen, "Social Responsibility vs. The Library Bill of Rights," *Library Journal* 97:3675–81 (Nov. 15, 1972).

business. Those involved in it will benefit from orderly minds and strong nervous systems.

This leads me to offer, very tentatively, Castagna's Theory of Daring Books. Theory because it has not been adequately tested and because I have enough ego to theorize but not enough to pose as a lawgiver. The theory goes like this: The same book, if it is daring or original in any way, will outrage the fundamentalist, worry the timid, challenge the open-minded, and stimulate the intelligent; but such a book will be a constant problem to the librarian, who must first decide whether to select it, then how to keep enough copies on hand to fill the reserves, while at the same time fending off those who are not only outraged and worried but want the librarian's hide. However, about ten years after the furor has died down, the book will be found on the assigned reading list of 85 percent of the colleges and universities and 2 percent of the high schools, and the editors of *Library Journal* will be hectoring the 38 percent of public librarians who still don't have a copy. The theory could easily be tested with titles that will come quickly to mind. It would make a good Ph.D. dissertation.

Dealing with Protests

Those closest to the public—the staff—usually are the first to hear protests about any part of the collections. Since they have presumably contributed to selection and are responsible for guidance to the public, they are in a good position to deal with complaints. Often they can be resolved through friendly discussion on the floor. Having a thorough understanding of the selection policy and assurance of backing by their supervisors, grass-roots staff should take initiative in making explanations to questioning patrons. It is important not to be confused by an attack when it comes, but to treat the complainant courteously— he or she has a right to complain, to be heard, and to have as full an explanation as possible.

All protests are not resolved on the floor. Supervisors and administrators should always be promptly available to take the heat. If it looks as if the protest will become public, it is a good idea to notify the media. Foresighted administrators, knowing that sooner or later something in the collection will be challenged, keep the public and the media informed through exhibits and releases

on how selection is done. Exhibitions of the countless classics that have been banned can be both interesting and informative.

One of the most effective ways of dealing with protests is the use of a printed form for the complainant to fill out. Figure 12.4 shows an example of such a form.

One obvious advantage of such a form is that it calls for a response in specific terms. A general statement of dissatisfaction will not do. Often, after looking over the form, the complainant will decide, having thought the matter over logically, that there is no basis for a reasonable protest. Another problem related to complaints is making provision for patron suggestions of material to be added to the library. Most librarians welcome such suggestions. Usually they can be taken informally by a staff member and forwarded for consideration. However, the form shown in figure 12.5 has been found useful.

Conclusion

This has been an attempt to report some of the best thinking on public library material selection and the building of collections. Some of the problems have been pointed out. The building and the nurturing of the library's collections are sensitive responsibilities. In order to discharge them effectively and to deal with the problems that are certain to occur, careful attention must be given to two basic factors. One of these is the establishment of a selection policy consistent with the Library Bill of Rights and based on the library's general objectives. Such a policy will assure those who support and use the library—the citizens—freedom in their search for facts, enlightenment, and recreation. The other factor is the commitment of all concerned—governing body, administrators, staff, and public—to defend the right of the people to read, see, and hear what they choose.

Those with responsibility for selection will benefit by recalling that it is our most courageous predecessors, and not the cautious ones, to whom we are indebted. It was those courageous librarians, sometimes hazarding their positions in their devotion to a principle, who made our public libraries highly regarded wherever freedom of thought and inquiry are valued.

ENOCH PRATT FREE LIBRARY

Book Selection Inquiry

Author: Publisher:

Title: Copyright Date:

Reader's Name:

Address:

Represents: [ ] Self

           [ ] Organization

    If complainant represents organization:

    Name of organization_____

    Address of organization_____

    Name of officer or person in charge_____

1. How did you learn of this book?

2. What are your objections to this book?

3. What harm do you feel might be the result of reading this book?

4. Did you read the entire book? Yes [ ] No [ ] If not, what parts did you read?

5. Is there anything worthwhile in this book?

6. Have you read any professional reviews of this book? Yes [ ] No [ ]

   If so, please list names of critics and sources of reviews.

   1.

   2.

   3.

7. What do you believe are the main ideas of this book?

8. What do you think was the author's purpose in writing this book?

9. In view of the author's purpose, would you say he had succeeded or failed?

10. What book with a similar purpose would you suggest in place of this book?

   Author:

   Title:

                           _____

                             Signature of Reader

Additional Comments:

Fig. 12.4. Form for use by a complainant. Reproduced by permission of the Enoch Pratt Free Library, Baltimore, Maryland.

```
                    ENOCH PRATT FREE LIBRARY
                      Book Selection Inquiry
                    (For Book Not in Library)

Author:                              Publisher:

Title:                               Copyright Date:

Reader's Name:

Address:

Represents:  [ ] Self

             [ ] Organization

     If complainant represents organization:

     Name of organization_____

     Address of organization_____

     Name of officer or person in charge_____

1.  How did you learn of this book?

2.  Have you read the book?  Yes [ ]   No [ ]

3.  Have you read any professional reviews of the book?  Yes [ ]   No [ ]
    If so, please list the names of critics and sources of reviews.

         1.

         2.

         3.

4.  What do you think are the main ideas of this book?

5.  What do you think was the author's purpose in writing this book?

6.  In view of the author's purpose, would you say he has succeeded or
    failed?

7.  Why do you think it is important for the Library to have this book?

8.  What book with a similar purpose would you suggest in place of this
    book?

    Author:

    Title:


                                   _____
                                      Signature of Reader


Additional comments:
```

Fig. 12.5. Form for patron suggestions. Reproduced by permission of the Enoch Pratt Free Library, Baltimore, Maryland.

13   Services Offered within the Library

DOROTHY SINCLAIR

In a broad sense, library service might be defined as whatever librarians do to assure successful use of the library by its clientele. This definition would include almost all aspects of the operation, since all are pointed, in the last analysis, toward the successful user transaction. Normally, however, library usage reserves the word *service* for those parts of the operation that involve direct staff interface with the public for the purpose of fulfilling the user's (and the library's) objectives. In this chapter, we shall attempt to come to grips with some of the major management decisions that must be made at various levels in connection with direct service.

The chapter is divided into two parts. The first section defines and describes service as it exists in today's public library. Here, in the interest of completeness, are included discussions of some levels and degrees of service more likely to be offered in larger than smaller libraries. A second section focuses on a few common problems and delves more deeply into possibilities for public library service, controlling its quality and incidence, and evaluating it.

Typical Services

When we view the library in its simplest terms, it might be described as a collection of objects containing messages. Most of the objects are books, but other types are increasingly found. The collection alone, however, is of little value unless the objects are used. Use, in turn, requires access, and library service is chiefly concerned with access—access, that is, of the user to the messages desired. Using these terms, we can define existing types of service as follows:

1. Access to the physical object, to facilitate self-service
2. Assistance in making a selection *among* objects (reader guidance)
3. Access to messages extracted for the user from within objects (reference or information service)

4. Interpretation of, or assistance in understanding of, messages within objects (also included in reference or information service; frequently given in the case of children or undereducated adults)
5. Provision of messages from objects, but without provision of the object itself (telephone service, storytelling, and the like)
6. Provision of messages, presumably derived at least in part from objects but considerably removed therefrom, to groups through programs with speakers, panels, discussion, etc.
7. Provision of information about alternative sources of messages and/or objects (referral of user)
8. Provision of messages and/or objects from an alternative source from which they have been transmitted as a result of institutional inquiry on behalf of the user (referral of inquiry).

Let us look in turn at each of these categories of service and what it entails.

Access to the Physical Object

The first and simplest type of access is physical access to the object. Normally, the user comes to the object. To facilitate this type of access, branches, bookmobiles, and other convenient outlets are provided. Within the library, means to promote easy access include arrangement, signs, catalogs, indexes, and other aids to self-help. Since many simple studies undertaken by individual libraries have indicated that a majority of users do not ask for help from a librarian, these aids are of major importance. Systematic and regular checks, to ensure that the user relying on his own efforts will not be misled or lost, should be made by every library regardless of size.

While a proportion of users' needs for specific items can be met through self-service, some cannot. It is important, therefore, that there be encouragement for the normally self-sufficient user to consult a librarian before assuming that an item

161

is not held by the library. One of the most frequent and distressing examples of nonsuccess in the use of the library, as found in surveys, is that people often leave unsatisfied, even when what they need is available but difficult to find without help. It is easy for librarians, naturally more aware of the users who do ask, to fail to take sufficiently into account those who do not. Signs ("Book Not Here? Ask at Desk" is an example) can be placed at intervals on shelves and at the catalog. Librarians on desk duty can approach browsing users unobtrusively with a casual "Are you finding what you want?" followed by the invitation, "Let me know if I can help."

Assistance in Making a Selection among Objects

The term *reader guidance* has been in use for some years, but it is not normally used directly with a reader. An older term, still in use in some libraries, is *reader's advisory service*—which is less likely to be offensive to the user. In addition to the somewhat condescending connotation of the current term, it can be objected to on the grounds that it is not strictly accurate. In the reader guidance transaction, the guidance is two way; the reader is guiding the librarian at least as much as the librarian is guiding the reader. The term *reader consultant* has a more modern ring and might well be considered as a substitute for both older terms.

In its older form, reader's advisory service required one or more interviews and resulted in custom-made reading lists or courses for individuals pursuing fairly serious educational goals. The service was expensive. Its early popularity created financial problems that in many libraries led to abandonment of such personalized in-depth service in favor of the mass-produced reading course, already available on a number of subjects. This type of course, extremely popular around the 1930s, was revived in the 1960s with the *Reading for an Age of Change* courses. Today, external degree or "university without walls" programs are becoming available throughout the nation, constituting a revival of the personally tailored reading course, completion of which may lead to university credit. The role of the public library in these ventures varies, but a number are actively involved. In some situations, the library's participation is auxiliary and does not involve the use of professional skills; the library publicizes the program, registers students, provides office space, hands out reading lists, supplies listed reading materials, and may even supervise examinations. In other cases, librarians are more deeply involved in the preparation of reading courses and are ex-

pected to advise students about additional or substitute materials. [1]

Most of today's public libraries have abandoned the older type of reader's advisory service in favor of less-formal advice about reading. While some readers are "regulars" whose interests are known, the type of reader service that is cumulative has apparently fallen somewhat into disuse. Good reader service today utilizes an interview technique in which the librarian goes to the shelves with the reader; identifies tastes, interests, and reading abilities; and, through a sort of three-cornered transaction in which reader, librarian, and collection are involved, arrives at what is needed. The librarian utilizes the collection in determining the user's need—individual items are described and offered, and, through the reader's verbal and nonverbal reaction, the librarian is guided toward a closer approximation of the appropriate material (figure 13.1).

The library-produced booklist frequently provides a substitute for the reader consultant interview; in this context it is a service tool rather than a public relations device. The variety of items listed and the notes presented often serve in place of the librarian's personal description of materials in the guidance interview. While the custom-selection element is lacking, a booklist offers some advantages in that it can be prepared carefully by the best-qualified staff members and can include materials for future use that may not be available on the shelves at any given time.

The old-style personal interview and in-depth personal service are still needed by some library users under some circumstances. Modern one-desk service brings to the same librarian a stream of inquiries of varying types, along with frequent interruptions by telephone. Such a system does not permit the full utilization of the librarian's knowledge when there is a need of some complexity and also perhaps an element of the confidential in the user's problem. Such circumstances are infrequent, but there ought to be an opportunity for a user in pursuit of assistance in seeking sensitive and complicated information to sit down in privacy with a skilled librarian. Further attention to this problem will be given later in this chapter.

Access to Messages Extracted for the User from within Objects

Regardless of the size of staff, and regardless of the level of subject specialization possible, librar-

1. Jean S. Brooks and David Reich, *The Public Library in Non-Traditional Education* (Homewood, Ill.: ETC Publications, 1974).

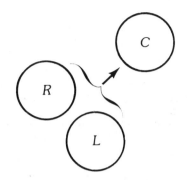

Step I. L. & R. approach C.

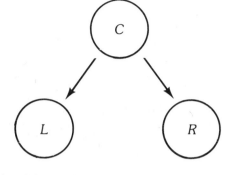

Step II. L. (suggests)
         (describes)
         (shows   )   item(s) of C. to R.

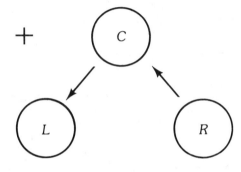

Step III. A.
R. reacts positively to C. and communicates satisfaction to L. (Transaction completed.)

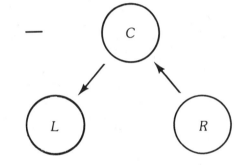

Step III. B.
R. reacts negatively to C. and communicates dissatisfaction to L.

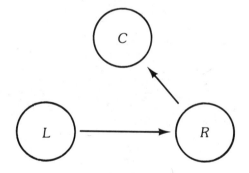

Step IV.
L. queries R. further as to reason for negative reaction.

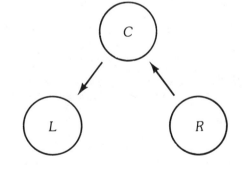

Step V.
R. responds in terms of C.

Cycle (Step II to V) is repeated until successful, with greater probability of success after each repetition.

Fig. 13.1. Interaction of librarian, reader, and collection in reader guidance transaction.

ians who give face-to-face reference service must have the following:

1. *Library skills*: knowledge of the tools and techniques of access to messages—catalogs, bibliographies, indexes, reference sources, the subject collection
2. *Subject knowledge:* ability to judge the soundness, up-to-dateness, and relevance to a particular inquiry of materials
3. *Human relations skills:* ability to interview the inquirer in order to determine the precise need, not only in terms of subject, but also in terms of user background, educational competence, and ability to use library materials.

Reference and information service depends heavily upon these qualities. It is almost impossible to overemphasize the importance of interviewing skill for the reference librarian. If a query is not clearly understood, much time may be wasted in searching for irrelevant materials. Such failures are not always identified; many courteous users may leave without satisfaction rather than press the librarian for a better performance. Variations in background and life-style further complicate the picture. What would seem an inoffensive question to a middle-class suburbanite, asked by a librarian of corresponding background, may not be acceptable to a minority user.[2] Similarly, a young, casually dressed, perhaps bearded male librarian may offend a more conservative user by his probing in the reference interview. Thus, while in some cases a direct question may be asked, often conclusions will be drawn by skillful conversation and listening. Sometimes the most helpful information a librarian can receive is the use to which the requested information is to be put, but, unless asked carefully, the question may seem to the user an invasion of privacy.

Techniques of searching also require skill. Here the librarian needs a knowledge of the reference apparatus, including the card catalog—a more complicated instrument, especially in a large library, than is commonly realized. Sequence is important in some searches, date in others. Where a specific fact is sought, imagination and experience will often call to mind sources intended primarily for an entirely different use. Experience and general familiarity with the literature will also help the librarian determine how widely to cast the net—whether to search a periodical index, for

example, under a general rather than specific topic.

Paradoxically, the larger the library, the more complex its collection, the more difficulty there may be in extracting messages to meet user needs. This statement may come as a surprise to some, since the larger library's more-specialized contents might be expected at first glance to be more likely to readily yield an appropriate message. It is true that, where the item needed is known by user or librarian, or where a volume on the specific subject needed is held, the large library will respond quickly and efficiently. However, when the message needed must be searched for, a large collection, while offering a better hope of final success, requires longer and more complex searches.

Interpretation of Messages within Objects

If the utilization of its resources by all who need them is one of the library's prime objectives, it will frequently be necessary to assist some users beyond the mere location and pointing out of the relevant message. Children and undereducated adults, for example, are frequently in need of further help. While the librarian attempts to find answers geared to the user's apparent educational level or knowledge in the field sought, it is not always possible to do so. Since it is axiomatic that a need is not satisfied until an answer is provided that the user can understand, it is sometimes necessary to give a brief explanation or interpretation of a page or paragraph of text.

In giving such service, the librarian must guard against several dangers. One obvious danger is a condesending manner that insults the user's intelligence. A second reflects a habit that may develop among young librarians unfamiliar with all the collection and genuinely trying to be helpful—that of giving a personal answer or opinion rather than paraphrasing the author for a user's benefit. A librarian is not a counselor, except in the fields of reading and recorded information, nor is a library a consultant service, except in those fields. Another possible danger occurs when a librarian goes too far in assisting a student to do work that is part of an assignment. It takes real skill to determine when help is needed, to offer it naturally and without transgressing professional boundaries, and to make sure the message is really received.

Provision of Messages from Objects without Provision of the Object Itself

Telephone service for information purposes, an increasing function especially in larger libraries,

2. Brenda Dervin has been engaged for several years on a study of information needs of minority library users and of sensitive areas in interviewing and means of dealing with them.

provides messages direct to the user. With parking and public transportation far from satisfactory in many communities, it is inevitable that people needing a fact or other brief information should telephone rather than visit the library. Over half the reference transactions handled by some city libraries come in over the telephone.[3]

Unfortunately, the great increase in telephone requests, superimposed on the more customary in-person inquiries, has been met in some libraries by an attempt to keep telephone service to a minimum. Time limits have been placed upon calls, arbitrary criteria for telephone queries have been imposed, and in general the user whose request comes via telephone has received far less satisfactory service than is given to the in-person user.

Reasons for this shortsighted approach are hard to find. Surely librarians are not influenced by the fact that the one type of question may result in a circulation, the other not. In the latter half of the twentieth century, the telephone is surely so much a part of everyday business operations that accommodation to its use may reasonably be expected! The old excuse, that the user who made the trip to the library deserves more of the librarian's attention than the telephoner does, cannot be upheld. Are librarians so lacking in ingenuity that they cannot find a way to accommodate both?

In some libraries, the answer to this problem has been the separate telephone service, with sufficient outside lines and staff to answer them. In addition, it is now possible, especially in larger libraries, for the caller to bypass a switchboard and be connected immediately with a telephone reference service, thereby avoiding the annoyance of one or more repetitions of the inquiry. The telephone company, will, on request, survey a library's telephone use pattern and report on the number of calls received, the number of callers who hung up before being connected with the proper line, the number receiving a busy signal, and the average wait for telephone service. A more efficient telephone service, perhaps with better equipment, may result from such a survey.

Other examples of provision of messages directly to the user are story hours, poetry and dramatic readings, and record concerts.

Provision of Messages to Groups

Services of both the reference and reader consultant type are often given to groups as well as to individuals. When a representative of a group approaches the service desk, there is frequently little difference from individual service. However, there are types of group service, falling generally into the reference and consultant category, that many libraries give in a different manner. After identifying those groups whose activities are consonant with the library's objectives, the library sets about creating a working relationship and setting up two-way communication. Library staff members may hold committee membership in the groups, participate in the planning of activities, learn in advance of important community information needs, and be in a position to offer services tailored to the group's requirements because of participation. Obviously, this type of involvement in group activity must be extremely selective, and groups concerned with serious community problems are usually those with whom the library cooperates in this extensive fashion.

In library-sponsored programs, another type of group activity is undertaken: the group is organized or gathered by the library. Such groups may remain together for some time or may merely be audiences for one occasion. For some librarians, this type of service holds special attractions because it is one in which the library definitely takes the initiative. *Active* versus *passive librarianship* are the terms sometimes used in this context, implying a value judgment whose validity others would question. Few, however, would disagree with the statement that such group activities are a legitimate library activity, related to its basic responsibility for information transfer and assurance of effective utilization of its collections.

Programs should be considered as service, since they do represent delivery of information or messages or are tied to utilization of library materials. It is true that they also serve a publicity function and may bring people into the library who have never previously come. But these values are secondary; the librarians who evaluate the success of a film program, for example, on the basis of the number of books circulated from the display offered, are missing the point. Viewing a film is direct exposure to library materials and thus constitutes library use in and of itself. Discussions, creative writing activities, drama for children, the increasingly popular use of multimedia techniques in creative activities especially for children and young people—all these activities are related to some degree to library materials. Programs with speakers are less closely materials oriented, but they do represent transfer of information, bypassing the object that is traditionally the library's stock-in-trade.

The role of the library as an educational agency is a commonplace in the profession, but that role has been variously defined. In the 1940s and

---

3. Ernest R. De Prospo et al., *Performance Measures for Public Libraries* (Chicago: Public Library Association, ALA, 1973), p. 51.

1950s there was considerable controversy about the library as an agency of adult education.[4] No question arose as to the appropriateness of its supplying the means of self-education, of stimulating this type of activity in various ways, and of offering it space and resources. However, there was only gradual acceptance of the library's more active role in offering opportunities, and often leadership, for group discussions, for drama groups, for creative writing groups, along with meetings or series of meetings at which outside speakers presented talks on matters of cultural, civic, or scientific importance. Today, few professionals consider such activity inappropriate for the library. However, libraries vary considerably in the amount of programming and also in the organization of the function within the library structure.

Recently, many libraries have begun special programs for the poor, bringing to bear the information in their collections on the informational or educational needs of a particular group. The point may be made, in connection with the philosophical justification for bypassing the message-containing *object*, that the library that offers programs or classes on consumerism, or counseling, or health-care information in poverty neighborhoods may be felt to be overstepping its bounds by other agencies in existence for these specific purposes. The problem is that many such agencies are semipublic and may receive a large proportion of their support from a United Appeal or similar funding agency. The entrance of the library into the field, therefore, is seen as a threat by the other agency, which may justify its continued support on the basis of numbers of attendants at various programs and classes. The publicly supported library's well-meant effort may seem to siphon away potential clients and potential statistical justification for continued funding.

Clearly, the best way to handle such a situation is cooperation. Cosponsorship of the program by library and agency will enable both to claim the attendance statistically and may well also lighten the load of each and result in a better program. Certainly, a cosponsored program has a better chance of attracting an audience large enough to justify the effort. Even if the effort of cosponsorship is great at the outset, long-range gains outweigh early problems.

Provision of Information about Alternative Sources of Messages and Objects

Referral of the user to another library or source of information should always be as specific and accurate as possible. Hours of opening of other libraries, limitations of service, charges, and other special circumstances should be made known to the inquirer. Such facts should be carefully updated at the library. On some occasions, a preliminary telephone call should be made. Some librarians, who may not hesitate to spend a great deal of time on a possibly fruitless search, are reluctant to spend the cost of a telephone call on behalf of a patron—a judgment that appears to reflect a faulty value system. If the library is to function as community information center, it must have at its fingertips, not only its own resources, but also access on its users' behalf to other community resources. It must consider the user's time and its own costs in moving quickly to the best source of information available.

Prominent among the services now offered by many libraries to residents of poverty areas is information and referral service connected with the various agencies, public and private, that assist with problems of daily living. Service may be given centrally, at branch libraries, or both. It may be chiefly telephone service, or it may provide space and staff for interviews. Some libraries employ a professional social worker for preliminary counseling in connection with some referrals, and to train the staff members who make the referrals. Problems encountered in such a service include:

1. Developing and updating the complex records of agencies and their services, which should include many cross-references under types of service. A computerized listing is ideal for such a record, as it permits easy access to multifaceted information. Through such a record, one could, for example, readily identify a nursing home for an elderly person in a desired location, within a price range, connected with a certain religion.
2. Overcoming reluctance of agencies to cooperate. Agencies may suspect that the library is moving into their field of expertise and may lack full understanding of the library's skills of interviewing and information searching. Personal contacts and actual experience of successful cooperation will help dispel this fear. There is so great a need, among the total population, for information about, and

4. Margaret Monroe, *Library Adult Education: The Biography of an Idea* (Metuchen, N.J.: Scarecrow, 1963).

referral to, service agencies that there is room in the field for the library as a point of entry.

Provision of Messages and/or Objects from an Alternative Source

The quality of all service depends to some extent on quantity—how many resources? How much staff? It is a mistake, however, to assume too readily that the size of a community will determine the depth of service that is needed and would be utilized if provided. Population size will, of course, affect the volume of need and may, in some degree, limit some specialized information needs related to occupational or professional concerns. With this one exception, however, individual needs in small communities may be as specialized as those in large. It is more likely that any differential experienced in demand for service in small communities is related to the services already given. What is expected, what is asked for, is determined by experience in library use; information needs may be in existence without being brought to the library. In spite of vigorous publicity efforts in many cases, we know in fact that even libraries that give specialized service in depth do not receive requests for more than a fraction of the information needs that the community actually generates and that the library is equipped to answer. Realistically, however, the small library must limit its direct services—and as a corollary, should step up its referral services to a high point of competence.

The concept of the public library as the community's intelligence center, or as an "information switching center,"[5] has two effects. First, it has narrowed the gap between larger and smaller libraries, insofar as their ultimate service capability is concerned. And second, it has recognized referral as a valuable and professionally acceptable method of meeting a need. Formerly, a referral to another source of information was felt by some libraries to be a confession of failure on the part of the library—to be resorted to only if all else failed. Today, libraries of every size and type have recognized the folly of attempting total self-sufficiency in the delivery of information. As a result, referral has become a respectable activity, and efforts are being made to increase its effectiveness and volume.

Efficient referral of a request for a known item—book, periodical, or article—is relatively simple.

Figure 13.2 shows how librarian, reader, and collection interact in a referral transaction. Professional practice requires that the entry be verified and that certain general rules be observed. Referral of a question or subject request without a bibliographic citation, a request for a message without citing a specific object, is more complex. In addition to the clarification of the nature of the query itself, which calls for a reference interview of the usual type, the librarian taking the request must attempt to tell the librarian who will have to handle it without an interview (1) all the facts about the user's need, ability, background that can be gathered; and (2) all the sources already checked, to avoid duplication of effort.

The increasing importance of systems and networks makes referral increasingly a routine affair for the smaller library that formerly had to limit its service to its own holdings and staff expertise. Experience has shown, however, that it is sometimes difficult to obtain referrals from libraries to a central resource or network. Small libraries with limited budgets tend sometimes to hesitate before using teletype or making a long-distance call, even if costs are fixed or absorbed by the system, unless the inquiry is one that appears to be of major importance. There is also occasionally a reluctance to admit limitations—a feeling that an inquiry not handled locally will reflect on the library or librarian. This reluctance is similar to that of the librarian of the larger library who refuses to call a local source for information until every conceivable internal possibility has been checked. Add to these problems the fact that the local user of the small library may need to be educated to use his library as a key to much greater resources elsewhere, and the magnitude of the referral problem becomes apparent. Librarians at both ends, as well as the public in general, must develop new habits if the full value of systems and networks is to be gained and unit costs reduced.

Management Problems

The services described above appear to include many uncontrollable elements. Since management necessarily implies some control, this section will consider whether they can indeed be managed in the sense of being controlled, and the degree of control. Specifically, we shall look at such problems as:

1. Determining limits and priorities. Assuming unlimited time and effort cannot be given to each need, how are these decisions arrived at?

---

5. Ervin J. Gaines, "The Information Switching Yard," *Library Journal* 95:641 (February 15, 1970).

(Compare with Figure 13.1, in which the same librarian is in constant personal contact with the reader.)

START

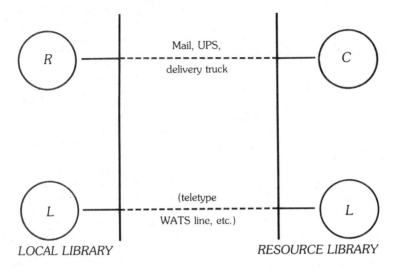

Fig. 13.2. Interaction of librarian, reader, and collection in a referral transaction

2. Achieving an appropriate balance between staff specialization and staff flexibility.
3. Utilizing staff time to greatest effect for service, especially so as to give service of approximately equal quality during slack and peak periods of use.
4. Assuring that best-qualified staff is utilized for most difficult service problems, and that simpler problems are, in general, handled by beginning staff. This is, of course, the familiar principle of classification of tasks. Here, it must be applied to degrees of one category of tasks, a much more difficult matter.

Objectives—Limits and Priorities

The services described previously, however legitimate as library activities, can be given somewhat superficially or in considerable depth. The average library administrator must give much attention to matters of cost and priority setting, because the budget will not stretch indefinitely and the jurisdiction cannot find funding for all the needs of all the public agencies, however socially desirable they may appear. Shall priority be given to an age group? To a social group or segment? To certain subjects or forms? Shall arbitrary limits be placed on certain services—like length of time spent on reference searches or length of telephone calls? Shall the service of referral more frequently replace direct service? Finding the best answers to questions such as these requires first a decision about, and commitment to, the library's service objectives.

Stating a public library's service objectives is difficult. Generalities abound in existing statements, which arouse no quarrel but provide little assistance in allocating funds and setting priorities. While there appears to be a good deal of agreement among libraries in terms of program and activity, the reasons given, the justifications offered, or the purposes expressed may differ a great deal.[6]

Critics within and without the profession, but chiefly outside local public library management, express impatience with the lack of clear-cut objectives. Local government officials, library associations and educators, state library agency personnel—all these groups urge more attention to objectives and priorities. Other public agencies, such as the public schools, find it practicable to state objectives in behavioral terms, and to determine readily whether these objectives have, in fact, been achieved. Formal education has developed such techniques to an advanced degree. Since in many jurisdictions there is a close structural relationship between the library and the formal education program, concern has been expressed from this sector over the library's failure to follow the same path.

6. Larry Earl Bone, "The Public Library Goals and Objectives Movement," *Library Journal* 101:1283-86 (July 1975).

Other friendly critics voice concerns that are chiefly social and political. Contributors to *The Public Library and the City*, notably Banfield and Ennis, appear to feel, not only that the library will accomplish more if it narrows its scope and deepens its efforts in a more focused fashion, but also that such a strategy will make it more visible and assist in the effort to obtain support.[7] From within the profession, the movement toward social responsibility, in a variety of ways and to varying degrees, urges commitment to social goals, emphasizing service to the poor and handicapped, and urging advocacy of particular viewpoints in collection building and programming.

In the face of such a broad and formidable group of promoters of specific and defined objectives, what are the reasons for the public library's reluctance to arrive at a more clear-cut definition of its role as a service agency? Some of the concerns stem from deep-seated commitments already made and accepted by the critics as well as those avoiding narrow priorities—to intellectual freedom, to the library as a highly individualized service whose goals must, in the final analysis, be set by each individual user. Some are expressed in terms of "demand" and a refusal to sit in judgment on the relative importance of each user's request. In terms of selection of library materials, these same questions are discussed, pro and con, in another chapter. Here, the point is that to many librarians it is inappropriate (not to say impossible) to enter into a subjective value judgment of the legitimacy, social value, and personal urgency underlying each request for service. Any effort to delineate library priorities in terms of subject, level, or group and to apply such priority policies in, for example, such a consideration as the length of time to be expended on a particular search would require them to make such a judgment. This group would claim that actual variations in quality and amount of service given do not reflect any priority judgments but are the result of factors over which the library has no control. This question will be discussed later in this chapter.

The problems involved in setting priorities are not easy ones. They reappear from time to time within librarianship in slightly varied forms but encompassing basically the same dilemma. They are sensitive problems that probe into commitments deeply held. Unlike the mass media, unlike even formal education to groups, the library's basic service is initiated by the individual, geared to that person's own need and level, and moves at the patron's own pace. It is individual in another sense; in the words of the National Book Committee, there is a

danger of imposition of the values served by the mass media and the concomitant importance of preserving and strengthening those media of communication (like the library) that aid individuals in forming their own values and strengthening individual autonomy and responsibility.[8]

While this characteristic—in fact, distinguishing mark—of the public library is sometimes the basis for librarians' refusal to set definite priorities, the result of such a refusal is often a set of actual, although unconsciously set, priorities that reflect existing demand, use, and values. It is this attention to "demand" that has often made the library the predominantly middle-class institution it is so frequently accused of being. "Demand," as every librarian knows, comes heavily from the middle-class public, oriented toward its children's education, toward best-seller reading that contains at least an element of keeping-up-with-the-literary-Joneses, or toward the current fashionable pursuits of suburbia, be they karate or astrological research. The demand-oriented library meets these needs unquestioningly and in volume. Over a period of time, the nature of the service tends to influence use; other needs, less frequently expressed, may not be met, and those who fail to find satisfaction at the library cease to try. Thus, the user group influences the service, which, in turn, tends to create a selected user group. The library is unaware of any discriminatory action and would, in fact, indignantly deny that any group is not receiving full service. The discrimination is implicit, unconscious, and made with the best intentions, in the name of a democratic principle that asserts "the public's" right to decide what its library service shall be.

The point here is not that the demands and topics cited are, or are not, appropriate; it is, rather, that decisions defining the library's objectives cannot be altogether abdicated to that segment of the public that now uses its services. Failure to make a decision *is* a decision in favor of: (1) the articulate, (2) the demanding, (3) the educated, (4) the library oriented. In terms of priorities of service, it is a decision to give priority on a basis

7. Ralph W. Conant, ed., *The Public Library and the City* (Cambridge, Mass.: M.I.T. Press, 1965). See Edward C. Banfield, "Needed: A Public Purpose," p. 102, and Philip H. Ennis, "The Library Consumer," p. 30.

8. National Book Committee, "Major Social Changes Affecting Library Service in the United States, 1955–1975," Attachment I, *Local Organization Handbook for the National Library Week Program* (New York: The National Library Week Program, 1967), p. 61.

of (1) former patterns of use, in terms of what is available; or (2) former patterns of use, in terms of staff expertise, staff manner, appearance, or lifestyle.

Many librarians, aware that they are in danger of allowing themselves to be caught up in such a spiral, are seeking a means to expand their services, introducing a larger element of conscious planning. This is done to clarify objectives and set priorities and to be better able to evaluate results, the latter often in response to governmental adoption of some type of program budgeting. To embark on such a program, with the necessary participation of a staff who may be in varying degrees of sympathy with or hostility to the change, is formidable. The necessity to do so is confronting more and more library administrators, both in response to authority and in the cause of improved service.

The library manager and staff who attempt to plan such a change do not, of course, fail to give attention to existing demand. Nor do they adopt a posture of "we know what is best for you." Rather they seek to follow the advice of Allie Beth Martin, who pointed out the need to know "How to develop plans—set goals, *with*, not *for*, users."[9] The responsibility to consult the needs of users—a variety of users, actual and potential—is clear. Equally clear is the ultimate responsibility of the library, including the boards, to coordinate all the information gained from and about the community, to weigh it, to develop tentative plans, to test these, and to implement them.[10]

Even if the above principles are accepted, the library administration may have trouble in making a beginning. There can be no one "correct" procedure. The following suggestion is offered as an illustration of one method of approaching the development of definite priorities. Use of matrix, one axis of which represents age groups, the other life roles, enables administration and staff to see at a glance the wide variety of information and reading needs from which priority services must be chosen and from which, equally but more painfully, services of low priority must be identified. Figure 13.3 shows such a grid.

Many of the cells will perhaps, as the process continues, be subdivided further. Subdivision by

9. Allie Beth Martin, *A Strategy for Public Library Change: Proposed Public Library Goals Feasibility Study* (Chicago: Public Library Association, ALA, 1972), p. 52.

10. The Public Library Association, a division of the American Library Association, has recently received a grant from the U.S. Office of Education, that will, it is hoped, lead to the preparation of standards for public libraries that will take into account variations in individual communities.

educational or economic level would enable the library to separate the needs of the "disadvantaged" in certain fields. Where there is a minority with a different language, this need might also be subdivided. An example of subdivision is given in figure 13.4.

The process of designing the matrix would first serve to identify those needs that the administration and staff consider appropriate for the library to fill, and then help to distinguish between those they wish to concentrate on at a given time and those they consider the major responsibility of another agency or library. Staff meetings would be required to reach agreement or compromise, but these would be of inestimable value in bringing to light and resolving variations in philosophy, in utilizing staff knowledge and insights, and ultimately in arriving at a more harmonious joint approach. The next step would be a study of each of the cells of the matrix—at least those tentatively agreed on as needs appropriate for library concern.

Staff knowledge related to information needs of a segment—for example, job information needs of the elderly, recreation needs of young adults—may be supplemented by assistance from the community itself. As a result of this study, some of the tentative decisions already made may be modified. Ultimately, however, the library will have a list of: (1) top priority needs—major emphasis (a limited number); (2) normal services; (3) needs to be met chiefly by referral or by inquiry to another library or to a system; and (4) needs to be met chiefly by referral of the user to another source, with the library accepting limited or supplementary responsibility only.

This list need not be a permanent one; circumstances may call for a change of emphasis. Use of such a device, however, will assist staff when decisions must be made as to:

1. How much time to spend on an inquiry
2. Whether or not to purchase an expensive but important book or film whose use may be limited
3. How much of the budget to spend on current topics, how much on less-popular but possibly longer-lived items
4. What types of expertise to seek for on the staff
5. The nature and extent of permitted staff self-development activities
6. What types of public programs and other group activities to concentrate on
7. Which of the many possible community agencies and organizations to call upon for cosponsorship or to seek representation upon

Child	Teenager	Younger Adult 20–35	Mature Adult	Senior Citizen	Role
					Family Member
					Home/Household
					Citizen—Local/State
					Citizen—World/Nation
					Consumer
					Physical Being (Health, etc.)
					Spiritual Being (Religion, etc.)
					Worker (Vocation, Occupation)
					Hobbyist (Indoor) (All recreation, etc.)
					Hobbyist (Outdoor)
					Student (Formal)
					Self-Educator
					Club/Organization Member (Not Covered by Above)

Fig. 13.3. Role and age group matrix for library planning

8. How much time to spend outside the library in working directly with the community, and with which segments
9. In what direction to aim publicity
10. What types of card files and special indexes to keep in the library for special needs.

It should be emphasized that such a priority list does not ignore demand. Certainly, needs of existing users and known emphases of this group will be taken into account. But the concept of demand is expanded to include the needs of others, and a reasonable, planned approach replaces the haphazard "priorities" created by former use patterns.

It is also important to realize that such a priority list will require frequent revision. Circumstances will change, new problems and needs will arise. Especially in the case of the organizations that receive special attention, foresight is needed. If new needs are to be met, either additional funds and staff must be sought, or some of the old high-priority needs must be demoted a rung on the ladder. Since the whole rationale of the procedure is lost when too many items are high priority, it is important to build into group relationships a plan for withdrawal to a position of less emphasis. For example, library-sponsored groups can be encouraged to develop their own leadership and thus need less library staff assistance.

Home/Household— Adult	High Income/ High Education/ Large Home, etc.	Medium Income/ Medium Education/ Medium-Size Home, etc.	Low Income/ Low Education/ Small Home, etc.
Budget			
Interior Decoration			
Gardening			
Home Repairs			
Entertaining			
Home Cookery			

Fig. 13.4. Example of subdivision of figure 13.3

Note that this example illustrates the need for flexibility in using the matrix forms. Staff working with the above segments of the matrix will be aware, for example, of high-income apartment complexes or of unemployed persons with a high level of education. These details do not invalidate the form, which exists only to assist the staff and administration in studying the community's needs. Noting an exception is one way of doing this. If the appropriate mix of books on houseplants and landscape gardens, of simple do-it-yourself repair manuals and extensive projects calling for a complete array of power tools, of low cost and exotic cookbooks are provided, the chart will have served its purpose. There are, in any case, overlapping interests. The elaborate decorating book may give the low-income homemaker ideas that can be adapted to a small budget. It is important, however, in communities where a sizable segment of the population is undereducated to make sure information is provided in easy-to-read vocabulary and format, at an adult level of interest.

Achieving Balance between Staff Specialization and Staff Flexibility

As the description of typical library services earlier in this chapter demonstrated, a community's investment in its library building and collection will not be utilized to the fullest without a skilled staff. Self-help, even by the best-educated user, can go only a short way toward extracting the messages relevant to a user's need. That is why librarians receive specialized education in reference sources and techniques. That is also the chief reason why libraries, especially larger ones, seek specialists among their staffs, for every graduate librarian is not equally prepared to serve children and the elderly, or to assist businessmen and musicians. The larger and more specialized the staff, the more probable that each user's needs will be satisfied with appropriate messages from the collection. In order to get full benefits from its collection, a library must make a further investment in personnel.

Thus managers are confronted with decisions of major importance, especially in an economy of rising costs and lagging income—how to balance investment in materials and staff and how to utilize both for the most effective service with, usually, an inadequate budget. Service specialists most often found in public libraries have expertise in one of the following categories.

1. *Age:* children's departments, young adult services, service to the elderly.
2. *Subject:* business, fine arts, etc. In the 1930s and 40s, adult services in most large libraries were organized almost completely by subject.
3. *Function:* Group services departments.
4. *Form:* Films, documents.
5. *User Category:* Service to labor, to foreign-language readers, to the disadvantaged.

As needs have been identified, new specialties have arisen to deal with them, and, in many cases, new units have been created. Too many units, however effective in meeting needs, are costly in a number of ways. For example, they lead to—

1. An increase in the number of stations to be manned. If departments are separated physically, each must have sufficient staff to cover all hours the department is open, regardless of workload.
2. An increase in the number of supervisors—relatively high-salaried personnel.
3. Duplication of materials.
4. Duplication of furniture and equipment.

While specialized departments are intended to provide superior service, and usually do, their existence in too great a number may at times actually contribute to service difficulties, for the following reasons.

1. The greater the number of departments, the more frequent the necessity of referring users from one to another, with resulting loss of continuity in service.
2. Referral of calls by switchboard operators becomes more difficult.
3. Selection of the proper department to meet a need is confusing for the user.
4. Variations in service philosophy and values may create conflict among departments. This is a problem common to all large organizations that develop specialties. It may take the form of attempts on the part of one segment of service to cling to users who should move to another. It may result in unwarranted criticism of one segment by another in connection with referred users. It may stem from subtle differences in quality of materials added, or from variations in size of collection and staff, which in turn result in variations in the amount of personal attention that can be given to an individual. To the user, such variations may create bewilderment, as the same individual seeks service from several departments that may differ somewhat in approach to direct assistance versus self-help assistance, in personalized cordiality versus a more businesslike approach, and so on. These inconsistencies result from the delegation of authority to a number of service department heads. It is hard for administrators to deal with them because they reflect no genuine fault, and because they relate to extremely tenuous

matters that cannot easily be regulated by statements of policy or instructions.

How best can the modern library administrator combine staff specialization with flexibility and consistency—not rigid uniformity—of service? How best can the complex and pluralistic needs of users be divided to advantage? These questions cannot be answered generally, as each situation is different. The size of the library, type of user, and internal building arrangements must all be taken into account in determining what specialties to offer and how to interrelate them.

A trend in new buildings appears to allow a reasonable compromise in medium-sized libraries. In the adult section, at least, a central core of stacks houses the entire collection. Around the periphery are the service agencies or departments, separated by furniture arrangements, carpet color, or low, display-type shelving so as to merge naturally into one another. These departments are usually fewer and broader in subject than those found in larger and older libraries—humanities; arts; social sciences; a combination of business, science, and technology; films or audiovisual materials; and fiction or popular reading. Each department staff member is prepared to assist any user, short of a need requiring considerable time and expertise. Each group uses the centrally located collection and may range throughout the entire scope of it. Selection of materials is performed by specialists within the department.

This type of arrangement is not usually extended to the major age-level divisions. Children's departments, the most common type of specialized division, also seem the most likely to remain separate physically, for a number of obvious reasons. However, as new subjects and treatments are learned in school, as persons of every age and educational level are encouraged to use the library, and as educational policies tend to keep students with their age groups, despite superior performance, there are beginning to be reasons why the total nonfiction collection, except easy books for small children, can be used increasingly by users of every age. Some smaller libraries have interfiled the nonfiction, so that age-level specialists, too, may draw on the entire collection. Thus, when a semiliterate adult finds a book that seems appropriate to meet an information need, the fact that it is a children's book is not embarrassingly apparent. Similarly, the adult seeking a simple explanation of the computer may find exactly what is needed in a children's book that might be missed without intershelving. On the other hand, the child whose interest in pygmies or dinosaurs or airplanes has exhausted the children's collection will be led to more specialized materials in the most natural and easy way.[11]

There is no one best way of mobilizing the staff for service. However, the trend does appear to be toward continued specialization within a flexible structure that allows the staff to serve the user's need and follow the user's requirements without the inhibition of rigid organizational barriers.

Another type of service division occasionally utilized in larger libraries is specialization by user groups, a grouping that does not supersede existing departments or create new ones but is superimposed on them. The specialist may concentrate on the total needs of a group of users (Spanish-speaking or other minority) or may work with a group defined by role. In the latter case, an analogy may be made with special services offered by department stores. For example, special service for brides calls upon the resources of the entire store—clothing, furniture, china, silver, kitchenware—as needed for a special use. In the same manner, the library may have a staff member or two devoted especially to the needs, for example, of consumers, parents, or persons engaged in high school or college equivalency programs. These staff members, found in only a few libraries as yet, are perhaps the modern successors to the old-fashioned reader's advisor, since they exist to devote more time to the needs of individuals in special categories selected as priorities than can the busy occupant of a regular service desk.

This specialist structure can be more flexible than a department. Since these specialists do not develop their own collections, they can utilize the entire collection. They need not be on duty at all times the library is open; appointments can be made in advance or through other staff. Their value and flexibility would diminish if they were tied to a departmental desk, a collection, or a schedule. They must be free to work outside the library walls as well as at their own desks. Since they are serving the total needs of a special public, or of a particular user role, rather than being tied to one subject, they can be extremely flexible. As the group's needs change, the special service librarian will readily adapt to the changes, a process much easier than changing the focus or direction of a formal department organized around a subject. Staff assignments of this type do offer the library the opportunity of specialization without the kinds

of duplication and extra costs noted above. One danger to be resisted firmly is the tendency to develop such individual specialists along departmental lines, with their own collections.

Regardless of the organization pattern of service decided upon, specialization, while it improves the quality of service and makes better use of the library's collections, takes its toll in compartmentalization, some inevitable duplication, and some confusion and overlappings. Communication, in-service training, perhaps rotation programs for staff, and certainly orientation visits of some duration are devices commonly utilized to overcome or diminish these difficulties. Committee responsibilities of a librarywide nature for staff members at all levels are helpful in preventing an undesirable narrowness of knowledge and viewpoint.

Variation in Staff Expertise

Simply stated, this problem relates to the fact that any library service desk is manned sometimes by an experienced, capable, knowledgeable staff member and sometimes by a beginner. Needs of individual users may be complex and difficult, calling for the assistance of the "expert." Or they may be relatively simple, easily handled by the junior staff. Add the fact that it is often impossible to immediately distinguish between a difficult or an easy inquiry, and the problem becomes more complex. Table 13.1 illustrates this point.

As posed by the user, all the questions in table 13.1 appear simple. A bright desk assistant or page ought to be able to handle them in the form in which they were asked. In actuality, each calls for an interview. A beginning librarian can probably deal with numbers 1, 2(a), 4, 5, and 6. Number 6, however, may require an interview in private, since it involves a sensitive personal subject. Numbers 2(b), 3, and 7 are likely to be better and more speedily handled by senior staff. Number 7, like number 6, may call for a private interview. Unfortunately even an experienced librarian cannot always tell how complicated a search may turn out to be until it progresses.

In a reasonably busy library, these and other complex inquiries will come to one service desk, presented in person or over the telephone, at any time of day. Ideally, the difficulty of the question should be matched by the expertise of the librarian dealing with it; that is, easier questions should come to newer staff and harder ones to senior staff members. Actually, the typical reference desk is manned by the staff in turn according to a schedule that places the department head there fewer hours than the new professional or the paraprofessional. There is no assurance in this arrangement that the least-qualified staff member will not be

---

11. Dorothy Sinclair, "The Preparation of Tomorrow's Public Librarian: Some Propositions, Principles, and Proposals," *Toward the Improvement of Library Education*, ed. Martha Boaz (Littleton, Colo.: Libraries Unlimited, 1973), pp. 68–83, contains a fuller discussion from another viewpoint of problems created by age-level divisions in public libraries.

Table 13.1. Examples of Apparently Simple Questions as Posed, with Possible Sources

Inquiry as Posed	Actual Need	Possible Source or Response
1. Where are the biographies of Lincoln?	A quotation	Quotation book
2. Where are the histories of Russia?	Information about Rasputin (saw TV movie) *or*	Biographies
	Material for dissertation on the Duma of 1905	Special bibliographies; Referral
3. Do you have a list of newspapers published in Africa?	To read story in a particular paper of a particular date	Address of the paper *or* (better) Address of a U.S. library that can supply a photocopy
4. Where are the books on electricity?	Material on how to repair home wiring—at amateur level *or*	Home repair manual. Local building code
	—at highly technical level	Oversize loose-leaf service with detailed blueprints, etc. (may require referral)
5. Do you have a Los Angeles directory?	Address of a professor at UCLA	(No recent directory, unlisted phone.) *Who's Who*, or *Directory of American Scholars*
6. Do you have a copy of the laws of Delaware?	Information on grounds for divorce in Delaware	Digest of state laws on special topics
7. Where is your child care section?	How to answer a six-year-old's sex questions	Expert staff knowledge of the materials, coupled with a tactful eliciting of questioner's sophistication, values, religious concerns, etc.

confronted by the most difficult inquiry, on the one hand, or, conversely, that the department head will not be called upon to spend time on a good many simple questions.

Other concerns that enter the picture are the need for privacy and a relaxed atmosphere for sensitive queries; the desirability of introducing the new staff to more complex queries gradually; the need for the supervising librarian to have direct contact with the public on the one hand, but to have time away from the public for administrative concerns; and the need to give attention to other users during complex interviews and service at shelves as shown in figure 13.1.

If sufficient staff are available, it is suggested that there be three levels of service points.

Desk 1. Manned chiefly (for two-hour tours of duty) by junior and intermediate staff. Services include giving directions, catalog assistance, quick reference from shelf at hand, advisory service from new-book shelf and other popular-type displays near at hand. May also include telephone service of the same types and taking of reserves. Many immediate referrals to Desk 2.

Desk 2. Manned by the same group, with occasional tours by senior staff. This staff member does the main "floor work" of the usual type. Goes to the shelves with users. Interviews users in some depth. Does more in-depth reference work, for users in person or on the phone. Works on holdover questions if time permits. Searches periodicals, documents, etc.; receives most queries referred from Desk 1. Utilizes judgment as to referrals to Desk 3.

Desk 3. In either a private office or a workroom with sufficient privacy for reasonably relaxed interviewing and counseling. Desk 3 is not actually a public desk in the same sense that Desks 1 and 2 are but is the working desk of one or more senior staff members who may also be age-level, subject, or role specialists. These staff members are working at normal away-from-desk activities such as materials selection and reports, but are on call for Desk 3-type service when need arises. Desk 3 may be called because the nature of the question is private, difficult, specialized, or complex, or the inquirer is a specialist, a member of a special public, semiliterate, or requires a protracted interview.

It is obvious that in actual situations, the work may not divide itself neatly among the service points as described. Another difficulty is that the user may have to explain the inquiry to three different staff members. Nevertheless, with all its imperfections, this arrangement attempts to tackle the problem that the typical staffing pattern ignores. It can be applied either to the medium-sized general library or to a subject department in a large library.

Telephone service in the larger library may be handled at a separate service point. In libraries with some volume of telephone use, it is desirable to have a separate number for service calls, so that these will come directly to a service desk and not require the user to repeat his problem more often than necessary. The first telephone service point should have basic reference materials. It should also refer calls freely to the equivalents of Desk 2 or Desk 3, so that telephone users will also have the advantage of skilled specialist service. It is a mistake to staff such telephone desks with non-professionals only. The librarian at a telephone desk is a busy person who must have a high degree of skill.

Peak and Slack Periods

Since most service given inside the library is initiated by the users, not the librarians, the workload is uncontrollable and may be highly variable. Deployment of staff and resources for service must take into account unforeseeable variations in amount of service requested.

The library, in its various units, can and should study use patterns: peak and slack times; effects of holidays, seasons, and the opening and closing of other services. Telephone use of the library may well have a different pattern than in-person use. In larger libraries with competent service to business and industry, the telephone calls from these sources tend to come about mid-morning and to be heaviest early in the week. The after-school rush is the heavy use period for many public libraries.

Nevertheless, there is a limit to the amount of planning possible on the basis of existing use patterns. Full-time staff cannot be expected to work every evening or to work many split days. Part-time staff, if they can be found and can be employed without disregarding personnel regulations, permit more flexibility as to the number of persons available to help the public in person.

As a result of variations in demand and available staff at a given time, service almost inevitably is inequitable. Persons asking for assistance during rush periods, in person or on the telephone, are likely to receive less help than those who come when the staff has more time to give them. On the resolution of this problem a good deal of the quality of a library unit's service will depend. There are several options:

1. Muddle through without attempting to cope with the problem, accepting the fact of variations in speed, amount, and quality of service.
2. Attempt to utilize slack time to prepare to give better service during peak periods.
3. Attempt to readjust the flow of work in order to create more equitable service.

The first option is not ordinarily recognized as an option; it is more likely to be considered a fact of life. The second, followed to some degree by most libraries, utilizes the time of the staff member on desk duty during slack periods to prepare for better and faster service during busy hours. This can take several forms: familiarization with materials, especially reference books; preparation of special indexes that will facilitate service, especially in the case of inquiries frequently received and difficult to fill; and a variety of professional tasks concerned with the collection and its location, such as subject-heading of clippings or pamphlets.

Public service librarians are constantly concerned that their work focuses heavily on giving out without a corresponding opportunity for taking in. If a librarian must know authors, titles, and the contents of books and other materials, and if in addition a specialty is expected in some area or subject, preparation time is necessary. But too many librarians have only minimal opportunity on library time to build up the requisite knowledge in any concentrated manner. Examining new books, familiarizing oneself with reference materials, and glancing through reviews and journals to bring up to date a specialty are sometimes frowned on by supervisors as not constituting "work." More acceptable are preparing a talk or story hour, writing annotations for a booklist or for an evaluation meeting, or attending a community meeting for the purpose of learning more about the community and its informational needs and concerns. Reading on library time is especially suspect, although condoned in special circumstances. It is assumed by superiors that all librarians will inevitably read and wish to read, that this activity is not only work related but also a personal satisfaction and refreshment, and that it should be done on the staff's own time. Undoubtedly, some staff members might, if allowed to do so, take advantage of the opportunity to read on the job. In many cases, the lack of time for intake is deplored but accepted as inevitable because insufficiency of staff necessitates immediately productive work.

If the principle is accepted that intake is a legitimate and necessary activity on library time, the principles of management by objectives might be invoked to confine it within acceptable limits. Together, the staff member and supervisor might agree to include among the staff member's objectives for a given period something like the following:

1. Become familiar with specified reference works (write a report on each, perhaps).
2. Utilizing bibliographies, the collection, and guides to the subject, become better acquainted with specified subjects with which the staff member is not now familiar—for example, sociology, Latin American history, modern art. (Again, a formal report may be required if the supervisor wishes, perhaps this time an in-person report to a senior staff member.)
3. Using maps, directories, annual reports, brief personal exploration tours (with permission), and the resources of the collection, become better acquainted with the community served by the library or branch—its geography, history, economy, and past library use. (This objective is especially appropriate for new staff and could be subject to a brief written quiz.)

These examples are merely illustrations of the type of planned intake program that might be developed. After the objectives have been agreed upon, the staff member is at liberty, according to the principles of management by objectives, to go about the program in any way suitable. An exception would be made in the case of outside-the-library activity, at least to the extent that some senior staff members would probably be informed of the staff member's departure.

This method would clarify what types of intake are expected and would remove from both sides any uncertainty as to the appropriateness of such a program of self-education. These objectives could also be combined, in the case of some libraries and staff members, with such necessary tasks as weeding the collection, recommending new titles, and preparing presentations for staff meetings. Such structured self-education, undertaken on an individual basis during slack periods, should gradually result in measurable improvement in performance. Service during peak periods should benefit in speed and quality.

While it may be easier to change staff workloads than to change user habits, the latter course, constituting the third option, also might be adopted to some degree. Few libraries have made a serious effort to redirect patterns of use to equalize the workload, although undoubtedly many librarians have informally advised readers that a morning or early afternoon visit would be pleasanter and more productive for users who can come at such times.

Better service for the user is, of course, the only basis on which a change can be justified. Many users have discovered that a preliminary telephone call will save them time on a library visit and, when it is combined with a drive-up book window, may also save a parking fee. The combination of telephoning ahead and personalized service has not, however, been exploited as much as it might be by the average public library.

What is suggested is a combination of the old reader's advisory file and the newer Selective Dissemination of Information (SDI) technique. In the former, a record of a reader's education, interests, reading, and reactions was kept; in the latter a similar profile is computerized and matched with new materials as they arrive. To receive the library's custom call-in service, a reader would fill out a form and have a personal interview during which various data would be gathered. A file would be started that would include, not only these preliminary facts, but also a record of materials selected for this reader and his or her reactions to them, pro and con. With such a record on file, the reader would call and present a request, and a librarian would consult the record and select materials according to the profile, place in each a reaction record sheet, and send the materials to the drive-up window (or to the user's branch or community library) to be picked up on the day indicated. Searches and selections for recommendation could be made by the best-qualified staff available during nonrush periods. The reader's reactions, if added to the file, would assure that changes in taste and interest would be known. Some approximation of this type of service is given to blind readers by the special service centers serving this group.

It is not to be expected that a great many readers would avail themselves of this type of service, but many of those served would be users whose needs would require a good deal of professional time. One problem would have to be explained to the reader—that of possible invasion of privacy, since this cumulative reading record would be on file for the use of the staff. Such a file should, if kept, be protected from unauthorized use and given to the reader on request.

Evaluation

Evaluation can occur at several levels. Under such a heading could be included the following: (1) justification for the library as a public, tax-supported service; (2) measurements of effectiveness of the service in general, or of specific services; and (3) assessment of quality of service of a given library, department, or individual.

The first type of evaluation can be made only in terms of society's values. It defies precise measurement. It concerns such basic but intangible topics as the value society gives to education: formal, informal, and continuing; society's perception of its need for authoritative and unbiased information; the importance in a free society of access to a variety of opinion, including new, unorthodox, unpopular views; the need society recognizes for a forum of dissent, including the type of dissent that acts as a watchdog to government itself; society's recognition of the importance of preserving and making available the records of the past and the acquired knowledge of its own predecessors; and society's acknowledgement of an obligation to encourage and preserve the literary and cinematic arts, as in other institutions it does the graphic and musical art forms.

These and similar values are held, consciously or unconsciously, by our society to such an extent that few will question the general value of a public library. However, it would be impossible to prove conclusively that the library does, in fact, promote these values. The best the library can do is show evidence that it offers support for them and that, on the basis of a surface judgment, use is occurring that may be assumed to contribute to them. To attempt to penetrate into the motives of individual users, their specific uses and needs, and the total effect of library use on the society it serves is not only so large a task as to be impossible, it is also repugnant in terms of invasion of individual privacy.

Nevertheless, a public-supported service must account to government and taxpayers for the funds it expends. Here we must deal, not with ultimate or penultimate effects, but with more immediate measures. The most important contribution to this effort in many decades is that of the Rutgers team's study on measurement of public library effectiveness, sponsored by the Public Library Association and published by the American Library Association.[13] Directed as it is toward library use, it offers a number of quantitative measures that are basically measures of service—or at least the elements of service. Use of the instruments it provides will permit the administrator to compare the home institution with others in the same general size group in a number of critical areas. In many cases, the results will prompt a reconsideration of priorities and allocation of funds.

Inevitably, however, such an instrument cannot provide more than information for decision making. If, for example, a library is making a special effort to reach the undereducated, it will in all probability show less of a statistical return in many categories in terms of expenditure, especially expenditure for personnel. The authors of the study warn against unwarranted assumptions on the basis of uncritical comparisons, and it is important that libraries using the instrument tie in their library profiles with their own service priorities and explain to budget officials the relationships that may affect the individual library's "score." If a library has identified service priorities, using the technique suggested above or some other device, there will exist both a clearly defined list of priorities and an awareness of response in the form of library use. Separate and more complete records may well be kept of such response to supplement general records.

Determination of quality of service as rendered by a department or an individual is different in nature from quantitative measurements. Internal controls will be set up by any good supervisor, and, even more important, pride in standards of performance will be developed. Spot checks, unannounced monitoring of telephone lines, inquiries by proxies whose results will be reported and studied—all these techniques are somewhat repugnant, with their taint of espionage or "bugging." It is true, nevertheless, that such unannounced checks have uncovered enough cases of inaccurate and incomplete reference services among public libraries to cause disquiet.[14] Taping of telephone calls, with the required "bleep" clearly audible so that the caller can request that the tape be turned off, will result in a body of data that can be studied and utilized for in-service training.[15] Individual responsibility for good performance, recognition of the need to ask others for assistance in order to give good service, a professional attitude toward quality of work, and especially a genuine interest in and desire to be of

---

12. See De Prospo et al., *Performance Measures* for methods of studying these factors.

13. De Prospo et al., *Performance Measures.*

14. Terence Crowley and Thomas A. Childers, *Information Service in Public Libraries* (Metuchen, N.J.: Scarecrow, 1971).

15. See Mary Jo Lynch, "Reference Interviews in Public Libraries: A Content Analysis of Matter and Method" (Ph.D. diss., Rutgers—The State University, 1976), for further information on taping.

service to each user are essentials in attaining service quality. The use of management by objectives and the careful development of the potential of each staff member are also valuable techniques. Detection of progress toward superior quality normally follows such lines; it is not strictly measurable, but one can measure the ingredients that produce it.

For Further Reading

The literature of public library service as a whole is relatively scanty, and it is in any case more appropriate for the service librarian than for the administrator. Below are suggested types of information with which the service administrator must attempt to keep current.

First, and foremost comes local information. Statistics from the census and reliable local sources are essential, broken down as far as possible both geographically and topically. Studies by chambers of commerce, local banks, regional planning agencies, utility companies, marketing research sources (if they can be obtained) provide a helpful basis for realistic planning of service. In addition to these general data, the printed (or mimeographed) output of local and regional organizations, which provides data about their current goals and programs and therefore is a helpful guide to their information needs, is of tremendous value. This sometimes enters the library collection directly, bypassing the administrative offices, which thereby fail to make use of it for planning.

Needless to say, local newspapers, including specialized neighborhood, minority, and foreign-language papers, are essential.

Much of the general literature on management, referred to in other chapters of this book and in their bibliographies, is applicable to the management of service. When used with caution, so is the literature of marketing.

Research studies are increasingly being published on the information needs of types of users or potential users of library services. For example, the series of investigations made under the general direction of M. B. Line of the the Bath University, U.K., concerns itself with informational requirements in the social sciences, and deals with the informational needs of not only academicians but also such groups as planners and social workers. This type of study may be useful in better focusing service programs toward such groups.

Finally, service-oriented planning requires some attention to trends and predictions. Here we find an area in which more reliable data are being gathered and published in such volumes as *The Human Meaning of Social Change* (Russell Sage Foundation, 1972); Herman Kahn's *The Year 2000*; or Raymond A. Bauer's *Social Indicators* (M.I.T. Press, 1966). The same title, *Social Indicators*, has been given to a new annual publication of the U.S. Bureau of the Census, which brings together statistical indications of social change from a variety of government sources. These indicators of long-range trends will be of use in a variety of ways to the creative planner of public library services.

14 Management Tools and Techniques for Support Services

GLENN MILLER

The visibility and drama of library public services usually outshine and overshadow the routine mechanical procedures of support services. Support service for our purpose here includes those necessary operations such as cataloging, book processing, circulation, or interlibrary loan, wherein the transactions are repetitive and usually out of the public eye. The fact that there are proportionately fewer librarians at work behind the scenes, rendering the actual impact of effort more difficult to observe, contributes to this lackluster image. Nevertheless, the support functions of libraries are frequently the basis for smooth-running library programs. In large part this can be attributed to the more tangible nature of support activity, which makes it susceptible to methodical, logical examination. In contrast, the very observation of a library user asking for assistance from a librarian will usually cause changes in the behavior of both to a degree that frustrates even general evaluation. The path and direction of both question and answer are subject to as much variation as the background and personalities of the participants. The tools of the social sciences are just not as precise as those of production methods or time-and-motion study. It is easier to understand and evaluate those activities that we can easily observe, touch, count, measure, and change.

Administrators have the opportunity to develop and exercise effective techniques in support services that will set patterns for the entire library operation. The regular demonstration of a philosophy that maximizes effectiveness will gain the wide participation of staff and result in a dynamic, aggressive service posture.

Environment

Of particular advantage to the administrator who would maximize the effectiveness of an organization is the fact that most support services take place out of the public eye. On its face, the opportunity for regular, uninterrupted observation and communication is a definite advantage. The sale of an idea, the study of a process, or the collection of data—all are more easily accommodated in an environment that is free of the priorities of public service. An easy demonstration is to place oneself at regular intervals in a typical day at the side of public-service and non-public-service personnel. One cannot and should not get the full attention of the public-service staff, for they must be conscious of the public activity around them. Indeed, if their full attention is given to colleague/visitor, the public is not being appropriately served. Not so, of course, in a nonpublic area where there is no such distraction. The full attention and concentration possible by support staff at any time certainly facilitate communication.

The creative and inspirational moments that can come over each staff member are precious. The administration and support staff can usually address them at the time they happen, augmenting and refining a concept or idea. Public-service staff have much less freedom and flexibility for the same type of follow-up. There is no value judgment involved here, merely note of administrators' need for full awareness and acknowledgment of this fact.

Perhaps more subtle but very real is the different nature of non-public- versus public-service work. For the majority of a working day, the reference librarian's time and activity is other oriented, dictated by an ever present and demanding public. Support staff, in contrast, are usually working on their own initiative and in control of what they think and do next. Overstated? Perhaps, but the administrator who is conscious of and sensitive to such subtle factors will find that the working environment plays a significant role in the development of strategies for improving services and understanding existing procedures.

Organization

Implications of the organizational framework should be reconsidered by every administrator in the context of support services. The objectives of the various support services (written or unwritten, understood or not) are established in relation to the overall institutional objectives. Desired results should determine how an administrator approaches the arrangement of various support functions within the organization. While each division is in operation, a pattern of continuous reappraisal of functions against objectives will occasionally indicate a need for change or realignment of functions. Thus, a table of organization should not impede getting the job done effectively.

The possibility does exist that an administrator can become enslaved to a theoretical organization chart and miss some of the better ways to meet objectives. Since the best overall results flow from a motivated and involved staff, it stands to reason that the administrator must play a direct role in encouraging such involvement. Frequently the most constructive and directly applicable suggestions for improvement will come from clerical staff. These staff members are crucial to the support functions, and an organization plan that isolates or tends to isolate the administrator from direct contact with them will work against all efforts to change and improve.

Administrative Resources

It is unfortunately true that many library administrators responsible for maintaining information resources do not take reasonable advantage of the professional literature. Even though every facet of library administrative practice is not described regularly in the literature, most are dealt with to some extent. It should not surprise the contemporary practitioner that most of the philosophical and many of the technical notions or concepts in libraries have been addressed earlier. At worst, searching the literature is an exercise valuable as continuing education. Knowing the path of development in some phase of technical services, for example, can only be helpful to the modern innovator. Most frequently, though, in routine library practices there is recorded experience that is directly applicable to the problem at hand. Even highly esoteric problem-solving techniques have been explored in detail by highly motivated colleagues in comparable institutions.

There are many other good sources for testing ideas. Probably the best of these are the other members of the profession. There are usually administrative counterparts in nearby libraries who are spending a good part of their working hours wrestling with the same or similar opportunities. The investment in a phone call across town or across the country to compare notes or discuss an idea may well be the best investment an administrator can make. Those who have not done so should test the technique at the next opportunity. An as-yet-unasked question, a fresh insight, a description of a discarded similar program, or a lead to where an approach is already being tried—all of these possibilities and many more may be learned by a phone call. As a bonus, there are few other types of conversations where one will receive immediate empathy and reassurance that others may also be paddling upstream.

Meetings, seminars, and conferences can provide the same stimulation. Many librarians attend conferences for no other reason than to spend a few hours with professional counterparts who provide some of the stimulation and ideas that will give direction to a program of service.

There are countless other sources of expertise available. Nearby academic folks from almost every field of study can sooner or later be tapped for particular knowledge. Few professional or business people will hesitate to respond to any reasonable request for assistance. Accountants, engineers, computer experts, and others have unique abilities and experience that are most appropriate to the support services in libraries. A good example of the appropriateness of these sources are the many labor- and money-saving recommendations that come from government documentation of management and efficiency studies conducted by interested citizens in all walks of life.

One set of experts doesn't even wait to be asked for help. In this group, of course, are representatives of companies in library and other book-related industries. With few exceptions, these men and women can offer a current and sophisticated view of their specific field. The occasional information or enthusiasm overkill from this segment can be tolerated in view of the whole.

The tendency to sometimes attempt to solve problems of support services in a vacuum is fraught with administrative dangers. A minimum of effort can yield help and advice quite appropriate to the task at hand, and there is no good justification for not seeking professional assistance.

Cooperative Support Services

The usual development patterns of library systems and networks inherently include the combined talents of a number of competent library managers. This fact alone strongly suggests that the resulting services and programs are worthy of serious consideration or evaluation by the local administrator. It is worthy of mention here, not only for a discussion of systems and networks per se, but because much of the impact of such efforts is directly related to the support service of libraries. It is usually the presence of opportunities or problems in the area of support services that stimulates a combined effort among agencies. In many circumstances, the apparent best solutions to problems can be addressed only by treatment on a larger scale or of a broader scope. Bibliographic control, cataloging, processing, and interlibrary loan are some of the most common examples. As with everything else, however, there are no guarantees, and the costs and benefits must be weighed carefully before commitment.

When looking beyond the local library for system or network solutions to a problem, it is well to consider that commercial agencies frequently provide equivalent services that may be better or more appropriate. Public and quasi-public organizations frequently fall victim to inefficient policies and procedures that could not exist long in business. That possibility is only mentioned because, once in a system, a library may have difficulty going back to prior or different procedures.

A Management Philosophy

"Necessary evils," "my biggest headache" are terms sometimes applied to support services by administrators. Although usually spoken in reference to a specific time-and-space problem, they sometimes are a reflection of attitude. Clearly no segment of an organization can work effectively if the front office doesn't care whether it does or not. Further, there is no more-logical source from which necessary encouragement should come than from the local administrator.

It must be acknowledged that the administrator is responsible for an overall view of the institution. And it must be true that no other person has a better vantage point from which to view the whole situation. From a simplistic perspective, then, it must be the administrator who will play the pivotal role in the evaluation of and planning for support services in libraries. The participation may not be constant and it may not be intensive, but the influence is inescapable. No matter how subtly this influence is wielded, it is a key factor. From the smallest library to the largest, the philosophy of the front office creates the working atmosphere. If efficiency and effectiveness are expected, then efforts in that direction will be acknowledged and fostered. If on the other hand an administration does not care or appear to care, every staff member will get the message. And that does not imply any direct negative communication; it rather means little or no communication on matters of evaluation or analysis.

Management Tools and Techniques

In a word, the indispensible need of persons in an administrative capacity is information—useful knowledge about how the organization is functioning. Decisions will be made as the problems and/or opportunities arise. The administrator who ducks a decision is effectively deciding to either leave matters as they are or trust the outcome to chance. The quality of decisions relating to support services, like other library decisions, essentially depends on the administrator and on whatever management information is available and utilized. One could alter the thrust of these comments by dwelling on the nature of administrators or organizational idiosyncrasies, but the focus here is on management information.

A lesson about information that is often learned too late is that, when it is needed, there may not be time to gather it. For example, when a funding authority insists upon more-convincing evidence or challenges the administrator's intuitive beliefs, there is usually not enough time to develop the supporting information. Deferral is the typical result. This shortcoming can be overcome by establishing a methodical program of analyzing the many facets of support services. The concept is simple enough. It means that administrators must understand their operations from a base of empirical evidence. Pure experience and intuition are frequently accurate, but the intellectual trauma brought on by having one's strongly held beliefs dispelled by hard data is an experience every administration should have. Another interesting aspect of management information is that it frequently raises as many questions as it answers. This frustration, however, would seem less serious in a situation where the people involved are actively engaged in the process of discovery.

As has already been implied, evaluation of support services involves more tangible processes than do public services. Therefore, it is easier to establish and maintain a pattern of analysis of support work. Start by taking stock of what is known of the efforts and procedures. What is each procedure meant to accomplish? Are the work station equipment and space appropriate to the task? Is the employee making good use of the motions and sequences? These are the kinds of questions in the mind of an analytical manager. Casual observation can usually bring to light some areas for examination. Deciding how to approach the specific problem, then, will bring into play one or a combination of management tools or techniques. Following are rudimentary explanations of some conventional management tools that are important to the problem-solving administrator.

Systems Analysis

Systems analysis is a continuous process of setting and challenging objectives, examining assumptions, and creating and testing alternatives. There is a large body of knowledge surrounding this concept, much of it steeped in economic theory. To some degree, every library administrator is involved in systems analysis. Its various aspects are engaged and utilized in subtle ways, usually in an informal or disjointed manner, so that the process is not really conceptualized as active and directed. However, for effective support services, managers should consciously consider the interrelationships of loose investigations. The very act will begin to bring the different examinations into perspective as forming an integrated, self-fulfilling process. Use of various techniques and employment of scientific tools will flow naturally from a recognition that systems analysis is one of the operational objectives of the library.

Management Information Systems

A management information system (MIS) is the product of sophisticated efforts to turn information to the use of managers. As the society we live in becomes more and more complex, there is ample recognition of the fact that information is the key to success, power, or just about any other goal. Broadly speaking, all of our library efforts are ultimately aimed at information—its collection, storage, retrieval, access, etc. By and large, though, we are an industry serving many masters; we serve a diverse public whose need for information is as varied as the population itself. In contrast, the information used in an MIS is sought for specific reasons and as a direct input to managerial decision making.

Information currently is addressed and utilized in many ways vis-à-vis support services. The conventional output measures of circulation, registration, materials cataloged, titles added, and all the others are in ample evidence. They can generally be described as historical data, routinely counted and certainly not dynamic. As such—and at the risk of insult—the conventional information generated by support services is not vital to aggressive, forward-looking administration. It helps to reveal where the institution has been. The thrust of an MIS is that it will yield active, exceptional, and futuristic information with which the administrator can make plans to maintain and increase the capacity of the organization. Which of the public libraries analyzes its processing function by comparing it with that of other libraries? Which administrators are quickly aware of a sharp increase in overdues, a decreasing fulfillment rate from a book jobber, or other exceptional facts?

Obviously the manager must be directly involved in selecting the key information to be sought. Too much or too little information is as useless or wasteful as having the wrong kind. Although sophisticated, MIS-utilizing computers and theoretical models are not within the means of many libraries, it is certainly possible for every library administrator to review the now-available information, evaluate its usefulness to creative decision making, and begin to see the unusual and enlightening trends and data that better serve the objectives.

Cost-Benefit Analysis

Cost-benefit analysis, like many other scientific management tools and techniques, rests on a simple logical concept. It is a process of gauging the effectiveness of alternative courses of action by comparing relative benefits and costs of the choices. Without getting into the intricacies of the engineer's operations research, librarians are regularly making decisions that lend themselves to the basic methodology of cost-benefit analysis.

Support service managers frequently must consider implementing new or different techniques for increasing productivity—for example, a new circulation system or an alternative processing possibility. All libraries are in the competition to maximize their effectiveness. Cost-benefit analysis lays out guidelines for approaching the choices. What are the benefits being sought? Can they be identified as necessary criteria for the new process? After establishing criteria against which to measure potential effectiveness, one must examine all of the alternative choices and, in doing so, include the factors of equipment, personnel, and materials. Following this step, cost estimates can reasonably be made. Following a coherent process to identify the various components of cost-benefit analysis will in itself result in improved choices. The administrator who achieves some adeptness at applying this technique can easily demonstrate its effectiveness.

Forms Analysis and Control

Analysis and control of the library's paperwork forms addresses one of the worst enemies of effective library support service. In order to process the information necessary to a technical services or circulation operation, a number of forms are used. If administrators desire changes or additional information, they may create a new form. Sometimes inefficiency comes through the use of too many copies of the same form. Regardless of the confidence placed in an institution's forms, it is reasonable to assume that there is room for improvement. Begin by challenging the very need for every form in the organization. If nothing else comes of it, the users of the forms will be forced to examine the reasons behind them. Review every bit of data required on every form for elimination of the unnecessary and clarification of the misleading. Stringently require sound justification for every additional copy that is created. Recognize the need to review forms on a continuous basis. There is ample literature addressing the question of forms, including many checklists of specific considerations.

Probability, Inference, and Sampling

The library administrator usually takes advantage of the broad concepts of probability, inference, and sampling on a regular basis. Frequently the use is essentially verbal and conveys an aura of authority that is then given the benfit of the doubt. Even casual, intuitive employment of the terms is frequently valid. Of course, many administrators utilize one or more of these techniques in a conscious, deliberate plan of management. The comments here are very brief and do not suffice as a technical description of any of these complex principles. Since the main purpose here is to elicit consideration, some license is taken.

Probability is a concept that we actually deal with every day. When we speculate on tomorrow's weather by inquiring "What are the chances?" we are really addressing the mathematical chance based upon present weather conditions. A solution to any uncertain situation can be sought by applying principles of mathematical chance. The soundness of the conclusions is generally dependent upon the quality of subjective judgments used as input. In library applications, judgments will often be required in projecting probability, even though activities that are repeated over and over for an extended period do of course lend themselves most objectively to calculations of probability.

Inference is another branch of statistics and is a technique useful to analysis of support services. It is nothing more than drawing conclusions—but with the important feature of recognizing limitations on those conclusions. A manager's estimate of the amount of library circulation generated by a specific user group—for example, the residents of one city in a service area—can be made within a range of accuracy. Samplings can be made and, with application of statistical methodology, the range of error or variance can be established with some confidence. A somewhat different use of the same theory is that of testing an hypothesis or, in other words, checking one's assumptions. Every administrator lives with a generous number of assumptions about aspects of support services.

The assumptions should be subjected to some experimental testing, even if the sample has admitted limitations. In many instances, even such simple testing can invalidate routine assumptions. To illustrate: How many regular users have library cards? Do more men use the library than women? What percentage of library users are students? Administrators assume answers to hundreds of such questions, and they do affect everyday judgments and decisions. Unfortunately many of the assumptions are false. Fortunately, inference and the use of sampling can be utilized to test these assumptions.

Samples and sampling have come to be very commonplace tools for the modern administrator. They have helped immeasurably in solving problems and answering questions. While it is likely that simple applications yield results that are valid within general limits, the user of sampling techniques has a responsibility to be aware of the implications. The theory and application of sampling in fact form a very sophisticated and technical branch of statistics that, used appropriately, can be invaluable to the library administrator.

Work Simplification

Time-and-motion study has probably been written about more than any of the other scientific techniques of management. Its nearly universal application in industry is no doubt largely responsible for industrial effectiveness in modern times. Ironically, there is an apparent hesitancy on the part of libraries to apply these techniques to support services. The production functions of book processing and circulation are the most likely candidates to benefit from such study. The objectives of time-and-motion study are to maximize workers' output and, at the same time, to minimize effort. It may be that failure to stress the latter, minimizing worker effort, has been a shortcoming in library approaches. There are degrees of complexity within the application of such analysis, but in any case, methodical and acute observation is of the essence. Beginning in a very informal way, managers could come up with significant tips and suggestions for improving work effort merely by being attentive to the processes in effect. As all concerned gained understanding of the process, a manager could employ more-sophisticated methods involving a stopwatch and process analysis.

All that has been discussed is relevant and useful only if it is applied. As a stimulus for the analysis of library support functions, a number of typical departments or activities are described conceptually. Comments and observations are meant, not as value judgments, but to provoke thought and investigation. Each library administrator has the challenge of applying these formulations on an individual basis and in light of personal value judgments.

Circulation Control

The public library's work output has been traditionally measured by numbers of books and other items circulated. The figures are usually impressive and, in fact, represent the scope of the circulation control function. The essence of the effort is to create a record of transactions with borrowers that will yield accurate tracking of what materials are not returned. The record will subsequently enable the staff to attempt retrieval of these materials. The nature of the work is repetitious and requires maximum accuracy. Of course, every institution is operating with some circulation system or other, but even so, care must be taken to be sure that analysis includes the very basic question, Why do we do this?

The range of available circulation systems is broad enough to give one serious pause. Frequently, however, the relative effectiveness of one over another is not even related to its basic design or concept—for example, photographic, mechanical, or computer-assisted charging. What happens locally to affect the system is more likely to influence the outcome in terms of results versus costs. Physical space, staff cost, staff training, volume, equipment maintenance, and overdue procedures are just some of the variables. Can they be reduced to their essentials for evaluation? Yes, they can—some more easily and more feasibly than others. Queuing theory may well be vital to a library that circulates fifty-thousand to one-hundred-thousand items per month, because of the volume of traffic or problems with layout, whereas a small library may never have more than a couple of people at the circulation desk at one time. A general grasp of time-and-motion study could earn considerable savings if applied to inefficient methods of circulation clerks. Ponder an unnecessary extra action that wastes a second or two each time a book is charged out. Cumulatively the process could be using hours every week and causing patron delays. Such effects are usually very subtle and willingly corrected by employees.

Will a new circulation system require continuous reliance on outside contracts or service companies? What is the effect of a roll of expired or lost film? Who controls the cost of a transaction slip–sorting contract? How much will it cost next year? These questions deal with choices not easily reduced to precise data. Talk to other users and review the literature. Ultimately, most review and analysis will require the making of judgments. The best administrators will plan and analyze with the intent of minimizing the risks or, conversely, of maximizing the possibility of making the wisest choice among alternatives.

Staff utilization and scheduling are extremely important in a circulation function. Because of the number of staff performing the same tasks, it is usually easier to observe and then test some managerial principles in that department. How does appropriate training affect work output? Does rotating jobs make any difference in the quality or consistency of staff response? Are traffic and circulation patterns during the day known from surveying and checking, or is the scheduling of an extra worker based on an intuitive guess? Up to a point, the more questions one can answer, the greater the quest for more and different information. The objective must be kept in mind, for an intimate understanding is desired in order to provide the best possible value in library services.

In the course of developing an ongoing evaluative posture, the question of performance standards is bound to arise again and again. In most industrial applications, the ability to measure performance against an acceptable standard is indispensable. The processes in libraries may be drastically different in appearance, but the very same principles apply. Any attempt to establish standards will abound with frustration and vagueness; there are no accepted norms, and the differences among libraries are great. The rewards in the long run will be worth the effort. How many books ought to be shelved in an hour? The mere fact of knowing such a figure could impact directly on scheduling through the week and certainly offer an easy method of spot-checking the performance of the shelvers. The development of standards for all aspects of circulation routines alone could provide the basis for a management information system that would gradually grow to encompass the whole situation. Yes, such standards would frequently be arbitrary and, yes, they would probably undergo change and adjustment on a regular basis. The lessons and insight gained in the experience would most assuredly carry over into analysis of support and other services that are not so easily measured.

Technical Services

Technical services, like circulation, require repetitive tasks, many of which are accomplished by clerical staff. Among institutions there are some differences as to just which activities are included here, but for the present purpose they include acquistion, cataloging, processing, catalog maintenance, and similar functions.

Possibly the strongest point that can be made about technical services is that the component processes—from selection through ordering, cataloging, and processing—are an integrated system. This notion is frequently dismissed or ignored. The economies of work to be exercised in this area can be applied to the processes separately, but the most profound results will come from analyzing them as a single, continuous, interrelated system. The acquisition or production of catalog cards is directly related to the selection process. The method and timing of book orders is inextricably entwined with the creation or acquisition of cataloging data. The processing function is haphazard unless it is in concert with a consolidated plan for selection and ordering. A systematic examination of the overall flow of activity will show ample evidence of these and other relationships.

A most common use of flow charting in libraries is in analysis of the technical services operation. Flowcharts usually show up when a systems analyst is studying existing procedures against the possibility of a data-processing application. While more is said about the computer elsewhere, it is interesting to consider that libraries do not avail themselves of efficiency experts until the prospects are so calamitous that an extremely expensive solution becomes the normal recourse. Ironically, the flowchart with its attendant logic and thoroughness is a technique that can be applied in at least a rudimentary fashion by any administrator. The objective of the examination, as with all analysis techniques, is an understanding of what is actually happening. The surface confusion and multiplicity of files, materials, and tasks can be reduced to logical and elementary steps within the mosaic of the whole department. The technique is admittedly tedious and time consuming, but it can be applied successfully to almost any procedure within the library.

Keeping in mind that the techniques and suggestions offered are illustrative and all have broad possibilities for application, consider next the challenge of forms analysis and control. While most support services could benefit from more awareness of it, the acquisitions function for books and the serials operation are areas that lend themselves to making the point. Most administrators are by nature inclined toward the elimination of unnecessary work and are conscious of the need for effective forms or work sheets that assist in getting the job done. At the same time, there are probably few institutions that escape the need for continual revision of some forms that are used every day. There is some whimsy in decisions for changes, but more often there are logical and

progressive reasons for it. All too often, unfortunately, the manager is victim to an incomplete evaluation of the full ramifications of the need for forms analysis. The multiple order form for book acquisition is an excellent example. These forms have probably saved millions of dollars through the efficiencies inherent in their use. What is not so evident is the corresponding misuse of them. Through enthusiasm or zeal, many libraries overuse multiple order forms by creating unnecessary additional copies, the handling of which offset the original gain. The symptoms are usually redundant files.

Over in the serials function, insight can be gleaned from the correspondence of publishers and subscription agencies. One can easily find both good and bad examples for study. Nonetheless, the intent is clear in a form that attempts to consolidate all pertinent information and even to anticipate a variety of customer responses, all on one sheet of paper. Can administrators afford to overlook the potential savings in efficiency that can be realized by acute examination of the purposes and design of the forms they use? If the right attitudes and general awareness are present, it may be that just a little more determination is needed.

For pure application of time-and-motion study, there are few library applications that are as obvious as those aspects of processing books that include pasting, stamping, and applying plastic jackets. All of the classic ingredients of production methods are present for analysis—work station, supply materials, distances, movements, lighting, distractions, etc.

In technical services there are wide variances in application of scientific principles because of the size differences among subject libraries. Choices may be more difficult for the administrator of a small library, who cannot achieve the relative economies made possible by processing large numbers of books, for example, or who may lack staff to carry the cataloging work load. Such limitations frequently force a reliance on services of library systems, cooperatives, or commercial sources. In such cases, the local administrator has the burden of evaluating those additional prospects.

The Card Catalog

Of all the support functions of the local library, the card catalog is probably the most interesting. It is the tool with which the public is most familiar, and it always commands a prominent place in the floor plan. The library staff, up to and including the administrator, take it for granted. Considering the amount of time and cost expended on this one tool, it is amazing how little challenge it receives. In many institutions, the card catalog has been converted to a book format that still contains essentially the same information as the old filing system. In others, significant progress has been made in on-line computer-data-base methodology, which has improved access. However, the concern for local administrators should be the limited amount of serious analysis aimed at the catalog. In this regard, the catalog represents an anachronism within modern administrative experience. The scope of services is now far beyond that available only in books, but the catalog persists. Or, rather, librarians persist in their allegiance to the catalog. The direct and subtle costs incurred in maintaining the catalog are enormous; the limitations are abundant. The probable reason that a replacement has not yet appeared lies in a combination of limited alternatives, high cost of conversion, and value systems. Consequently, when adminstrators deal with the card catalog, they must eventually make professional and economic choices that could very well affect their own jobs.

All that aside, the administrator must have a position vis-à-vis the catalog. How often is it used, how is it used, and by whom? Some limited attempts to determine answers to these questions will demonstrate the complexity of the problem. Insight into the methodology of social science research will prove valuable in this and other areas where the public is involved, because expectations of users and similar intangibles are extremely difficult to assess. Ultimately the administrator will come to grips with the reassuring fact that value judgments by the practitioners are indeed a key element in evaluation. Fortunately, the route of expanded awareness and application of scientific principles will automatically improve the information from which the judgments are made.

Computer Applications

The use of computer applications in library support services has made dramatic advancements possible. Among public libraries, the largest systems have naturally led the way, but academic institutions have had more experience. The efforts to automate certain library functions are not limited to an identifiable department or separate function, but they are serious enough to warrant specific consideration here. The byword should be judicious caution—the stakes are high.

Change generally in library support services has occurred slowly. The dramatic, rapid changes in routine and procedure dictated by computer applications can produce trauma. Employees most directly affected must be aware throughout the process of just what is being planned. Giving thoughtful attention to staff undercurrents is a necessary responsibility for the administrator. The process of investigation and study of computer applications will require much of the administrator's time, and some routines will suffer. But it would be a serious strategic mistake to neglect staff relationships at such a time.

But what of the planning process and the decision environment leading to computerization? In fact, if an administrator is utilizing scientific principles in a continuous review and evaluation of operations, there is little difference from normal other than the scale of the impact. The same need to know and understand what is happening in the existing process is applicable here. Since the effectiveness of the computer is based upon simple logical manipulation of data, the system analysis that is the preliminary investigation will merely attempt to produce what the administrator should already have available: a record of what exactly is taking place and the objectives of each element. This is the appropriate place for a reminder that the adminstrator's role here is extremely crucial because the decisions made will encumber future choices. The toughest decisions are those requiring value judgments. To include or not a certain capability, to assume that the library's needs will continue in a certain pattern, to limit because of overall cost—these are the kinds of choices that only the administrator should make. And it is at these points in the life of the library that the administrators are separated from the pretenders. The cumulative experience and available knowledge that go into these value judgments form the real determinants of success or failure. Thus the attitudes and approaches that were developed in earlier years and that formed the basis for management awareness are the key factors in ongoing improvement. On the other hand, if scientific principles and techniques have not been utilized, the need for them will become evident during and after the fact, when it may be to late.

Computer technology itself serves to underline the need for caution. The advances and improvements come so quickly that significant changes in capability occur even within the planning or development phase of one project. How different from the decades when the card catalog, for example, was a mature, constant component of service and not subject to rapid advances and general revisions! Nonetheless, the potential benefits and advantages of the new technology are so great that all administrators will sooner or later face the issue of automating. It will provide some assurance to note that the development of library computer applications is maturing to the point of routine acceptance, just like the payroll and financial applications that already affect everyone on a daily basis.

The administrator's responsibility stretches to include understanding the computer. While admittedly the details and maintenance of hardware and software will fall to experts, there is no way to sidestep the issues by deferring completely to subordinates or consultants. The options in computer application are many. Using computer capability already possessed by the parent government is one option that must be considered, regardless of some potential drawbacks. Frequently librarians have a dim view of their priority within local government and are disinclined to look there for solutions. Failure to assess the possibility of using city or county hardware could result in justifiable priority shortcomings. Time-sharing relationships with computer service companies is a practice that is widely used in business and becoming fashionable in libraries as well. There are many variations on the theme, which amounts to a number of clients together supporting the capital and overhead of one center. It is increasingly feasible for a library to support and maintain its own mini-computer. The minis are now finding their place, and indications are that decreasing cost of hardware will favor them over the larger systems, particularly since most applications do not require the big capability. Progressing further, a combination of mini-computers with one larger computer is bringing very attractive possibilities into play. The library may have a relatively expensive mini-computer that takes care of daily routine and small programs and could be tied directly to a large unit to satisfy occasional larger need. The relationship could also satisfy a desire for ongoing backup maintenance and support. The latter is an obvious need for the library that cannot support any depth in computer technical expertise.

The analysis leading to a computer decision is complex, and there is always a clear danger of cost escalating; but so much for waving danger flags. What areas of support services are most appropriate for computer assistance? Most visible are bibliographic control and access through the big data bases with remote terminals. Then there are numerous applications that simplify work through on-line access to lists of local holdings or book catalogs. Such a conversion has been made by many commercial services that cater to libraries, notably book jobbers and subscription agencies. It appears that the circulation-control function has gained the spotlight for a time. It may well be that this emphasis was the result of a combination of factors, among them a narrower range of local variation in circulation requirements and an easier package to put together. Surely it is especially salable because of the visibility of circulation and

the ability of more people to identify with that application.

Technical services support activity is where the most savings will be made in improving efficiency. As mentioned before, there is the need to recognize that acquisitions practices are entwined with bibliographic control and even circulation. For this reason, it is well to ensure that planning is farsighted enough to include the possibility, if not likelihood, of integrating most of the computer applications. It is viewed by some as a disappointment that acquisitions packages seem to be waiting for the circulation market to run its course, but, everything considered, it must be acknowledged that library administrators play the key role in making such a determination. They are the individuals whose decisions and choices will regulate the development.

Again, of all the applications of scientific methodology in library support services, none will require as much investigation and awareness as that of embarking on a plan of computer assistance.

Other Support Services

There are of course numerous other support services, and they vary in importance. Without dwelling on them, it is well to make a few observations about their susceptibility to scientific management principles. Collection security systems are a relatively new development in library practice; serious loss of materials was the causal factor. Like so many possible solutions to problems, designing this type of system requires a good deal of planning information. While the assumption is that losses must be reduced, it doesn't necessarily follow that the taxpayers' interest is best served by installing a collection security system. Is the actual value of book losses known? What will a system add to normal operating costs in processing as well as in circulation control? What are the intangibles of public response or staff apprehension of change? In some cases the security system is primarily a psychological deterrent and makes no attempt to establish a specific savings.

Interlibrary loan is frequently placed under the auspices of other functions and, as a consequence, it is one of these services that just grows and grows until it requires a significant amount of effort and resources. Some other functions that may be classified as support activities are books by mail, reserves, building security, mail, and delivery. These activities often suffer from benign neglect. Administrators do acknowledge the important roles they play, but because they have a relatively small scope of activity, there is no routine monitoring procedure. In the array of reports the manager sees, there ought to be some measures that will yield enough information to maintain an awareness of these functions. Also, the report data must be chosen very carefully. Too many data are usually worse than not enough, because the expense of collecting them may outweigh the savings they could effect. The need is, of course, to keep the managers aware of the operations. There are enough demands on the administrator's time that the use of every hour relates to overall effectiveness.

One technique that often provides useful information related to support services is that of surveying the users. Literally ask the public for their concerns and observations. Generally this technique is most useful for direct public services, but all too often the information gained is related to support services. There is no substitute for such direct feedback from the end user. Many large and well-run service organizations develop sophisticated internal evaluation techniques. In such cases they usually use standards established by the staff of the various functions and regularly measure the performance. A not-so-subtle twist is to have peers in other functions perform the inspections or checking.

Graphic arts, printing, reproduction, even copying machines are support functions that must pass the tests of effectiveness and relationship to objectives. At some levels, a single copying machine can cause more disruption and frustration than a major service decision. On the one hand, the evaluation is tied to quality and quantity of output. This is difficult enough, but the tough cost-benefit evaluation should respond to these questions: Should it be in the library at all? Are the dollars spent and the additional logistical burden fully warranted by the need? Would it actually cost more on the outside considering the relative quality? Is it fair for the taxpayer to assume there are valid answers to these and similar questions?

Conclusion

Library support services may lack the glamour of public service, but the work objectives are as vital as any in the institution. In addition, there are several facets of environment that lend to support services a greater latitude for applying scientific management principles. But the environment is not enough. Each library administrator has to develop attitudes and a philosophy that will provide direction and motivation for all other staff. The philosophy must hold as a central notion that understanding and evaluation are continuous and routine aspects of the institutional effort.

It is inescapable that the administrator is the central figure in the library and that the style and enthusiasm for utilizing scientific techniques will emanate from that person. The administrator's success in applying the techniques depends in some measure on the advice and assistance that are drawn upon. The literature, colleagues, local experts, consultants, and many other sources of help are readily at hand. Some problems of library support services are large and complex enough that libraries need to combine efforts in systems or networks in order to develop reasonable solutions.

The manager should formalize the use of scientific techniques as much as the institution will permit. All staff should be aware of the import of continual analysis and so participate in it more fully. Library support services have appropriate applications for virtually every scientific management tool and technique that is available: systems analysis, management information systems, and cost-benefit review of the organization. Forms control, sampling, and time-and-motion study offer methodologies for improved effectiveness and efficiency for a small component or procedure within the library. There are many others, of course, and it is incumbent on the administrator to become aware of them.

Circulation control and collection maintenance are the two areas of support services currently undergoing the most dramatic changes and improvements as a result of scientific analysis. On the other hand, many administrators are using the techniques but doing it so casually that the results are minimized.

Great potential for applying scientific analysis often occurs in conjunction with the computer. However, the stakes are usually very high in that the decisions are costly. It is vital, therefore, that the administrator have the clearest possible understanding of the library's actual operation and objectives before embarking on automated solutions.

Awareness and use of scientific tools and techniques in support services is paramount in the decision-making process. This conclusion cannot be overstated. Each administrator of a public library will increase effectiveness through application of measures of analysis and evaluation.

15   *Extension Services*

PEGGY SULLIVAN

The commitment of the public library to serve the public wherever that public may be has led to the development of a wide range of extension services. If these are defined as public services provided to the users and potential users of the library throughout the area served by the library but excluding those services offered in a central downtown or research library, we have a good working definition. The distinction may be unclear or meaningless in a library system that is a federation of local autonomous libraries, each of them having some of the features of an extension service, each having some of the features of a central library. It may also be blurred when, as in some newer, larger systems, the development of a pattern of community libraries in a variety of locations has occurred without the establishment of the central or main library that has been a typical feature for generations.

Branch libraries are probably the first thing one associates with extension services, bookmobiles the second, and deposit collections of some sort the third. But there are others. Service to the homebound, which may be administered from some central location, is really an aspect of extension services. So is service to those in institutions, including hospitals, correctional facilities, schools, and nursing homes, among others. Outreach programs, most prevalent in the period of the Great Society of the 1960s, have been in existence in some form for a long time, if we consider them as efforts on the part of public libraries to reach people wherever they are. The visit of a librarian with a bag of books to a union hall or the cooperative planning of a storytelling series with park and recreation staff members are instances of outreach that have been traditional. What was generally added in the 1960s was better funding and increased support of staff. These made possible the undertaking of more assignments of this kind without the burden of neglecting other responsibilities. Service to the blind and physically handicapped—at least those who fit the definition of the Library of Congress—is another aspect of extension service, usually funded through the federal program for this purpose.

Elements of Extension Services

The development of a concept of library extension services is relatively easy. Its interpretation and implementation are the problems. Most of those responsible for the administration of public libraries would agree that service needs to be provided to as many people as possible, as effectively and efficiently as possible, with consideration of the needs, interests, and convenience of that public. Then come the questions: What is library service? How is the public defined and located? What are the trade-offs between efficiency and convenience? What are reasonable steps toward provision of better service? To what extent does the community served need to participate in the development of plans and goals? And these are only the beginning.

If one were to list all the services that some extension library agency provides somewhere and indicate the frequency with which they are provided, the number and variety would probably surprise and perhaps even shock many. Most people expect libraries to provide books for loan, and they can extend that expectation to a variety of other media if they are encouraged, either by the library or their own needs, to do so. While they may pay lip service to the idea of a library as an information center, they are less likely to expect reference service from their own neighborhood or community library and may be unaware of its possibilities for telephone reference requests, verification of availability of materials elsewhere, or requests for interlibrary loans. Library-sponsored programs may first come to the public's awareness through publicity about programs for children, and the idea of having lecture series or film programs for adults may be new to many, just as the possibility of using a library's facilities for community meetings may be unknown to many.

While the above activities and services can be readily understood as a part of a library's program of service, there are many more that are grayer areas, both in practice of librarians and in the minds of the public. Sales of the library's used materials, service on a local library's advisory committee or Friends of the Library group, and the library's participation in an art fair or community show are not uncommon, but neither are they taken for granted. And, in its energetic efforts to reach a variety of publics, the library itself must have defined what its real purpose is and the avenues it may be justified in taking to achieve that purpose. Library staff members who have exhausted themselves in cooperative programs to provide social activities for young adults, for example, have often wondered later whether the effort was justified in terms of making the young adults aware of what the library had to offer them. On a narrower base, there are those who seem to want to have every effort pay off in increased attendance at the library, rising circulation statistics, or some other tangible gain. Somewhere between the two lies reason. When sponsorship of an activity that is not clearly library related is suggested, the personnel of extension services need to decide whether the effort is worth it, but they may also need to adjust and readjust their measurement of values. It may be most reasonable, for example, for a new branch library to be the site for medical testing if that would make it more visible to its community. On the other hand, it might be disastrous for an overcrowded, high-traffic library to take on the same program if it would only hinder the library services it is committed to offering.

The Public for Extension Services

There are frameworks for fairly elaborate studies of how to locate and define the library's public. There are firmly held ideas to the effect that those above educational and socioeconomic medians use public libraries more extensively. And there is general recognition of the fact that one of the love affairs of childhood is with the public library. Community groups may respond warmly to the prospect of having libraries located in their areas without having any individual interest in using them. On the other hand, newcomers to a locality may be much more open to finding and using libraries that have collections and services that match their tastes, almost regardless of the library's location. In dealing with all these aspects, a library needs to have a sense of its actual and potential public and a recognition of the fact that at different times different parts of that public need to be targeted for special effort. An awareness of changes in a community's composition is essential for the librarian serving it. An influx of apartment dwellers, a change of transit routes, the removal of a hospital, an increase in the average age, or a change in the ethnic composition should be considered, not only by the staff of the local library, but by the administration that has the responsibility to offer the best service to each community. It often happens that a librarian who is enthusiastically attuned to a mix of families using the library in fairly traditional ways is woefully inadequate when it comes to responding to the requests coming from young singles who have life-styles and values varying sharply with the librarian's. It may make more sense for the librarian to change jobs or locations than to attempt to change that person's attitudes or background. The real problem is that, in matters of change like this, the change is often unobserved and unreported by the library staff until the shift has been so dramatic that much more effort is needed to serve the new members of the community.

The love affair between the child and the public library, mentioned above, did not just happen. Public libraries have made constant efforts to reach children and to make them feel at home in libraries. Visits by classes, story hours, film programs, puppet plays, craft programs, and summer reading clubs are only a few of the traditional efforts made. Children's librarians have usually had the freedom to visit schools and playgrounds to reach children where they were most likely to be. The cultural pattern that has made every generation willing to sacrifice for those who come after it has caused immigrant parents and those from newer minorities to ask for services for their children that they could not imagine—or thought they might not be able to use effectively—for themselves. There are two ironies in this: public library extension service has become too often identified with full service for children and inadequate service for adults; and, in violation of a classic gambling maneuver, libraries have tended to support their successes and pull back on their failures. Programs and services for children are often stressed to the detriment of similar offerings for adults, and the result in many metropolitan library systems is an attitude that suggests it is appropriate for extension services to be designated for children, and for reference services at a central library or major libraries to be targeted toward adults. Because extension library agencies such as branches or bookmobiles are likely to be small, competent staff members will be few in number, and, if the emphasis is placed on children's programming and collections, planning for adults may be overlooked or seen only as another task for the librarian who has major responsibility for supervision and overall planning for the library.

There is another facet to the question of what library service is, and it has particular relevance for extension services. If library service implies access to all the benefits of major libraries—large collections, public programs, good reference service, space for study, and equitable access to other library services both within and outside the system—then it is clear that small units of service are inequitable. The difficult thing is to find the balance between what is practical to provide in a location convenient to a small or isolated community and what that public should be able to consider total library service. This difficulty has appeared in many guises in public libraries in the United States. Librarians in the South who prided themselves on having provided some form of library service, on a separate but equal basis, to Negroes in the 1920s through the 1940s were dismayed when those services were repudiated as being of poorer quality than those available to the white communities served by the same library. Similar efforts to establish outreach programs in urban slums or ghettos have also been rejected by the audience they were intended to attract on the basis of being something less than the total service available in larger libraries or for other publics. Each library system needs to decide for itself such matters as what a minimum staff or collection will be, what a reasonable distance is between libraries and what factors should be considered in making exceptions to it, and how the benefits of the system can effectively be extended to every library in it.

Planning Service Facilities

The real problem is that few public libraries have the luxury of time and talent and intellectual and social climate to develop a plan of extension services. Too often, when a throughway threatens a branch library, there is a site nearby that can be hastily taken over, and the action is taken without judgment of that action in reference to other priorities. A new apartment development is planned, and the library is offered space in it for a permanent branch. The offer is accepted because it is a good idea to have a library there, but the specific location may be poor. It is axiomatic that it is at least as hard to move a library location as it is to change an educational curriculum, and that, in turn, is like moving a cemetery. One never knows how many friends the dead have until one attempts such a move. It is difficult to determine whether it is better to take some risks by investing in more-experienced staff or special collections or exceptional services in order to revive a library that may appear to be languishing, or to decide that nothing can rescue the location. Decisions like this are fraught with political implications, for the local community groups that see the demise of a library

as the equivalent of desertion by the powers that be, and also for the powers that be themselves, who may be reluctant to admit that an earlier location was in error or who may feel that the library should still "show the flag" when a business area is dying or a community is becoming one of factories rather than families.

In instances where thoughtful plans for the establishment of extension services have been developed, they have often not been implemented in the way or to the extent of the original plan. Philadelphia, Dallas, and Chicago are among major city library systems that have had such plans in the years since World War II, and the time consumed in implementing them has led to major changes, usually reductions, in achieving them. Constantly rising costs are the major problem, but changes in other plans closely related to the library have their effect also.

There are few absolutes in the matter of planning for locations of library extension services, but among the few are these: (1) Traffic patterns and attitudes toward them need to be considered. (2) Communities and their library needs change, and the library must be able to respond as well as to lead. (3) Bigness is not always an economy when the ongoing costs of maintenance and staffing are the continuing budget items. (4) The library's plan needs to be consonant with those of other public agencies as well as with its own overall plan and priorities. (5) It is desirable to have some minimal and optimal needs established for each location in terms of square footage, collection, parking, and other physical requirements. Policies specifying minimal space requirements or locations in separate facilities (e.g., not in schools, not in community centers), or ground-level locations for most public service points may need to be developed and integrated into the planning of new facilities as well as the evaluation of the old.

The nature of the community surrounding the library has much to do with what can be reasonable access. Where automobiles proliferate, parking is, of course, essential, but it may be possible to anticipate that users will travel farther to use the library. In densely populated areas of apartment buildings, parking may not be as important, and the cost of land may be so high that less square footage is available to the library.

The scale of permanence of library buildings ranges from those owned by the library to those rented, those designed for portability, and bookmobiles, the "traveling libraries" of our time, which were once the sign of a rural library but which became, largely thanks to funding through the Library Services and Construction Act and other federal programs, the regular visitors to many urban and suburban areas. In recent years, budget cutbacks have often removed bookmobiles from service, but experience and expert opinion suggests that coming years may see their reemergence as service posts. Arguments about them are reminiscent of arguments about the utility of aircraft carriers in an era of supersonic fighters. They seem bulky and heavy when compared to other means of service, but, when scheduled appropriately, with their mobility made a strength, they are the library's best response to shifts of population and to areas that may, because of geographic isolation, make limited use of a library building but can use the bookmobile to good effect. When book collections for bookmobiles are well developed and when the reserve store of them is tapped with the interests of a particular stop's clientele in mind, they can cover many more needs than the necessarily more-static collections of other libraries. They may be used in interim or emergency locations or when permanent libraries are in the planning stages, closed because of such emergencies as fire damage, or in the process of being closed permanently. To the extent that the mobility of the bookmobiles is stressed, they can be an asset to the library's planning and a valuable part of the library's program of public service.

While some libraries have provided programs such as story hours or film showings in conjunction with bookmobile stops, the bookmobile service is usually more limited, stressing the loan of materials. Bookmobile stops at shopping centers may stress collections for adults, those at schools may cater to children's interests, and the flexibility of the collection can serve both clienteles well. A flexible, competent staff able to work in the varied locations and at close quarters with their publics is almost a must.

Recently, branches or small libraries with features of portability are being used in some areas. These also are primarily used as centers for circulation of materials rather than for reference, study, or extensive research. Described as kiosk libraries, these can be erected in a short time on concrete bases, but they have the potential of being moved to other locations if the location proves to be inappropriate or when time suggests a change. Public space is the greatest part of these small libraries, and they may require backup or storage collections elsewhere, just as bookmobiles do. An argument in their favor is the fact that they can be available on a much more extensive basis than bookmobiles in terms of a regular weekly schedule, and varying life-styles with irregular hours may be better served by such library facilities than by small, permanent locations. Better evaluation of the effectiveness and convenience of these facilities can be made when they are used in a greater variety of geographic and social settings, including urban locations where building codes and other requirements are certainly not encouraging to their use.

Rental locations offer some of the options of impermanence and may seem to be reasonable ways to test locations or to provide interim service when building plans are in abeyance. Leases of from three to five years are probably most reasonable. The conversion of typical rental properties to libraries may require the strengthening of floors for the weight requirements of the collection, introduction of such features as ramps or special rest rooms for the physically handicapped, and change of such features as extensive window areas when shelving or public seating areas may have a higher priority than displays. The cost of initial renovation of a building, the development of a location's identity, and the costs associated with moving into and out of a facility all need to be considered carefully when rental locations are evaluated.

One kind of location for a library is often suggested as a very logical and economical possibility. That is space rented or, occasionally, provided free in another facility. Schools and community service centers are often available on this basis, but the history of such locations has not been high on success. There are public libraries that are or were associated with boards of education, and in many instances it seemed desirable to have joint facilities. Several studies of public libraries housed in public school buildings have pointed up generally unsatisfactory experiences. Problems range from those of establishing appropriate but different goals and reaching different publics to those associated with collection development and deployment. If curricular emphases or insistence on a collection limited to materials appropriate only for school-age users dictates the scope of the collection, the public library is crippled before it even begins. There can also be problems of limited access due to location within the facility. While there are few inviolable guidelines for hours of opening of libraries, it is important that the library be available at times when most of the public can use it, and that is not likely to be the case if limited school hours with some extensions are the model or baseline. In community centers, there are other trade-offs: other activities scheduled there may attract to the library users who might not otherwise come, but there are also likely to be parts of the public who totally miss the information that the library is a part of the larger complex of activities within such a building.

Matters of administration are the major points, however. The library needs the freedom to plan its programs, reach its public, and set its hours to fit its own goals and objectives, and, even with the best cooperative planning, this may be hard to do when it is housed with other facilities. Access to public exhibition galleries, lecture halls, rest rooms, or similar facilities may seem to be an asset, but these are assets only to the extent that they are fully accessible for library users, and limitations may not be clear at the time of the planning. Cooperative housing may seem most appropriate for communities where funding is limited and populations are isolated, but in every instance such planning should be undertaken with care and with consideration of the library's unique needs and purposes. Nothing should be taken for granted in the negotiations for such a cooperative enterprise.

Library locations that are owned by the library or the governmental unit supporting the library are probably the most common and the most permanent. Over a period of years, the trend from monumental (even when erected on a small scale) to the functional but uninteresting has continued toward moderation, with esthetic features considered along with those affecting function and accessibility. Precise location is of prime importance when the library is committing itself to one property. Plans for the neighboring area, access to parking, traffic patterns, and requirements for buildings in the community all need to be considered carefully in choosing a site. Most often, libraries with public areas located at ground level will be preferred if enough space is available at reasonable cost.

Patterns of Service

The physical facility is, after all, only the setting for the library; it is not, in itself, the library. A central administrative staff and the overall community may determine the library's goals in a given location. Planning for the interrelationships of a variety of libraries is essential. Regional centers or larger libraries strategically located throughout the area may be a part of the planning, as may be the division of a number of smaller units into geographic regions. Neighborhood libraries may have the responsibility of providing staff, storage space, or other needs for smaller libraries or bookmobiles in the area, and there may be a natural clustering for cooperative purchasing and/or staffing of libraries in similiar localities or with similiar kinds of patrons. Administrative relationships may not have to be formal if cooperative planning is effective—that is, an experienced librarian at a major branch library may provide leadership to other libraries nearby without having specific responsibility for supervision or evaluation of their collections or staffs. In some instances, the designation of some regional supervisor may be most desirable in order to provide guidance and support for libraries that may be somewhat remote from the central administration. It may be desirable for these supervisors to be persons other than those heading the largest libraries in the area, even though this establishes another layer of administration and supervision, a feature usually to be avoided.

Management and Supervision

Fortunately, management is becoming more widely recognized as a skill of librarians, and supervision is a major part of it, not just in terms of evaluation of staff members and assignment of tasks, but also in terms of the handling of almost all aspects of the library's program at a given location: public relations, maintenance of the physical facility, collection development, information and reference service, public programming, etc. Supervision and management are not necessarily more complex in ratio to the numbers of people or amount of space or budget to be supervised and managed. There is a need to assign one's own time wisely and to make decisions about allocations of resources that will provide the best service for the community to be served, no matter how small the library may be. Extension service libraries usually provide the opportunity for individuals to develop these skills without removing themselves from the immediately satisfying work of dealing with the public, and therein lie both frustration and reward. Librarians who enjoy working with the public may resent the time that must be spent on recruiting and scheduling staff or assignment of budget, but the opportunity to acquire such experience on a limited scale without making a commitment that pulls the individual away from direct public service entirely is an opportunity to be enjoyed.

Internal Communication and Cooperation

Every public library has its own tone and quality of public service, and there is need for consistency among its various extension programs. Decisions about such matters as length of loan, procedures for interlibrary loan, hours of opening, employee requirements and perquisites need to be made centrally and followed with general consistency throughout the library, but there is usually more room for freedom in the various extension units than most supervisors associated with them appreciate or enjoy. Patrons using a variety of libraries in one system should be able to adjust themselves to general practices while still appreciating some of the differences in programming that make up the unique character of individual libraries.

There is also usually more possibility for centralized services, such as production of book lists or cooperative public programs, than individual libraries in extension services use effectively. Cooperative planning is very inertial. It is not easy to start, or to stop once it has been well started, but it does require thought and effort. Stimulus by one leader may be important in its early stages, but some distribution of tasks among the staff members engaged in the cooperative effort is also important. Ideas as well as work should be shared, and communication should be consistent. One aspect of cooperation among extension service agencies can be the opportunity to learn from the mistakes of others, but that can occur only when open communication prevails and when the atmosphere of learning and growth is stressed. Competition among various libraries, in regard to circulation, public relations results, or appearance, can coexist with cooperation and may even stimulate greater cooperation. The provision of a new service, such as the free exchange of sewing patterns, may be offered in one library and picked up as an idea, given another twist such as organization of the patterns by size or style, and initiated elsewhere. Feedback from the seond library can in turn suggest improvements or adaptation to the first.

Probably the areas where cooperation can have its greatest impact in relation to service is development and use of the collection. Almost by definition, extension services are made up of a number of small collections; and it should be noted that great skill and understanding are needed to make these collections as useful and as good as they can be. An efficient transportation system is essential if materials are to be loaned among the various libraries, and that system must, in turn, be supported by good communications including the provision of information about what is available elsewhere in the system and about other factors that affect availability, such as hours of service, limitations on loans, etc.

The public library's technical services, such as cataloging, circulation and processing, are of critical importance for extension service. The development of automated service in these areas is certain to have great impact on extension services. Access to information about what is in the entire library system can be provided in each of its units, and circulation systems can inform the would-be user whether the item is immediately available or not. It can be reasonably predicted that individual extension service points will become locations used by patrons to locate what they want and that information about the availability of materials elsewhere will cause dramatic increases in the requests for lending among libraries. To some extent, this has already occurred, but the future promises to increase the possibilities for efficient, economical exchanges of materials and to provide better access to information about their availability at the very time that many libraries may be limiting their purchasing of materials.

Collection Development and Maintenance

It is superficial to think that small libraries, such as those included in extension services, can exist with more general collections and simply request more specifics from other, larger units of service. Requests are as likely to be specific in a small library as in a large one, and the alert and competent librarian who can predict and respond to such requests is the one who will provide the most effective service. An example can illustrate this. The head of one small branch library points out that, with his small space, it makes more sense for him to purchase one book on all kinds of breeds of dogs, rather than to attempt to have one each on several breeds. True, but if even a nonscientific survey of the community reveals that cocker spaniels and beagles predominate, it can make sense to provide individual titles about them for the community that is likely to want them. The same concern for precision and prediction of use can work in the selection of poetry, mysteries, economics texts—any part of the collection where anthologies or general introductions are not necessarily the best choices if interest and potential use can be well predicted.

The support of extension service collections must include some storage for materials needed occasionally but not often enough to justify inclusion in the small units of service. Regional libraries may fill part of this need, serving as backup collections. But there may also be the need for nonpublic storage areas where staff members in extension services can periodically select materials for their collections, either on a long-term loan basis or for short-term use by an individual patron. Literary classics, foreign-language titles, large-print books, sixteen-millimeter films are among the kinds of items best utilized by this kind of access. Procedures for circulating entire collections among a number of branch libraries or other service centers may be the best way to provide the variety that an individual library needs along with the economy with which it must be concerned. In other words, if twenty titles in large print can be shifted from one agency to another, and be replaced by a different set of twenty titles, the public in both places has, over a period of time, access to forty titles, but the individual library has not had to purchase that many. Typically, active readers chafe at small collections, which they may read through all too rapidly, at least in the areas that interest them. This phenomenon is the major reason for the appeal of rental collections, which libraries can lease on a regular basis and return to the vendor while continuing to get current titles. These rental plans provide delivery on or near publication date of new books, and they allow for turnover. Some studies indicate they may not justify their cost, but each library differs also in the rapidity with which it can provide new materials, so rental plans may offer more to them than they can provide for themselves in terms of rapid acquisition and processing, for example.

When one considers that a major argument for having a variety of service points in a library system is to provide for the different needs of varied publics, it is surprising that collections, arrangement, public programming, and staff deployment are as similar as they are. In some public library systems, one can enter a library blindfolded and know exactly where the bulletin boards are going to be, where the picture-book tables and charging desks are located, and what signs will be posted at which points throughout the building. Even librarians who pride themselves on finding and serving the needs and interests of their communities are likely to make the libraries for which they are responsible too much like other libraries. What is needed is a balance between the traditionally good aspects of library organization and the good ways to approach and please a given community.

Identification of Publics

Division of service responsibilities by age levels of users is, for example, a traditional library pattern. Adults and children were the early broad groups. Young adults, usually teenagers, were the next group to be distinguished. More recent years have seen the development of more programs for senior citizens as the numbers and power of this part of the public have grown. Service to preschool children and their parents has become more recognized also. Nevertheless, it does not make sense for every library to divide its programs

of service in these ways, nor to assign staff responsibilities on the basis of age levels. Similarly, many libraries that have fairly small collections have improved access by combining into one arrangement the formerly separated children's and adult collections of nonfiction materials. This is certainly not the appropriate arrangement for every library, but the arguments for it—the ease of finding simple treatments of topics near more advanced treatments, possible elimination of duplication in the collection, and reduction of the embarassment of older readers who cannot read well—are arguments for recognition of a community's special needs that can be accommodated without sabotaging the library's need for some logical arrangement.

No library is static in its services or in its collections. Yet there is a tendency for libraries to retain their initial forms even as new materials or services are incorporated so that the latter are never well integrated into the library. This observation applies to paperback collections, which are generally accepted but often treated so separately that much of the value of having them is lost. Mass-market paperbacks are important to most public library extension services, but the staff need to keep their unique characteristics in mind. They should be discarded when they have become grimy and unattractive unless there is some compelling reason for maintaining them in the collection. It should be possible to provide access to them for patrons who do not "just want a paperback" but who want to find a specific title or kind of book, and they should be displayed in ways that stress their good points. Racks where their covers can be viewed easily increase their usefulness. However, paperbacks are often displayed so separately and so differently from the rest of the book collection that they do not encourage readers to move from one part of the collection to the other, and the paperback racks may simply look like some kind of permanently fixed afterthought to the library. Media such as audio cassettes, pamphlets, sound filmstrips, to name a few, are often treated similarly and not integrated well enough into the collection to achieve their full usefulness.

Coordination of Services

Extension services must replicate, perhaps on different scales, some services that are coordinated throughout the library system. Too often, individual staff members think that a time will come when some activities will not have to be initiated or repeated, but that is not likely to happen. Even with the best coordination of effort, individual extension service units need to be informed about and in communication with such parts of their communities as schools, churches, businesses, neighborhood organizations, and other public agencies. And the communication needs to be maintained and evaluated. Librarians may naively assume that their service areas have the same boundaries as other agencies and groups nearby, but that is seldom the case. There may be several community organizations served by a single library, and the librarian needs to maintain cordial relations with them all, even when they may be unaware of each other or, worse yet, not in accord with each other. The real problem for librarians in working with community groups is not a general failure to do so, but a failure to work among several of them equitably without becoming identified with only one or two.

Schools are often assigned, as a matter of responsibility, to the staff members responsible for work with children or young people. Simple courtesy visits to the principals or school librarians are important and may need to be repeated frequently. Provision of information about the library and its ability to respond to special needs of students is essential in service to schools, and coordinated effort for summer reading programs and other events can be one aspect of continuing cooperation. The point here, as in other aspects of community relations, is that the individual service unit must be aggressive and consistent in its own pattern of communication and cooperation and must be able to use, without relying exclusively on, such backup assistance as may be provided by coordinators or administrators on a systemwide basis.

Some parts of every community are traditionally neglected by library extension services. The businesses are likely to be among these, although they may be sought out when donations are needed for refreshments or decorations. When library communities are defined, many staff members think of residents rather than workers within the community, although some studies have indicated that people who work near a library may make up a major portion of its users. The work-related needs of this public have often been ignored or served only incidentally by community libraries, but there appears to be a growing awareness of the need to serve this part of the community and, on the other hand, a growing awareness on the part of community business personnel of what the library can and should provide. This emphasis, as it grows and spreads, can be a major means of causing the library to develop into a more general community resource rather than being typed as the provider of children's materials and services and of recreational resources.

Reference and Information Service

The information and reference services of individual community libraries are customarily underused and, in a spiral of neglect, when they are underused, they are not provided or not maintained as effectively, and thus the underuse increases. Telephone reference requests in a library system are often almost automatically directed to a central library; yet many could be satisfactorily handled in some of the smaller units. Except for school assignments, there is limited use of branch libraries for subject-related reference work, but much more might well be provided. Community history may be a strong part of the collection in an extension service unit, and this can be ironic, since it may often be argued that better security and preservation systems at a central resource can be utilized to provide better location for the collection and that it should be possible for interested persons to have access, in one place, to all community-related materials, rather than having to go from one location to another to get information on a number of communities in one library system's area.

The underuse of reference and information services has many reasons. Since many extension service units are small and cannot provide much reference service, it has been generalized that few or none of the others can. It is as fast and easy to telephone to a farther point as to a closer one, and if a central or regional library has publicized its reference service, potential users will tend to think of that source rather than a nearer but smaller library. And, in the pattern of publicizing successes, extension services have tended to encourage greater use of services already in demand rather than of those that might well be developed.

Personnel

The staff of extension services have special needs and opportunities. Some may be specialists in one aspect of the service, such as service to institutional residents, to senior citizens, or to young adults. Their career orientation may be toward positions in those specializations within or outside librarianship, but not necessarily within the public library. They need to have access to the same continuing education opportunities as are available to staff members in more general areas, such as branch library supervision of children's or reference services. All deserve the opportunity to advance in responsibility and status as their competencies permit, even though in some instances this may suggest a change of specialization.

An especially sore point in the matter of promotional opportunity concerns children's librarians. They often contend that they are systematically excluded from advanced positions unless they are willing to transfer into adult services. Even when that is not a requirement, many of them seek such transfers because they believe the work of supervision is more compatible with work in adult services than in children's services. On the face of it, there is no reason why this should be true, but because programming and planning for children are more precisely developed in most library systems and because adult services have in the past been more compatible with branch library management, the pattern is continued.

Special requirements for extension service staff members are often related to their work settings. The ability to work well with others in a limited physical space, an enthusiasm for diverse communities and life-styles, a willingness to acquire experience in a variety of locations, and ability to adapt to necessary security measures in some locations may be among the characteristics that these staff members need to possess. Bookmobile service, work with persons in institutions, and general outreach work through other community agencies may call for specific technical and psychological strengths and for stamina. One advantage of the typical diversity of assignments available in extension services is that other options may be available when the strains of one kind of work become too great for a staff member. However, the work still needs to be done, and no extension service can support more than a minimal number of staff members who cannot carry their full share of responsibility.

Privacy and pomp are usually nonexistent in extension service assignments. Freedom from close administrative supervision and the opportunity to sample a variety of experiences and to gain information about a variety of kinds of life are among the compensations.

The communication patterns among extension service units that are essential for public service—for example, interlibrary loan or reference referral—are also important for staff morale. Chiefly because extension service units tend to be small and numerous, the staff members can readily develop feelings of isolation and neglect. Efforts to inform them promptly of administrative decisions and to respond promptly to their inquiries and concerns about such matters as their own personnel requirements can help to overcome those feelings. Inclusion of extension service personnel in such activities as staff association committees, in-service planning sessions, and continuing education programs under the library's sponsorship are among the best ways to integrate the staff more effectively into the system.

It has been observed that a characteristic of American librarianship is the development of theory in practice. In public library extension services, this kind of development is occurring regularly. Basic service and purposes are continued, but they are expanded and adapted for new publics, and technlogical developments make better service possible. In the long run, however, it is the staff of extension services who determine the quality and kind of library service to be offered to most people by public libraries. Their abilities, including their imaginations and their openness to experience, shape and determine the quality and quantity of the service.

16 The Role of Library Systems and Networks

JOHN A. McCROSSAN

An increasing number of local libraries belong to library systems and receive services from the systems and from the networks to which the systems belong. The level of development varies from state to state, but in a number of states almost all public libraries are now members of library systems—a great change from the 1960s, when many systems were just beginning. The major reason for the rapid growth of systems is that they provide many services of value to local librarians and library users, services offered in a particular area being dependent on the perceived needs of the area. System services often include liberal interlibrary loan; centralized reference service; consultant help on a variety of library programs and administrative matters; technical processing; continuing education programs for librarians and trustees; and reciprocal borrowing programs that have made it possible for people who live in one community to freely borrow materials from all libraries in the system area.

In this chapter the different types of library systems and networks are defined and discussed, and their role in local library development is considered. Since local libraries relate most directly to regional library systems and receive most services from or through them rather than from networks, most of the discussion relates to the former types of organizations. Networks, which generally offer services to systems rather than directly to local public libraries, are considered insofar as their programs affect local library services.

Historical Development

In the nineteenth century and throughout much of the twentieth, independent public libraries were established in local communities—cities, towns, and villages. Most of these libraries were very small and inadequately supported because their service areas had small populations. The vast majority of communities did not then, and do not now, have the population or wealth necessary to provide adequate library service. The American Library Association has estimated that a popula-

tion of between 100,000 and 150,000 is needed to support such service. According to the latest census of governments, there was a total of 18,862 municipalities nationally, and only 393 had more than 50,000 population; 514 had between 25,000 and 50,000. The large majority—17,955—were of less than 25,000, and 9,614 of these had fewer than 1,000 people.[1]

Adequacy, of course, is a matter of definition. The current movement in professional circles is to attempt to define adequacy in terms of specific community needs rather than on an arbitrary basis. Nevertheless, with the great variety of informational needs in even the most stable and homogeneous communities, the population base mentioned above can still be considered as valid to avoid exorbitant per capita cost.

In order to remedy the problems inherent in small, poorly supported libraries, beginning early in this century the library profession and interested community leaders took steps to organize public library service by "larger units of service"—library organizations that were funded by and that provided services to an area larger than one municipality, often consisting of an entire county or a larger area.

In areas with few libraries or without library service, consolidated library systems were organized on a county or multicounty basis. One of the most successful efforts was undertaken in California under the dynamic leadership of the state librarian, James B. Gillis. Gillis, a prominent railroad lobbyist, was appointed state librarian in 1900. Between 1911 and 1917, thirty-seven county libraries were organized in California.[2] In those counties that had relatively large populations, the county libraries were usually very successful. However, many counties, in California and most other states, are very small in popula-

---

1. U.S. Bureau of the Census, *1977 Census of Governments*, Vol. 5, *Local Government in Metropolitan Areas* (Washington, D.C.: Govt. Print Off., 1980), p. 4.
2. Oliver Garceau, *The Public Library in the Political Process* (New York: Columbia Univ. Pr., 1949), p. 41.

tion, so a larger library unit was needed. As noted in the *Census of Governments*, of a total of 3,044 counties, over half—1,840—have fewer than 25,000 people.[3] Thus, by the 1920s library leaders were turning their attention towards establishment of multicounty and regional libraries, and a number of such library systems were successfully established in various states, especially where there were large unserved areas and few existing local libraries.

Many states, however, had a proliferation of very small, poorly supported public libraries, and attempts to bring those libraries into consolidated county or regional library systems often failed because local libraries did not want to give up their autonomy. Therefore, in recent decades great emphasis has been placed on development of cooperative library systems. By joining these systems, local libraries can retain their independence while at the same time benefiting from sytem services.

For a time it was thought that large city or county libraries could function fairly well by themselves and did not necessarily need to be involved in a library system. However, the fallacy of this notion has long been apparent. Not even the largest libraries can afford to purchase or house all the library materials or provide all the services needed by their users. They must belong to organizations that provide for sharing of resources, especially in this time of rapidly rising costs. Moreover, the growth in volume of published materials, print and nonprint, and the increased demand from the public for a variety of types of media have made it essential for even the largest libraries to participate in resource sharing.

Defining Systems and Networks

The terms *library system* and *library network* both denote some kind of formal organization that has the purpose of promoting better library services through sharing of resources, either library materials or less tangible resources, such as the expertise of specialized personnel. Defining and distinguishing between these terms is not an easy task, especially at a time when systems are changing by admitting not only public libraries but also other types of libraries into their organizations. Moreover, a variety of types of library networks are rapidly developing.

While a library system could be considered simply a particular type of library network, a sys-

tem has certain characteristics that distinguish it from other types of networks.

The term library system generally means an organization that is made up solely or primarily of public libraries that are located in a particular area of a state and that have a formal basis or organization in state statutes, state regulations, or contract. Many of these systems have now admitted other types of libraries. However, the nonpublic libraries usually do not participate fully in all systems programs but only take part in such programs that are of mutual value to different types of libraries, such as liberal interlibrary loan and reference service.

"American National Standards for Library Statistics" contains a useful and often quoted definition of a library system, which is as follows:

1. An organization based on a plan or procedure in which library units work together, sharing services and resources in a manner which results in improved service to library users.
2. A central library and all of its other service outlets, i.e. branches, deposit stations, bookmobiles.[4]

The first part of the definition in general refers to a cooperative library system made up of a number of independent local libraries, such as town, city, or county libraries. While maintaining their autonomy, these libraries join a system that usually has a central administration and provides services to member libraries and sometimes to the public. The second part of the definition refers to a consolidated library system, such as a city library or a single county library, that has one central administration and in which the system outlets are branches administered by the system rather than independent libraries.

A library network usually includes subgroups such as library systems in its membership. Generally different types of libraries participate fully in network services, and usually a network covers an entire state or a larger area. A report prepared for the National Commission on Libraries and Information Science defined a library network as a

formal organization among libraries for cooperating and sharing of resources, usually with an explicitly hierarchical structure, in which the group as a whole is organized into subgroups with the expectation that most of the needs of a

---

3. U.S. Bureau of the Census, *Governmental Organization*, p. 2.

4. American National Standards Institute, "American National Standards for Library Statistics; Approved Aug. 22, 1968" (New York: The Institute, 1969).

library will be satisfied within the subgroup of which it is a member.[5]

One way to illustrate the difference between library systems and networks is to describe the organization in a particular state. Illinois has eighteen library systems, each serving a particular section of the state. Seventeen of these systems are cooperatives made up of independent public libraries and of other types of libraries that are affiliate members. The other system, the Chicago Public Library, is a consolidated municipal library system. The Illinois State Library coordinates the statewide Illinois Library Information Network (ILLINET), and four large libraries have been designated as research and reference centers. Those libraries receive state funds to lend specialized materials to the library systems and system members. Most of the needs of local libraries, such as interlibrary loan and reference, are met at the systems level, and the network centers are usually tapped only for special needs that the systems cannot meet.

Types of Systems and Networks

Distinctions between types of systems are usually made on the basis of their organizational and administrative structure, the most common being: (1) single-jurisdiction systems, (2) multijurisdiction systems, (3) cooperative systems, and (4) state hierarchical systems, now more commonly called networks since they generally include library systems and different types of libraries in their membership.

Library systems and networks are also classified as to whether they are general purpose or special purpose. A general purpose library system provides a variety of basic library services to libraries and users within the system area, such as reference and interlibrary loan, free reciprocal borrowing privileges, rotating collections of materials, and centralized processing. The majority of public library systems are of the general purpose type.

A special purpose system is one that offers one or two selected services but less than a full range of basic services. One example is an area reference system that assists local libraries in providing answers to reference questions and furnishes specific books and other interlibrary loan materials. Other examples are film centers, processing cen-

ters, and storage centers for little-used materials, which may involve only public libraries or different types of libraries.

Most statewide and national networks to date are of the special purpose type, as they generally provide a few selected services that seem most needed.

Single-Jurisdiction System

A single-jursidiction library system is a library organization that is responsible to only one authority, such as a city or county, and provides general purpose library services to the one library jurisdiction—i.e. the area to which the library authority has legal responsibility to provide service. City libraries and single-county libraries are examples of this type of system. They are consolidated in that they operate under one central policy-making body, such as a library board, and have one central administration that is responsible for management of all units of the library system, including the central library and other outlets such as branches, deposit stations, and bookmobiles.

Multijurisdiction System

This type of system is one that provides library services in two or more jurisdictions and is responsible to the authorities of those jurisdictions. As in single-jurisdiction systems, local service outlets are not independent libraries, but are operated by the system. The city-county library is one example of such a system. Usually a city library, in addition to administering library services within the city, also provides library services to the surrounding county under contract. The Tampa–Hillsborough County Library System in Florida, for example, is operated by the city library. The city of Tampa appropriated funds to support library services within the city limits. In addition, Hillsborough County contracts with and provides an annual appropriation to the city library to provide library services in the area of the county located outside the city. The system is managed in a consolidated manner with one central administration responsible for all service outlets in both the city and county. However, the county retains ownership of branch library buildings located in the county area.

The LeSueur-Waseca Regional Library in Minnesota is another type of multijurisdictional system, serving the counties of LeSueur and Waseca and the city of Waseca and receiving funds from all three governmental units.

---

5. Vernon E. Palmer et al., "Resources and Bibliographic Support for a Nationwide Library Program," (Washington, D.C.: National Commission of Libraries and Information Science, 1974).

Cooperative System

A cooperative library system is made up of independent libraries that voluntarily organize to provide cooperative or centralized library services. There are both special purpose and general purpose cooperatives, the former types being those that provide only one or a few selected services to members, such as reference cooperatives. General purpose cooperatives usually provide a wide range of library services and are a very fast growing type of system.

In cooperative systems, each member library remains completely autonomous, retains its own governing board and budget, hires its own personnel, but freely joins the system in order to receive services that are beneficial to its own community. These systems range in size from those that cover a small part of one county and involve only two or three libraries to those that serve many libraries and large areas, including a number of counties.

Cooperative systems are governed by boards representative of the member libraries. In many of these systems, each local library board designates one or more of its members to serve on the system board, which is responsible for system activities, hires and supervises the system director, and sets policy for the system.

In recent years, many cooperative systems have been formed in such states as New York, California, Illinois, New Jersey, Colorado, Michigan, and Minnesota. In some cases the development of these systems has been statewide and has been the result of vigorous activity by the state's library community to secure state legislation providing authority and state funds for systems. For example, librarians and friends of libraries in Illinois worked intensively for several years and were successful in obtaining state legislation authorizing the development and state funding of such systems in 1965. By 1967 the state had eighteen library systems that serve the entire state, all but one of these being cooperatives. The vast majority of public libraries and many libraries of other types now belong to these systems.

There are several reasons for the rapid growth of cooperative systems. One reason, noted above, is that independent libraries do not have to give up their autonomy when they join such a system. They retain the freedom to assess needs and develop service programs on a very immediate local level. Another reason is that, once favorable state legislation is enacted, such systems can be formed relatively easily by action of local library boards wishing to participate. Experience shows that, once the legal framework is established, most boards do want to obtain the benefits of coopera-

tive systems for their own population. Some other types of systems can be formed only after approval by governing bodies, such as county commissioners, which are often very reluctant to approve any new program that might increase taxes.

The fact that cooperative systems can often be formed to cover whichever contiguous geographic area seems most reasonable to area libraries, rather than being restricted by artificial political boundaries, can also be an advantage. Thus a community library located in County A but near County B might decide to join a system in County B because the library in question is related more closely to libraries and population centers in County B than County A due to transportation or business patterns.

Another major reason for the rapid growth of cooperative systems is that most of them are now funded entirely or primarily with state money, as is the case in such states as New York, California, Illinois, and Minnesota. State funding has the advantage, not only of relieving local government of a financial burden, but also of making possible the provision of system services on an equalized basis throughout the service area without consideration of the amount of money coming from a particular locality.

In the past many systems received substantial funding from local sources in addition to state funds and Library Services and Construction Act grants. For example, local libraries were often asked to pay at least part of the cost of particular services—e.g., technical processing and film service. County or other local governments sometimes made a general appropriation to assist in paying for system services.

The requirement of substantial local support of systems proved to be very unsatisfactory in most areas, however. Local libraries and local government might be confronted each year with the decision as to whether to support a local library service or to contribute to a system service. This kind of decision has been especially difficult in recent years as local government financial problems have become increasingly severe. Therefore it is not surprising that the portion of state support of systems has been growing while the local portion has been declining.

One of the disadvantages of cooperative systems is that it is not always easy to extend library services to unserved or underserved areas since the system boards are made up of representatives of communities that have libraries; the other areas have little or no representation. This problem can sometimes be remedied by securing county or state funds specifically earmarked for bookmobile or other service to areas without libraries. Of course, if the entire area of the system is within the service area of one of the member libraries, this matter does not usually become a problem.

Some librarians feel that the decision-making process is extremely difficult in a cooperative situation since consensus often must be sought in a board representative of diverse libraries and communities. Others, however, do not see this as a major problem and believe group decision making can be a healthy, fruitful process.

There is some evidence and considerable opinion that a system having a separate administrative staff can give a better return on cost than a system that utilizes staff of existing libraries. In the latter situation, there is sometimes a tendency for staff to spend undue effort on responsibilities in their home library and to neglect system duties. For example, a librarian who is head of the children's department of the headquarters library and also the system consultant on children's services might be tempted to spend too much time at the headquarters and too little in the field. Problems of this type are not usually insurmountable, however, and can usually be resolved if the system has a strong board that is willing to deal with them.

The Nassau Library System in New York State is a large, general purpose cooperative system composed of fifty-four independent member libraries located in Nassau County, which has a population of approximately 1½ million. The system is governed by a nine-member board, each board member representing a particular geographic area of the county. Chartered in May, 1959, as a cooperative library system under Section 255 of the New York State Education Law, with thirty-two libraries as charter members, the system derives its funding mainly from the state, which provides annual grants to each of New York's public library systems.

The San Joaquin Valley Library System serves a four-county area in central California. It is composed of four county libraries, two city libraries, and one district library and is governed by an administrative council made up of the directors of the seven member libraries. The Fresno County Public Library is the administrative headquarters for the system, and the Fresno County librarian is the system administrative librarian. Federal, state, and local funding is used to support the system. In fiscal 1978, funding was 45.5 percent federal, 16.7 percent state, and 37.8 percent local. In 1977, a revised California Library Services Act was passed, and as a result considerably greater state funding for systems should be available in the future.

The Area Reference Resource Center (ARRC) headquartered in the Greenville County Library in South Carolina is an example of a special purpose system. This system may not be a cooperative in the strictest sense, as it is administered by the county library under the terms of a contract between that library and the South Carolina State Library, funding being provided by the latter agency. Nonetheless, the program has various cooperative aspects. For example, local libraries are encouraged to provide basic reference services and to refer users to the center for more specialized information and materials. Also, local library representatives serve on a council that advises the center on budget and programs. A major recent thrust of the center has been in-service training of the staff of member libraries in provision of reference services. Since South Carolina has a statewide library network coordinated by the state library, requests for information or materials not available at ARRC can be referred to the state library, to other county or regional library systems, or to participating academic or special libraries.

State Hierarchical Systems and Networks

State hierarchical systems or networks are generally statewide and administered or coordinated by the state library agency. Their purpose is to provide an effective structure that enables residents of all areas of a state to have access to a wide range of library materials and information and not be limited to those in their local libraries or system areas. In some states, these networks are made up primarily of public libraries, but in an increasing number of states other types of libraries are also members of the systems and thus have access to network services. In many states, large academic or special libraries, as well as the state library and large public libraries, also serve as resource centers for the networks.

These networks must have at least two levels—local and state—but some have a number of levels, e.g., local, county, district, region, and state. The number of levels is generally related to characteristics of a given state, such as state geography; size and density of population; and number, size and distribution of local libraries.

One state that has a number of levels is New York. In some areas independent local libraries belong to county library systems, which in turn are members of cooperative regional systems that include more than one county and are state funded. These regional systems participate in the 3R's systems (Reference, Research, and Resource Systems), which generally cover an area served by two or more regional public library systems and include academic, special, and public libraries in their membership. The 3R's systems provide specialized materials to libraries throughout their area. If needed materials are not available within the area of a given 3R's system, requests may be sent to the next level, which consists of a small number of large research libraries that have been designated as statewide resource centers.

Vermont is a state that has few levels in its hierarchy for library services. Like some other small states, Vermont is a one-library system or network state, the program being coordinated by the state library agency. Local libraries are independent agencies maintained by cities, towns, and villages. They receive certain types of service directly from the headquarters of the State Department of Libraries, which is located in the state's capital city, and other types of services from the five regional libraries that the state agency administers.

Networks beyond the State Level

Various library and information networks are developing beyond the state level. While most of these networks have relatively little impact on local library services at the present time, this situation could change greatly in the future since some of these networks are expected to grow quite rapidly in the years ahead.

Multistate networks exist in several parts of the country, such as the New England Library Network (NELINET) and the Southeastern Library Network (SOLINET). A major service of these organizations, which are made up of different types of libraries, is acting as brokers for providing member libraries with computerized, on-line cataloging data from OCLC, Inc., in Columbus, Ohio. Relatively few local public libraries are members of such networks, but some systems do belong and have at system headquarters a computer terminal connected with OCLC. Thus the ongoing cataloging data are used by some systems for centralized cataloging and processing for member libraries.

At the national level a number of networks are developing, some of which will undoubtedly have considerable impact on local libraries in the future. These programs are receiving strong encouragement from the National Commission on Libraries and Information Science, which is working towards development of a "full-service" national network. This network will involve participation by all types of libraries and by the various levels of library agencies—local, system, state, and region.

National networks include bibliographic programs such as the Library of Congress's MARC services, and OCLC, Inc., which is fast becoming a national program. The Continuing Library Education Network and Exchange (CLENE) is a national network, developing programs that should assist local librarians in securing the kinds of continuing education needed to keep abreast of the many changes rapidly occurring in library and information sciences.

The Library of Congress Division for the Blind and Physically Handicapped coordinates a national network of special library services for those people who have difficulty using regular printed materials because of blindness or some other physical limitation. The DBPH designates one or two regional libraries per state and sometimes a number of subregional libraries. Many state libraries and large public libraries have been designated as regional libraries, and many public libraries of various sizes have been designated as subregionals. The DBPH provides free talking books to those libraries, but other costs of the program must be borne by the state or locally.

Goals and Objectives

Briefly stated, the major goal of a library system or network is to make possible the provision of improved library services to the public through the sharing of resources, either materials or personnel. As noted above, few if any communities are sufficiently large and wealthy to support fully adequate library services by themselves. Therefore, agencies are needed to promote cooperative or coordinated programs that facilitate various types of resource sharing. Voluntary, informal cooperation among independent libraries can be very useful, but it is rarely as effective as an organized system or network that facilitates unified planning for a full-service library program in a particular area and has funds to support the cooperative or centralized services that are needed.

System and network goals should support and supplement the goals of local libraries. Thus a major goal of a library system or network is to provide materials and services that will assist local libraries to fulfill their goal of offering the best possible service to users in their respective communities.

The *Minimum Standards for Public Library Systems, 1966* indicate that library systems facilitate improved services at the local level and that "libraries working together, sharing their services and materials, can meet the full needs of their users."[6]

---

6. Standards Committee and Subcommittee, American Library Association, *Minimum Standards for Public Library Systems, 1966* (Chicago: ALA, 1967), p. 10.

"A Mission Statement for Public Libraries," adopted by the Public Library Association of the American Library Association in 1978, strongly emphasizes that the goal of public libraries is to bring every person, regardless of such factors as age, education, and cultural background, into effective contact with the information they need and desire. That document further indicates that this ideal can be met only through systems and networks that link "collections in the region, state, nation, and the world."[7]

In 1975 the National Commission on Libraries and Information Science published *Toward a National Program for Library and Information Services: Goals for Action*. That document states very broadly the goal of library service nationwide as being "to eventually provide every individual in the United States with equal opportunity of access to that part of the total information resource which will satisfy the individual's educational, working, cultural and leisure-time needs and interests, regardless of the location, social or physical condition or level of intellectual achievement."[8]

The NCLIS statement indicates that this ideal can be achieved through the creation of a national network of library and information services that would not be monolithic or authoritarian in structure but that would be a framework for families of geographic and functional networks and systems "interconnected according to a comprehensive plan."[9]

Thus, in order to reach the national goal enunciated by NCLIS, it is imperative that each library system and network analyze the particular needs of its constituency, since these needs can vary considerably from one area to another, and establish its own service goals and objectives. These goals and objectives should, insofar as possible, be developed so that they will complement other systems and networks.

Many library systems have developed their own statements of goals and objectives. Some of these statements are quite short, while others are very long and detailed and include a long list of major and minor goals and objectives with specific steps to be taken to implement them. Regardless of length, the idea of improving library services to the public through cooperative action is almost always paramount in these documents, and the differ-

ence in the role of the system and of local libraries is generally given considerable attention.

The Monroe County, New York, Library System has developed a very detailed goals statement that has been approved by the system board of trustees. The MCLS statement begins by indicating that the mission of the system is "to serve its member libraries and, through them, the people of Monroe County." The two general goals are (1) to centralize those supportive operations that could be best performed at the system level, and (2) to continue decentralization of direct services for which member libraries have primary responsibility.

Fourteen specific goals follow the general goals, and each of the specific goals is followed by lists of particular programs and services that have been undertaken to implement a given goal. For example, one specific goal is "to enable the residents of Monroe County to have free access" to library materials not only in the county but in a large region. Programs undertaken to make such access a reality include (1) issuing a reciprocal borrowing card to all Monroe County residents that can be used in any public library in Monroe County and in a number of other counties; (2) picking up and delivering library materials that borrowers have returned to libraries other than those from which the materials were borrowed; (3) providing borrow-by-mail services for the homebound; and (4) publishing addresses, phone numbers, and service hours of member libraries.

Detailed goals statements of this kind, carefully developed and adopted by a systems board, can be extremely useful to the library system and to local libraries for such purposes as planning programs, developing priorities, and informing funding bodies and the public about library services and the need for financial support.

Services Offered by Library Systems

General purpose library systems provide a variety of programs for libraries and library users in the system area, while special purpose systems provide selected specific services as noted above. The variety of service possibilities of general purpose systems would be almost limitless if sufficient funding were available. Since all systems operate on limited budgets, however, priorities for services must be carefully established among the many potentially useful programs. Moreover, the need for particular types of services can vary greatly from one area to another, so regional and local needs must be carefully considered before decisions are made about which programs should be made available.

7. "A Mission Statement for Public Libraries: Guidelines for Service, Part I," *American Libraries* 8:619 (Dec. 1977).

8. National Commission on Libraries and Information Science, *Toward a National Program for Library and Information Services: Goals for Action* (Washington, D.C.: The Commission, 1975), p. xi.

9. Ibid.

System services may be grouped in the categories listed below. Most general purpose library systems offer some services in most of these areas, the depth of such services dependent on such factors as area needs, funding, and staff available.

1. Direct user access to collections
2. Interlibrary loan and reference services
3. Supplementary collections of books and other materials for local libraries
4. Professional assistance to local library staffs and boards
5. Services to special groups
6. Centralized technical services
7. Administrative services.

Direct User Access

Perhaps the greatest contribution of library systems to public library service is that they have made possible much greater direct user access to library collections, both to basic collections and to strong, in-depth collections. This greater access has been achieved in several ways. The creation of county and regional library systems has resulted in extending public library services to vast areas that previously had no libraries or were very inadequately served.

Cooperative systems have opened up the collections of existing libraries in the system by arranging for reciprocal borrowing privileges so that everyone living in the area may freely borrow books and other materials from any member library, and in many systems users may return materials to whichever library is most convenient, with interlibrary delivery systems providing for final return to the library owing the material.

Before the creation of systems, people often did not have legal access to libraries in neighboring communities or could use them only upon payment of a nonresident fee. This created artificial barriers and discouraged use, especially by groups of people especially in need of public library services—the disadvantaged, children and young people, and the aged. Also, in a mobile age many people find it convenient to use various libraries, since so many live in one community, work in another community, and perhaps shop in several communities.

In many systems, headquarters libraries or other strong libraries are designated as resource libraries that have responsibility for maintaining strong collections to be made freely available to the entire system. The libraries often receive special financial assistance to carry out this type of responsibility. In some cases a library is designated as a general resource on the full range of subjects,

while in others a library is asked to serve as the resource for one or two subjects. In the Nassau Library System in Uniondale, New York, for example, two strong libraries are designated as co-central libraries and given responsibility for providing in-depth reference service to patrons of all member libraries. Several other libraries have been designated as resources for materials on particular subjects or in particular forms. For example, one library has a very strong collection of materials on art and music, and another houses a special collection of books in twenty foreign languages.

The Traverse des Sioux Library System headquartered in Mankato, Minnesota, provides an example of a very progressive reciprocal borrowing system. Each public library that is a member of the system issues a borrower's card that is honored by every other member library in the nine-county area. Thus patrons may borrow books from any public library in the area and return them to whichever library is most convenient. A regular courier service picks up books returned to libraries other than those from which they were borrowed and delivers them to the library of origination. In addition library users may also borrow books from academic and special libraries that, along with the public libraries, belong to SMILE (South-Central Minnesota Inter-Library Exchange). Moreover, a number of Minnesota's public library systems have entered into reciprocal borrowing agreements so that a borrower's card may be used in sixty Minnesota counties—a great convenience for people who travel in their work, for education, or when on vacation.

Beginning April 1, 1978, seventeen of New York's public library systems entered into a cooperative agreement called NYLIB (New York Libraries Inter-Borrowing Cooperative). Probably the largest such arrangement in the nation, this organization extends reciprocal borrowing privileges to residents of 53.5 of New York's 62 counties!

Interlibrary Loan and Reference Service

The effectiveness of system interlibrary loan and reference service is strongly evidenced by the fact that libraries often cite these services as major reasons for joining or remaining in systems.

Interlibrary loan has existed for many years, but traditionally it was quite restricted. Eventually, systems worked out liberal arrangements, with funding often used to pay resource libraries that provide a high proportion of loans to libraries in a system. Interlibrary reference was minimal or nonexistent in many areas until the establishment of centralized reference service by systems. The success of such services is readily apparent from statistics from many systems, which indicate that the number of interlibrary loan and reference requests has increased dramatically in recent years. For example, the number of requests in the Monroe County, New York, Library System was only 963 in 1953. By 1967 this figure had jumped to 36,577; and by 1976, 83,123 requests were received.

In many states there is a hierarchical interlibrary loan and reference network that, in general, works in the following way. When a local library cannot fill a request, it contacts the system headquarters, which searches for the needed item within the system. In some systems a headquarters library or another large library is designated as reference and interlibrary loan center, and most requests are filled from its collections. In other systems, the headquarters maintains a union catalog that lists the holdings of various system libraries, and the catalog is searched to discover which library has a requested item.

In adequately developed systems, most requests can be filled from system resources. When they cannot, the system staff contacts the state library or another designated state resource library for the needed information or materials. Occasionally, a request cannot be filled from state resources, and then a library outside the state may be contacted.

In addition to printed materials, systems often maintain strong collections of films and other audiovisual materials for loan to member libraries and sometimes directly to users. Central film collections are especially useful to local libraries, since films are very popular with library users, yet most libraries cannot afford to purchase more than a very few. Film services are also very much valued by member libraries. In a 1977 survey of the members of Suffolk Cooperative Library System in New York, film service was given second priority out of fourteen types of services listed.

Supplementary Collections

Most library systems provide supplementary collections of books and other library materials to local libraries. These collections may be made up at the system and rotated from one member library to another, or local librarians may make up their own collections from bookmobiles or by visiting system central book depositories.

These kinds of collections have been provided by library systems for many years, and they have proven to be very welcome to local libraries, especially small libraries, since they contain useful materials for library patrons that a local library

could not afford, including specialized and expensive materials. Also, the effect of rotating parts of the collection is most valuable in providing "new" materials for the frequent user of a library having a low rate of local acquisitions.

Rolling Prairie Libraries in Illinois has a collection of over 81,000 volumes that is used for rotating collections as well as for interlibrary loan. In addition the system rotates collections of framed art prints from its collection of more than 1,000 prints.

In Vermont local librarians may visit one of the five regional libraries and pick out their own collections. They may take the books back to their libraries in their own vehicles or request that they be delivered by a state department of libraries van. Both public libraries and school libraries use this service.

Another way some systems assist local libraries in supplementing their collections is by providing funds for purchase of library materials. The Monroe County Library System in New York, for example, provides about $125,000 annually to local libraries as materials grants.

Professional Assistance

Systems provide a variety of types of professional assistance to member libraries. Types of such assistance may include (1) advisory help on library service and administrative matters; (2) organization of workshops and other training programs for local librarians and trustees; and (3) preparation of public relations materials useful to local libraries, such as exhibits, posters, reading lists, and news releases.

This type of assistance dates from the turn of the century when the newly established state library commissions began work with local groups on establishment and improvement of public libraries. In general, however, the state agencies were not able to do an adequate job in these areas since they were usually small, poorly supported agencies. Thus, in states in which strong library systems have developed, most direct contact with local libraries is carried out by system staff, and the state agencies generally work with and through the systems.

Many system staffs include consultants who are specialists in particular areas of public library service, such as children's, young adult, and adult services; reference and information service; and technical service. These consultants advise local librarians on methods of improving services of their local libraries and on use of services provided by the system. Their work is done in personal visits, telephone conversations, and letters. In some cases a consultant initiates the contact by calling or visiting a library and offering to help. In many systems it is a policy to offer assistance only when asked to do so in order not to give the impression that the system wants to dictate to a local library.

System directors and other administrative staff also often provide advisory help to local libraries. Many administrative staff are very knowledgeable about such matters as library policies, budgets, buildings, personnel, public relations, and automation and will make their expertise available to local librarians and trustees.

In some states, state library agencies have designated systems to assist local libraries in filling out forms that are required for receipt of state aid in preparing proposals that local libraries may wish to submit to the state agency for receipt of Library Services and Construction Act grant funds. Moreover, the state agencies also sometimes expect system staff to monitor the use of state aid and of grant funds by local libraries and to assist those libraries in problems that may arise in carrying out state-funded programs. Some systems also will advise local libraries on applying for grants from foundations, and some have offered intensive workshops on grants, including training in identifying appropriate funding agencies and developing and writing proposals.

Since the knowledge required of local librarians and trustees is constantly growing and changing, in-service training and continuing education are becoming more and more important for them; many systems are making a real contribution to filling these educational needs. Not too many years ago, the majority of local librarians in many areas were untrained, so systems offered workshops that taught the fundamentals of cataloging, reference, and other basic library processes. These types of training programs are still needed in many systems. In others, especially those that have fairly large member libraries with professional staffs, more sophisticated continuing education programs are needed, and systems are attempting to assist by organizing seminars on matters of current interest, such as new, experimental types of service programs and new budgeting techniques. However, few if any library systems could justify attempting to provide for all the continuing education needs of member libraries. Fortunately, other agencies do provide for some of these needs, especially state library agencies, which sponsor educational programs that both local librarians and system staff are encouraged to attend.

Many systems prepare or purchase public relations materials that are distributed to local libraries either for permanent use or as rotating items. These include exhibits, posters, reading lists,

brochures, and sample news releases. These kinds of items can be useful to local libraries in particular programs or for general distribution to the public.

Services to Special Groups

Members of special groups often are relatively few in number, are scattered over a large area, and have need of quite specialized kinds of library materials and information. Therefore, since it is not economically feasible for most local libraries to provide the full range of services to such groups, special services are often organized on the system level or even on a statewide level. Special user groups include the blind and physically handicapped, the institutionalized, the homebound, and those who use English as a second language.

Traditionally, library services for the blind and physically handicapped were organized on a state or multistate level. The Library of Congress generally designated not more than one Regional Library for the Blind per state, and a number of states had none. Their readers were served by mail from a regional library located in another state.

Because of the expansion of the program in recent years to serve the physically handicapped in addition to the blind, and because of growing awareness that the library needs of both the blind and the physically handicapped were not being adequately met, many additional libraries have been designated to serve as regional libraries or subregional libraries. At the present time, most states have at least one regional library and a number of subregionals, and in many systems, one of the system libraries is either a regional or subregional agency. These libraries all receive free talking books from the Library of Congress for circulation to users in their areas. Some, but not all, receive Braille materials; Braille is very bulky and expensive to house, and only about 10 percent of the blind currently read Braille.

Although most of the circulation of these materials is done by mail, many of the libraries maintain a small reading room for patrons who wish to visit the library for such purposes as browsing or obtaining reading guidance.

Local libraries that are not regional or subregional libraries often play an important role in these services by (1) maintaining small sample collections of talking books and Braille books for display and browsing purposes; and (2) by identifying and referring eligible readers to the proper library. This latter task is particularly important since the handicapped are largely a "hidden" population, and the majority of them are unaware of the free special library services for which they are eligible.

In many states the state library agency coordinates services to state-operated institutions, while library systems coordinate services to county and municipal institutions and to private agencies, such as nursing homes. In some areas the system headquarters serves these agencies directly, while in others member libraries take responsibility for such service. The pattern for delivery of these services can vary a great deal from one system to another depending on local conditions and needs.

An increasing number of library systems provide books-by-mail services to the homebound, those in nursing homes and institutions, isolated rural people, and others who find it difficult or impossible to visit a public library. Unlike the special library materials for the blind and physically handicapped, discussed above, these are traditional printed books for those who do not have difficulty using print. In most of these programs a catalog, often looking like a Sunday newspaper supplement, is distributed to private homes, institutions, etc. People send their requests through the mail, and the requests are mailed to the patrons. In other cases, users may write or call a library and request any book in the collection. Usually the library pays the mail charge at least one way and sometimes both ways.

The North Central Regional Library in Washington State was a pioneer in this kind of service. An illustrated catalog is distributed on all rural postal routes and also to other residents throughout the library district who find it difficult to use library facilities. The service has been so successful that several additional regional library districts have contracted with the North Central Regional Library to provide books-by-mail service to residents of their areas.

In Vermont, the State Department of Libraries maintains a books-by-mail service for the entire state, servicing more than 10,000 homebound, rural, and isolated people. When the service was initiated several years ago, some people thought it might result in diminished use of local libraries. However, this did not happen, and many local librarians and trustees believe the mail service supplements and complements the service of local libraries and encourages greater use of those libraries.

The Orlando, Florida, Public Library System, which serves three counties in central Florida, provides a books-by-mail program that gives access to the total central library collection. Patrons simply call or write the library, and the requested material is mailed to them.

For many years library systems have used bookmobiles to extend library services to isolated rural communities. In some areas general bookmobiles have been discontinued because of their cost and the belief that books-by-mail programs

offer a viable alternative. However, bookmobiles and smaller vehicles are now being used to distribute library materials to special groups, such as the aged in nursing homes, and to bilingual minorities who live in scattered small communities throughout a large area.

Centralized Technical Services

Centralized ordering, cataloging, and physical preparation of books has been a very important and popular service of library systems. While some systems have discontinued this service due to rising costs and competition from commercial agencies, other systems continue to provide effective technical services for their members.

The processing center was one of the first widespread types of cooperative projects that made public libraries aware of tangible values of library systems, and some systems can trace their beginnings to such centers. A number of processing centers began in the 1950s and 1960s and received Library Services and Construction Act grants from state library agencies to assist in their support. They proved to be very popular with local librarians, whom they freed from the rigors of technical services to work with the public. Also, at that time it was extremely difficult for small local libraries to employ trained librarians, and the untrained staff who had little expertise in technical services welcomed having a processing center that did expert cataloging and classification for them.

At the present time a number of commercial agencies offer cataloging and processing services for libraries, and some of them can provide such services more quickly and cheaply than some library systems. As these agencies deal in a very large volume of materials, often serving libraries in a number of states, they are able to automate and can take other steps that reduce costs.

It seems likely that only large library systems will be able to maintain cost-effective technical service centers in the future. Most smaller systems and unaffiliated libraries will probably have to buy such service from large systems or the commercial sector.

The effectiveness of commercial cataloging and processing remains to be evaluated. While some librarians feel the commercial services compare favorably with system processing service, others believe the commercial services are not so good. For example, some librarians report that the commercial agencies will not catalog and process as large a proportion of books purchased as a system processing center; for example, the vendor may not wish to handle the less-popular books. This has forced local libraries that previously did little or no cataloging to devote additional staff time to technical services.

A related criticism is that it is much more difficult for local libraries to influence the decisions of commercial agencies than those of library systems on such matters as whether to process a larger proportion of the books the local library wishes to add to its collection. The commercial area is not subject to the same degree of control as a system, which usually has representatives of local libraries in policy-making positions on its board.

All this is not meant to say that commercial processing is not effective. It does mean that such agencies should make a greater effort to discover the kinds of services libraries need and respond to criticisms of services offered. Furthermore, library systems should continually evaluate the quality of technical processing service, as well as other services, in order to make informed decisions about future directions of system programs.

Administrative Services

Some library systems offer a variety of administrative services for local libraries. Many of these are activities that a system can carry out efficiently and cost effectively but that a member library acting alone, especially a small- or medium-sized rural or suburban library, would find too costly.

A wide range of administrative services are possible, the kinds offered being limited only by funding available and the needs of member libraries. A number of systems provide printing service to produce signs, brochures, booklists, and other materials requested by member libraries. Some systems keep payroll records for member libraries and issue checks as directed by the libraries concerned. A number of systems have developed systemwide book or microform catalogs, in some cases computer-produced works. These catalogs often list the holdings of all member libraries in a system, and they sometimes include holdings of neighboring systems as well. They can be produced in multiple copies and distributed to all service points for the convenience of users. Some systems have secured automated circulation systems that may be used by member libraries.

Another type of valuable service of this type provided by some systems is coordination of legislative information or lobbying efforts of librarians, trustees, and community leaders in the system area. These efforts often tie in with a statewide legislative network coordinated by the state library agency or state library association. The value of such an activity is obvious. Concerted, coopera-tive legislative information activity has great potential for securing legislation favorable to libraries, including laws that authorize greater federal or state funding for library programs.

State Library Agencies

The role of state library agencies in development of local libraries and library systems has been alluded to throughout this discussion. However, since these agencies occupy a unique position in library development, their activities will be summarized here.

Each of the states has a state library agency, and the major responsibilities of those agencies include the following:

1. Administration and monitoring of state aid and federal LSCA funds granted to library systems and local libraries
2. Planning for and coordination of a statewide network of library services
3. Provision of services to libraries, especially services that would not be feasible for individual systems to provide.

Since the beginning of programs of state financial aid to public libraries at the turn of the century, state library agencies have been charged with responsibility for administration of such aid. At the present time all but eleven states have state aid programs for public libraries or public library systems, and state laws and regulations provide that the state library agencies should administer these funds, monitor their use by libraries, and require reports from the libraries specifying how the money is being used.

Federal laws and regulations indicate that state library agencies have responsibility for administration of Library Services and Construction Act funds. This federal program, begun in 1956, has made available relatively large sums of money to each of the states for development of library services throughout the state. A portion of these funds is used to support the state library agencies and centralized programs managed by those agencies. In most states, however, the bulk of the money is granted to local libraries or library systems for extension and improvement of library services in the different areas of the state. The federal government requires the state agencies to oversee use of these funds and to make regular reports to the U.S. Office of Education detailing how they are used. A further requirement is that the state agencies involve representatives of all types of libraries and of the public in planning for and evaluation of the use of federal funds.

Planning for and coordination of development of library services throughout the states are perhaps the most important functions of state library agencies because of their potential impact on library programs. The state library agency's responsibility in this area is, of course, strongly supported by its authority to administer state and federal funds for library development, particularly since these aid programs require considerable planning and evaluation.

Although the federal government has developed national priorities for library programs, the U.S. Office of Education recognizes that there are wide demographic and other variations among the states, requiring intensive planning at the state level, and that library and community leaders must be represented in these processes, as noted above.

The National Commission on Libraries and Information Science, which is taking the lead in development of a "full-service" national library and information network, has indicated that state library agencies are the logical agencies for this activity. The commission document *Toward a National Program for Library and Information Services* states that the state library agency is "the natural focus for statewide planning and coordination of cooperative library and information services and for coordinating statewide plans with those of the Federal Government."[10] That document also recommends that the state agencies involve the "library, information, and user communities" in this process.[11]

The types of services that the state agencies provide to libraries and library systems vary a great deal from one state to another and depend largely on the needs of a state's libraries as related to the development of library systems in the state. In states that have well-developed library systems throughout the state, the state agency is mainly a planning, coordinating, and funding agency. In states in which systems are not well developed, the state agency also provides a number of centralized services for libraries, such as film service, technical processing, consultant help, and in-service training for librarians.

The Federal Role

While the states have had a large impact on development of public library services, the federal government has had relatively little such impact, largely because of the traditional division of responsibility between the states and the federal government as specified in the Constitution. The most notable contribution of the federal government to public library development to date has been the Library Services and Construction Act, which is administered by the states.

The national library and information network, which is beginning to develop with the encouragement of the National Commission on Libraries and Information Science, has great potential for the future. All local libraries stand to gain a great deal from development of such a network, which could make easily available to them a variety of bibliographic services that they do not now have.

It also appears that the federal role in funding library programs will grow significantly. The national network, of course, will need federal funding. Moreover, additional federal funds are needed to assure the provision of adequate library services at the local level, since municipalities and states vary a great deal in their ability to support such services.

It seems that a real federal-state partnership in providing quality library and information services will develop, that the federal government will coordinate activities nationally, and that state library agencies will have responsibility for development of library services within the states and for coordination of those services with national programs.

Conclusion

Through the years library systems have proved their value in development of local public library services in many ways, particularly by making possible the extension and improvement of library services to large areas previously unserved or inadequately served. With the development of statewide and national networks involving all types of libraries, it appears that systems and networks will have an even greater role to play in connecting the local user to needed resources. As is noted in the National Commission's statement of goals, the national network will "form a shelter and framework for families of geographic and functional networks developed and interconnected according to a comprehensive plan."[12]

This does not mean that all systems and networks or their programs are necessarily good or worthy of support or that programs that are successful today will be successful, or even needed, tomorrow. Systems and networks have changed greatly over the years in such matters as organization, financing, and services provided, and they

---

10. Ibid., p. 62.
11. Ibid.

12. Ibid., p. xi.

will undoubtedly need to continue to change to meet the changing needs of libraries and the public in our dynamic society.

How successful systems and networks will be in providing for future needs depends to a great extent on the library community and interested lay leaders. Careful and frequent planning and evaluation will be necessary to make sure that a given system or network provides the kinds of services most needed by libraries and library users in the area served.

17 Planning and Construction of Buildings

EDWIN P. BECKERMAN

In recent years the list of funding sources that have been used to construct public libraries has grown to truly massive proportions. Local financing (largely through the issuance of bonds), private subscription, foundation grants, aid to Appalachia legislation, federal community development grants, Library Service and Construction Act (LSCA) grants, revenue sharing, state building grants, and just recently Commerce Department Economic Development Act (EDA) grants have all assisted in library construction.

Anyone with any direct experience in connection with the above funding programs will testify to the sometimes quixotic nature of their experience. Specifically, grant opportunities often require direct, vigorous, and almost immediate action if funding opportunities are to be realized. The long period of lead time necessary to the preparation of an effective building program is too often unavailable. In effect, the choice may well be between a great set of plans and no funding, or no plans and adequate funding. Under such conditions I have seen plans, preliminaries to be sure, completed in ten days, with no serious consideration given previously to the function of the building. The results are not always felicitous.

Given present funding possibilities, and projecting a variety of such possibilities into the future, it seems axiomatic that no library can afford to function today without some firm idea of its capital construction needs and funding opportunities.

Overview

Preliminary building planning often begins with the question, What kind of building do we want? Wrong question! A more appropriate question would be, What kind of services do we want to offer? Too often building design is seen as a thing apart from the library's service pattern. Planning for a new building is then structured as a separate activity, distinct from the library's formal planning activities. Ideally, the planning of the structure flows directly from the normal consideration of services, which should be part of a total, ongoing planning process. A library building is not a thing apart, but rather a concrete, three-dimensional representation of a service concept. If the concept is unclear or nonexistent, the resulting building is likely to fall short of satisfying the needs of the institution.

A few examples of service concepts and their effect on building program development should suffice:

1. At what age or grade do children gain access to adult facilities? Do we want to encourage an easy flow of children into the adult area? The answers to such questions will affect the size, location, and other physical characteristics of the children's room. Don't answer such questions after the building has been designed.
2. What is the library's philosophy vis-à-vis young adults? Does the library approach young adult service in terms of a large, separate collection and well-identified service area, or is service approached largely through an integration of young adult material into the adult collection, the focus of such service essentially based on specialized staffing? The library's outlook on young adult service will impact directly on the kind of space required.
3. The persistent issue of the library as materials reservoir versus cultural center must be addressed. Emphasis on providing a wide range of cultural activities within a public library setting must obviously be reflected in the amount and kind of space provided.

It is not my purpose at this point to urge any specific answers to the difficult questions that confront community libraries. Rather, I wish to suggest that a long and often tortuous process confronts libraries before they can even begin to ask such basic building questions as, How much space do we need, and How many levels shall we construct?

The Building Cycle

In the ensuing portions of this chapter, I shall examine in some detail the various stages of a building project, with some emphasis on issues that I feel are critical.

Phase 1—preliminary planning. This initial phase of planning involves all preliminary efforts to outline library objectives, including the building program that will make explicit library goals and objectives.

Phase 2—design development phase. The second phase in the planning cycle involves the translation of the written program statement into a set of building plans that reflect the service objectives of the library. The culmination of this phase in planning occurs when construction documents are produced, the building is bid, and contracts for construction are awarded.

Phase 3—construction phase. The final stage in the building cycle usually begins with a flourish at goundbreaking ceremonies and ends with a flourish at dedication ceremonies. What occurs in between will require steady nerves and the ability to smile in the face of disaster.

Looking at the entire structure of the building cycle, I am struck by the thought that, of the three phases in the process, the single phase that almost always receives inadequate attention is perhaps the most critical phase—preliminary planning. Preliminary planning involves complex assessments, a good deal of consultation, and, above all, time. Commonly, little solid planning is done before a commitment has been made to build a library. Then, for a variety of reasons, not enough time may remain to complete the preliminary phase of planning before beginning the building design. Serious building planning should begin from the moment the need is assessed, whether or not any commitment has been received from funding authorities. It is never too early to plan.

Phase 1—Preliminary Planning

As previously stated, I believe the building planning process properly begins even when there is no formal building project as such in existence. This is to say that a library's service objectives should be the object of constant review, and that the library as an institution should always have a clear perception of where it is, where it wants to go, and how it intends to get there. Part of this perception includes an assessment of buildings— their current status and future needs. Of critical importance at this preliminary planning stage and throughout a building project is the question of who does the planning.

Who Plans?

What is planned (the service, the programs, the building) results directly from who plans it. Most buildings are an amalgam of the views of the many individuals who participated in their planning or, on occasion, a reflection of the views of a limited few who "called the shots." Often, one's view of a building is conditioned by one's perspective. Thus, staff may focus on certain kinds of problems, trustees on others, and architects and municipal officials on still others. While this view is, of course, somewhat oversimplified and ignores individual differences, it is true enough to be worth stressing. A planning process that culminates in a community library building should provide for input from a wide variety of community perspectives. In essence, effective planning results from the development of a planning team that provides for the expression of a variety of interests and reflects a variety of perspectives in its composition.

The power to act in a public library is normally vested in either a library board of trustees or a municipality itself. In either case, it would be normal for certain kinds of planning and organizing responsibilities to be delegated to another individual or group in the interests of efficiently pursuing the project, with final authority reserved. This delegation of authority, of course, assumes many different patterns since circumstances vary. As one possible model for an executive group I suggest the following as a pattern that would allow for a wide range of input.

Library Building Team

Development of a sophisticated construction project requires the efforts of a limited group of individuals with the capacity to focus on issues and reach at least tentative conclusions. Quite obviously, the architect chosen to design a new building is a key member of the building team. Equally, the director of the library should also be a key member. The building team should also include a representative of the policy-making body: when the library is governed by a library board, either the president of the board or the chairperson of the board's building committee; when the library operates as a municipal department, a key representative of the municipality. A fourth key member of the building team would be the library building consultant, where the library has elected to engage the services of such a consultant. Usually a librarian or other consultant with expertise in the field of librarianship, the building consultant normally acts as a kind of bridge, assisting in the translation of service concepts into concrete building plans.

The building team, as I conceive it, should have broad responsibility in the following areas:

1. Development of a written building program outlining in some detail the general philosophy of library service in the community to be reflected in the building plan; the amount and kind of space required; the amount and kind of furniture and equipment to be utilized; and comments on all other critical areas that need to be considered, for example, site characteristics, parking, etc.
2. Development of building plans reflecting the concepts outlined in the written building program.
3. Construction of the building as designed and approved.
4. At every stage of planning and construction, the building team must act to explain the project to governing authorities and other interested parties as well as to secure necessary approvals that are required as the project progresses.

While the building team would have broad responsibilities with respect to a building project, it is important to emphasize that such a group would not operate in a vacuum. While crucial decisions must constantly be made, they should always be taken with careful reference to several other key groups:

1. Final authority for decision making is always vested in the library's governing authority. At all critical points during the life of the project, the views of the governing body must be solicited and accommodated within the final plan and approvals secured. This is, of course, only common sense, since the governing authority is charged by the law with responsibility for the provision of library service within the community.
2. The views of the library staff should also be carefully weighed at every juncture. It has been my experience that, although the views of governing bodies are rarely ignored, library staffs are too often bypassed as a building plan develops. This is not to say that all suggestions of staff members are always useful. However, staff members have a unique perspective from which to view library objectives and building plans, for they will have to live with the results. The staff can apply their own individual yardsticks to a thousand details of the building plan, subjecting it to a critical analysis from a perspective that no other group can duplicate. Ignore the staff at your peril!

3. It would appear useful to me, when planning new facilities, to constitute a citizens' advisory committee to provide input from library users as plans emerge designed to serve these same users. Periodic meetings with the citizens' advisory committee at critical stages in the design process should help to assure the development of a building that is responsive to the needs of all the citizens of a community.

A word of warning, however, is in order regarding the above suggestions. Opening up the design process for critical review by a large number of people does not provide the easiest route to library design. At best the process is time consuming, at worst it can be frustrating and exhausting. However, I can think of no other practical way to elicit such a wide variety of perspectives and to raise so many important issues. Given the time to explore properly all facets of a building program, a careful examination of all issues by a varied group of concerned individuals should produce the most thoughtful result.

Selecting the Architect and Consultant

Few choices facing library governing bodies are as critical as the choice of an architect and a consultant for a new building project. The most pertinent advice is to select your architect and consultant early enough for both to participate in the entire building cycle, and to check carefully into their previous work experience. The governing body should feel comfortable with both parties, since the working relationship will be long and subject to many stresses. The governing body should also check carefully with previous clients to assure that past performance was successful. While previous experience with library design is useful on the part of an architect, intelligence, flexibility, taste, and ability to design for public purposes in the long run offer the best criteria upon which to base a choice.

Funding the Library Building

I began with a recommendation that libraries be prepared to take strong action on short notice to construct needed facilities, due to the significant number of funding possibilities that exist today. If a library is to compete for scarce building resources on the federal, state, or local level in today's market, a reasonably sophisticated level of planning will be required. Such planning will have to address, for example, such issues as the following:

1. The planning team must clearly focus on the character of the community to be served. What impact does the geography of the community have upon service patterns? What are the characteristics of the population to be served? What can one anticipate in terms of population growth, shifts in population characteristics, and growth of community resources?.

2. What kind of library service is currently available to community residents? In order to build a strong case for a new library building, the library must convince all concerned that a new building is necessary. To do so requires a careful examination of what is currently being done, with careful attention to the way in which facilities currently available limit the services provided.

3. In light of our knowledge of the community as it exists today and our projection of how it will grow in the future, what kinds of objectives are we setting for the future that can best be realized through construction of a new library?

4. What are the alternatives to construction of a new library? The building needs that seem so apparent to the library professional may not in fact be apparent to anyone else. Such alternatives as renting of facilities or an addition to an existing structure should be considered. Nor is this simply a matter of cosmetics. The objective should be to find the best solution to a service problem at the most reasonable cost, and this solution may not always involve construction.

Let us assume at this juncture that you have made a good case for construction of a new building—you are clear on your service objectives and why a new building offers you the best means of achieving these objectives, all alternatives considered. Where do you go from here in terms of funding?

There is, of course, no single simple answer. Any approach to solving funding problems proceeds from the unique nature of each individual community. Every community has its own hierarchy of values. Libraries compete with a whole host of other municipal services, and our success or lack of it in the end is determined by where we are placed in this scale of values. Having said this, there are several hints that may help in planning a campaign:

1. No two communities are exactly alike, although they often may seem to be. The task of those who would promote library interests is to understand the unique process in each community by which decisions are made. This involves an understanding of the political life of the community, what forces shape municipal decisions, and the responsiveness or resistance of local government to public pressure. What individuals and groups within the community are most likely to be persuasive to local officials? Does local government view the library as one of the "municipal family," or is it regarded as an outsider? The answers to such questions as these will help to suggest a line of approach with the best chance of success. For example, the problem of eliciting support for a new building in a community in which decision making is narrowly based and tends to be concentrated in town hall, and in which the library is considered part of the family, would suggest to me a heavy concentration of effort in convincing the municipal power structure of the need for a new building. As a member of the family, the library can argue its case from within the structure itself. The same library, if it were considered by local officials to be outside of the family structure, would of necessity be required to mobilize a far greater outpouring of public sentiment to put pressure on local officials from the outside. Unfortunately, too many public libraries are regarded as outsiders by local officials, and this too often creates an adversary condition in which each side views the other with some suspicion and not a little hostility. From a library standpoint, this is self-defeating, and one can only hope that librarians and trustees will come to understand that they are part of the political process and can with some skill and tact maintain their scruples and integrity, virtually intact, while drawing closer to the decision-making political forces of the community. In any event, learn the way the game is played in your community, and learn to play it effectively yourself.

2. In the last analysis, the surest ground upon which the library can stand is the quality of the library itself. All other things being equal, a good library is easier to sell than a bad one. Effective public relations programs are often spoken of as a thing apart. Legitimately, an effective public relations effort begins, or dies, with an effective library. An effective library that accomplishes explicitly and implicitly its objectives in a highly visible way stands a better chance of securing support than an irrelevant institution.

3. Regardless of the closeness of relations between municipal and library officials, one of

the keys to the funding of the local library is the ability to focus the general support that an effective library commands into effective political support. To be sure, the way in which such support is articulated may differ depending upon the basic sympathies of local officials, but even the most sympathetic local administration will welcome some demonstration of public support where funding of public facilities is involved. In short, count your friends and see that others do, as well!

4. On the local scene, a small monument will always be raised to someone who puts up a building with nonlocal funding. Make sure you are current on all possible sources, governmental and private. Your state library agency may assist all public libraries in the state in this sometimes arduous business.

5. Try to emphasize the funding of your building in as graphic a manner as possible. A $700,000 building will normally not involve the immediate expenditure of so large a sum. In fact, the annual expenditure may be in the range of $50,000, depending on interest rates and duration of the bonding period. What is most relevant to average persons is their share of this cost, which may amount to $15 annually for the average home owner. Dealing with library construction in this way presents a more balanced picture. After all, the average person is being asked to spend $15 a year for perhaps twenty or thirty years rather than to plunk down $700,000.

6. Often, success in raising capital construction funds is a matter of timing. As a library advocate, you should always have a reasonably precise idea of what public construction is pending in your community and what kind of construction schedule is anticipated. Try to avoid conflicts between scheduling of library construction and the construction of other essential projects. However, rest assured, the time is never right to try to raise money. Raise it anyway, but give yourself every break by avoiding avoidable conflicts.

Selecting a Site

A good deal has been written about the importance of carefully selecting a library site before building. Conventional wisdom holds that a library site should be located at the busiest intersection of the downtown area of any given community. Essentially the library is viewed from the same

perspective as in any retail business. Maximum return on investment, in this case usage, requires that as high a volume of traffic be encouraged as possible, and this is at least partially affected by location. While it is recognized that such an optimum site will be expensive—at times exorbitant—it is felt that in the long haul the cost of the site will be an acceptable burden in view of the higher value of usage such a site will attract. Put in other terms, the unit cost of operation will decline as greater volume of traffic outweighs higher site acquisition costs.

While in general I subscribe to the above theory of site location, it is a bit simplistic. Particularly in light of the development of the modern motor vehicle orientation of suburban and rural communities, it fails to come to grips with what is actually occurring.

In the first instance, while it is true that retail establishments attempt to maximize their volume of traffic in order to maximize potential profit, this factor must always be viewed in the context of the cost of the site as well as the cost of building on a particular site. While one should attempt to select the busiest site, this factor must be evaluated together with other key site characteristics such as cost, size, shape of the lot, and other factors that impact on the difficulties of construction on a given site. An additional factor that must be carefully weighed in site selection involves the parking, actual or potential, available in the vicinity of the site. However much public transportation is available to the area of the site, the importance of automobile transportation to the location cannot be overemphasized. Particularly in communities of any geographical size, a substantial part of the traffic is likely to be carried by the automobile, and this must be reckoned with as a factor in final site selection.

In selecting a site for a suburban or rural community, the concept of locating a building in the busiest downtown area may be of limited use, since there may be no downtown area in the traditional sense. One is confronted rather with shopping centers and strip development along major traffic routes. In some cases small "downtown" areas do exist, but these often have ceased to be viable areas economically. In such cases, I believe, one must substitute "most heavily travelled vehicular route" for "busiest downtown intersection" as a guiding concept. Two other factors that should be weighed in viewing the suitability of a site on a heavily traveled roadway are the centrality, or lack of it, to the total service area and the ease with which traffic moves along the route. Suburban communities are notorious for their lack of proper design standards for developing vehicular routes, and at times this reaches such crisis proportions that it is questionable if any additional load should be added to the already snarled traffic.

In general, in selecting any site, care should be exercised to assure both that the site is large enough to accommodate the structure needed for today's purpose, as well as the future, and that potential construction problems inherent in the site are carefully evaluated. Excessive slope (over 15 percent) and problem soil or drainage conditions can add significantly to the cost of site preparation, and all of these potential site problems should be understood before a final commitment for use of the site is made.

Writing the Building Program

Earlier I stated my view that a wide variety of opinions should be sought from different perspectives concerning the library needs of the community and the kind of building these needs suggested. In view of the broad input to be solicited, the building team would do well to carefully structure the dialogue concerning the building so that issues are brought into focus and problems attacked and resolved. The basic building block of this effort should be the written building program.

An effective building program should indicate such specifics as the recommended size and location of the library site, the amount of parking required, the kind and amount of space required for all library functions, and the amounts and kinds of furniture and equipment required. It should do even more. An effective building program should convey the spirit of the library to the reader so that it suggests design directions to the architect, trustees, and all others who read it. In essence, the function of the space outlined should be clear from a reading of the program, and, even in the absence of specific recommendations covering all issues, reasonable solutions should be inferable from the written document. Essentially then the design phase of the building program should seek both to solicit a wide variety of opinion and to take the raw material that results from this dialogue and focus on specific design solutions. If we fail to solicit the widest range of opinion, we are likely to design in a vacuum. If we fail to focus on solutions, we can become involved in an endless dialogue that never evolves into any solutions. Both results can be intensely frustrating to all concerned.

In order to structure the dialogue along fruitful lines, it is wise to prepare a draft of the building program at an early point in the project. Preparation of such a document will require a broad understanding of the field of librarianship, broad knowledge of the community, a firm understanding of the objectives and "style" of the local library organization, and some understanding of the way in which abstract goals and objectives are best translated into concrete and steel. In practice, the specific skills needed for such an undertaking require the training and background of a professional librarian, and with rare exceptions the writing of a building program should be undertaken by the library director or a library consultant engaged for that purpose. If a consultant is hired, that person should be engaged to participate with the building team for the duration of a project. The writing of the building program is the commencement of a process rather than an end in itself, and many changes will occur during the process of discussion. As one would not engage a physician or lawyer to perform half of the services required, one should not hire a consultant to perform only the first of many services that will be required.

Completion of the draft of the building program will provide all of those concerned with a framework around which to structure a discussion of the library's building needs. The program should be discussed with the staff, the library's board of trustees if there is one, governing officials of the library if other than a board, any advisory groups that may be involved with the library, and representatives of the public. The views and suggestions of all of these parties should be solicited. In addition, the library architect should be chosen at an early point in the project so as to be a party to this process.

Upon completion of this review, the draft of the building program should be revised in light of the determination of the building team, and copies of the revised program circulated among all of the above concerned parties. Upon solicitation of further comment, a final draft of the building program should be prepared and submitted to the governing body of the library for approval. Upon approval, the building program becomes the conceptual blueprint for development of the building design.

Phase 2—Design Development

It is assumed that, by the beginning of this second phase in the building cycle, architect and consultant have been chosen and library objectives, including building objectives, have been articulated. The next steps to be taken will be determined by such factors as whether a site has been selected and whether funding has been assured. If both site and funding have been secured, activity during the design development will center around the technical problem of creating a set of building plans that carry out the intent of the building program. However, in the event that action on securing a site or funding is incomplete, the design development phase must deal with both the technical problems of creating building plans and the practical problems of securing funding.

When funding the cost of the building becomes a major activity during this phase of the work, development of a preliminary set of plans—including floor layout, elevations, an artist's conception of the project, or even a scale model—may prove useful. In such a case, considerable work will have to be undertaken before any bond money becomes available. Thus in the absence of a firm commitment for bonding funds from a municipality or other funding source, a substantial amount of seed money may be required to secure funding authorization. On occasion, securing the seed money may be as difficult as securing final approval of the project.

Aspects of Basic Design

Form and function. If there is any single aspect of library building design that can elicit universal support among building consultants, it is surely the simple notion that form follows function. A library building must first of all be designed to fulfill a well-defined purpose. The purpose will itself begin to suggest appropriate design forms as one begins to put flesh on the skeleton.

Style. A good deal has been written in recent years concerning the need to design more comfortable, intimate, and inviting buildings than had perhaps been the vogue in the past. This change in the style of library design reflects similar changes in the design of public buildings generally. While previous generations expressed themselves by re-creating the heritage of the past, our generation seems intent in exploring the possibilities inherent in new technology—for example, creating new shapes it has made possible and utilizing new materials it has created. Above all, stylistic changes in library design are aimed at creating flexible structures, recognizing the tentative quality of social planning, and structures that in taste and design reflect the culture of the society as a whole. Thus, library buildings today do tend to be somewhat informal, do tend toward a more open style of construction with fewer fixed, load-bearing partitions than was previously true, and do tend toward greater use of color and more comfortable seating in interior design. In general, I think this tendency to develop more flexible, inviting buildings has been healthy and properly reflects changes that have occurred in the library world and in American society.

Space allotments. The experience formulas developed over the years by the late Joseph Wheeler are widely used and offer a good point of departure in considering space needs (Joseph L.

Wheeler and Herbert Goldhor, *Practical Administration of Public Libraries* (Harper and Row, 1962).

Wheeler suggests that, if anything, these formulas may be overly generous, perhaps by as much as 15 percent. In fact, I find on the basis of my experience that they are overly confining. This is true particularly as one increases the population served. Let us consider a service area of 101,000 population. I would contend that a seating capacity of 202 is minimal for such a large population, that a book collection of 202,000 volumes is inadequate, and that a total building of 50,000 square feet is totally inadequate. More recent base figures recommend 3 volumes per capita for a minimum collection for any size population, and 5 seats per 1,000 people served.[1] In overall terms, as building plans are developed incrementally, allowing for all planned purposes, I find that a scale of from .5 square foot per capita to as much as a foot or more is really required. I would include in this assessment, however, the space available in branches of a multibranch system.

The important thing in outlining space needs is to recognize that, in building terms, space exists to realize objectives. The crucial questions relate to service program objectives rather than what any authority has suggested is a minimal book collection for your community. The experience and opinion of others provides a useful point of departure in considering local needs, but standards are of necessity somewhat arbitrary and need to be carefully weighed in terms of local knowledge. Once needs and program objectives can be determined, the space to carry out program objectives can be reflected in preliminary and working drawings without real difficulty.

Needs of the Handicapped. In building design and construction, it is essential to recognize that libraries are utilized not only by patrons with varying interests and service needs, but by individuals with varying physical capacities as well. While public libraries may not be used by all, lack of use must be a matter of choice, rather than the result of physical limitations imposed by the building.

A variety of statutes at all levels of government currently apply to public library construction, designed to assure that patrons with physical handicaps will be guaranteed equal access to library facilities and programs. When building new facilities or remodeling, it is important to review pertinent state and local statutes, and to be aware of

---

1. Nolan Lushington and Willis N. Mills, *Libraries Designed for Users: A Planning Handbook* (Syracuse: Gaylord, 1979).

such relevant federal statutes as Section 504 of the Rehabilitation Act.

While specific standards and space requirements are quite detailed, they generally attempt to accomplish the following:

1. Ensure that patrons confined to wheel chairs, those without sight, and the hearing impaired can move easily throughout a library building. Thus all levels of a library must be connected by elevators large enough to accommodate wheelchairs.
2. Rest room facilities and water fountains specifically designed to accommodate wheelchairs should be located on all public service levels of a building.
3. Ground level or ramp access should be provided for every library building.
4. Site development should be designed to accommodate needs of the handicapped by eliminating sharp grades or other barriers inhibiting to traffic.

Shelving. Approximately 1 square foot of space will be required to shelve ten volumes; 1 linear foot of shelving can hold approximately eight volumes (remembering that the average reference volume is somewhat larger than the average picture book). Public area stack isles should be a minimum of 4 feet wide (4½ to 5 feet is even better). Closed stack areas can be planned with 3-foot aisles, and calculations can be made on the basis of fifteen volumes per square foot available. In general, I question the use of any substantial closed stack areas in medium-sized and smaller libraries. Much library use, I believe, is associated with browsing, and the greater the percentage of the collection in closed stacks, the more limited is the browsing potential in that library. In general, as well, adult stacks should be limited to eighty-two inches in height (sixty inches in children's areas). Approximately fifty long-play records can be shelved per linear foot.

Seating. As a general framework for planning seating areas, the Wheeler and Goldhor experience formulas appear sound. I would suggest some modifications, however.

Recommendations for seating at the lower end of each population grouping appear too restrictive. Thus, 55 reader seats for a population of 11,000 and 108 seats for a population of 36,000 will not in my judgment be adequate for most libraries serving such populations. Similarly, the formulas may be overly generous at the higher end of the scale. Thus 90 seats for a library serving 9,000 population (higher than the requirement for a library serving 11,000) would be somewhat high. An allowance of 6 or 7 seats per 1,000

served for both the library serving 9,000 and 11,000 would be closer to the mark, on the basis of my experience.

An allowance of thirty square feet per adult readers' seat has been found adequate, and while twenty square feet per juvenile seat has been widely used, I prefer twenty-five as a more realistic figure.

As a basic element of table seating, I prefer the four-seat table to the six, it being easier to supervise such a seating area. In keeping with a general trend toward greater informality, I think it is desirable to include casual lounge seating in informal groupings in modern libraries, the extent to which this is done depending on how you view your library program locally. I would suggest, however, that consideration be given to the control of lounge areas. For example, single lounge chairs are to be preferred to sofas for control reasons. Decide early if your lounge area is to be a group experience or a comfortable area for singles. Your purpose will affect the kind of furniture and equipment you buy.

Staff space. It is unwise to generalize too much regarding formulas for allocation of staff space. In essence staff space must be planned incrementally, with the particular purpose of each space in mind and with specific allowance needs for all items of equipment and furniture. In general, it has been found that work space of approximately 100 square feet per staff member has usually been adequate for most libraries.

Staff size, as projected for future needs, is obviously a vital question in staff space allocation. This question must be considered in developing the building program, with careful attention to future needs.

Meeting-room space. Perhaps no other spaces in the library so clearly reflect the impact of program philosophy on space utilization as do meeting rooms. Although most public libraries do provide some meeting-room area, the amount of space provided ranges from the minuscule to the palatial, depending on program philosophy.

In my own experience, few areas in a library have been as open to challenge by municipal authorities and at times by the public as meeting-room and multipurpose area facilities. Particularly in libraries with limited previous experience in group programming, meeting-room facilities have been suspect.

Yet, for a variety of reasons, meeting rooms, auditoriums, activity rooms, and similar kinds of spaces can be as important as any other spaces in the library. In addition to being a center of learning within a local community, a public library can become a center of broad-cultural activity, in some communities the only center of such activity likely to develop. It seems appropriate to me to extend the cultural role of the library to include all kinds of communications beyond the written word, which has traditionally been the focus of library interests.

In addition to providing the framework that can permit the library to perform a number of varied, socially useful tasks, a library program that is oriented toward group programming, including the performing arts, offers some practical political advantage. Some librarians have questioned the wisdom of much nontraditional library activity on the basis that such activity detracts from the central purpose of the library, that of providing print materials and related services for their publics. My own view is that all library programs stand a much better chance of adequate support if the library is perceived as a dynamic institution generating a wide range of interest and involvement. One way of generating such a perception on the part of the general public and municipal officials is through a wide range of cultural programming.

In planning multipurpose facilities, the wide range of activities that may be generated should be carefully considered. Provision of kitchen facilities adjacent to meeting facilities has often encouraged use by diverse groups. Acoustics should be carefully considered with all potential uses in mind. Usually an oblong rather than a square room is desirable for audiovisual purposes. Consider the possibility of a projection room or booth in rooms of any size. While audiovisual equipment is quieter than it used to be, I have yet to hear a projector that wasn't distracting to some extent.

Generally, an allowance of ten square feet per meeting room seat has been found adequate. In a multipurpose room, care must be exercised to provide adequate storage space for all chairs and tables to be utilized for all programmed activities.

Architectural space. In calculating space needs, inadequate allowances are often projected for a variety of purposes, including wall thicknesses, stairways, halls, toilets, elevators, heating and air conditioning equipment, and closets. It is likely that an allowance of 20 percent will be required to provide for the above needs.

Arrangement of space. In addition to providing the amount of space needed to accomplish the major purposes of the library, it is essential that spaces be organized in a way that allows for the most effective provision of service. It is necessary that the planner imagine being in the position of the library user, the library worker, or those delivering materials or supplies to the library, so that the space is arranged from the users' perspective. For example, from the users' perspective, the shorter the distance from the parking lot to the front entrance, the better; a building with a street-level front entrance is easier to enter than one with front steps; some guidance as to the organization of the building is useful upon entering, .as are clearly worded and legible signs directing one to the desired location. In general, in a multilevel building, as many public services as possible should be located on the ground level. More-casual browsing functions of the library should be located in more heavily used areas, while care should be exercised to remove reference functions to quieter areas.

From a staff perspective, great care should be given to designing a structure that is as easy to supervise as possible. Thus cul-de-sacs are to be avoided; toilets are to be located where they can be easily supervised, as must public phones. Sight lines must be carefully plotted to assure maximum supervision from the charge desk and information desks. Care must be given also to planning the way both staff and materials move throughout the building so that space is located properly.

Flexibility. In my experience, few libraries are constructed with adequate room for expansion. In rapidly developing rural or suburban areas, it is doubly important to allow adequately for future expansion and alteration. Trying to construct facilities with built-in expansion room for the next ten years is highly desirable, but at the very least a definite plan for expansion of the facility should be included in every building program. Limiting the number of load-bearing partitions and confining toilets, elevators, and similar building service areas to fringe areas or central cores can also serve to lend flexibility to building design.

Remodeling. As with new construction, remodeling an existing structure for library purposes should proceed within the framework of a written building program outlining the philosophy and space needs of the library. In almost all cases, the benefits and disadvantages of remodeling an existing structure for library use will have to be weighed in terms of alternatives. It has been my experience that, when the alternatives are viewed side by side in concrete terms, many conflicts disappear; the most desirable course of action becomes apparent.

Probably few issues stir as much discussion, and at times dissension, as the suggestion that, rather than build a new library as proposed by the library board, the old Millard Fillmore Elementary School should be converted for use as a library. I have seen such helpful suggestions surface at the last minute on numerous occasions, and the results are often disastrous, at the very least to community interpersonal relationships.

Essentially, the last-minute helpful suggestion for remodeling an existing building should rarely occur. The building team, at a very early stage in their deliberations, when the general requirements for the building become clear, should examine the various alternatives available to meet these needs. This would include utilization of various sites as well as an examination of the possibility of using existing structures remodeled for library purposes. One should not be too quick to accept suggestions for use of existing structures by well-intentioned and sometimes not-so-well-intentioned observers, but, on the other hand, the possibilities of using existing structures should be viewed with an open mind. In general the following issues should be addressed in reviewing remodeling possibilities:

1. *Advantages and disadvantages of the site must be viewed carefully.* The same test that one would apply to establishing a retail business on a proposed site is valid for the establishment of a library. Usually, possible buildings and sites suggested to the library by interested observers are badly located and/or dilapidated. Librarians will recognize the syndrome. If you don't know what to do with your dust-covered collection of old college textbooks, donate them to the library. The same often applies to buildings. Worn-out school buildings in particular are often offered for this purpose, and almost as often, they are badly located for public library purposes.

   Size and physical attributes of the site must be evaluated as well. This is particularly important if extensive rehabilitation of the building is projected or if any other plans require changes in the way the site is used. Thus if new parking areas are needed, the size and shape of the site must be considered as well as the projected cost of altering the lot.

2. *The amount and kinds of spaces required by the library must be clearly in view* as the merits and deficiencies of a building proposed for remodeling is considered. In general, large, open spaces are preferred for modern library use, since this kind of space offers maximum flexibility and greatest economy in ease of supervision. This usually translates into a minimum of levels in a multilevel structure, since more floors in a building will usually require a larger staff to serve the public and supervise public areas.

   Often the buildings offered as candidates for remodeling, particularly in the case of schools, are multistoried structures with many classroom-size spaces and the kind of solid construction reminiscent of the Magi-

not Line. While one can in fact convert a given structure into something totally alien, the cost of opening up a solidly built structure with many smaller spaces incorporated into its design may well exceed the cost of building an entirely new structure from scratch. Clearly at an early stage in consideration of remodeling, an architect with the assistance of qualified engineers should be asked to estimate the cost of converting the structure to library purposes, as outlined in the building program.

3. *The condition of the existing structure should be carefully assessed* at the same time alterations are considered by the building team. Needed replacement of a roof or boiler can be important considerations as one evaluates the viability of proposed alterations. Consider all the requirements of local codes as well as state regulations when estimating cost. For example, you may ideally want a one-level structure, but you are evaluating the possibility of remodeling an existing two-level structure. If, in such an instance, state regulations required that any new or remodeled public building utilizing two levels provide an elevator, such an expense would have to be calculated into the cost of remodeling. Of course, similar calculations would have to be made when considering the cost of new construction.

   To sum up, it is the responsibility of the building team, and ultimately of the library's governing body, to reasonably examine the alternatives available as a means of reaching selected objectives. It is not the job of the library to aid the community in the disposal of unwanted municipal facilities. Nor is it the job of the library to build monuments to the governing body, the library administration, or the political administration currently in power. It is the job of all concerned to provide structures that are needed to accomplish objectives at the most reasonable cost possible. This should, at times, involve the remodeling of existing structures.

   A final word regarding style. Many buildings have a unique charm and dignity reflecting the taste and intent of their designers. At times those who have guided remodeling efforts have not always respected the basic building and have taken great liberties in remodeling. While alterations are needed in older buildings to make them more nearly conform to modern needs, greater care can and should be exercised to preserve the best in our older buildings and to provide for modern needs in a way that does justice to the heritage of the past.

Parking. I have suggested that all kinds of libraries—urban, suburban, and rural—need to be concerned about the provision of adequate parking space since we live in an automobile-oriented society. Specifically, how much parking is enough?

In calculating requirements for public parking, it is difficult to be both arbitrary and sensible at one and the same time. In calculating parking requirements in the past, I have found the following scale, which relates number of spaces to number of feet constructed, to be useful:

Add—five parking spaces per 1,000 square feet constructed up to 20,000 square feet. Minimum number of spaces required is twenty-five.

Add—four parking spaces per 1,000 square feet constructed for all space constructed between 20,000 square feet and 40,000 square feet.

Add—three parking spaces per 1,000 square feet constructed for all space constructed between 40,000 square feet and 75,000 square feet.

Add—two parking spaces per 1,000 square feet constructed for all space over 75,000 square feet.

If possible, an allowance of 325 square feet per space would be desirable, although as little as 300 square feet could be utilized if necessary.

Phase 3—Construction

The difficulties that the library will experience during the construction of a building are hard to overestimate. In public projects, the bidding process designed to secure the lowest possible price while still preserving quality of construction often acts to protect marginal contractors with shaky credentials. The following suggestions may prove useful and, together with daily prayer, may guide you through your time of trouble:

1. *The key to a successful construction job is good contractors.* To the extent that state laws will permit, a careful review of proposed contractors should be undertaken, with contract documents designed to weed out contractors with poor records of performance on previous jobs. Recognize that it may be difficult to base such a judgment on the recommendations of previous clients, who may be reluctant to give candid appraisals of

past performance. However, one can often judge performance on a more objective basis, such as whether the job was completed on time, if not why not, and whether any of the completed work had to be redone at a later date. In assessing references, try to make initial contacts by phone or in person for a more candid view. Remember, however, no contractor currently building can be totally immune to criticism.

2. *Part of the review of contractors should include a thorough financial review* of the company to determine if the contractor's assets are adequate.

3. *The building team must be as familiar as possible with the contract documents,* including the bid specifications. The entire team—not just the architect—should be familiar with and understand the terms of the contract before the job is bid. While all members of the building team are not experts in construction, a great deal of the difficulty that occurs on many construction projects is traceable, not to obscure technical language in the contract, but to a basic lack of attention on the part of responsible library officials.

4. *A clerk-of-the-works should be engaged to protect library interests on a project of any size* (to be arbitrary, let us say a building of more than 15,000 square feet). Such a clerk is normally hired by the library, working in cooperation with the architect, to be present at the building site during the hours when construction proceeds. The clerk-of-the-works must be thoroughly conversant with all phases of general construction and must also be entirely familiar with the contract documents to assure that all materials and methods of construction are as specified and that, where deviations are noted, rapid corrective action can be taken. While it is true that one function of the architect is to provide direct supervision of the construction job, this general supervision should not be confused with the close supervision that can only be provided by a representative of the owner who is on the job site at all times.

5. *If possible, I think it wise to choose a single contractor with overall responsibility for the entire job.* In some states, the library may have a choice between one general contractor to perform all of the work or letting separate contracts for major portions of the work, such as general construction, electrical, heating and ventilating, etc. Having a single contractor could add something to the cost

of construction, since it is likely that a general contractor would subcontract out major areas of work, and both contractor and subcontractor would require a profit on a single area of work. However, this could be minimized by greater efficiency with only one contractor scheduling and supervising. From a library point of view, clear lines of responsibility would enable the library to hold one contractor accountable in a way that is difficult with multiple contractors.

6. *Several steps can be taken to avoid delays.* Perhaps one of the most frustrating areas with which we deal in construction is the difficulty of pressing work through to completion when there are four or five major contractors. To the normal delays of construction (strikes; floods; fire; inability to secure raw materials, supplies, and equipment) we now add the difficulty of assigning definite responsibility for delays. For example, the general contractor cannot pour a cement floor until the electrical contractor places his conduit. The electrical contractor has an agreement to permit the plumbing contractor to lay pipe in the area before conduit is placed. The plumbing contractor says that he has not scheduled the laying of pipe for another two weeks, as agreed to by the general contractor. In the meanwhile work on the job virtually ceases.

The kind of situation cited above is normal on most jobs. Several steps can be taken by the library to help reduce conflict. A schedule of all work to be performed by all contractors during the life of the project must be

prepared before work begins. In a job involving more than one contractor, the general contractor is normally responsible for preparing such a schedule. The clerk-of-the-works should be alert to all field decisions and agreements arrived at between contractors, and these agreements must be carefully recorded by the clerk. In fact, the clerk must be extremely careful to record all occurrences on the job, since these records may be extremely important in forcing the job to completion or at some later time in a court of law in deciding who was at fault in specific situations.

Summary

If there is one single piece of advice that can be given to those about to become involved with library building for the first time, I think it would be not to check your common sense at the front door before entering. Yes, there is special knowledge involved in building a library, but most of the knowledge you will need you can acquire as you proceed. Choose your experts—architect and consultants—carefully, and you will protect yourself in highly technical areas, but never be afraid to raise the issues you feel are important, even if it runs counter to the expert advice you receive. Above all, remember that every building team, governing body, and staff went through the same torture you are about to endure and that most of the time the frustration is left far behind the moment the front door at last opens on your gleaming new library building.

18   *Physical Facilities and Environmental Control*

RONALD TOLLAFIELD

The experienced librarian accepting the position of top administrator is aware of the high percentage of total budget assigned to salaries and materials. These are the primary requirements of library operation. The remaining portion of the budget is allocated to various fixed or estimated expenses. The new administrator may not fully appreciate the magnitude of such building-maintenance costs as repairs and janitorial supplies. In addition, *preventive* maintenance must be a part of the philosophy of budgeting procedure. A continually low maintenance level will result in relatively swift building deterioration and high repair costs. Regular planned maintenance will extend the usefulness of equipment and furnishings and delay necessary replacement. It can prolong the life of a building, as minor upkeep can often prevent major repairs. A well-maintained building also indicates the pride of the whole staff in its facility and is one of the less-obvious reasons for good staff morale. The public has a right to expect reasonable maintenance of its property, not only to promote long use but also to express pride of ownership.

Planning for Building Maintenance

In planning a new building, the architect will develop space for building maintenance, including janitors' closets, storage, and workrooms for the maintenance staff. The administrator must be cognizant that maintenance requirements will increase with building size and that staff may need to be enlarged. It is at this time that the architect must be told of expected space requirements for a carpentry shop and custodian's office. At the same time, the architect may find it necessary to remind the book-oriented librarian that not all the building space can be allocated to book stacks. Both administrator and architect must balance the esthetics of a building with the practical knowledge of the amount and costs of maintenance required and the useful life of the building materials.

The method of maintenance will be an administrative consideration in preparing the budget allocation and may affect planning in relation to space requirements in a new building. In general, custodial services will be of one of three types: in-house staff, local government maintenance pool, or contract maintenance.

In-house staff. Where the library employs its own staff, consideration must be given to the effectiveness of full- or part-time employees, their salaries, fringe benefits, training, and supervision. Local conditions may require trade union personnel. Or a library may employ a "handyman" for janitorial services and minor repairs, using outside help for special purposes on a contractual or bid basis. Where trade union help is required, a decision may have to be made regarding the trade most useful as part of the staff, such as custodial and carpentry areas. Repairs requiring plumbing and electrical work may then be jobbed to outside help.

Local government maintenance pool. The maintenance of government buildings may be the responsibility of one department with employees supervised by this department and requests for special services made through departmental channels. The library administration must inspect the quality of the work to maintain its own standard. This method relieves the library budget of custodial salaries, but there may be some charge based on hours of work or square feet maintained.

Contract maintenance. The library may contract with a commercial firm for all specified maintenance routines. Bids should be taken for the selection of this contractor even where not required by law. Specifications for the contract should be carefully worked out since the bid may be based on cost, or cost plus supplies. However, the selection should be based on bid plus a careful consideration of other factors. These include quality of work, number of work hours used in computing costs, and past performance as determined through references or experience.

A contract fixes budget items for maintenance salaries and equipment, and it provides relief from the details of maintenance, training, and coverage of schedules. Disadvantages may lie in the quality of cleaning, costs, need for inspection and super-

225

vision, and dissatisfaction of the library staff. It may be necessary to carry in-house employees in addition to a maintenance contract to cover emergencies or routines not handled by the contractor.

The hourly costs of various kinds of custodial help will differ. Total costs should be compared by computing yearly in-house expenses (salaries, equipment, supplies) for the square footage of areas maintained, and the contractor's annual cost for the same area.[1]

Administration of Building Maintenance

Budgeting

The administrator may underestimate annual maintenance costs because of size and age or deterioration of the building or buildings in the library system. The size, condition, design, and furnishings of a building will dictate the number of hours needed for good maintenance. Age and condition are not necessarily related. Even if a building is well maintained, its age may indicate expected repairs or replacement of equipment. On the other hand, the deterioration of a structure only a few years old may indicate a poor history of maintenance. Either of these conditions will have to be considered, and the budget adjusted if necessary to allow increased expense.

A budget for maintenance including building repairs and supplies, but not salaries for staff, may be 9 to 12 percent of the total library budget. Expected large repairs or replacement of such major equipment as a furnace might increase the budget allocation. Usually the year's allocation will be increased slightly, and additional costs will be covered by slighting expenditures for regular items and postponing minor maintenance items for a future budget. If the latter condition is necessary, the administration should keep these items in mind for the following year.

Maintenance Personnel

Regardless of the size of the library, it will have maintenance personnel. A village library may require only a part-time janitor. A large urban system will probably have a superintendent of maintenance with a staff of several custodians and perhaps some representatives of the various trades. Salaries for the individuals will be based on the local rates for commensurate work. The salary needed to attract a responsible and knowledgeable individual as a head custodian and supervisor may seem high; however, this individual must have experience and leadership qualities comparable to those of a department head of the library staff. Such an individual can relieve the administrator of everyday operational problems. The maintenance superintendent should be responsible for general daily maintenance, repairs to buildings and equipment, and training of the custodial staff and should report directly to the librarian.

In a small library, the custodian will have little authority or decision-making responsibility, although the administrator may act on the custodian's recommendation. In a larger organization, this position carries greater decision-making authority. The head of the building department will set priorities for maintenance and repair, authorize purchase of supplies and small equipment, and carry out or supervise work without immediately reporting to the administration. The custodial supervisor will consult along organization lines with a branch supervisor or other line officers, since, in practice, agencies will request services directly. Recommendations for large purchases or capital expenditure will be made in the custodian's annual report to the librarian, and requests for purchases made as required. The administrator will be the arbiter of the need and cost of new equipment and must of necessity become acquainted with maintenance problems, the tools of the staff, and the terminology.

Selecting and training the new employee. In the past anyone who could push a mop across a room qualified to be a janitor. The physically handicapped and those with limited mental achievement were often hired but seldom trained to do the work. With today's technologies and automated equipment, a custodian must be able to understand and appreciate the purpose and quality of the tools and machines utilized. These include even soaps and waxes developed for specific purposes and materials with relatively small, measured amounts necessary per unit of water. An untrained or untrainable individual may assume that greater quantities will do the job more easily. It may be difficult to make such an individual understand that, not only are large amounts unnecessary and wasteful, but they can shorten the life of the material to be cleaned. Heating and cooling equipment is highly sophisticated today; even though it is largely automatic with built-in safety devices, a mishandled valve or electrical switch may necessitate expensive repairs. The motors of vacuum cleaners burn out if overworked because of the failure of the operator to change the dust bag. These methods require a thinking person, and the administrator should be willing to take the time and steps to find one.

1. Douglas W. Beach, "Readers Rate Contract and Staff Cleaning," pp. 50–53.

The selection and training of a custodian are as important as for any other new employee and should follow the normal procedure of the library. A job description for the custodial position should include the following information:

1. *Selection criteria.* The custodian should be pleasant, affable, physically able to do the work, and literate. These are the personal attributes most noted by the rest of the staff.
2. *Compensation.* The salary, pay period, fringe benefits, hours of work, and other details of the library routine should be described.
3. *Schedule of requirements.* These should include: (a) all duties to be done daily, weekly, monthly, or seasonally. (b) Time requirements for specific duties. These may be developed by the staff or adapted from lists found in various sources such as *School Maintenance and Operation* by Joseph Baker, or in state and government publications or maintenance standards. These usually are expressed as minutes required per square foot of floor or wall. (c) time of day to do the job.

Training will usually be done by the head custodian and can be effective if six simple steps are followed.

1. *Give a general orientation.* Show the new employee the area assigned, equipment, storage room, staff lounge, and the library building in general. Explain the schedule of work and duties required.
2. *Explain the whole job in detail.* The job to be covered may be limited to using a mop over a tile floor. Much time and energy can be saved if the job is done correctly.
3. *Demonstrate.* The head custodian uses the mop in the fashion described and encourages questions. The employee should be asked to repeat the instructions in his or her own words. It is important to remember that the employee may be hearing new words and doing new things. Communication between supervisor and employee must be clear to make sure there are no misunderstandings.
4. *Supervise.* Have the employee try out the job under the supervision of the head custodian. At least three hours of supervision will be necessary before the employee works alone.
5. *Follow up.* Inspect the employee's work.
6. *Use refresher consultation.* In a few days, check to see that the employee is following instructions and is not making mistakes or taking shortcuts.

When there is no one on the staff to train the new employee, the administrator might direct inquiries to the local government or school district officials or to the state vocational education department concerning training sessions for new custodians. Most states issue a training handbook, and local districts may have them available for their own use. These usually discuss the use of equipment, schedules, job time requirements, and operational tasks.

Employee Morale and Staff Relationships

A library administrator may realize that there is a relatively heavy turnover in the maintenance staff and assume the cause to be dissatisfaction with pay or work load. In fact, the employee may cite these as reasons for resigning, not recognizing that the real cause is low morale and a subconscious feeling of inferiority. Except in large organizations, the maintenance position may be a dead-end job. Even if this is so, fringe benefits may be found to help maintain high morale among the custodial staff. Assigning the individual to a fixed responsibility or encouraging improvement in carrying out responsibilities may be enough.

Every individual takes pride in self, wanting to be recognized as performing a job that is important and worthwhile. The job of janitor often connotes menial work performed by an individual unfit for anything better. Changing the job title to custodian confers some dignity. The holding of a master key indicates trust and dependability in the position. The employee is assured that the job is important to the operation of the library. Even if the value of the library as an educational institution is not fully apparent to the custodian, the monetary value of the building in tax dollars may be. It can "belong" to the employee, who will develop a sense of pride in its appearance in the public's eyes.

The basic elements in supervision are motivation and criticism. Understanding the reasons for doing a job and its place in the overall picture of the organization will start the employee in the right direction. Criticizing by questions and suggestions can be done so as to make the employee feel that he or she has originated ideas and contributed to the job.

The attitude of the rest of the library staff toward the custodian's position is also important to the latter's morale. If the staff acknowledges that this position is important to the library, the custodian is recognized as a staff member and as an individual. This can be accomplished by appointing members of the maintenance department to staff committees. To be respected by fellow workers for the job done will boost self-esteem. Compliments on the neat lawn or a newly cleaned floor are a reward for a good job. While people enjoy the informal friendliness of being known by their first names, the use of "Mister" when in public or in formal meetings indicates a respect for the individual, regardless of position.

Maintenance Quarters

Space for maintenance quarters may be fixed, and the possibility for expansion limited. However, in planning a new library, consideration should be given to the impact of greater floor space and perhaps landscaping on the problems of maintenance. Although information will be written into the building program, the administrator and architect should consult maintenance people concerning work and storage space necessary for supplies and equipment while the building is in the planning stage.

Plans for maintenance shop size must include space for administration, work area and machinery, supply storage, storage for items in process of repair, and storage for combustibles. Space for supply storage should be in addition to that necessary for regular library supplies of paper, cards, and forms. Minimum space for a small library would provide for a desk and file cabinet, a six-foot work bench, shelves for supplies such as light bulbs and soaps, and wall space for brooms, rakes, and shovels. Floor space will be needed for storage of vacuum cleaners, cleaning pails, lawnmower, plus enough open area to allow repair work to be done. A sink with hot and cold water should also be in this area. Too often the custodian is cramped into a room noted on the plans as the "janitor's closet," with space only for a small table, a few shelves, and hooks for brooms, with work room and supply storage sharing space with the furnace. During the building planning, it may have been the intent that repair work would be sent out, so consideration of maintenance space was unnecessary. Regardless of the size of the library, the custodian must have a headquarters to serve as a quiet area for paperwork and a work area for small repairs.

In large units or systems, the floor space allotted to maintenance might include a separate office for the department head; separate work and storage areas for carpentry, plumbing and electrical repairs; plus storage for supplies. A dust-free enclosure for spray painting will be useful for a large maintenance operation. Sufficient light and electrical outlets will be needed. A large staff will appreciate a shower area, not considering it a luxury after repairing roofs on a hot summer day.

The architect will have to be informed of the expected use of the maintenance workroom and equipment to be installed, such as table saws, racks for wood supply, tool and parts storage. If space is available, the workroom and supply storage for cartons and drums of cleaning liquids may be in a separate but nearby area. The storage of combustibles will be dictated by the local or state safety codes. Generally, they must be stored in safety cans away from flame in a well-ventilated area. Fire inspectors discourage the storage of gasoline and paint in the furnace room.

In multifloor buildings, provision for a custodial closet on each floor should be made by the architect. The size of the closet will obviously depend on equipment and material to be stored. However, it should be supplied with a floor sink for hot and cold water in a single wall fixture with a five-foot length of hose. Sinks are available in rectangular or corner shapes from twenty-four inches to sixty inches, allowing the sink to fill space between walls in small areas. Specifications should require caulking around the edges to prevent water seepage to the ceiling below. Space for shelving, pails, mops, brooms, spare cleaning materials, and perhaps a vacuum cleaner will be required. A ventilator grill in the floor will provide air circulation for drying.

One university has developed a standard closet size of six by eight feet for each floor of a new building.[2] Specifications for this room call for glazed tile on walls and floor, ventilation, fifty footcandles of illumination, and at least twelve square feet of shelving.

Maintenance space in new buildings should not be underestimated. Providing good janitorial facilities will not only produce more efficient work but will maintain the morale of the staff. If well located, such facilities can reduce the time spent to prepare for the job and to complete it.

Maintenance Schedules

The single word that defines the purpose of maintenance procedures is *preventive*. Preventive maintenance is concerned with the kinds of renovation and upkeep tasks that will protect equipment from failure and consequent need for replacement or extreme remedial maintenance.[3] Essentially it is a program of service, inspection, and correction carried out according to a predetermined schedule and at regular intervals.

---

2. John Gardner, "Planning a Building? Don't Overlook Maintenance," p.7.

3. Joseph J. Baker and S. J. Peters, *School Maintenance and Operations*.

The planning of maintenance begins with the architect. The intent is to design a building that is both functional and esthetically pleasing internally and externally, at the same time keeping in mind the problem of upkeep of materials used. As noted previously, the library administrator will inevitably play devil's advocate to the architect, whose strong esthetic leanings may overshadow the commonsense reality of costs and life of materials. This is not to say that costs of particular items are always the prime consideration, since a higher initial cost may mean low maintenance costs for the life of the building. The librarian, with the staff, must scrutinize the plans for exteriors that require painting and interior walls difficult to clean, judging whether ultimate usefulness outweighs original cost.

A program of scheduled preventive maintenance will mean savings in operating costs over a period of years. An immediate result will be a reduction of calls for emergency service by outside personnel. Such calls may not be eliminated, since mechanical failures are always a possibility; regular inspections may help keep breakdowns and plant failure to a minimum. The value of the building will be maintained at a high level, and the safety of the staff and patrons will be increased.

When setting up a maintenance schedule, it may be found that maintenance people are not equipped to service some equipment in the building. Today's increased automation demands great technical background, probably necessitating the use of outside maintenance contracts. Elevator systems, for instance, must operate within state and local certification requirements, and the training and experience needed to maintain this equipment make it mandatory that a service contract be carried by the library. The same may be said for a sophisticated air system and some office equipment. A regular schedule of upkeep of machinery, tools, and buildings will prolong the time before obsolescence—when an item is irreparable or repair parts are unavailable—and deterioration through use or weather is reached.

Another aspect of preventive maintenance is the anticipation of problems before emergencies occur. The administrator should expect the annual report of the head of the maintenance department to include not only a summary of the work of the previous year, but also a statement or a list of items planned for the coming year. The director should be warned of possible problems so that agreement can be reached on priorities. A schedule of major goals for a period of several years will serve as a guideline for budgetary planning. Large expenditures for repairs and new equipment will be expected, and the budget adjusted accordingly. While a contingency fund may be a source for emergency expenses, a scheduled maintenance plan may prevent unavoidable allocations to it.

Planning Maintenance Work Schedules

An efficient maintenance routine requires that a schedule of work be developed that will eventually cover all items needing maintenance. A detailed schedule is not only a corollary of good management but enables the administrator to distribute the work load without overlapping job assignments. The staff will appreciate knowing what is expected of them: they can work individually at their various tasks following lists that will prevent overlooking duties. Other members of the library staff often request maintenance people to perform immediate jobs, thus interrupting the maintenance routine and adding to the time required to complete the work. A work schedule informs all the staff that the maintenance people have specific duties that must be done first. The training of new personnel is simplified for the administrator and the new employee when a list of duties is available for reference.

Organizing a maintenance schedule begins with recognizing the total job to be done. Using a set of plans for the building or rough sketches, a list of items or areas and their condition is drawn up. This will include numbers of tables, chairs, counters, hung pictures, etc., as well as the room size and types of flooring and walls. Using this list it will be possible to assign the items to a schedule of jobs to be done daily, weekly, or over longer regular periods. These individual duties are then assigned a length of time required for completion and a time during the day when they should be done. After breaking the total duties into equal loads, a separate schedule is assigned to each of the maintenance personnel as an individual responsibility. The custodian of the building or of one floor of a building will find that certain of the assigned duties can be grouped. For instance, wastebaskets around the room can be emptied into a large wheeled container as one moves about the room to dust tables. By coordinating planning, the custodian can accomplish two jobs with less time and effort than if both were done separately. A capable custodian will find methods that are time saving without reducing the standard of maintenance.

When setting up the work schedule, the administrator will have to be cognizant of the time required to complete a specific job. It may be necessary and advisable to carry out an informal time-and-motion study using several individuals and a stopwatch to find an average period required to complete one job. Times per operation will be expressed as minutes or seconds necessary for the completion of a task, or time per square foot required. Table 18.1 illustrates such a list.

The number of custodians required to carry out the maintenance work satisfactorily, that is, to maintain a schedule designed to provide an accepted standard, may be a decision based on funds available, individuals available, size of building, and the number of floors of the building. Recommendations of several sources vary from one custodian for 11,000 to 15,000 square feet. One recommendation of some years ago suggests one custodian per 16,000 square feet of floor space. Because of the advances in equipment through the years, this ratio may not be too high, since types of materials used in recent construction must also be considered. The use of carpeting in public areas rather than vinyl title reduces the daily operation time of the custodian. On the other hand, this advantage may be lost in the trend to large expanses of glass in interiors and exteriors.

A simple janitor's schedule for a branch of 4,900 square feet is shown in table 18.2. It illustrates the relation of jobs to be done to a time requirement for the work, on a year's basis.

The author of the article presenting this schedule qualifies it as perhaps "somewhat below the maximum ideal. It is a practical arrangement which permits us to keep the building clean and presentable but not necessarily highly polished."[4]

It should be obvious that variations in the size of areas, flooring materials, light fixtures, and so forth will affect the frequency of cleaning and working times. A building located in regions of winter snow will require time for snow clearance. Use of snow melters on streets will require at least a monthly washing of exterior windows, since salt-bearing droplets are carried by the wind to windows high above the street. The use of salt may also mean that entrances must be mopped daily to pick up the white residue.

In this schedule for a California branch, the time allocated to the care of cork, linoleum tile is 154 hours a year, or about 13 percent of the total janitor hours. On the other hand, table 18.3 shows that, on a national average, cleaning crews spend 52 percent of the time on floor care and carpet maintenance.[5]

Mechanization of floor care will help prevent the schedule and yearly costs from getting top-heavy in this area and will help get the most from the labor hour. Although there is little mechanization of many cleaning jobs in a building, such as windows or light fixtures, machines for floor care are common, and the administrator should become acquainted with the types available. An initial investment in equipment can help hold down the growth of the salary budget over a period of years.

It is important to remember that compiling a list of maintenance operations serves two purposes: (1) it indicates what maintenance operations are required, and the average time period of each;

4. W. S. Geller, "Practical Aspects of Building Equipment and Maintenance," p. 552–69.

5. Beach, "Readers Rate Contract."

Table 18.1 Operation Time for Vinyl or Linoleum Floor Maintenance (Minutes per 1,000 square feet)

	Unobstructed	Slightly Obstructed	Obstructed	Heavily Obstructed
Sweeping	7	9	10	14
Wet Mop and Rinse	35	45	50	55
Machine Scrub 16″ Machine	27	38	44	49
Strip and Rewax	100	120	140	180

SOURCE: Adopted from Ohio State Dept. of Education, Division of Vocational Education, Ohio Trade and Industrial Education Service, *Custodial Training* (Columbus: Ohio State Department of Education, 1962), p. 16.

and (2) it enables the administrator or the head custodian to establish a fair load for each maintenance employee.

If the total work load is evenly distributed, the result will be a smoother operation with greater efficiency, and one cause of low morale will be eliminated.

Table 18.2 Janitor's Schedule for a 4,900-Square-Foot Branch Library

Janitor hours
per year

780	Daily cleaning (interior) Clean floor; dust chairs, tables, shelves; dump trash; sweep steps; replace paper towels and toilet paper
70	Books and shelves Dust books and shelves every 60 days (remove all books and magazines and dust shelves)
64	Windows Wash all windows 3 times per year
	Floor (cork Linoleum)
104	Mop floor weekly
24	Wax floor every 6 months
36	Buff every 30 days
34	Furniture Polish chairs, tables, desks, etc., every 30 days
36	Light fixtures Clean globes and shades every 60 days
16	Drapes Vacuum every 90 days
26	Miscellaneous work Clean kitchen sink and toilets Replace light bulbs
18	General Cleaning Dust walls, tops of shelves, 2 times per year
1,188	Total hours per year

Table 18.3 Percent of Maintenance Time Required for Various Tasks

Floor and carpeting	52
Fixtures and equipment	19
Walls and woodwork	13
Ceilings	6
Windows	6
Lights	4
	100

SOURCE: Douglas W. Beach, "Readers Rate Contract and Staff Cleaning," *Buildings* 66:50–53 (Feb. 1972).

Guidelines for General Maintenance

The administration of maintenance procedures demands knowledge of tools, supplies available, and qualities and care of materials used in the building. The various types and location of these materials will have been inventoried in the process of compiling the maintenance schedules.

Periodicals devoted to, or concerned with, building and maintenance problems are available. Discussions of new products and procedures will be of interest to the administrator and the maintenance staff. The neophyte head librarian can quickly become acquainted with the jargon of the field by scanning the advertisements—but cautiously, since the acquisition of equipment depends on need and on type or size best fitted for the building. A few books in print pertain primarily to school plants. These are excellent guides and require little extrapolation to apply to libraries. Catalogs and brochures from manufacturers are readily available if requested, complete with follow-up by a salesperson with a demonstration or free samples. This is not mentioned facetiously, for these people are experienced in the field, and advice from several, weighed for pertinent facts, will supplement material from other sources. It is also well to maintain a file of operating manuals supplied with equipment. These will serve as training manuals for new employees. The plans, exploded views, and schematic drawings are normally accompanied by a parts list to simplify repair problems. When a new piece of equipment or replacement part is received, the model and serial numbers should be noted on the manual to expedite reordering at a later date.

Space available will help determine the quantity of supplies kept in inventory stock. Unit costs are usually reduced for quantity purchases, and orders for dozens, cases, or drums will also avoid excessive small invoices and clerical work. The cost-conscious administrator will investigate several alternatives for bulk supply purchases, some of which may be:

1. Requesting bids from suppliers for specific items or related groups of supplies—soaps, wax, cleaning equipment.
2. Seeking commercial discounts at local stores. The use of a charge card and monthly billing will obviate cash purchases and the issuing of individual purchase orders. The department head should submit requisitions for single purchases or combinations of items so accounts can be controlled and invoices verified.

3. Purchasing stock from a municipal purchasing office as needed.
4. Submitting orders annually or as called for to the municipal purchasing department for combined ordering.
5. Ascertaining if the local government of school districts of the area have combined supply orders for quantity purchasing based on bids. Although many items in bulk or quantity, such as tires or notepaper, may not be of interest to the library, substantial savings may be realized in incandescent lamps, fluorescent tubes, and paper products.

Common replacement parts and supplies for equipment must be kept on hand for immediate use, and the stock replaced before the last part is used. Belts for drive motors, vacuum cleaner bags, toilet valves, and the like often are needed quickly and should be part of the standard inventory. For new buildings, the architect may specify equipment that may become obsolete within a three-to-four-year period. Manufacturers may turn out a quantity of a particular design, then change the model slightly. When the original quantity is gone, correct replacement parts may be difficult if not impossible to locate. A careful study of the plans and discussion with the architect may point out equipment for which spare parts should be acquired and held for future need. Lack of a unique latch, special frame-holding springs, unusual chair casters, and other seemingly minor items may put the equipment out of use for months until a source of supply can be found or a substitute adapted.

Problems of Exterior Maintenance

The maintenance of a building and grounds is as important for the impression it creates as for the preservation of the building. Unkempt landscaping, broken or missing letters on signs, cracked glass, and other minor elements, when combined, give any building a rundown appearance.

Landscape work for the maintenance staff should begin in early spring in northern climates. Lawns need to be seeded and fertilized, and shrubbery should be pruned. A check of garden books helps in this, as the correct season for pruning varies among plants; some need cutting after growth stops. The correct fertilizer must be used for each planting: the application of a type for acid-loving evergreens would eventually kill other types of shrubs and perennials. The care of lawns requires a mowing schedule to prevent an overgrowth; however, the type of grass will indicate the mowed height to be maintained. In dry areas,

plantings will require regular waterings. An underground sprinkler system is a help, providing plantings do not grow to interfere with the watering pattern. In water-short areas the architect or landscape contractor may foresee the maintenance problem and use fine stone or concrete in lawn space, interspersed with green islands of plantings that subsist with little water. In urban areas where air pollution is a problem, plantings should be washed regularly by spraying to clean leaves of chemical deposit. Trees should be watered through the root system by use of a hollow rod attachment to the hose. They may be fertilized by spray or root feeding during the growth season.

Proper seasonal landscape care creates custodial work in addition to normal summer building maintenance. Library systems may find it expedient to contract this work to a professional landscaper or perhaps knowledgeable students or teachers. Part-time branch custodians may be allowed time for lawn care, or arrangements made with a neighborhood youngster for regular mowing.

Staffs in most geographical areas will tend to adjust maintenance routines to allow time for outside work when weather permits. Roofs should be inspected early in the spring, debris removed, and drains and gutters cleaned. Exterior painting should be done, and asphalt parking lots should be repaired, recoated, and re-marked. Small details should be attended to, such as repair of bike racks, broken stone walls, vandalized exterior light fixtures, etc. Here again, the administration may make a decision between using the custodial staff and an outside contractor for special jobs.

Problems of Interior Maintenance

Information on the care of materials and equipment is available from a number of sources; therefore, only a brief comment need be attempted here. The new administrator will find it necessary to expand his or her scope of knowledge beyond the usual limits of university training. While the details of maintenance may not be of concern, an understanding of problems, materials, and methods should be acquired. Anyone may recognize that a floor is not clean; however, an administrator may also need to recognize that the floor is being damaged by the use of strong chemicals.

General items of the physical plant that will concern the administrator should be mentioned briefly:

Furniture. The standard library furniture of oak and maple was known for its durability and ease of repair, and much wood is still used in combination with newer materials. Metal-and-plastic chairs are often chosen for their pleasing lines but may not have the useful life of all-wood or all-metal chairs. Chairs and tables may be cleaned with a damp cloth, although some cleanser may be added for an accumulation of heavy soil. The plastic upholstery of lounge chairs should be checked occasionally for loose seams and slashed cushions. Knife cuts may be repaired by patching, but recent equipment may be worth the cost of recovering with a durable material.

Shelving. Steel shelving in a variety of colors is now used in many new installations. Care needed for upkeep is minimal. Student assistants may dust shelves in assigned sections as part of their responsibility, but the maintenance department should dust the tops of covered sections at least twice a year. A dry mop bent at an angle to the handle is a useful tool for this job. Wood shelving may be enhanced by the application of a stain-liquid wax, covering scratches and nicks.

Floors. Information on floor materials, care, and equipment is readily available, so only a brief discussion of types is necessary.

Solid vinyl and vinyl asbestos materials are common in floor construction. Vinyl tile or sheet is available in a variety of styles and colors. It is easily maintained by daily dry mopping and gives long service in heavy traffic areas. One early problem with vinyl was the tendency to indent under chair or table legs. Today there are several types that resist permanent indentation.

Rubber has a natural resilience. It is used in commercial or heavy traffic areas.

Cork tile has gained a new popularity for use as flooring since it has been sold with urethane finish. This type of cork is more durable and easier to maintain than early types.

Carpet use in public buildings has increased in recent years due to the new materials and methods used in production. Many styles and colors are available in wool and man-made fibers. Carpet may be more easily maintained than other types of flooring, needing only a daily vacuuming and steam cleaning once a year. The latter process is best done by professional carpet cleaners, although a library having a large maintenance staff may find it expedient to train an employee to use one of several small steam cleaners recently developed. Steam cleaning is really a misnomer, as the cleaning is done by hot water. Care must be taken in the amount of water used. Overwetting permits water to soak through to the padding, causing mildew. The water vapor released may also damage books on lower shelves by wetting top edges or loosening bindings.

When considering equipment for carpet care,

the hand-pushed sweepers should not be overlooked for fast convenient pickup. Among electrical cleaners, an upright machine using a revolving brush is slower but should pick up more dirt than a tank model. On the other hand, the tank type may be usable for wet or dry pickup—an advantage when pipes burst.

Ceramic is one of the oldest construction materials, but new shapes and colors have made it one of the most versatile for use on decorative walls. Available glazed or unglazed, it is one of the easiest materials to maintain. There are three types:

1. Glazed wall tile.
2. Ceramic mosaic tile glazed or unglazed. Commonly referred to as "floor tile," it can be used for both interior and exterior surfaces.
3. Quarry tile is used in lobbies and factories, both indoors and out.

The two latter types are maintained with the application of a damp mop. No protective coating is necessary, and wax need not be used unless the high gloss of a carnuba coat is desired. However, this may defeat the purpose of the tile—ease of maintenance. When ceramic is used in entrances, outside dirt falls on the easily cleaned tile before it reaches the vinyl or carpet areas.

Marble may have a polished or a honed (dull) finish. In either case, the overuse of abrasives should be prohibited. Clean hot water with a soluble cleaner, or a mild abrasive for stains, will keep the stone in good condition. For floors the abrasive may be sprinkled sparingly on the damp surface, or a handful put into the pail of hot water.

Terrazo is a composite of marble, quartz, or granite chips mixed with cement or another grout and poured in place on the building subfloor. It is then ground and polished. Specialty items, such as stairs, may be precast.

Wood can be beautiful, but old flooring tends to carry noise. A new form is the acrylic/wood tile, a composite material of hardwood and acrylic plastic. These parquet panels require little more than dry mopping and buffing, with an occasional cleansing with a foam cleanser and buffing with a nylon pad.

Concrete floors may be painted with a urethane floor finish at any time, providing all dirt and grease are carefully removed.[6] On new floors, the oil-free urethane coating stops concrete from "dusting" or surface wearing, making dry mopping or washing easier and extending the life of the

---

6. Jake J. Skala, "One Answer to Floor Care Problems: Urethane Floor Finishes," pp. 52 + .

floor. The process may also be used on wood floors if they are well prepared by sanding.

Walls. Most painted walls may be washed with a mild soap solution. There is a trend to cover walls with a variety of materials for design and sound-proofing. Cork, carpet, or vinyl in tile or sheets may be used by the architect to create a pattern for visual effect. Appropriate floor-cleaning products may be used for these wall coverings. Cloth-backed wall coverings should be washed with a mild soap, and abrasives and hand rubbing used with caution.

General Cleaning Methods

The library's maintenance personnel may become so conditioned to routine that they fail to see accumulations of soil, especially on wooden chairs and fronts of catalog trays and in corners of rooms. Legs of chairs and tables on tiled floors show a buildup of soil from mopping and waxing. Cobwebs in ceiling corners or between hanging light fixtures tend to be ignored by the janitorial staff. The total effect presents a slovenly appearance that reflects not only on the custodial staff, but on the administration as well. An occasional inspection by a sharp-eyed staff member will point out areas for special attention. Much of this can be alleviated by a continual but superficial cleaning. Custodians should be made aware of the value of a damp cloth for wiping soiled surfaces regularly. Cleansers will be needed to remove heavy soil and grease once or twice a year.

Much use is now being made of plastic laminates on tops of tables and counters. Wood grains and other patterns in recent products extend to some depth, but in older products they may be printed on the surface. The finish of these may wear through use and abrasive cleansers. The use of furniture wax on plastic may do little or nothing to preserve the material, but the use of products especially prepared for laminates will cover scratches to some extent and provide a coating that may protect the surface.

Glass may be cleaned with many products available for the purpose; however, a mixture of water and vinegar (weak acetic acid) cuts the oil from fingerprints and provides a liquid to pick up dust. Any good book of formulas will list a variety of mixtures for glass cleaning. The secret of polishing glass lies in the use of a clean cloth for damp wiping and paper toweling for finishing (newspaper will do as well).

Methods of cleaning metal letters on exterior signs depend on the material. Commercial cleansers are available for aluminum, but labels must be checked for limitations. Some may etch the polished surfaces of oxidized aluminum. A more certain method for any polished metal surfaces is the use of very fine emery cloth, or rubbing compound on a soft cloth, wrapped around a wood block and rubbed vertically on the figure.

Elementary Safety Precautions

While libraries may rank low among hazardous places to work, carelessness and sloppy house-keeping can result in serious accidents. Just as an office employee should think of the consequences of a low file drawer left open, so the custodial staff should beware of hazardous situations and minimal safety habits.

Tools used by maintenance people should be returned to their proper storage place and not left in passageways. The correct method of storage should be maintained—not only for neatness but also for the purpose of prolonging the life of the item. Brooms should be hung so that the bristles will not be flattened against the floor. Hanging mops dry faster and are less apt to become mildewed with air circulating about them. Mop buckets should be emptied and stored upside down where possible. Damp cloths are hung to dry rather than thrown into a corner. These are commonsense requirements for the care of equipment, but custodians may have to be frequently reminded of them.

Equipment in regular use should be constantly checked for loose nuts and bolts, wood screws, belts, wheels, and wiring. This is a part of preventive maintenance as necessary as regular inspection of the heating system. Often, downtime of equipment can be prevented if minor repairs are made. Many fasteners and parts are difficult to obtain locally; one must ship the tool to a distant service center or at least order the part and wait for delivery. A custodian who can plan ahead will check seasonal equipment in expectation of its use. Lawn mowers, snowplows, lawn sprinkler systems, hoses, and the like can be serviced and ready for use when needed.

The custodial staff must keep aware of situations likely to become unsafe to the public and staff. Inside the building, a waxed floor with a water spill can present a slick surface and may cause a fall. Covers on the ceiling lights can work loose due to vibrations in the air system and drop to the floor. Exterior walks often become uneven and present danger to pedestrians. Dangerous or hazardous conditions must be anticipated.

Although aware of the safety of others, custodians often neglect or ignore their own. For instance, when using a grinding wheel for sharpening tools, they may feel that looking for and wearing safety goggles is an unnecessary aggravation. Carelessness when using portable saws, electric cutting tools, soldering irons, and torches may exact a penalty that could have been avoided.

Stepladders deteriorate slowly, but often no one takes the responsibility or the time to repair lost braces or a broken step. When using a stepladder, the top step should not be used, nor should one attempt to reach too far to the side. Likewise, in using extension ladders, the worker should leave two rungs above his feet for handholds. This also provides working room against the surface of the wall.

For interior work, a portable, adjustable scaffold should be considered, especially in buildings with ceiling lights having large plastic covers, or for systems using in-house painters. The platform should be large enough to provide space for two people. When choosing a portable scaffold, it would be wise to consider a model with short-angle crossbracing, which can be raised to pass over a book stack, and of a length to allow its use perpendicular to the stack aisles. The ceiling can then be reached without standing on the stack tops or overreaching from the platform.

Fire Prevention and Procedures

A picture of a library's total operation is not really complete until the administration surveys the building from the viewpoint of fire prevention and procedures. Even where the community does not have an inspector assigned, the chief of the local fire department will be most cooperative if asked to help in a fire inspection. Through experience and training, the fireman will recognize dangerous practices or situations and advise on possible solutions.

Basic fire prevention practices include the safe storage and use of combustible materials such as gasoline, cleaning fluids, paints, and flammable adhesives. Fire inspectors will disapprove of the storage in closed areas of lawn mowers and snowplows with gasoline remaining in the tank. Flammable liquids should be stored in a safety can approved by the Underwriters Laboratory.

The fire inspector will point out storage areas to be cleaned and may recommend that certain locations no longer be used for storage or trash. Oil-soaked rags should not be allowed to accumulate in a pile or waste can because of the possibility of spontaneous combustion. This may be prevented by hanging rags individually on hooks or by draping them over a clothesline, so that air can circulate around them. Vents in the doors of janitor's closets may be required by local building codes to permit air circulation in these small, confined spaces.

Although newer libraries will probably be constructed of fire-retardant materials, local regulations may require wall-mounted fire extinguishers. Two types are in general use—the water pressurized and the dry chemical. The first is suitable for Class A fires (wood, paper, carpeting). If potassium is added by the manufacturer, this water-chemical mixture is rated as safe for Class B fires, or flammable liquids. The dry chemical, in various forms, is suitable not only for Class A and B but also for Class C (electrical wiring and equipment). Since this second type is suitable for all types of fires, due to its smothering ability, it might be advantageous to purchase only this type. If fire does occur, the average employee may not be clearheaded enough to make a correct choice among several kinds of extinguishers. Water under pressure will only spread an oil fire, while the chemical type will cover it with powder to close off the air and stop combustion.

Early warning of fire is essential for safety of life and property. Automatic fire detection devices are built into new construction but may not be difficult to install in older buildings. Heat and smoke detectors give early warning of trouble by light or bell signal. In larger communities the library administration may ask to be linked directly to the central fire department signal system. The department will probably specify the equipment and wiring necessary for the connection.

Sprinkler systems may be required in open areas between floors, if not over all spaces; however, in stack areas the water damage to library materials may be greater than that caused by heat and smoke. Building planning should include smoke detectors in such spaces.

A plan for the evacuation of staff and patrons should be developed, with concise instructions posted directing people to the nearest exit. If the building has an automatic coded alarm, the code and area information should be posted for staff action. Employees should be instructed to leave the building quickly without panic. Unless the shelf list and other card units are involved in direct flame for some time, the cases will probably prevent most cards from being more than scorched at the edges. Water may produce more damage. In brief, educate the staff to call the fire department and leave the building.

Natural disasters indigenous to geographic areas will call for special plans for safety and personnel evacuation. Construction methods may be regulated where earthquakes are frequent, but immediate evacuation, based on local recommendations, would be necessary. Likewise, in areas where tornados are frequent, advice should be sought at the local level.

Lighting

The lighting installation for a new library will probably be based on the recommendation for a minimum of thirty lumens for ordinary reading and seventy lumens for study, card catalogs, and circulation desks.[7] However, the instant the lights are turned on they begin to lose their efficiency. The life span of an incandescent lamp is computed as the total hours of burning before the candle-power drops to 80 percent of the initial intensity. A lamp will begin to burn faster after reaching 70 percent of the rated life. Fluorescent tubes have a much longer rated life, usually computed on the basis of three hours per start.[8] A standard forty-watt fluorescent tube has a rated life of approximately 15,000 hours with 3,120 initial lumens. At about 40 percent of its rated life (or 6,000 hours) it will produce approximately 2,840 lumens. Another factor contributing to dimness is dust on globes and diffusers.

Preventive maintenance for lighting is a planned program of lamp replacement. This can be done by spot (individual) replacement or as a group replacement. For incandescent lamps, spot replacement may be preferred since individual bulbs burn out at various periods before approaching "rated life," and they are usually easily accessible. Fluorescent tubes may last for two to four years before burnout, so that a program of group replacement for one floor, or office space, can be scheduled on a twenty-four–month, thirty-six–month, or other time period. It may seem wasteful and inefficient to remove and clean diffusers, remove and install new tubes, and reassemble before the bulbs are burned out, but this expense will be offset by the efficiency of setting up a ladder or scaffold and gathering equipment for all units at once. In addition, the luminosity is kept high. If one fluorescent lamp does go dark, causing the tube wired with it to fail, the bad bulb should be changed. If it is not, the ballast (transformer) will burn out, and its cost of replacement is approximately four times the cost of the tube. A combination of spot and group replacement may be used when one tube in a single fixture of four to eight tubes burns out and all tubes in the fixture are replaced. A darkening on one or both ends of a fluorescent tube indicates that it is near the end of its useful life and should be replaced.

Heating and Air Conditioning

Since the 1950s, practically all new library buildings have been constructed with air conditioning as original equipment. Air conditioning is usually thought of as limited to cooling; however, the process, especially in regard to libraries, may be considered as conditioning the air; that is, heating or cooling outside air after filtering out dust and fumes. Dirt and chemicals in urban air are detrimental to book life, a factor to consider when planning new construction. The effect of cooling on patrons and staff during periods of high daytime temperature is, of course, obvious.

There are two general types of equipment now used in air conditioning:

1. Packaged air conditioners
   a. Cooling unit only, ranging in size from a window box to a five-to-thirty-ton unit used in restaurants and stores. This type might be suitable for a storefront branch library. In some climates, a water-cooled system may be feasible, depending on the plumbing and the local water supply.
   b. Heating-cooling unit. Operated by motors and a heat pump or furnace, this type provides energy for heating or cooling air through the same duct work.
   c. Winter air conditioning. This type uses a heat exchanger in conjunction with a furnace, fans, and filter.
2. Separate units for heating and cooling.[9]

The architect, in consultation with heating engineers, will evaluate these types, basing the final choice on building space, purpose, and energy supply. A recent development is a system reclaiming heat given off by ceiling lights. Heat pumps, which make hot water for heating and cold for chilling, are finding increasing favor among architects. These may be driven by a variety of energy sources.

Unless the library is large enough to employ a trained heating/air conditioning mechanic, a contract maintenance agreement is the most practical solution for all units. Air conditioning has become so automated and complex that a trained specialist is necessary for full understanding of the equipment. Continued regular maintenance by knowledgeable service people will relieve the house staff of this work and be less expensive over a

---

7. John H. Wall, ed., *American Electrician's Handbook*.

8. Ibid., chapters 10–64.

---

9. "Air Conditioning," pp. 10–13.

period of years. Service should include boiler cleaning and adjustment, inspection of fans, pumps, and compressors, inspection and chemical treatment of water systems, resupplying refrigerant, and inspection of control systems.

The library maintenance staff must become acquainted with the operations so as to recognize indicators of trouble and possible failure. However, when a contract gives the contractor responsibility for the continued operation of equipment, the administrator should be firm in maintaining a "hands-off" policy for the library staff, except in operations cleared by the service people. For instance, changing settings of temperature or humidity may interfere with the periodic gauge readings the contractor may be evaluating. In the case of highly sophisticated equipment, the contractor will welcome telephone calls concerning unusual gauge readings, internal noises, or temporary water shutoff. Some seemingly minor signals may mean serious trouble. The contractor usually assumes responsibility for parts replacement in the contract fee and so is most interested in keeping the equipment running smoothly.

Energy Conservation

Administrators have always been aware of the conservation of energy, but usually only in relation to the effect of high costs in the budget. In recent years, conserving fuels has become a public policy because of supply shortages and distribution problems. This emphasis has resulted in a drastic change in the design of buildings. Where architects used glass walls as a design concept, they now use tinted glass, metal panels, or masonry. A truly temperature-controlled building requires no windows, and many nearly reach this ultimate form; however, the human desire for a view and freedom from claustrophobia require some glass, if only to permit employees to check the weather.

Where seasonal temperatures vary, outside air may circulate through the building, thus relieving the heat-control unit. In new construction the administrator should ask the architect to give work areas windows that can be opened. The architect should avoid large glass areas on the south and west so as to reduce the effect of the sun on interiors and the resulting necessity for cooling. In addition, the absence of glass at ground level increases building security and discourages vandalism.

In older buildings, various improvements and additions to the heating system may provide energy-conserving benefits:

1. Install two-bulb indoor/outdoor controls, thus automatically adjusting the system to the need produced by outside temperatures.
2. Set up zone controls for areas that have different loads because of location or occupancy. Such controls would adjust for temperature variation between sunny and shady sides of the building. They would also permit reduction of heat to empty work areas and little-used storage areas.
3. Many older buildings utilized steam radiators operating on the convection principle. Change these to air-handling units with a fan blowing across heat coils for better heat distribution.
4. Update older heating units by replacing manual on/off controls with automatic controls.
5. Shut down the outside air intake during extremely cold weather. Sufficient fresh air will usually be pulled in to satisfy the system. Varify this with the architect or the service contractor.
6. Check to see that all exterior door closures are fully operative. Tighten springs, or have them serviced if necessary.
7. Add storm windows to reduce loss of heat through glass areas.[10]

In spite of good original planning and improvements to old air systems, one must contend with the human element, which is often the most difficult to control. Five employees in a work space may feel the need of five different environmental situations. Regardless of the thermometer reading, the area will be too warm, too cold, too drafty, or too stuffy for some individual. Such a situation can try the administrator's soul. An interest in the employees' welfare must be shown, but there is often little that can be done, due to the design of the air system or controls. Where there is zone control by a thermostat, employees can waste electrical energy by constant readjustment. Employees must be constantly reminded not to change the control but to send complaints to the administrator or the maintenance personnel.

Conservation of electrical energy in lights is a concept all the staff can understand. If lights are on in an area not being used, then the power is wasted. A campaign of using only necessary illumination and extinguishing lights when not in use will need to be a continuous program. Lighting in new construction should be wired so that fixtures can be turned on in groups or alternate panels

10. "Nine Ways to Conserve Gas Energy," p. 28.

when areas have low use or when outside light is sufficient. However, it should be kept in mind that fluorescent lights may burn less energy if burned continuously rather than intermittently, because a surge of power is needed to relight the tube.

It may be possible to use exterior lights for fewer hours, except those needed for security purposes. The installation of a simple time clock will relieve staff of responsibility for exterior lighting and pay for itself in a short time.

Waste Control

Libraries are not exempt from modern problems of waste disposal and pollution control. In addition to discarded books and newspapers, libraries now have punched cards, plastic cups, and metal soft-drink cans filling waste containers.

Many buildings are equipped with incinerators of a size thought adequate at the time of construction. Through the years, however, the amount of waste may have outgrown the ability of the incinerator to handle it. In addition, many states and localities have adopted statutes to prevent the use of incinerators and the possible consequences of airborne smoke and odors.

Balers for newspapers and other paper trash have been used in the past, and their principle has been applied in modern waste compactors. These machines are available in portable models as well as in large, fixed-mount units. They may be manually operated or automatic, the latter actuated by material entering a chute. Refuse is compacted into a relatively small, easily handled cube of paper, plastic and glass. This may be ejected into a plastic bag placed over the chute or into a long plastic tube that can be tied off into sections of any length.[11]

The maintenance staff should be supplied with canvas collecting bags on carts for trash pickup about the building. Large paper drums and a can dolly may be substituted for bags. A wheeled cart slightly larger than the drum diameter can easily be made from scrap lumber. Such carts serve a dual purpose and will be found useful when moving furniture about the building.

Renovation, Remodeling, and Improving

Soon after an individual begins a new position as administrator or departmental supervisor, he or she will notice possibilities for change in physical facilities or arrangement of furniture and equip-

ment. The staff may even suggest changes that they have been requesting for years with no success. This desire for change is not limited to older buildings but will be found to varying degrees in libraries occupied only a few months. Regardless of the discussion and staff consultation involved in planning a new building, errors of judgment will be made. Space allocated for workrooms may prove to be too small, or public areas may be more than adequate. The staff and public may create traffic patterns not anticipated by the staff or architect.

An architect planning a library has the building program of the administration in mind. The architect and an interior designer together plan the floor areas and suggest furniture, flooring, and color to attain a pleasing effect. Space is designated for use, furniture is placed for ease of movement within the space, while color accentuates or blends for definite purposes. Before moving items within a space, consideration must be given to the effect on the overall design intended by the architect. Is a change or addition of new items really necessary because of planning errors? The ability of departmental staffs to present reasonable arguments for the addition of a desk, table, card box, etc., is often a match for the administrator's ability to evaluate the real need and the effect on the total design concept. Perhaps the elapsed time in the new surroundings has been too brief for the staff to acclimate to the arrangements, or new routines have not been completely accepted. If the need for an additional desk or chair is real, the administrator will have to approve the appearance and usefulness of the item. The placement in public areas of used, worn furniture should be discouraged, for the old equipment not only appears shabby, but its material or finish may be an anachronism readily apparent. Under such conditions, an entire area assumes a sloppy appearance; the interior designer's and architect's aesthetic values become distorted or destroyed.

Libraries that have aged more or less gracefully may be improved with remodeling and additions. When considering changes, features of the existing building should be kept in mind—for example, location of load-bearing walls, construction materials, hookups for new water or electrical lines, and problems of their installation. Consideration must be given to site grading, removal of windows, steps to another level, or the value of an addition as opposed to a new building.

Often simple changes can do much to renovate a room or area. Old floors can be retiled or carpeted, and wall surfaces repainted. Books and articles are available concerning the effect of color on the human temperament. A basic understanding of the psychological effect of color is essential to decorating. People feel comfortable or cool

---

11. "Facing the Trash Explosion," pp. 20+.

surrounded by blue but taut and warm in red. Color may also be used to advantage to make rooms appear larger or smaller. Light tones tend to "push out" walls, while dark tones seem to bring them in. Colors are used as a temperature control on exterior surfaces, where light colors reflect the sun's rays and dark shades absorb heat.[12] On interior surfaces color can be chosen for its reflective qualities to reduce the illumination needed for an area.

Where conditions have become so crowded that staff workrooms disturb patrons in nearby public areas, the use of acoustical tile on ceilings will do much to absorb noise. Modern, attractive patterns of this tile or lengths of carpeting can also be used as a sound-reducing wall covering on at least one side of a room, presenting a pleasing effect through use of color or pattern. Its overuse may be too heavy for a small area and have the effect of "closing up" a room. We are conditioned to seeing carpet underfoot, so its use as a wall covering may cause some individuals to be uncomfortable before they learn to accept it.

Remodeling will permit the administrator and architect to correct lacks in construction caused by the passage of time and by new building regulations. The architect is aware of changes in building code requirements, while the administrator can observe innovations in new buildings. State and local requirements have changed to accept new materials and methods of construction. Many of these changes are the result of federal regulations for remodeling and new building financed with federal aid.[13] The influence of federal assistance can be seen in schools, libraries, public buildings, and apartments.

One of the most obvious new requirements comprises provisions for the handicapped. Main entrance doors must now be at ground level or be accessible by means of a ramp and handrails. People in wheelchairs or with walking difficulties can thus enter a building easily. In contrast with libraries of the Carnegie design, with rows of steps leading to the entrance, the new designs provide a pointed example of the advances made in planning buildings for *all* people. Entrance doors must also be wide enough as a single unit (thirty-two inches) to permit passage of wheelchairs. Double-leaf doors, though wider, are not acceptable unless they may both operate with a single effort. Wider access may also serve another purpose for

the library, since it may be necessary to remove a stricken patron on an ambulance stretcher.

Many recent multistory buildings are provided with escalators as well as elevators and stairs for passage between floors. All are perhaps necessary, for many individuals fear one or the other of the mechanical conveyances. Escalators may be used only between primary levels to move traffic quickly. At least one elevator in a building should service all floors to provide for vertical movement of books and mechanical equipment. At least one must also be accessible to the physically handicapped on the level they enter the building.[14]

Federal standards specify space and access requirements for toilet facilities, water fountains, public telephones, room indentification signs, and obstructions. Toilet rooms should have at least one toilet stall that is three feet wide and four feet, eight inches deep, with a swinging door thirty-two inches wide and handrails on each side. Mirrors and shelves mounted as low as possible but with the bottom of the mirror no higher than forty inches above the floor are required.[15]

Child-height drinking fountains have been a part of original equipment in libraries for many years, usually in or near the children's area. Standards for the disabled accept many of these providing they are easily accessible and operable by hand or foot control. The architect may place two drinking fountains side by side at different heights in public traffic areas, in line vertically on the various floor levels to simplify installation of water pipes.

The decision to build an addition to the library requires consideration of changes in the old building to modernize color, lighting, materials, and facilities. Often such work is required in any case, not only because the use of space may be changed by the new construction, but also because the old space may be drab and clash with the new. If the addition is to provide new public and staff areas, the architect will plan to coordinate both buildings, but a short statement of purpose, use, and function will be needed as a guide. While this statement need not be as extensive as a building program for a new library, the library board and administration should consider space allotments and use of special equipment such as a drive-in window for public service; wall connectors between film projectors and speakers; outlets for equipment, charging machines, and typewriters; and other specialized items having to do with library services to the public or work of the staff.

Grasp of the total picture of physical plant maintenance, including knowledge of equipment

---

12. James C. O'Connor, "Maintenance Painting and Color," pp. 26–28.

13. American Standards Institute, "Specifications for Making Buildings and Facilities Accessible to, and Usable by, the Physically Handicapped" (New York: The Institute, 1961).

14. *Ibid.*

15. *Ibid.*

and its proper use, and the ability to work with the maintenance staff as an understanding and fair supervisor should be the administrator's goals. If the staff has been well chosen and well trained and has the confidence of the librarian in day-to-day duties, the administrator will have the help needed for major maintenance decisions. The administra-

tor's job is to see that the library policies, budget, and total staff serve the public to make the library an educational and informational institution. Maintenance of the physical plant is a part of the overall program and should receive its proper recognition, but in the perspective of total service.

Bibliography

"Air Conditioning." *Building Operating Management* 17:10–13 (July 1970).

Arco Editorial Board. *Building Custodian*. 6th ed. New York: Arco, 1976.

Association of School Business Officials. *Procedures*. Vol. 53. Chicago: The Association, 1967.

Baker, Joseph, and Peters, S. J. *School Maintenance and Operations*. Danville, Ill.: Interstate, 1963.

Beach, Douglas W. "Readers Rate Contract and Staff Cleaning." *Buildings* 66:50–53 (Feb. 1972).

Berkeley, Bernard. *Floors: Selection and Maintenance*. Library Technology Program Publication no. 13. Chicago: ALA, 1968.

Cleaning Consulting Services, Inc. *The Comprehensive Custodial Training Manual*. Seattle, Wash.: Cleaning Consultant Services. 1975.

"Facing the Trash Explosion." *Building Operating Management* 17:20 + (Oct. 1970).

Falk, Bernard H. "Efficiency without Sacrifice." *Building Operating Management* 25:14 + (May 1978).

Gardner, J. C. "Estimating the Amount of Housekeeping Work." *American School and University* 45:8 + (Oct. 1972).

"Planning a Building? Don't Overlook Maintenance." *American School and University* 44:7 + (July 1972).

Geller, W. S. "Practical Aspects of Building Equipment and Maintenance." *News Notes of California Libraries* 52:552–69 (July 1957).

L'Hote, J. D. "How to Put Good Thinking into Maintenance Staffing." *Nation's Schools* 81:195–96 (Feb. 1968).

"Nine Ways to Conserve Gas Energy." *American School and University* 44:28 + (Jan. 1972).

O'Connor, James C. "Maintenance Painting and Color." *Building Operating Management* 20:26–28 (Aug. 1973).

Ohio State Board of Vocational Education. Division of Trades and Industries. *Custodial Training*. Edited by Trade and Industrial Education Instructional Materials Laboratory. Columbus: Ohio State University, 1962.

Ostrander, R. E. "Maintenance and the Medium Sized Library." *New Jersey Libraries*. New Series 1:20–22 (Fall 1968).

Skala, Jake J. "One Answer to Floor Care Problems: Urethane Floor Finishes." *Building Operating Management* 20:52 (Nov. 1973).

Tonigan, R. F. "Contract More Operations and Maintenance Work." *School Management* 16:8 (Oct. 1972).

Wall, John H., ed. *American Electrician's Handbook*. 9th ed. New York: McGraw-Hill, 1970.

Young, J. F. et al. "They Didn't Teach Me This in Library School: Tips on Maintenance—A Discussion." *Wisconsin Library Bulletin* 64:21–23 (Jan. 1968).

Periodicals carrying articles concerning maintenance of buildings, training, and special problems:

American School and University
Building Operating Management
Nation's Schools
National Elementary Principal
Plant Engineering
School Management

The Contributors

Ellen Altman is Director of the Graduate Library School, University of Arizona. She has been working in and teaching librarianship since 1963 and has served as a consultant on library management for the Urban Institute and Public Administration Services. Altman is the coauthor of two books on performance measures for public libraries. Some of her articles have appeared in *Library Quarterly, Library Journal,* and *Journal of Academic Librarianship.* She has been a featured speaker on the subject of library evaluation at conferences of the American Library Association, the Canadian Library Association, and many state library associations. She has also held a number of offices in the American Library Association, including Chairperson of the Committee on Research and the Library Research Round Table (LRRT) Publications Committee. She is a former member of the editorial board of the *Journal of Academic Librarianship* and an associate editor of *Library Research Quarterly.*

James M. Banovetz is Professor and Chairman, Department of Political Science, Northern Illinois University, where he established the graduate program in public administration and municipal management. Banovetz has frequently worked as a consultant to local government, edited *Managing the Modern City,* and was named an honorary member of the International City Management Association in 1978.

Edwin P. Beckerman is Director, Free Public Library, Woodbridge, New Jersey. Beckerman has had extensive experience in public libraries and as a library consultant, in addition to teaching courses in library administration and library planning. Formerly a member of the ALA Council, Beckerman is active in state and national professional associations.

Edwin Castagna served as chief administrator of four public libraries prior to his fifteen-year administration of the Enoch Pratt Free Library of Baltimore. Additional contributions to the profession include: service as a visiting professor at several library schools; consultation for surveys and planning studies for nine California public library systems; leadership in the Nevada and California library associations, as well as ALA; and publication of four books and dozens of articles, chapters in books, and other contributions to the professional literature.

Ralph W. Conant is President, Unity College, Unity, Maine. His previous positions in higher education include serving as President of both Shimer College and the Southwestern Center for Urban Research; as Associate Director for the Lemberg Center for the Study of Violence, Brandeis University; and as Assistant Director of the Joint Center for Urban Studies, MIT. His publications of particular relevance to public librarians are *The Public Library and the City, The Metropolitan Library* (with Kathleen Molz), and *Urban Perspectives, Politics and Policies* (with Alan Shank).

Byron Cooper is a law librarian, Indiana University, School of Law. Cooper holds an A.B. in classical languages and an M.L.S. from Indiana University, as well as the J.D. from the Indiana University School of Law. Cooper taught classical languages before the completion of his professional degrees.

Phyllis I. Dalton is a free-lance library consultant working in the areas of planning, evaluation, and measurement of library services. Currently Copresident of the Association of Specialized and Cooperative Library Agencies, Dalton has served as Assistant State Librarian of California and as President of the California Library Association and the Association of State Libraries. Dalton received an award for Distinguished Professional Achievement from the University of Denver Alumni Association.

Melvin J. LeBaron is President of Team Associates, a management/team development consulting firm. A faculty member of the University of Southern California School of Public Administration for nineteen years, LeBaron pioneered, developed, and conducted numerous team-building and management-development programs. In addition to his administrative and professorial service at USC,

241

LeBaron has been a part-time faculty member at eight universities and is the author of fifteen books.

John A. McCrossan is Associate Professor of Library Science, University of South Florida. McCrossan has had extensive experience in public libraries, as State Librarian of Vermont, and in library education, in addition to his research on public library services and administration. At South Florida, he is currently developing curricular offerings covering public and state libraries.

Glenn Miller is Director, Orlando (Florida) Library System. Before assuming this position, Miller worked with two public libraries in Michigan. He held various library support positions for ten years previous to the receipt of his AMLS. Active in ALA, the Florida Library Association, and the Public Library Association, Miller has served on the boards of public television, a hospital, Kiwanis, and school volunteers in his local community.

Alice Norton is a librarian, an accredited member of the Public Relations Society of America, and the owner-operator of a public relations firm. Her clients include public and state libraries, library associations, and other library-related organizations. In addition to conducting workshops for library schools and library associations, she has been president of the Library Public Relations Council and Chairperson of ALA's Public Relations Section and the National Library Week Committee. Among her publications are *Public Relations: A Guide to Information Sources* and *Measuring Potential/ Evaluating Results.*

Alan Shank is Associate Professor of Political Science, State University of New York, College at Geneseo. Shank is a recent NASPAA (National Association of Schools of Public Affairs and Administration) Faculty Fellow at the U.S. Department of Housing and Urban Development. He is coauthor of *Urban Perspectives, Politics and Policies* with Ralph W. Conant and recently completed a manuscript on the domestic policies of President John F. Kennedy.

Ira Sharkansky is Professor of Political Science and Public Administration, University of Wisconsin—Madison and Hebrew University of Jerusalem. His publications include *Public Administration: Policy-Making in Government Agencies; The United States: A Study of a Developing Country; The Routines of Politics;* and *The Maligned States: Policy Accomplishments, Problems, and Opportunities.*

Dorothy Sinclair is Professor and Program Director for the Public Library Program, School of Library Science, Case Western Reserve University, where she has been on the faculty since 1965. Formerly with Enoch Pratt Free Library of Baltimore, Sinclair served as Bureau Chief of the Library Consultant Bureau of the California State Library and is a past president of two ALA divisions. She is the author of *Administration of the Small Public Library*, in addition to contributions to symposia and professional journals.

Peggy Sullivan has served as Assistant Commissioner for Extension Services, The Chicago Public Library, since 1977. In addition to her services at the ALA headquarters, Sullivan has taught at several library schools, directed the Knapp School Libraries Project, and worked as a children's librarian, supervisor, specialist, and project director in public and school libraries. A prolific author, she is active in ALA, the Chicago Library Club, the Illinois Library Association, and the Special Libraries Association.

F. William Summers is Dean of the library school at the University of South Carolina. Before assuming this position, Summers worked in public libraries, served as State Librarian of Florida, and taught in the library school as Assistant Dean. Chairperson of the ALA Code of Ethics Committee, he has been active on the ALA Council and the Committee on Accreditation.

Roderick G. Swartz is the State Librarian of Washington State and Executive Officer of the Washington Library Network. His professional accomplishments include: former Deputy Director of the National Commission of Libraries and Information Service, former Deputy Director of the Tulsa City-County Library, Assistant to the Executive Director of the Library Administration Division of ALA, Professor at the Institute of Library and Information Science in Tampere, Finland, and various other consultative and administrative library positions.

Ronald C. Tollafield is Director of the Franklin Sylvester Library, Medina, Ohio. Before assuming this position, Tollafield was Extension Department Assistant Librarian (Branches and Extension Services, Personnel, Maintenance), Akron Public Library, Group Service Department, Firestone Branch, 1953–74.

Douglas Zweizig is Assitant Professor, School of Librarianship, University of Washington and a consultant for the Public Library Association standards Development Project. He writes primarily in the areas of communication, user studies, and research. He has performed investigations of information needs and seeking, library service evaluation, and library staff development.

Index

Compiled by Wayne Moquin

Designed by Vladimir Reichl
Composed by Modern Typographers Inc.
  in Linotron 202 Souvenir
  with Helvetica display type
Printed on Antique Glatfelter,
  a pH neutral stock, by
  Chicago Press Corporation
and bound by Zonne Bookbinders Inc.